D1829215

DYNAMIC FAIR DEALING

Creating Canadian Culture Online

Dynamic Fair Dealing argues that only a dynamic, flexible, and equitable approach to cultural ownership can accommodate the astonishing range of ways that we create, circulate, manage, attribute, and make use of digital cultural objects.

The Canadian legal tradition strives to balance the rights of copyright holders with the public's need to engage with copyright-protected material, but there is now a substantial gap between what people actually do with the various cultural forms and how the law understands those practices. Digital technologies continue to shape new forms of cultural production, circulation, and distribution that challenge both the practicality and the desirability of Canada's fair dealing provisions.

Dynamic Fair Dealing presents a range of insightful and provocative essays that rethink our relationship to this policy. With contributions from scholars, activists, and artists from across disciplines, professions, and creative practices, this book explores the extent to which copyright has expanded into every facet of society and reveals how our capacities to deal *fairly* with cultural goods has suffered in the process. In order to drive conversations about the cultural worlds Canadians imagine and the policy reforms we need to realize these visions, we need *Dynamic Fair Dealing*.

ROSEMARY J. COOMBE is Canada Research Chair in Law, Communication, and Culture in the Department of Social Sciences at York University and an internationally known legal anthropologist.

DARREN WERSHLER is Concordia University Research Chair in Media and Contemporary Literature in Montreal and a published poet.

MARTIN ZEILINGER is SSHRC Banting Postdoctoral Fellow in Law and Culture at York University.

Dynamic Fair Dealing

Creating Canadian Culture Online

EDITED BY
ROSEMARY J. COOMBE, DARREN WERSHLER,
AND MARTIN ZEILINGER

UNIVERSITY OF TORONTO PRESS
Toronto Buffalo London

Toronto Buffalo London
www.utppublishing.com
Printed in the U.S.A.

ISBN 978-1-4426-4640-7 (cloth)
ISBN 978-1-4426-1441-3 (paper)

Printed on acid-free, 100% post-consumer recycled paper with vegetable-based inks.

Library and Archives Canada Cataloguing in Publication

Dynamic fair dealing : creating Canadian culture online/edited by Rosemary J. Coombe, Darren Wershler, and Martin Zeilinger.

Includes bibliographical references and index.
ISBN 978-1-4426-4640-7 (bound) ISBN 978-1-4426-1441-3 (pbk.)

1. Copyright – Canada. 2. Copyright and electronic data processing – Canada. 3. Electronic information resources – Fair use (Copyright) – Canada. I. Coombe, Rosemary J. (Rosemary Jane), editor of compilation II. Wershler-Henry, Darren S. (Darren Sean), 1966–, editor of compilation III. Zeilinger, Martin, 1978–, editor of compilation

KE2799.D95 2014 346.7104'82 C2014-901204-7
KF2995.D95 2014

University of Toronto Press acknowledges the financial assistance to its publishing program of the Canada Council for the Arts and the Ontario Arts Council.

Canada Council for the Arts Conseil des Arts du Canada

ONTARIO ARTS COUNCIL
CONSEIL DES ARTS DE L'ONTARIO
50 YEARS OF ONTARIO GOVERNMENT SUPPORT OF THE ARTS
50 ANS DE SOUTIEN DU GOUVERNEMENT DE L'ONTARIO AUX ARTS

This book has been published with the help of a grant from the Canadian Federation for the Humanities and Social Sciences, through the Awards to Scholarly Publications Program, using funds provided by the Social Sciences and Humanities Research Council of Canada.

University of Toronto Press acknowledges the financial support of the Government of Canada through the Canada Book Fund for its publishing activities.

Contents

Introducing Dynamic Fair Dealing: Creating Canadian Digital Culture 3
ROSEMARY J. COOMBE, DARREN WERSHLER, AND MARTIN ZEILINGER

A THE CANADIAN COPYRIGHT CONTEXT

I Provocations: Fair Dealing as Right, Speech, Duty, and Practice

1 Copyright and Freedom of Expression: Fair Dealing between Work and Play 43
BITA AMANI

2 From the Right to Copy to Practices of Copying 56
MARCUS BOON

II Recognizing the Canadian Public Domain

3 The Canadian Public Domain: What, Where, and to What End? 65
CARYS J. CRAIG

4 Dynamic Fair Dealing with Orphan Works: Lessons from "Real" Property 82
REN BUCHOLZ

5 Publicly Funded, Then Locked Away: The Work of the Canadian Broadcasting Corporation 90
KYLE ASQUITH

III Infrastructures for Fair Dealing

6 Resisting Enclosure: Licences, Authorship, and the Commons 100
JOHN W. MAXWELL

7 Weaving an Open Web: Innovation and Ethics in the Virtual Commons 113
ELIOT CHE

8 "This Content Is Not Available in Your Region": Geoblocking Culture in Canada 124
IRA WAGMAN AND PETER URQUHART

9 Net Neutrality and the Threat to Open Cultural Expression 133
STEVE ANDERSON

IV Experiments in Pedagogy and Diversity

10 Copyright and Access to Media for People with Perceptual Disabilities 144
J.P. UDO AND DEBORAH FELS

11 If You're Asking, It's Not Fair Dealing: Animating Canadian Copyright Issues in a "Read-Write" Classroom 154
MATT SOAR

12 Hacking Education: How Openness and Sharing Can Transform Learning 164
ALEC V. COUROS

B MEDIATIONS

I Digital Publishing

13 Open Access Publishing and Academic Research 177
ROWLAND LORIMER

14 Open Access Mandates and the Fair Dealing Button 189
ARTHUR SALE, MARC COUTURE, ELOY RODRIGUES, LESLIE CARR, AND STEVAN HARNAD

II Principles and Practices of Heritage Management

15 The Evolution of Cultural Heritage Ethics via Human Rights Norms 201
ROSEMARY J. COOMBE AND NICOLE AYLWIN

16 Indigenous Cultural Heritage in the Age of Technological Reproducibility: Towards a Postcolonial Ethic of the Public Domain 213
GEORGE NICHOLAS

17 Cultural Diversity: A Central Dimension of Canadian Cultural Heritage? 225
NICOLE AYLWIN

III The Work of Poetics

18 Parodists' Rights and Copyright in a Digital Canada 237
GRAHAM REYNOLDS

19 Robin Hood of the Avant-Garde 251
KENNETH GOLDSMITH

20 Remixing bpNichol: Direct Dealing and Recombinatory Art Practices 261
JUSTIN STEPHENSON

C MAKING OUR DIGITAL HERITAGE A DYNAMIC ONE

I Documenting Pasts and Assessing Virtual Futures

21 Copyright Dramas: Theatre Archives and Collections Online 273
DAVID M. MEURER

22 Streaming a Digital Scream: Archiving Toronto's Barbaric Yawp 284
SUZANNE ZELAZO

23 The NFB, Canada's Experimental Documentary Tradition, and Found Futures 294
MARTIN ZEILINGER AND ELI HORWATT

II Recombinant Creativity

24 Chipmusic, Out of Tune: Crystal Castles and the Misappropriation of Creative Commons–Licensed Music 305
MARTIN ZEILINGER

25 "My Real'll Make Yours a Rental": Hip Hop and Canadian Copyright 317
ALEXANDRA BOUTROS

26 Friction over Fan Fiction 327
GRACE WESTCOTT

27 Child-Generated Content: Children's Authorship and Interpretive Practices in Digital Gaming Cultures 336
SARA M. GRIMES

AFTERWORD: REFLECTIONS

Deal with It 349
LAURA J. MURRAY

Pull Up the Stakes and Fill in the Ditches: The Materiality of Intellectual Property 354
DARIN BARNEY

References 361

Acknowledgments 417

Contributors 419

Index 429

DYNAMIC FAIR DEALING

Creating Canadian Culture Online

Introducing Dynamic Fair Dealing: Creating Canadian Digital Culture

ROSEMARY J. COOMBE, DARREN WERSHLER, AND MARTIN ZEILINGER

A Manifesto for a Robust Culture of Fair Dealing Online

The call for the papers that comprise this volume began as a manifesto: a call to arms for academics, artists, and activists to defend Canada's emerging digital culture. We posed a series of queries, declarations, and provocations that distilled into a single question: given the legal, social, and practical contours of cultural life in a digital era, how can we collectively ensure that digital technologies best serve the creative and social needs of Canadians?

To answer this question, we need to better understand the activities and aspirations that animate the work that Canadians actually *do* in digital environments. We are all aware that networked digital technologies provide significant tools and unique opportunities for democratically transforming cultural life. Nonetheless, as critics such as Darin Barney (2000) remind us, the progressive possibilities of such technologies are not inherent, but shaped by their social regulation. Thus, our manifesto:

> The process of "dealing" itself – that is, the dynamic, complex, contingent, and shifting set of relationships and practices characteristic of the space *between* digital cultural creation and regimes of law and social regulation – has eluded the attention of scholars for too long. This is not surprising, because the fair dealing provisions in Canada's Copyright Act have been "poorly applied and underused" (Handa 2002: 288). Dealing with cultural goods and conducting social negotiations about their propriety shapes the quality and experience of digital culture in Canada. What constitutes "fairness" within digital networks is constantly and contextually evolving, and

demands a greater degree of attention than we currently afford it. Critics, activists, librarians, scholars, creators, and citizens' groups everywhere are embroiled in complex debates over intellectual property (IP) rights' extensions, corporate enforcement practices, and exercises of digital rights management. Many believe that as forms and exercises of power, such attempts to extend the reach of IP rights are illegitimate, excessive, or simply out of step with the realities of contemporary cultural expression, production, and exchange in digital environments. In short, despite the capacity for collaborative creation that digital technology affords, and despite the ostensible commitment from all levels of government to make Canadian cultural content more accessible, IP laws in Canada pose unnecessarily punitive prospects for potential liability.

Through the concept of fair dealing, the Canadian Copyright Act is supposed to enable Canadians to access and engage with copyright-protected cultural works. Such engagement is a necessary part of learning, creativity, cultural productivity, scholarship, critical conversation, and expressive collaboration. Nonetheless, many creators, educators, and researchers experience the Copyright Act as obstructing rather than facilitating access to works. Ironically, the rights created under copyright law often obstruct what they are traditionally designed to enable: fair access to cultural expressions, with the aim of encouraging innovation and creativity to the benefit of society at large. It's not simply that they don't adequately serve the needs of Canadian creators, the cultural industries, and everyday users of cultural goods in digital contexts. They may also be used to exert a chilling effect on Canadian cultural exchange.

If we really want to encourage democratic, dialogic, pluralist, and polyvocal forms of cultural practice in digital environments, we are faced with several urgent tasks. We must explore the potentials and limits of existing practices, while developing new forms of knowledge, negotiation, and techniques that articulate and honour the rights of both creators and users of cultural content, and, to ensure the viability of these new practices, we must insist upon the protection and elaboration of a robust and vibrant public domain. To accomplish this work, it is necessary to assert the primacy of fair dealing as a human capability, an individual responsibility, and a citizen's right. Fair dealing cannot be a limited default category based on the assumption that *any* digitization of protected material is a reproduction and therefore an infringement. Such an assumption deprives us of the critical capacity for digital literacy. Instead, we aim to define, assert, and defend fair dealing as the affirmative practice in which we engage when we actively encounter, critically consider, and/or transform

> cultural content online. Moreover, we need to find ways of using such practices to drive conversations about the cultural worlds we envision and aspire to as Canadians, and the cultural policy reform necessary to meet these objectives.

When we issued this provocation and invited others to help us map the terrain of this volume, we received a wealth of responses. The following chapters were written as a collaborative project by thirty-four scholars, activists, and creative practitioners from a range of disciplines and professions, with experiences in many different fields and genres. These essays place particular emphasis on practices of what we call *dynamic fair dealing* – emergent approaches to the creation, circulation, and management of digital cultural objects that challenge traditional paradigms of intellectual property or pose alternatives to them. Legal theorists and policy makers face a tremendous task in their aim to achieve a balance between owners' and users' rights. The contributors approach this challenge by asking how we do so in a fashion that fairly accommodates the opportunities for collaboration, copying, sharing, and creative reuse that digital media afford Canadians – opportunities that many citizens now perceive as rights.

One of the tasks of this book is to provide significant grassroots case studies and empirical evidence of open content strategies, alternative models, and successful cultural practices. As a means to inform, educate, and persuade critics, policy makers, and custodians of cultural content, we would rather proceed by way of example than by abstract theory or polemic. Our approach is explicitly micro-political, focused on building progressive cultural policy from the bottom up. This is especially important in a Canadian context, where the borders between artists, academics, audiences, and arts administrators are particularly permeable, and individuals act in all of these capacities simultaneously or by turns. Rather than accepting shouting matches between consumers and the cultural industries as the norm, this book explores possibilities for new arrangements that redefine interests in the very activities of circulation, use, modification, attribution, criticism, research, review, and reporting – fair dealing, in short – that digital technology enables and that online communications invite.

The adjective "dynamic" emphasizes that fair dealing is a dialogic, performative, and continuous activity. As performers par excellence, artists and cultural creators can and should participate in this dialogue with all of the zeal and ingenuity that they bring to their work itself.

There is too little public input and too little empirical evidence to inform the direction of Canadian cultural policy. As artists, librarians, writers, publishers, students, scholars, historians, activists, consumers, and citizens, Canadians need to have their interests considered, their practices documented, and their aspirations voiced. We should share social and technological innovations that meet our diverse needs in digital environments and explore the greater prospects and limits of such practices so that we can disseminate and improve on them. Our ultimate goal is to foster the creation of knowledge, practices, and innovations that will contribute to the creation of a dynamic and dialogic Canadian cultural heritage in new media environments.

This book constitutes an interdisciplinary conversation about the opportunities and constraints that Canadian intellectual property laws pose for cultural activities in digital environments. Our focus is not on Canadian cultural content per se, but on the specific policy issues that arise when engaging with digital content in a Canadian context. How do the particularities of Canadian IP laws, educational and cultural institutions, media forms, creators' collectives, geographical diversity, technologies, traditions, and audience expectations create problems or shape opportunities for more open and democratic approaches to the use of digital culture? We provide a wide range of critical perspectives on what it means and what it *should* mean to deal fairly in Canada. Rather than treat fair dealing as an abstract legal concept, our authors reframe it as a practice in which all participants in digital cultural exchange necessarily engage during the course of their daily activities. What the contributions to this book share is the conviction that if we want to bring Canada's IP laws back into step with the everyday norms and practices of Canadian cultural production, then copyright reform is necessary and inevitable, if far from simple and self-evident. Accordingly, this volume provides an inclusive, interdisciplinary venue for a discussion of how everyday practices are relevant to IP reform as a matter of cultural policy.

We understand this effort as a continuation of a project that Laura Murray and Sam Trosow began in *Canadian Copyright: A Citizen's Guide* (2007, 2013), a general primer on Canadian copyright that familiarized the Canadian public with our national legislation and its interpretation by focusing popular attention on the importance of users' rights. Despite the existence of a number of digital venues for journalistic writing on the need for law reform (such as the blog *Excess Copyright*, maintained by copyright advocate Howard Knopf, *IP Osgoode's IPilogue*, and

Michael Geist's blog at michaelgeist.ca, which leads the field) there has been little sustained interdisciplinary conversation about copyright in Canada generally, or about fair dealing in particular. We seek to consider these issues in a fashion more sensitive to the specificities of Canadian digital infrastructures, educational institutions, funding bodies, cultural policy, and popular culture, which are missing in more purely legal accounts. Economic and technological barriers have restricted the ability of many in the arts and non-profit sectors from sharing materials online, even when the legal issues have been resolved.

Debates about copyright, author's rights, and their appropriate limits are attracting an increasing amount of public attention, but few works address the range and diversity of positions and perspectives on copyright that characterize Canadian public interest and activity. We thus seek to add to what Ysolde Gendreau and her collaborators (2008) refer to as "an emerging intellectual property paradigm" by acknowledging the creative practical work that Canadians do in managing cultural goods in digital environments. We also seek to add new dimensions to both the practice and concept of copyright reform. Michael Geist's collections of essays on proposed reforms to the Canadian Copyright Act (2005, 2010b), for instance, were timely and important efforts to bring a legal academic perspective on copyright reform to the attention of the wider public, an agenda Geist pioneered through his well-known columns in the *Toronto Star*. Our interventions contribute a broader range of academic and practical expertise to this endeavour.

Although legal scholars (Bita Amani, Carys Craig, Graham Reynolds) are well represented in this volume, we have juxtaposed their voices with those of scholars in communications (Kyle Asquith, Alexandra Boutros, David Meurer, Matt Soar, Peter Urqhuart, Ira Wagman), cultural policy (Nicole Aylwin), publishing (Rowland Lorimer, John Maxwell), literature (Marcus Boon), film studies (Eli Horwatt) information management and pedagogy (Alec Couros, Deborah Fels, J.P. Udo), anthropology (George Nicholas), information technology (Sara Grimes), computer science and software design (Leslie Carr, Marc Couture, Eloy Rodrigues, Arthur Sale), digital production, design, and administration (Steve Anderson, Eliot Che, Justin Stephenson), lawyers (Ren Bucholz, Grace Westcott), and artist-activists in the cultural sector (Kenneth Goldsmith, Suzanne Zelazo). As such, our contributors express distinctive perspectives and propose unique practices and ethics to take advantage of the tremendous cultural opportunities that digital technologies have enabled. Our own backgrounds in anthropology, law, and cultural studies (Coombe), literature, publishing, and communication studies (Wershler), as well as comparative literature, film, and new media (Zeilinger), informed our choices.

Given the American dominance of news media, Canadians are accustomed to critiques of copyright that have their origins in the United States. Such criticisms presuppose the American constitutional tradition, which, in terms of the limits it poses to copyright's reach, privileges freedom of speech. The nature and consequences of the potential conflict between freedom of speech and the copyright power is the subject of great concern, much of it critical of the overreach of corporate copyright and trademark holders into the public realm of expressive freedoms (Benkler 1999, Coombe and Herman 2001, McLeod 2005, Vaidhyanathan 2001; however, see Netanel 2008). Although this conflict was first addressed in the US constitutional context, the issue has also surfaced and attracted critical attention in Europe (Bonadio 2011, Hugenholtz 2001, Montero and Van Enis 2011, Porsdam 2009, Voorhoof and Cannie 2010), the United Kingdom (Akester 2010), and South Africa (Haupt 2008, Nwauche 2008). As Bita Amani's essay in this volume shows, despite the prescient scholarship of David Fewer (1997), the Canadian tradition of considering the intersection of intellectual property and freedom of expression is far less developed.

A series of books, ranging from Jane Gaines' and Rosemary Coombe's early volumes, *Contested Culture: The Image, the Voice and the Law* (1991) and *The Cultural Life of Intellectual Properties: Authorship, Appropriation, and the Law* (1998), respectively, through to Lawrence Lessig's renowned *Free Culture: How Big Media Uses Technology and the Law to Lock Down Culture and Control Creativity* (2004), have extensively documented the obstacles that copyright and the more general legal terrain of intellectual property pose to creativity, cultural critique, and democratic dialogue. The opportunities and limits that the American doctrine of fair use poses to culturally expressive activities have been addressed by Siva Vaidhyanathan (2001, 2004) and William Patry (1985, 2009), and memorably spoofed and satirized by scholars, activists, and musicians (Demers 2006; Levin 2003; McLeod 2001, 2005, 2007; Negativland 2003, 2009). Critics deem the concept of fair use to be in dire need of reconceptualization and reform in the digital era (e.g., Aufderheide and Jaszi, 2011, Gillespie 2007). Most critics are frustrated by the lack of any overarching American cultural policy principles to balance the voracious appetites of corporate IP holders. As we shall discuss, they have founded initiatives such as the Creative Commons (CC), open source (OS), and the access to knowledge (A2K) movements, in order to stimulate civil society practices of cultural policy making in the absence of decisive government political activity that addresses public needs.

The Canadian common law concept of fair dealing, rarely considered in juxtaposition to freedom of expression as a human right, has received far less critical academic attention than the American fair use doctrine. In part, this may be because Canadian legal history provides little assurance with respect to the likely success of a fair dealing argument and the concept received relatively little attention during most of the twentieth century. Rather than engaging in risky copying activities, authors, publishers, creators, and users chose to, or were advised to, err on the side of caution.

The concept was included in Canada's first Copyright Act of 1921, which came into force in 1924 and provided, without much deliberation, that no copyright infringement was constituted by fair dealings "for the purposes of private study, research, criticism, review, or newspaper summary" (c. 24). Although insubstantially amended by statute in 1993, fair dealing remained stable, little invoked, and largely uncontested. In 1997, Bill C-32 introduced a series of exemptions that pertained to educational institutions, libraries, and uses by and for perceptually challenged individuals. These exemptions provided detailed language that could potentially have strengthened a fair dealing defence; they were also, however, perceived to limit the concept's usefulness by outlining very specific limits on available exemptions that could thus be interpreted more narrowly.

Prior to 2012, the most important indication that new perspectives on fair dealing were needed and emerging, was the 1997 *Allen* v. *Toronto Star Newspapers Ltd.* case and the landmark Supreme Court decision in *CCH Canadian Ltd. et al.* v. *Law Society of Upper Canada* (2004). In the first case, the Ontario Divisional Court allowed a fair dealing defence to apply to the copying and reproduction of an entire photograph, effectively reversing *Zamacois* v. *Douville* (1943), in which it was established and later accepted – in cases including the infamous *Michelin* v. *CAW* (1997), which Reynolds examines in this volume – that a fair dealing defence was not available for activities that involved the use of a complete work. *CCH* continued this trend and, significantly, established that fair dealing was a substantive users' right that "should not be given a restrictive interpretation" (para. 54).

The *CCH* case concerned photocopying and document delivery services offered by the Law Society of Upper Canada's library, which were alleged to infringe the copyrights of several law publishers. The Law Society invoked fair dealing as their defence, but in the initial 1999 trial court ruling, fair dealing was strictly construed and found inapplicable to the copying practices in question. When this decision was reversed by the Federal Court of Appeal, and this reversal confirmed by the Supreme Court in 2004, an important step in the direction of stronger fair dealing in Canada had been taken. Fair dealing, as the Supreme Court now clearly stated,

> is perhaps more properly understood as an integral part of the *Act* than simply a defence. Any act falling within the fair dealing exception will not be an infringement of copyright. The fair dealing exception, like other exceptions in the *Act*, is a user's right. In order to maintain the proper balance between the rights of a copyright owner and users' interests, it must not be interpreted restrictively. (para. 48)

The *CCH* decision is today widely viewed as having provided a much-needed and long overdue indication that fair dealing was to be taken seriously and that users could have some faith that at least some of their dealings with copyright-protected works that involved their reproduction would be permitted. Nevertheless, because the Supreme Court also asserted that fair dealing was "impossible to define" (para. 52) and that it required a careful case-by-case re-examination to definitively conclude, no great clarity was provided to the public as to what dealings were, in fact, permitted. The language employed by the Supreme Court was not, moreover, implemented in other significant decisions, interpreted by institutions, or propounded by government institutions, with the consequence that individual users continued to shy away from activities that might later require them to invoke their rights of fair dealing. This situation was exacerbated by the growing power of Access Copyright (formerly the Canadian Copyright Licensing Agency), which generally overstated the strictness of the Copyright Act and continued to assert that no uses that could be paid for were fair dealing; causing educational institutions, in particular, to convey overly restrictive copyright guidelines to their users (see Trosow et al. 2012).

As many of our contributors note here, fair use is a broad and general category animated by general principles that enable the judiciary to exercise discretion in deciding whether acts are infringing, whereas fair dealing exceptions, in comparison, are narrowly defined and precisely enumerated activities. The former is commended for its flexibility but decried for its uncertainty, while the latter has the virtues of certainty. However, the enumerated activities of fair dealing are generally too static to encompass continuing social and technological changes in the ways that Canadians use culture and knowledge – a shortcoming profoundly exacerbated by the advent of online activities.

Clearly, we are not alone in this recognition. As we finished this introduction in the summer of 2012, the Copyright Modernization Act Bill C-11 received royal assent, and five major Supreme Court of Canada judgments pertaining to copyright (the so-called pentology) were released. The imminent legislative amendments spell some improvements for creators and users of content in digital environments by expanding fair dealing to include some limited educational purposes and for parodic and satirical uses. It has also established other important users' rights, such as the right to make backup copies and shift content between formats. However, the Bill's strong protection of "digital locks" (technological means of digital rights management) threatens all of these user rights by treating the circumvention of such locks as an act of infringement despite the otherwise lawful nature of the use, suggesting ongoing legislative ambivalence about the fundamental importance of fair dealing in digital environments.

The Supreme Court pentology contains no such ambivalence, greatly increasing optimism for the future of fair dealing in Canada (Geist 2013). These cases reiterate the Court's continued insistence that a "large and liberal interpretation" should be applied when interpreting whether practices fall within the category of fair dealing to ensure that user rights "are not unduly constrained" (citing *CCH*, para. 51). Significantly, in a 5–4 split decision, in *Alberta (Education)* v. *Access Copyright*, the Court rejected the argument raised by Access Copyright that copies of works made for students by teachers at their own initiative for classroom use should not be considered as private study or research, but rather as instruction, which Access Copyright argued should not qualify as fair dealing (see Crowne 2012a). The Court decided that such copying was, indeed, done for the accepted purposes of research and private study, because, as a user's right, the relevant perspective from which to consider the purpose of the use was the user, in this case the student, whose research and private study was facilitated by the teacher's instructional use of the copy. This decision calls into question the much-debated model licence agreements between Access Copyright and several Canadian universities (Geist 2012), a critique anticipated and elaborated upon by our contributor Marcus Boon.

The same insistence on a liberal, user-centred interpretation of fair dealing characterizes the Supreme Court's unanimous decision in *SOCAN* v. *Bell Canada*, which found that the provision of online song previews, streamed to consumers before they decided to purchase and download musical works, was protected as fair dealing for the purposes of research (see Crowne 2012b). The Court rejected SOCAN's argument that research must serve to foster creativity and affirmed, instead, that research can "be piecemeal, informal, or confirmatory" and can "be undertaken for no purpose except personal interest" (para. 22), significantly because the dissemination of works – not merely the promotion of creativity – is one of the Copyright Act's purposes and in the public interest.

In these landmark decisions, the Supreme Court reaffirms the significance of fair dealing in digital environments as the exercise of users' rights that must be largely and liberally interpreted. In these welcome judgments, the Court also stressed the objective of technological neutrality, that is, the propriety of having the Copyright Act applied in a way that operates consistently, regardless of the form of media involved or its technological sophistication. This principle is of particular relevance to academic observers, activists, and user groups concerned with opportunities for dealing fairly in digital contexts. Nonetheless, the ongoing demand for royalties for digital fair dealing activity by licensing collectives for eight years after the *CCH* decision acknowledged the integral nature of fair dealing in the copyright system and the public interests the system is designed to serve, suggests that the social and economic landscape does not immediately change as a consequence of appellate-level legal decisions, which are optimistically interpreted by copyright owners as restricted to their own narrow facts. Ultimately, the statutory formation of fair dealing still frames it "as a narrow exception to copyright rules" and one that for too long has been "encumbered with an apparent, if unarticulated sense that use of another's work without permission [is] *de facto* unfair" (Craig 2005: 438, 443).

Many Commonwealth jurisdictions, including Australia, Canada, India, and Singapore, adopted the 1911 UK Copyright Act, the basis for the fair dealing exceptions, either directly, or as a model for their own laws (Burrell and Coleman, 2005: 249), which have been variously updated or amended in different jurisdictions (e.g., Handler and Rolph 2003, McLay 1999). Significantly, the Australian government considered moving from a fair dealing to a fair use defence in 2005, in response to growing demands for copyright reform. These demands included the pressures of a fair trade agreement with the United States, as well as civil society interests in a more balanced relationship between owners' and users' rights perceived as likely to be further undermined by compliance with US trade dictates. The proposal was rejected and the amended legislation included a long and detailed list of exempted fair dealing activities rather than a more general and flexible fair use defence. A flurry of critical scholarship quickly followed; most critics despaired of the lost opportunity to counteract the expansion of copyright holder privileges (Weatherall 2007) and the flexibilities lost through rejection of fair use (Baron 2007), but others argued that some of the newly delineated usages might actually provide greater scope for user activity in digital environments (Austin 2010), a prospect that Bill C-11 might also hold for Canadians, were it not for the spectre of users having their rights foreclosed by ever more sophisticated technological locks. Despite the fact that Canada is subject to many of the same pressures that Australia faces and shares a similar legislative history, Canadian fair dealing has been neglected as a subject of critical scholarship, subjected to far less public inquiry and less policy scrutiny than can continue to be warranted. The rapid transformations of the ways in which culture is used and generated through digital technology suggests that strictly defined fair dealing exceptions will continue to privilege holders of legal rights while disregarding public benefits. Our authors explain why this is the case and what might be done about it in a digital world characterized by dynamic fair dealing. In this way, they make a specifically Canadian contribution to one of the major reform efforts currently pursued by the A2K movement: the rebalancing of copyright regimes through the formulation of an international legal instrument to create minimum mandatory limitations and exceptions to copyright powers (Franz 2010).

Overview of the Volume and the Contributions

This book consists of an introduction and three distinct parts, each of which provides a distinct perspective from which to consider the context, conditions, process, and practice of fair dealing in Canadian digital culture.

Part A The Canadian Copyright Context

The first part of the volume provides theoretical context for the chapters to follow, and stakes out the major issues to be addressed throughout the book. It serves the purpose of (re)familiarizing readers with the legal concept and interpretation of fair dealing and offers a broader context for understanding Canadian copyright law by placing particular emphasis on the public domain in which fair dealing functions. The two chapters contained in the first section of Part A address provocative issues around the definition and implementation of fair dealing. These include the concept's impact upon expressive liberties, the uncertainties it poses in everyday activities, and the obstructions its enforcement by collectives pose to learning and creativity (Striphas and McLeod 2006). Law professor Bita Amani argues that to meaningfully update the existing, flawed fair dealing doctrine, we must take seriously the ways in which copyright law contravenes Canada's Charter of Rights and Freedoms – significantly, rights to freedom of expression. She proposes that the Charter, as well as the Copyright Act be invoked in intellectual property disputes, and strongly argues against the misconception that the two are unrelated. Like John Tehranian (2011), Amani points to the unseemly amount of infringement liability an average person inadvertently accomplishes in a single day, the counter-intuitive role of fair use and fair dealing in actually expanding the copyright monopoly, and the important expressive interests at play in many unauthorized uses of copyright works. Although proposed legislative amendments will exempt non-commercial uses of published works for the purpose of creating new ones from copyright infringement, the qualifying conditions are likely to be difficult for youth to understand or interpret. Amani reiterates Lawrence Lessig's (2008) important point that inherently reproductive digital technologies provide the most important tools of creativity for a new generation for whom digital remixing is a fundamental form of speech, thought, and identity.

Among youth, now the targets of increasingly didactic and moralistic "anti-piracy" campaigns (Bently, Davis, and Ginsberg 2010, Gantz and Rochester 2005, Logie 2003, Yar 2008), the legitimacy of copyright law has reached a new nadir, while important new forms of creativity are imperilled (Reyman 2009). The study of social rhetoric around copyright in digital environments, both by those who are fearful of the new technology and fuelling moral panics (Patry 2009), and by activists promulgating new user's rights (Collins 2010, Postigo 2008b), is an important area of emerging concern for those concerned with the ways in which language shapes the interests we recognize in public policy disputes (Murray 2005, Silbey 2010). The necessity to achieve a balance between access to and protection for intellectual property has preoccupied a full generation of IP scholars, led by the groundbreaking work of

David Vaver (1990). Aware that copyright reform historically tended to be dominated by small groups of industry stakeholders, leaving the public to be represented by educational and library representatives (Geist 2005, Sheppard 2009), these scholars ask whether digital technologies do not demand that the broader public have their interests more fully represented, as users and creators of cultural content (Craig 2005, Drassinower 2005).

Starting from his position in a university classroom, literary theorist Marcus Boon answers this question affirmatively, taking as his point of departure the question of whether Access Copyright (the Canadian agency charged with administering permissions and fees on behalf of copyright holders) interferes with fair access to intellectual property. The question is not merely theoretical; in 2011, a group of Canadian universities collectively rejected the tariff structure proposed by this agency, its assumed monopoly over educational materials, and its interpretation of fair dealing recently legitimated by the *Alberta Education* decision. Boon argues provocatively that copying, an inherent and crucial aspect of human expressivity, is throttled by copyright law and the limited exceptions it recognizes and asserts; in their current and proposed manifestations, these exceptions are not meaningfully related to practices of creative expression. This is particularly true in a networked digital milieu that facilitates copying, sharing, and new forms of collaboration – a contention that other authors in this volume further elaborate, refine, or qualify. Boon's contribution moves us into the notoriously amorphous concept of the public domain, which, although legislatively unacknowledged, is fundamental to understanding how fair dealing functions.

Historically, the public domain was the subject of a scant few prescient books and law review articles (Patterson 1968, Patterson and Lindberg 1991, Lange 1981, Litman 1990). Since the turn of the millennium, the ubiquity of digital technology in consumer societies has renewed critical interest in the concept, and the term "public domain" has attracted enormous new energies (e.g., Dreier 2001, Coombe 2003, Drahos and Braithwaite 2002, Frow 2000, Hemmungs Wirtén 2008, Macmillan 2007a, Waelde and MacQueen 2007). The public domain has variously been characterized as those intangible goods and forms that lack IP protection (Boyle 2003), equated with a cultural "commons" (Gross 2006, Lessig 2001, Starr 2000) or a commonwealth (Bollier 2002), described as a realm of socially shared informational goods lacking commodity status (Therien 2001), or defined by gift relations (Frow 1996), and is occasionally considered a dimension of the public sphere (Halbert 2005). Definitional and "mapping" efforts (Dutfield 2000, Guibault and Hugenholtz 2006, Samuelson 2003) abound.

The next section of Part A addresses the concept of the public domain and its dimensions as a space of cultural activity. Legal theorist Carys Craig argues that the power of the public domain stems directly from its protean nature as a concept. She suggests that asking what the public domain *is* represents a sort of cognitive error. The relevant question is what we *need* the public domain to be. Craig makes the case for expanding the use of the term "public domain" beyond works publicly available because copyright protection has expired and suggests that existing case law points to a more positive rendering of the public domain as an enlarged space of cultural productivity that serves the public interest. Strengthening and elaborating the concept of the public domain in Canada's legal culture, Craig claims, is closely linked to the development of a robust and dynamic concept of fair dealing.

The next two chapters examine central ambiguities around the status of what might be considered border objects in the public domain. Lawyer Ren Bucholz addresses difficulties that emerge from the public's lack of capacity to access and use orphan works. These works enjoy legal protection but belong to corporate or private entities that cannot be located, making it nearly impossible to obtain licences to take social and creative advantage of them. To remove such works from this legal limbo, and facilitate access to them, Bucholz proposes that Canada's fair dealing provisions encompass and validate the activities of people like amateur curators of "abandonware" (software whose corporate copyright holders no longer exist or cannot be located) who ensure that such works can be accessed and used fairly.

Kyle Asquith is also concerned with issues of access, focusing on publicly funded cultural works that are withheld from public access, by considering Jesse Brown's successful CBC Radio One show *The Contrarians*. Although the CBC hosts freely accessible episodes of many of its shows on its website, this is not one they had made available. As the show's original creator, Jesse Brown wanted to share these episodes with the online public, and consequently, he attempted to host free digital copies as a series of MP3 files on his personal website. The CBC insisted that he had no right to do so. In the course of this dispute, it became evident that despite its national public service mandate, the CBC outsources its IP monitoring to an American corporation, which thereby polices Canadian use of public culture at the Canadian taxpayer's expense. The result is that content paid for by Canadian tax dollars is unavailable to Canadians. The individual interviews Brown sought to make accessible comprise a very small portion of the CBC's output; nevertheless, the policy precedent that this incident sets is a matter of democratic concern. Asquith calls for the use of public licensing schemes by public institutions such as the CBC as part of a more clearly developed principle of user's rights in Canadian law and culture generally.

As the example of the thwarted hosting of *The Contrarians* MP3 files illustrates, technological innovations are not necessarily useful to members of the public unless they are paired with clear policies that render their use open and democratic. In *Always Already New: Media, History and the Data of Culture* (2006), media historian Lisa Gitelman argues that a medium consists of more than technology itself; it also includes the relationship of that technology to the protocols that shape the ways in which we perceive and make use of it. For example, the first decade of this century witnessed conflicting protocols regarding the use of MP3 technology. The Recording Industry Association of America (RIAA) infamously sued both file-sharing networks such as Napster and a range of US citizens, contending that downloading MP3s was an illegal act. When the Canadian Recording Industry Association (CRIA), attempted to launch a similar series of lawsuits in Canada, the courts denied the request (*BMG Canada Inc.* v. *John Doe*, 2004). Nonetheless, during the same period, Apple sold computers using their "Rip. Mix. Burn." advertising campaign in both countries. As Tarleton Gillespie (2007: 14) asserts:

> technologies can powerfully shape the social activities in which they intervene, sometimes with significant political consequences; at the same time, technologies are also powerfully shaped by the individuals and institutions that produce them and reshaped in powerful ways by users, suggesting that their impact has a lot to do with the meanings that are negotiated and the cultural contexts in which that negotiation occurs.

Thus, the third section of our general contextual grounding of fair dealing focuses on the practices and policies that shape the infrastructures for fair dealing in Canadian digital environments.

In the wake of copyright restrictions that might otherwise inhibit creativity in digital environments, a whole range of new protocols for dealing with digital cultural objects has emerged in the revolutionary operating systems and applications programmed by Free/Libre and

Open Source Software (FLOSS) thinkers and activists like Richard Stallman (2009), Eric Raymond (1997) and Linus Torvalds (1991). Their chief argument is that although strengthening IP regimes stifles democratic debate, their software supports both the creative process and the public discourse vital to democracy: "If people cannot 'speak' without buying the rights to the underlying property, then the needs of democratic citizens are necessarily silenced" (Berry 2008: 32). The most significant of the protocols introduced was the public licence, such as the GNU General Public License (GPL), which encourages the use of copyright powers to enforce sharing rather than restrict it (Kelty 2008). Initially designed to ensure that the source code of a program circulated openly, along with the compiled, executable version of that program (hence, the term "open source"), the GPL also ensures that no one can corral a piece of open code and use it in her or his own commercial products without also sharing her or his own derivative creations, keeping code available, and ensuring the common pool of open code continues to grow in size and complexity (Wershler-Henry 2002: 26–9). People quickly saw the value of the public licensing paradigm for things that did not have source code, such as books, comics, and paintings and adapted the GPL to apply to non-programmed digitized objects. The CC licence is the best-known example. Due, in part, to pundits like Lawrence Lessig and Cory Doctorow (2008), the popularity of public licensing has expanded to include cultural objects of all sorts (Kelty 2011).

Canadian publishing scholar John W. Maxwell, in his chapter, examines public licensing and the development of the concept of "user's rights" as responses to the vast increase in the scope and duration of copyright powers during the past century that has created an unbalanced legal regime (Scassa 2005, Lametti 2005, Tawfik 2005). Arguing against a "pay per use" culture in which every cultural work is owned so as to require clearance before it can be used (Therien 2001), Maxwell advocates the global adoption of the practices and conventions of peer-production–based communities such as Flickr and Wikipedia. Such practices are built on principles of collaboration, sharing, and the providing, rather than the limiting, of access to informational goods. The novel exercise of such rights has helped to forge new communities and legitimize and popularize new norms.

Website developer Eliot Che revisits the importance of open source movements in developing contemporary norms of online sharing and collaboration in his chapter. As the ethos of sharing developed by these movements spreads to the larger cultural sector through wiki-style knowledge repositories, social networking platforms, and image-sharing sites, Che argues that it is necessary to reconsider the qualities that define the usability of digital goods. Although we often think of digitally provided goods as simply available for public use, the capacity of end users to actually employ digital products such as software is often possible only because of intense, collaborative, cooperative efforts that must continue in order for these goods to produce social benefits. Che proposes that we think of this characteristic of digital products as "social usability," pointing to the benefits that a society draws from the accessibility of social capital represented by software and other collaboratively authored cultural expressions.

In response to the astounding popularity of peer-to-peer (P2P) file sharing, the traditional content industries responded with new technological means and new protocols for concentrating and restricting the online circulation and use of digital cultural objects (Zittrain 2008, Wu 2010, David 2010). Digital rights management (DRM) systems, which encrypt content in order to limit access to it, present a "technological fix" to this problem, enabling producers to physically control and manage digitally distributed information by using contract law to enforce these limitations. The emerging digital landscape is increasingly governed by privately generated norms backed up by legislative bodies, privileging private ordering and displacing public deliberations around the scope of copyright and its limits: "the immediate outcome of this process is to turn large chunks of what was once in the public domain into private goods" (Elkin-Koren 2001: 192). Deployments of DRM can and do result in violation of users' rights of fair use and freedom of expression:

> The attempts thus far to impose technological solutions onto the promiscuity of the Internet have all faced intrepid users who refuse these constraints: from the casual users of peer-to-peer networks to the amateur DJs creating innovative forms of digitally reworked music; from the widespread use of "black market" technologies to the hackers that take on every new system; from academic critics who challenge these strategies to the campus activists who mobilize against them. (Gillespie 2007: 18)

Various solutions to this standoff have been proposed by advocates of methods to provide compensation to owners without controlling the behaviour of users (Fisher 2004, Lessig 2004, Litman 2004, Netanel 2003). Although capabilities for preventing unauthorized file sharing are still under development, and their long-term viability is uncertain, "right holders are still betting on exclusivity in cyberspace" (Peukert 2009: 153).

Communications scholars Ira Wagman and Peter Urquhart further extend the argument that the part of the Internet we know as the Web has never actually been open. As evidence, they discuss the widespread practice of geoblocking – denying access to a Web address based on the geographical location of the user's computer – which is ever more common when real-time streaming video is the means to access digital audiovisual content. Wagman and Urquhart examine the regional imbalance in access to cultural goods that the practice creates in Canada, and question the fairness of this approach. In the final contribution in this section, open media advocate Steve Anderson tracks the accelerating movement of Canadian Internet service providers away from "net neutrality" principles, through their adoption of practices such as the shaping and throttling of traffic and the prioritization of information flow for customers prepared to pay a premium. Overall, the contributions to this section indicate that if some parts of the Web have never been open, other parts are becoming less open than they used to be, a development that has profoundly negative consequences for a supposedly egalitarian public domain.

The accessibility of digital public culture is of great concern in education. Section IV of Part A explores practices of pedagogy and scholarship in which intellectual property rights limit opportunities for learning. The academy is a bellwether for IP management practices; what happens there generally has consequences for the other learning communities that digital media serve. Canadian cultural policy, however, seems oblivious to the academy's innovative efforts to improve and ensure the accessibility of knowledge (Lorimer et. al. 2011). Eroding notions of fair dealing and fair use may adversely affect the sorts of texts that students are encouraged to read and instructed to produce in the classroom (Westbrook, 2009). Legislative allowance for education as a fair dealing purpose must be publicly as well as judicially interpreted in a capacious manner. Education as a public good is non-rivalrous in nature in that students benefit from it without reducing the amount that is available to others; moreover, the more educated the public, the greater the market for copyright-protected goods. Nonetheless, "cases which deal with the exceptions and limitations of copyright law – particularly in determining what is fair – seem to take a restrictive and narrow interpretation" (Wahid 2011: 86, 93). Here, the need for a practical ethos of fair dealing is especially pressing, as the ability to study society and culture is fundamentally predicated on open access (OA) to texts and other cultural objects.

Given the current limited exceptions to copyright liability, encouraging Canadian educational institutions to take full advantage of the learning opportunities that digital technologies afford is a huge challenge. For example, for audiences with impaired hearing or vision, as J.P. Udo and Deborah Fels show in their chapter, the addition of closed captioning and audio descriptions provide the only means of accessing cultural works. Creating such useful interfaces is virtually impossible to do, however, without engaging in a transformative use of the copyright-protected content, which requires bypassing the access restrictions that copyright puts in place. Udo and Fels argue that to accommodate such activities and the important social functions they serve, we require either a broadening of fair dealing rules to enable accessibility for the perceptually challenged or a commitment by creators, producers, and distributors to guarantee improved accessibility to their works. Such changes are essential to recognizing the cultural rights of people who would be otherwise socially marginalized.

Whereas Udo and Fels are concerned with access to digital works for the general educational needs of disabled learners, the last two chapters in this section deal specifically with issues concerning the study of digital objects in the university classroom. Communications scholar Matt Soar confronts the uncertainties that instructors face when teaching students with and about digital media. This is especially true in classes that have a production component, which necessarily entail using the reproductive capacities of the technology at hand. Alec Couros continues in this vein, presenting his achievements in moving from a conventional passive "teacher network," towards a philosophy of teaching based on openness. Grounding his discussion in his own teaching experience, Couros outlines philosophies and methodologies that are useful in establishing digital pedagogical practices in which students are invited to share in the structuring of university courses and redefine their engagement with and dissemination of course content. As demand for the study of digital materials increases, and more classrooms become equipped with "smart" technologies, an ethos of fair dealing in the classroom becomes a more pressing need.

As our colleague Meera Nair reminded us in an email, much has happened since the call for papers for this volume was first circulated: "In the summer of 2009 Canadians were invited to contribute their opinion on copyright to the federal Government. The depth and breadth of the response was extraordinary. Thousands of Canadians participated and it became evident that the subject of copyright has moved beyond an archaic specialty within the law to a policy field recognized as having broad public relevance. Many Canadians are now aware of the potential of fair dealing to mediate between the claims of property and the access called for by creators and communities. Yet the nuance of fair dealing has yet to be fully appreciated by universities and publishers – the very institutions that are best positioned to educate all Canadians."

Part B Mediations: Professional Practice and Creative Activity in Three Fields

The second part of the book, "Mediations," considers three fields of professional practice and creative activity: digital publishing, heritage management, and poetics. In each of these fields, the ubiquity of digital technologies ensures that questions of fair dealing continually arise and, due to the historical lack of progressive legislative reform, need to be addressed by committed practitioners, often in innovative and sometimes startling ways.

Publishing is a field that has been reinventing itself since the emergence of networked digital media. In a realm where the profit margin is already much narrower than the music industry, film, or television, publishers simultaneously have to master new technologies while contending with dwindling physical sales and the increasing concentration of digital sales through online portals and e-reader manufacturers like Amazon and Apple, all of whom demand a cut of the retail price. One of the earliest assertions about the effect of digital media on publishing, Stewart Brand's epigrammatic claim at the first Hackers Conference in 1984 that "information wants to be free" (which continues to be misinterpreted as a call for a the total abandonment of copyright), still has a surprising amount of traction. What Brand actually said still holds true: networked digital media creates a deadlock between the increasing value of information and the ease with which we can copy and redistribute it (Clarke 2000). Although the idea that copyright would simply become irrelevant in an era of networked digital publishing was debunked fairly early (by Mark Stefik in 1997), the first serious forays into the question of what digital publishing would become were largely hypothetical exercises in economic theory (e.g., Kahin and Varian 2000). The market for digital books would not really take off for another decade.

Our contributor Stevan Harnad (1998) was one of the first to argue that digital media would affect fair dealing in the academy, by insisting that the "theft" of scholarly text is a victimless crime. Since authors of refereed papers receive no remuneration for them, what needs to be protected against is not the theft of the papers per se, but the loss of attribution of authorship, suggesting that moral rights have particular significance in digital worlds (Rajan 2011). One implication of Harnad's prescient argument is that traditional trade models of publication such as subscriptions or pay-per-use might be replaced by much smaller charges on behalf of the author, in exchange for making the text freely and openly available in perpetuity, so long as attributions remain intact. On this basis, Harnad (1998, 2001) made early arguments in favour of institutionally based open archives of scholarly literature.

The proliferation of digital repositories and OA journals (Brown, Griffiths, and Rascoff, 2007) is presented by its advocates as an antidote to the prohibitive institutional pricing schemes, firewalls, and draconian copyright practices characteristic of many prominent academic journals (Willinsky 2006). Where high-quality digital copies of scholarly materials are available, their usage tends to displace the use of traditional print materials (Joint 2008) and OA digital research is between two and four times more likely to be cited than research published solely in print (Hall 2008: 47). Although implementations of open access have existed since 1969, less than 15 per cent of all peer-reviewed scientific journals are open access, and the majority of academic libraries have yet to implement OA repositories (Theodorou 2010). In the meantime, three companies (Elsevier, Springer, and Wiley) control the publication of 42 per cent of journal articles, and their profit margins have hovered at around 40 per cent for over a decade, a practice of limiting access to research that has been described as "pure rentier capitalism: monopolising a public resource then charging exorbitant fees to use it" (Monbiot 2011). These academic publishers control many of the leading journals; to maintain their reputations and stay on top of the work in their fields, many scholars are simply unable to stop reading or publishing in them. From the perspective of public institutions and at the policy level, conflicts abound. Public institutions cannot afford the price of these subscriptions, but they cannot uphold excellence if they deny faculty and students access to them. The licensing agreements of many databases and electronic journals often specify who is and who is not authorized to use the information they contain. Fair dealing, however, makes no such distinction between authorized and unauthorized users, creating potential conflicts between academics and librarians about the appropriate use of digital materials (Masango 2009: 234).

Even as OA journals and repositories continue to spread, openness and the free circulation of knowledge as public goods – values traditionally championed by the academy and Internet users in general – are coming into increasing conflict with corporate publishers' appeals for entrenched or even stronger owners' rights. Activists involved in the fight against enclosing "the commons of the mind" are supporters of the basic principle of copyright because it protects and maintains the rights of both the public and individual authors (Willinsky 2006: 41). However, maintaining a balance between owners' rights and those of educators working in the public interest is proving to be difficult because owners increasingly treat all educational uses as simple markets (Herrington, 2001). FLOSS movements, for example, have had little influence in commercial publishing realms.

Early experiments in open commercial science fiction publishing, such as Baen Books' Baen Free Library, suggested that making full-text versions of books available online for free could boost sales of print editions (Flint 2002, Suber 2006: 22–3), an argument later popularized by Chris Anderson's *The Long Tail: Why the Future of Business Is Selling Less of More* (2006). Science fiction authors and editors continue to be leaders in the field; TOR/Forge books recently announced the launch of a DRM-free e-book store for its titles (Tor Management Services). Some mainstream commercial publishers recognized that the circulation of digital versions of a text could serve to increase sales of paper books (Hall 2008: 51) and e-book publishing looked like a promising arena for the development of a regime of fair dealing that served publishers', authors', and readers' needs. Alas, such initiatives were abandoned in favour of competitive, proprietary infrastructure. The current digital publishing environment is dominated by short-lived hardware platforms, competing and conflicting file formats, cumbersome technical protection measures, and increasingly concentrated commercial distribution channels with draconian terms of service, none of which is conducive to fair dealing.

The basic tensions that Stewart Brand described are still very much in operation. At the same time that the OA paradigm is taking hold, the accessibility, ownership, and user rights that we have come to expect from books (such as "first sale" – the right to resell a used book – or the right to share personal copies), along with the cultural political values that scholars and students have traditionally supported (such as the free circulation of knowledge), are unlikely to continue to exist in the world of Amazon Kindles, Apple iBooks, and Sony eReaders (Striphas 2009). As in the realm of pedagogy, the degree to which digital texts will remain proprietary and the extent to which fair dealing practices will be legitimated is still unclear.

In the interest of providing some context for current discussions, preeminent Canadian publishing scholar Rowland Lorimer traces the modern history of academic publishing from its post–Second World War status as a service industry to its contemporary status as a commercial enterprise and addresses the implications of this transformation for access to scholarly research. Like other scholars and activists concerned about the practice of creating artificial scarcity by using copyright to restrict access to research (see Rees 2010), in his chapter, Lorimer argues the merits of OA publishing as a mechanism to increase both openness and competitiveness in academic publishing.

One of the factors that will determine how open or closed the future of publishing will be is the software that we use to manage digital publishing. Arthur Sale, Marc Couture, Eloy Rodrigues, Leslie Carr, and Stevan Harnad believe that if something isn't part of our digital desktop, it is often too easy to ignore, and that an invisible opportunity to access information often seems like no opportunity at all. Their contribution to this volume describes a tool that helps to instantiate fair dealing practices directly into the fabric of the digital media interface: a software button that allows readers of digital documents to request the author email the text to them for individual research purposes under the provisions of fair dealing.

Rights to particular measures of control over how works are used are clearly matters of concern for a wide range of creators. Practices of fair dealing, like those of intellectual property enforcement, take place in contexts shaped by historical inequalities. Not all peoples have been able to take advantage of the law's categories. Historically, IP law has privileged European categorical systems, and to that extent, it may further entrench socially specific values and world views. Dichotomies between the public and the private developed in early modernity; as many scholars have shown, they served particular interests and delegitimated others (Bowrey and Anderson 2009, Graham and McJohn 2005). Within IP debates, critics have placed particular emphasis on the ways in which a so-called public domain enables and encourages the appropriation of intangible resources held by non-Western others, particularly Indigenous peoples and those in the Global South (Biagioli,

Jaszi, and Woodmansee 2011). This is a dilemma well understood by the World Intellectual Property Organization, which recognized over a decade ago that a singular and wholly unregulated public domain would not meet the needs of many Indigenous peoples and local communities (WIPO, 2003).

Most IP regimes operate on the assumption that creative works circulate through standard forms of publication supported by markets. Rarely do we consider that channels of communication other than arm's-length licensing transactions may be necessary for the sharing of cultural work. Access to and the sharing of benefits from traditional knowledge and traditional cultural expressions may require distinctive forms of relationship involving trust, collaboration, and close apprenticeship. When it comes to traditional forms of cultural work, "the goal of providing and protecting public goods cannot be met by simply assuming their position in a singular public domain populated by cultural resources free for general appropriation" (Coombe 2005: 603). Indigenous peoples, in particular, often hold rights with respect to intangible cultural goods that are coupled with distinctive forms of obligation that constitute their identity as a people and pose new challenges to IP regimes (Brown 2003, 2005; Bowrey 2011; Geismar 2012; Gibson 2007; Graber and Burri-Nenova 2008). Finding means of respecting Indigenous responsibilities with respect to cultural goods also entails a consideration of Indigenous customary law, which, like any new IP consideration, must be tied to global norms (Drahos 2005).

The international human rights framework is the only global normative framework of sufficient legitimacy to engage these issues. Intellectual property rights are positioned as cultural rights within the global human rights framework, and are thus integrally related to rights to cultural heritage, to cultural diversity and the maintenance of cultural identity, as well as to rights of participation and cooperation (Coombe 1998; Ahmed, Aylwin, and Coombe 2009), although the appropriate articulation of these rights is ongoing (Helfer 2007, Macmillan 2008, Wong 2008, Yu 2007). Recognizing, appreciating, and maintaining cultural diversity pose new challenges for copyright law and fair dealing (Wong, Torsen, and Fernandini 2010). The next section of Part B focuses on issues of heritage management, an area in which Canada is emerging as a leader. The essays in this section illustrate the need to formulate policy attentive to issues of multiculturalism and intercultural dialogue in the management of collective cultural heritage.

As cultural policy scholars Rosemary Coombe and Nicole Aylwin remind us, Canada needs to place its fair dealing considerations into a wider cultural policy framework attentive to our human rights commitments. In their chapter, they ask that we reimagine cultural heritage as a dynamic, dialogic activity rather than the appreciation of static works of history – a shift that will bring new responsibilities as well as new rights. Contemporary heritage practice illustrates the emergence of a new cross-cultural ethics of care with respect to cultural properties. Recognizing that property is a relationship between people and that cultural goods are enmeshed in relations of historical identity, practitioners have moved beyond the commodity logic of intellectual property to embrace notions of guardianship and mutual responsibility (Coombe 2009). Putting this ethos into practice is manifest in new employment opportunities, benefit-sharing arrangements, and resource management structures that contribute to new forms of sustainable development based on an acknowledgment of collective cultural rights.

Cultural rights are too often absent from national and international conversations around the ownership of culture, because they concern the rights of groups as well as those of individuals. The overwhelming pervasiveness of digital technologies underlines the need to take cultural rights into account, because such technologies offer both a greater potential for the abuse of cultural rights and new opportunities for cross-cultural dialogue and deliberation (Christen 2005, Graber and Burri-Nenova 2008). Archaeologist George Nicholas illustrates this point in his chapter by focusing directly on the issues that digital media raise with respect to the cultural heritage of Indigenous peoples. He explains why Indigenous cultural heritage should not be considered part of the public domain, and argues for a new postcolonial research ethic to ensure that our use of digital technologies does not exacerbate the injuries inflicted on Indigenous peoples during our colonial past.

Nicole Aylwin closes this section by examining the precarious position that Canada inhabits as a leader in the field of cultural diversity management, ambiguously suspended between commitments to economic stimulation and social objectives that recognize public goods. She points out that policy discourse almost always invokes copyright law as an economic rather than a cultural vehicle, a tendency that calls into question Canada's ostensible objectives of maintaining multiculturalism and furthering intercultural dialogue. Aylwin reminds us of Canadian commitments to human rights as the appropriate normative framework for appreciating cultural diversity (Donders 2010) and a more responsible way forward with regard to issues of Canadian cultural policy.

Section III, "The Work of Poetics," focuses on how creative expression interfaces with issues of IP rights in literature and avant-garde art. As Marshall McLuhan's useful notion of artists as an "early warning system" in *Understanding Media* (1964) suggests, many of the issues pertaining to fair dealing and the discourse around intellectual property that have become relevant to cultural production and cultural policy at large first surfaced in poetic and artistic practice. Surrealism, Futurism, Cubism, Situationism, Warhol's Pop art, Fluxus and the neo–avant-garde, the conceptual art of the 1960s, contemporary literature and poetry, and virtually all of postmodern art established collage, bricolage, copying, and appropriation as major techniques of twentieth-century artistic production. These techniques also helped to inculcate a strong structure of feeling among artists, critics, and audiences that challenged traditional assumptions about the propriety of asserting property in cultural expressions.

A continuous stream of humanities scholars have reflected on the significance of copying practices in all areas of contemporary human creativity – Benjamin Buchloh (1982), Rosalind Krauss (1985), Frederic Jameson (1991), Jean Baudrillard (1994), and Hillel Schwartz (1996), to name but a few illustrious examples. In the Canadian context, literary theorist Linda Hutcheon (1989) approached the tension between the established canon of expressive works and the copyings and repetitions to which these were subjected in postmodern art (the focus of many ongoing copyright trials). She did so by formulating an influential theory of "complicit critiques" which function by changing the meanings of the originals from which they quote by repurposing their contents. The success of such critique depends on the recognizable invocation and hence the "copying" of these same originals. As Kembrew McLeod and Rudolf Kuenzli (2011) remind us, practices of reproducing cultural texts that critically comment on their cultural meaning are fundamentally important to the projects of creators in virtually all expressive media, from the early twentieth-century avant-gardes and the textual and musical subversion of blues and folk music traditions to contemporary architecture, culture jamming, and digital sampling. Despite ever more convincing theoretical explanations of the critical work that acts of creative appropriation accomplish, the legal landscape around contemporary appropriation art is far from settled (Aufderheide and Jaszi 2011).

The new non-commercial transformative use exemption for consumers, which requires attribution of source, use of a legal copy, and a determination that the use will have "no substantial effect on the exploitation of the original work" is unlikely to counter the chilling effects that threats of copyright infringement proceedings have had on such expression.

Parody has played a historically important role in shaping public understanding of permissible cultural appropriation in the visual and audible arts. As one of the oldest forms of creative expression in which the use of another's work is regarded as a creative act that uniquely conveys expressive value, it marks an important intersection between artistic and legal discourse. Parody represents an important component of the American fair use doctrine, and other national jurisdictions, such as Australia (see Australian Copyright Act 1968, McCutcheon 2008) have amended their copyright legislation to include it. As Carys Craig (2005: 445) suggests, "the transformative value of parody and the power that it wields as a means of social critique make a strong case for its inclusion in the fair dealing defence." In his contribution, legal scholar Graham Reynolds explores the long Canadian history of judicial lack of recognition for parody as a form of fair dealing by way of explaining why an explicit legislative amendment was ultimately deemed necessary, while assessing the prospects of such legislation for protecting parodic expressive practices in digital environments.

Kenneth Goldsmith – writer, artist, and administrator of UbuWeb (one of the largest and longest-standing freely accessible repositories of avant-garde materials on the Internet, including visual and concrete poetry, critical texts, spoken word pieces, films, and videos) – however, eschews law reform and embraces a strikingly different approach in his discussion of his management of online cultural content. Most of the material on UbuWeb was digitized and posted without the permission of its creators. It is kept publicly available thanks to Goldsmith's strenuous efforts to argue for the fairness of his "dealing" on a case-by-case basis, personally negotiating permissions with all creators and rights holders who send him cease-and-desist notices. Goldsmith reports that he is usually able to convince rights holders that it is in their own best interests to leave their materials in the archive, especially when the materials in question are nowhere else available. "Radical works deserve radical distribution," Goldsmith argues – an extreme position that might be considered one end of the spectrum of practices that constitute dynamic "dealing" with respect to copyright-protected objects in digital environments.

Filmmaker and digital media designer Justin Stephenson rounds off this section with an account of his experience with handling permissions while constructing a digital video project based on the creative work of famous Canadian experimental poet bpNichol. Recounting details of personal negotiations with the rights holders of the materials used, he suggests that there is a "third way," suspended, like Goldsmith's more radical approach, between the formal securing of licences and the conscious practising of infringement, based on respectful deliberations with creators (and their estates) about the intentions, desires, and perspectives of the original author as well as those of the creator who seeks to reuse the material. "Direct dealing," so easily facilitated by digital technology, may be quite effective in enabling consensual, fair access to protected cultural expressions. Unfortunately, Stephenson laments, such negotiations remain largely invisible to the institutions that manage copyright and forge cultural policy for Canadians.

The contributors to this part of the volume thus speak to the dynamism of fair dealing as a Canadian artistic practice that contrasts starkly with the static category our legislation bestows upon us. The essays contribute to an emerging field of scholarship that goes beyond general criticism of the law's failure to keep up with the communications and cultural transformations wrought by technological change to consider alternative moral economies or norm-based forms of culture and knowledge that operate outside of, in the shadow of, or as an alternative to formal IP systems (Biagioli, Jaszi, and Woodmansee 2011; Dreyfuss 2010; Zeilinger 2012). Building upon sociological and anthropological studies of communal forms of resource management, a new ethnography of what we might call "vernacular forms of intellectual property" is now emerging (e.g., Buccafusco 2007, Fagundes 2011, Fauchart and von Hippel 2008, Loshin 2008, Oliar and Springman 2011, Raustiala and Sprigman 2006).

A renewed interest in community norms among scholars of intellectual property is similar to the revitalization of interest in customary law among heritage practitioners and museum curators. Both add new dimensions to what is increasingly an interdisciplinary field of scholarship and practice concerned with emerging ethics for governing cultural access and circulation in digital environments. To achieve viable, broadly beneficial reforms in cultural policy, we need to attend to such ethics, which illustrate that alternatives to the current impasse between digital "piracy" and the "clearance culture" are not only necessary, but feasible and perhaps even inevitable (Zeilinger 2011). Whether and to what extent such empirical knowledge of viable ethical practices will serve to inform legal understandings of intellectual property and the necessary qualities of law reform is an important (if open) question.

Part C Making Our Heritage a Dynamic One

The final part of the volume explores relationships between Canada's cultural past and its cultural futures. Our contributors outline new challenges, and invite readers to consider the new opportunities that digital technology and digital creativity offer for restructuring interactions between creators and communities of users, be they audiences, researchers, or consumers. Coombe and Wershler have long been convinced that digital technologies enable online archives to uniquely balance the rights of creators, cultural institutions, and members of the public as users and creators in their own right. To that end, and with the support of the Canadian Foundation for Innovation and the Ontario Research Fund, they have developed an OS, online content management system (CMS) called Artmob for cultural institutions wishing to make their archives of cultural content digitally available to a broad public. Artmob fulfils and surpasses Canada's fair dealing requirements by fostering collaborative engagements between institutions and Canadian users – be they students, researchers, fans, or consumers – while facilitating the greater range of attribution, criticism, news reporting, and review that the Internet enables.

Artmob is designed to educate the public about copyright and more fully represent the complexity of contemporary cultural production practices while providing institutions with a greater sense of security in posting digitized cultural works. To take but one example: a video recording of a dramatic performance will involve individual performances as well as the reproduction of musical, dramatic, and possibly underlying literary works, each of which is distinct, and all of which may be associated with distinctive rights. Representing them as both singular and bound together within the online presentation of the composite work is important for attribution, licensing, informational, and educational purposes. Although this embedding of works and rights in composite works may be self-evident to IP lawyers, it is far from intuitive for cultural institutions holding archives of such works or to members of the public.

The Artmob project involves the development of innovative software that creates new interfaces to enable institutions to easily identify both works and rights holders (and others considered worthy of credit in distinctive fields of cultural production) and to make such attribution information available to the public. When such information is incomplete, or where it turns out to be incorrect, the Artmob system enables interested Internet users to provide archive administrators and future users with further context about a work's creation. In this way, the system fulfils twin objectives; not only do we potentially gain a more accurate understanding of the field of actors who hold rights in works, but we learn far more about the social and historical conditions under which works have been created by using the dialogic capacities of digital technology to augment our understanding of our cultural heritage.

Finally, Artmob is structured to invite and enable users to engage in online news reporting, criticism, and review. It encourages those who want to put digitally archived works to new purposes to negotiate directly with archivists and rights holders. In so doing, new and innovative licences for the use of cultural work may be forged and shared. Through the online use of this CMS, the very architecture of publicly available digital cultural archives can incorporate and encourage practices of dynamic fair dealing. The Artmob project is still in its infancy, and the public launch of its OS software is pending as this book goes to press. The remaining essays in the volume explain how and why we consider such a new and dynamic approach to fair dealing in digital environments to be long overdue.

The essays in Section I, "Documenting Pasts and Assessing Virtual Futures," ask difficult questions about popular access to the cultural works and public collections that arguably define Canadian cultural heritage, and illustrate how existing IP law impedes the maintenance and creation of new digital platforms for making this work available. The creation of databases of historically significant, collaboratively authored cultural works is an important example of the kind of activity that fair dealing exemptions should enable. However, as the surveys and case studies in this section show, it can be exceedingly difficult to develop such archives in the current culture of licences and permissions.

Using case studies of digital collections of Canadian theatre materials, sociolegal researcher David Meurer argues that the likely enforcement of Canadian copyright law increasingly puts it into direct conflict with the mandates of libraries, archives, and museums, which are obliged to make materials broadly accessible to the Canadian public. In his chapter, Meurer's chief concern is that the current discourse around copyright pits users against the creators and owners of cultural materials, with the result that public institutions such as libraries and archives, which should ideally mediate and facilitate access to cultural materials, are given no leverage or voice in public dialogue. Observing the recent development of a legally shaped cultural landscape that does not allow for the creation and dissemination of precisely the kinds of cultural archives most desired by students, researchers, and artists, Meurer concludes that controls on educational and not-for-profit uses of cultural materials need to be loosened in order to allow publicly held material to be made available for activities in the public interest. It was precisely to help arts administrators address these kinds of difficulties that the arts content management software, Artmob, discussed above, was designed.

In her chapter, literary scholar and arts practitioner Suzanne Zelazo examines the logistics around creating large, complex arts websites such as that of Toronto's Scream literary festival, and she explores the difficulty of negotiating permissions to access and reuse cultural works. Citing the increasing number of electronic recording devices, communications tools, and digital storage options now available to creators, festival organizers, and audiences, Zelazo illustrates how basic assumptions among participants and organizers concerning permissible uses for recordings of literary performances have changed over the past decade. With a multitude of different potential rights holders involved in the production and documentation of festivals such as Scream (poets, performers, videographers, curators, designers, etc.), the ways in which our digital cultural heritage is being built are by necessity characterized by dialogic negotiation and significant collaboration. This ethos needs to be reflected in Canada's fair dealing provisions, Zelazo suggests, if we want to ensure the continued survival of cultural events designed to spread and circulate cultural heritage.

In a white paper prepared for the Documentary Organization of Canada (2006a), lawyer Howard Knopf, a prolific and provocative advocate on copyright matters, drew attention to similar problems facing Canada's filmmaking community, by outlining a series of problems facing Canadian creators of documentary films because of the assumption that paid-for permissions are necessary for all uses of protected content. Knopf showed that the work of documentary filmmakers embodies the struggles that face many contemporary cultural creators, since their chosen form of creative expression inevitably relies on the use of materials protected as intellectual property. Nevertheless, Knopf considered the work that documentary filmmakers do as already constituting fair dealing, anticipating the emergence of a more flexible and far-reaching fair dealing model that the Supreme Court pentology arguably legitimates. Fully functional models of fair dealing, however, will also require the courage of creators of appropriative expressive works to confidently assert and defend their own dynamic acts of fair dealing, which seems particularly desirable when they are making cultural works that educate Canadians about their own cultural history.

The joint contribution of Martin Zeilinger and film scholar Eli Horwatt builds on the concerns outlined by Meurer and in Knopf's white paper. They consider how copyright can obstruct the availability not only of privately owned creative expressions, but also, as Asquith alerted us, of publicly funded works, even when the institutions controlling these works – such as the National Film Board (NFB) of Canada – hold a mandate to ensure public access to the creative expressions they manage. Under any conception of fair dealing, it would seem that publicly funded culturally expressive works should be made available and accessible in the public sphere. Taking as their example Canada's NFB, Zeilinger and Horwatt illustrate how the public access mandates of cultural institutions are inevitably at odds with the conditions through which they produce and distribute cultural works. These institutions become unnecessarily entangled in a larger clearance culture that puts their legal obligations to rights holders above their statutory obligations to public audiences. The authors argue that certain art forms – in this case, experimental cinema based on the reuse of existing film footage – foreground the difficulties that IP rights pose for creators, producers, and distributors. They conclude that a more comprehensive and flexible fair dealing model is needed to enable public institutions to fulfil their mandates to provide the public with broad access to the cultural creations they finance.

Works such as those discussed by Zeilinger and Horwatt often provoke legal conflicts because, like much of contemporary poetry and visual art, they represent acts of cultural appropriation, which remains a contentious practice in North American copyright law. The "recombinant creativity" that marks such creations is the focus of the last section of this volume, which features case studies from digital media contexts that prompt critical discussions of how conventional understandings of fair dealing fare on the playgrounds (or battlefields) of contemporary cultural production. As we have noted, appropriation and creative reuse of existing work has a long history in the literary and fine arts. These practices have been established as vehicles for dissenting political expression and the critique of commodification in critical thought at least since Walter Benjamin's work in the 1930s pointed to the potential of technologies of mechanical reproduction to provide users with new capacities to participate in production processes and thereby to resist the control of information by dominant elites (Benjamin 1968 [1936]). Practices of appropriation are recognized as a viable route of critical intervention within copyright regimes (Coombe 1998, Jaszi and Woodmansee 1994, 1996) and have proliferated in digital contexts (McClean and Schubert 2002, McLeod and Kuenzli 2011). As Lev Manovich (2002) argues, practices of reusing and copying, once primarily the critical tools of the artistic avant-garde, are now employed by all users and consumers of digital media, because they are implicit in the basic "cut and paste" operations we perform in digital contexts hundreds of time a day (Reynolds 2009).

Sampling, a contemporary reiteration of older forms such as collage and bricolage, is arguably the dominant mode of recombinant composition involving digital technologies. Manovich (2002: 135) suggests that the disc jockey rather than the poet is now the paradigmatic figure of the contemporary author. Martin Zeilinger's contribution considers how Canadian laws and their interpretation may affect such compositional practices and the communities who adopt them. He observes that even public licensing systems that are designed to facilitate fair dealing and online sampling proceed from the assumption that these licences will be used in good faith. Zeilinger considers the internationally successful Canadian band Crystal Castles and the alternative music community's reaction to their repeated misappropriation of electronic music distributed under CC licences. In light of the difficulty of enforcing such open licensing models, he suggests that artistic communities increasingly establish alternative ethics and protocols for fair dealing, rather than rely on legal models that fail to accommodate their practices and philosophies of creativity, collaboration, and sharing.

Hip hop is one of the most popular musical forms to have negotiated similar questions – not only in the creative underground but also in mainstream contexts. The cultural practice has an uneasy relationship with intellectual property for social and technical reasons alike: it is both a politicized form of creative resistance and a component of affirmative mass culture (Haupt 2008, McLeod and diCola 2011) that relies heavily on sampling and textual referencing. Since the first legal proceedings against hip hop artists in the late 1970s (see George 1998), cases involving sampling artists, record labels, and rights holders have been heard before the highest courts in many legal systems (Vaidhyanathan 2001,

McLeod 2005, Schur 2009). Not only are there ambiguities surrounding the legality of sampling in most legislation, there is no shared philosophy of sampling among practitioners. Musicians can be observed both bragging about the thrill of appropriating samples without having cleared rights *and* the luxury of being able to afford astronomical licensing fees (Demers 2006). In her chapter, communications scholar Alexandra Boutros focuses specifically on the relationship of Canadian hip hop practitioners to collaborative processes of cultural production that foreground "belonging" rather than "owning." Reading hip hop's history as a utopian narrative of collective, open concepts of creative expression that "might have been," Boutros argues that in order to address current cultural inequities, we need more than "technologically facilitated access to the public sphere." She suggests that sampling is a way for Canadian hip hop to index the histories both of the genre and of the individuals involved, while simultaneously exploring how the use of the term "piracy" has kept Canadian hip hop from receiving wider circulation.

Grace Westcott's contribution to this volume focuses on the phenomenon of fan fiction, which raises particularly thorny issues for ascertaining the equities of compensating for creative endeavour. In this area of creative play – in which copyright works are redeveloped and deployed by fans of the original in new creative directions – distinctions between producers, creators, users, and consumers of cultural texts are increasingly difficult to uphold (Jenkins 2006, Collins 2010, Schwabach 2011, McKay 2011). Intellectual property legislation, however, is not being amended to adequately reflect such developments, despite the fact that digital technology renders such positions ever more anachronistic (Jenkins 2008). The potential for unwitting copyright infringement, confusion about the meaning of invited access to intellectual property, permitted uses, and the ownership of new content that emerge here are increasingly evident in many other digital entertainment contexts (Coombe, Herman, and Kaye 2006; Lee, 2009; Postigo 2008a, 2008b). Rights holders in some branches of the entertainment industry, such as distributors of video and online games, are beginning to embrace and even encourage fan-produced derivative works, but this usually occurs within the parameters of strict copyright rules and permissions, with the ultimate purpose of generating further profit (Hayes 2008).

In response, scholars call for policy reform that eases restrictions and takes into account the important functions that the digital realm represents as a creative and learning environment (Livingstone and Brake

2010), or, in the absence of such reform, that we explore and defend the ways in which users assert their determination to create by circumventing technological barriers (Tushnet 2010). By contesting, renegotiating, and in some cases rejecting the equities and ethics of copyright, Westcott argues, fan fiction makes important contributions to a cultural landscape otherwise marketed (and owned) by the entertainment industry. Fan fiction is no longer a marginal subaltern phenomenon, but a popular facet of everyday life in commercial cultures. Nonetheless, unfortunate conflicts between copyright holders and their audiences frequently ensue because most of the works that fan fictions engage are still under copyright. Westcott thus urges the development of "a new kind of digital civility, an online code of respect in engaging with cultural works that recognizes and addresses authors' rights and legitimate concerns," so that it becomes easier for both authors and rights holders to recognize the contributions represented by user-created content. As scholars such as Penalver and Katyal (2009) have demonstrated, those who ignore IP law, protest it, or create alternatives to it, often serve inadvertently to improve its design and operation if their activities are taken seriously.

As a sociologist of information technology, Sara Grimes also approaches problematic encounters between the culture industries and their audiences by scrutinizing the little-explored but increasingly prevalent corporate appropriation of child's play in digital game worlds. Canadian new media scholars Dyer-Witheford and de Peuter (2009: 210) have pointed out the "deep *disparity* between the real conditions of digital production and existing property laws" in digital games. Creativity in this field relies heavily on the adaptation and modification of existing works. So-called consumers often produce much of the games' content. In such cases, the only possible way to ensure that no copyright infringement occurs is through invasions of children's privacy and the hobbling of digital tools to restrict their play. Children's play in these branded virtual worlds, "produces the information and cultural content of the commodity," to use Maurizio Lazzarato's (1996) seminal definition of "immaterial labour," thus providing valuable unremunerated content to cultural industries, which may then sequester it as their own intellectual property.

Grimes responds to the recent call by theorists of immaterial labour to move beyond the preoccupation with individual users as producers to appreciate the value of the work of those peoples whose creative energies are systematically exploited in creating corporately owned intellectual property and generating its profits (see also Coté and Pybus 2007, Dyer-Witheford, Burston, and Hearn 2010). Children's digital play clearly complicates the division between free and exploited labour (Hesmondhalgh 2011). As parents and educators, we might ask how well do we understand children's online interactions and how often do we reflect upon the nature of their play? How child-appropriate are branded digital playgrounds in which intellectual property functions to prevent children from freely expressing themselves, alienates them from the results of their creative play, and teaches them to be loyal, subordinate consumers (cf. Bakan 2011)? As the last chapter in Part C, Grimes' cautionary tale draws our attention to the potential power that rests with a budding generation of youth increasingly at home in digital worlds and the importance of creating policy that honours their need for a digital cultural landscape that truly encourages, rather than impedes or alienates their creativity, freedom of expression, learning, and citizenship.

Conclusion

Despite the promises of digital technologies, we are currently witnessing a clear shift towards a dramatically less open culture on a variety of fronts: closing bookstores; growing concentration and centralization in the production, circulation, and sales of electronic texts; and unsympathetic governments eager to replace the subvention of culture as a public good with the rhetoric of cultural industry that addresses a narrow range of purely economic concerns. The chilling effects of potential enforcement of copyright in all areas of online activity, the withholding of publicly financed research and creative work, constraints on learning, limitations of constitutional rights, the failure to consider issues of human rights and cultural policy, the marginalization of recombinant creativity, the potential criminalization of new forms of expressive play, and the extension of corporate control over digital creative work that we have explored in this volume illustrate that this tendency to control and contain culture is extending into all dimensions of Canadian social life.

This volume grew out of a concern with the ways in which the interpretation of intellectual property with respect to digital technologies was shaping everyday cultural life in the Canadian context. The characterization of many of the everyday digital "dealings" of Canadians as simply unlawful is both inappropriate and inopportune. As our contributors have illustrated, Canadians involved in creating online culture have done so with goodwill and a sophisticated and evolving ethics with respect to authors' rights, moral rights, users' rights, and human rights. Copyright laws that contain narrow and rigid fair dealing provisions not only make it difficult to read, write, learn, and create, they make it impossible for our culture to evolve in a fashion that respects the work we do as creators, students, scholars, consumers, and citizens. They serve primarily to protect corporate investments rather than public interests. If this opinion seems alarmist, consider that as we wrote the first draft of this introduction, Canadians discovered that officials in the Harper government were taking instruction from US officials representing industry interests in lengthening and expanding copyright protections (Geist 2011). Once again, it would appear that copyright reform in Canada was being driven by foreign interests and corporate agendas. New case law and some very limited legislative reform have, nonetheless, provided Canadians with some reason for optimism that narrow economic interests will no longer fully dominate policy conversations.

At the very least, we hope we have shown how fundamental intellectual property is, not merely to the Canadian economy but to the Canadian public interest and how important fair dealing is in Canadian cultural life and heritage. In the longer term, we hope that the inherent tendency of digital technologies to facilitate copying, sharing, and cultural exchange will be embraced as a positive quality, which may also encourage a principled return to copyright law's original purpose of enabling learning, creativity, cultural productivity, scholarship, critical conversation, and expressive collaboration, while furthering cultural policy objectives and supporting cultural rights. In such a world, the practice of fair dealing would be considered a fundamental cultural right rather than a mere exemption to the economic privileges of others.

The essays collected here speak to the difficulties that face Canadian cultural practitioners, researchers, educators, citizens, and activists in today's prohibitive culture of licences and permissions. Taken individually, the contributions may appear to paint dire pictures of the current status of digital cultural production and creativity. As a whole, however, they point to a shared conviction that our collective desires to create, to share, and to learn by fairly engaging the wealth of expression and the communication channels available to us is sufficiently powerful to challenge and change the status quo. If the legal difficulties we face when dealing fairly are real ones, we nonetheless have robust traditions of cultural exchange, negotiation, and intercultural dialogue that illustrate that we are forging a dynamic and evolving digital cultural heritage. Whether these practices avoid the law, challenge it, work in its shadow, or ultimately succeed in changing and shaping it, they suggest that the future of fair dealing is already at hand. The Canadian cultural landscape depends on this field of dynamic practice.

PART A

The Canadian Copyright Context

1 Copyright and Freedom of Expression: Fair Dealing between Work and Play

BITA AMANI

Copyright, a creature of statute, provides explicit rights and remedies that are exhaustively defined in the Canadian Copyright Act. Copyright law has a dual purpose: to promote the creation and broad dissemination of works while expanding the "expressed universe" (McCutcheon 2007: 141). To this end, copyright protects original expressions rather than ideas. Owners have the exclusive right to reproduce a "work" (s. 3), but not the exclusive right to use it. Copyright is also subject to certain exceptions and limitations – including the fair dealing provisions – that implicitly acknowledge that the public needs to be able to use works for specific purposes. Nevertheless, how a person may use protected expression in further expressive activity is a source of significant legal contention, stemming both from uncertainties in the law and from the practical obstacles that face parties engaged in litigation.

The difficulty with copyright is the inability of anyone to know, at any given time or with certainty, what cultural content is fenced in as a protected *work*, and what is available for *play* in the protean space beyond. Just as any copyright-protected work contains both idea and expression, the line between the private and the public is also internal and traverses the work even as it "separate[s] protectable from non-protectable elements" (Craig 2010: 225). Moreover, copyright law continues to struggle with the spurious exercise of determining whether a work is original, no matter how low the threshold for this definition. To the extent that only that part of an expression that originates with an author constitutes a protected work, the boundaries of a copyright-protected work can only be approximately imagined. Generally, assertions of intellectual property (IP) rights are given priority, against which the expressive rights of others struggle to find voice. Copyright's function is not exhausted, however, by what it prevents people from doing with copyrighted expressive work. Equally important is its fundamental role in facilitating permissible and, indeed, desirable uses of such expression by establishing and enforcing the boundaries of these state-sanctioned rights. When and how, for example, can you "remix" the cultural content of a work, recreate it, or critically reproduce it? This chapter develops the argument that certain playful expressive activities, while not always producing copyrightable works per se, are defensible exercises of constitutional rights within the ambit of s. 2(b) of the Charter of Rights and Freedoms (hereinafter, the Charter) which protects freedom of expression over and above copyright's belaboured classifications.

If a cultural creation is both original and expressive, and thus deemed a work, it is not only a constitutionally protected form of expression but also protected by copyright. What is often overlooked in copyright disputes, however, is that the same constitutional protection must be extended to meaningful forms of expressive play, even when and perhaps especially when they will not qualify for proprietary protection. With its propensity to value work and vilify play, copyright law has proven to be no fun at all, and continues to artificially construct value through the rhetorical deployment of a romanticized trope of authorship that serves primarily to protect commercial investment. Moreover, expression – particularly in the digital realm – is simply not all about work. From the perspective of those engaged at ground zero – the YouTube generation of fan fiction writers, gamers, mashers, samplers, jammers, and transformers of popular culture – digital culture is, in fact, all about play. "Work" characterizes only a sliver of expressive activity within digital environments and does not capture its motivations; if Girl Talk – a pre-eminent mash-up artist and champion of the playful use of protected works – quit his day job as a biomechanical engineer to pursue remixing full-time, it was presumably because he had more fun engaged in such play. However, the burden of proof may be too costly for the author of expressions that creatively draw upon the expressions of others; it may render the justification of the exercise of expressive freedom simply too much work. Or, to put this another way, if expression automatically equals work, then many authors continue to be dispossessed from their means of production, since the resources with which they labour and the expressive inputs into their meaning-making are tied up with state-sanctioned property rights.

Although this has yet to have a full chilling effect on digital play, it does pose ominous limits and shifts policy conversation from balancing rights to enforcing absolute rights. As a society, we need to renegotiate the permissibility of playful engagement with protected cultural artefacts to ensure fair access to cultural expression and equal access to the constitutional right to express ourselves.

Monopolies on Freedom of Expression: All That Is (Un)Fair in Copyright Wars

Although expressive freedom is constitutionally protected in Canada, copyright law subordinates such freedom by clearly privileging the rights of copyright owners as property. In the current "copyright wars" (Patry 2009, Yu 2005), an owner's duly protected freedom of expression has greater power in the universe of expressive freedom because it contains the ever-latent capacity to subvert the cultural uses of creative practitioners in digital play by rendering these infringements of copyright. Federal law confers on copyright owners not only an exclusive right to control the communication of the expressive work, but by corollary, the nature of the monopoly confers an exclusivity that serves to undermine the very expressive freedom of others. In short, copyright law not only grants exclusive rights as specific privileges, but also privileges a particular elitist vision of culture in which only creators and distributors of works speak expressively and, in turn, use these privileges to silence the playful expressions of others. Copyright owners have become, effectively, cultural managers by authority of the Copyright Act. By an Act of Parliament, freedom of expression has, thus, been transformed from a constitutionally protected right in public law to an issue of peripheral management for private parties imposing their copyrights through licensing, rent collection, or litigation. With the assistance of the judiciary in enforcing these property arrangements, owners are delegated regulatory discretion to administer our constitutional rights. In the process, freedom of expression is rendered anathema to IP rights – copyright's foe.

In digitally networked environments, expression is fluid and expansive. Adaptable and adapted to the ecology of the World Wide Web, expression involves relational processes that produce creative content and resist binary classifications of work and play. The shifting structure of control over communications systems in digital environments, moreover, has practically contested the traditional capacity of copyright owners to enforce their rights. Copyright laws were "drafted with a particular model of mass communications in mind: one in which all copies issued from the centre, with the media owner at the centre and a passive, receiving public at the end nodes" (Cahir 2007: 73). In digital worlds of networked communications, however, any dealing with a work requires some reproduction, however transient (Litman 1994), meaning that copyright and its limits are implicated nearly every time users of cultural goods communicate and disseminate expression. Not surprisingly, new mechanisms for proprietary management have emerged in response, dramatically altering the dynamics of copyright's "war game" from defining the scope of the rights that authors and their assignees actually have to ensuring legal protections for digital rights management (DRM) mechanisms. These new tools technologically *impose* the copyright holder's expansive interpretation of his own proprietary rights on all users, regardless of what entitlements the latter might have in their own right. Law reform efforts in Canada have sought to entrench such remedial market responses into further statutory protections for copyright owners.

The battle continues and the rhetoric of "war" commonly espoused by copyright owners in this debate has turned the regime into a parody of expressive freedom. Peter Yu (2005: 681) notes that in the United States "[in its] desperate attempt to protect itself against digital piracy, the recording industry has sued, or threatened to sue, virtually everybody – telecommunications service providers, consumer electronics, corporate employers, universities, lawyers, college researchers, hackers and cryptographers, and students" (citations omitted). Such strong enforcement pursuits have proven to be both unpopular and provocative, fostering a countercultural movement of enormous energy and conviction (Vaidhyanathan 2004). Against the litigious agenda of copyright owners, it is left to our fair dealing provisions to define the permissibility of copying processes and outcomes to be negotiated by settlement or litigation.

To that end, the 2004 Supreme Court of Canada (SCC) decision in *CCH Canadian Ltd. et al.* v. *Law Society of Upper Canada*, and public discussions on copyright reform since, have raised public hopes that a more socially instrumental approach to copyright might finally have achieved legitimacy, if not primacy in legal analyses of infringement. The judgment in *CCH* indicated, as no Canadian case had before, that the function of copyright was a social one in which individual private rights must be balanced with social benefits. Recognizing fair dealing as an "integral part to the *Copyright Act*" (para. 48), the Court affirmed it as a *users' right* (see also Craig and Maxwell, this volume). Practically speaking, however, it continues to be the defendant to a copyright suit who is burdened with defending the propriety of his expression as fair dealing. She must prove that her expression not only falls within the scope of one of the specifically enumerated exceptions, but also that her use of it was actually fair (*CCH* para. 50). As fairness is not defined in the Act, this remains a contextual inquiry: "whether something is fair is a question of fact and depends on the facts of each case" (para. 52), leaving enormous discretion with the judiciary and impossible evidentiary obstacles to face defendants.

Given these impediments, it becomes important to ask whether the assertion of copyright infringement does not unduly impinge upon constitutionally protected expression. In other words, we might first ask whether copyright's limitation on constitutionally protected expression is justified under section 1 of the Charter, rather than whether dealings with the contents of the protected work are permissible under copyright's defence of fair dealing. The current approach defers analysis of the propriety of the defendant's conduct from consideration of her constitutionally prior expressive freedoms to focus on the appropriate limits upon the owner's exclusive property rights. This approach makes it difficult to give any real credence to the much-vaunted principle of balance between the interests of owners and users. For example, despite the evident sympathies towards the public indicated in *CCH*, the net result of the judgment as legal precedent was: first, a relatively low threshold for granting rights, based not on creativity but on skill and judgment; and second, a clear but lesser statement of judicial opinion affirming the need for more nuanced determination of appropriate limits to these rights. In the alternative vision proposed here, the broad definition of freedom of expression in the Charter would significantly change the dynamics of the copyright balance by facilitating a potential finding of breach of expressive freedom. Whether the expression is work or play would be immaterial under the Charter analysis as a legal measure of worth for protecting freedom of expression. The balance of proof would be shifted to its rightful holder, the copyright owner, to justify copyright's limits upon constitutionally protected rights.

Nevertheless, the *CCH* decision was a welcome and timely judicial endeavour to explicitly adopt the language of users' rights in the context of copyright disputes, and more so for resisting the urge to narrow the range of permissible dealings on account of the commercial context. For those in the digital space, it was especially important given the subculture of commonplace but culpable infringement in which everyday users of cultural texts playfully work to transform the meanings of cultural goods, to undermine corporate and state hegemony and to challenge dominant meanings as well as the legal authority to engage in meaning making. Users who are now more accurately described as productive players (be they primarily authors, artists, bloggers, consumers, creative workers, gamers, or software developers) thereby threaten to trigger a cultural revolution. Such a revolution may compel a re-examination of our very ideas of culture – from the conservative view of the authentic representation of an aesthetic reinforced by the conversion of expressive activity into fixed works and ultimately commodity goods, to a greater appreciation for the social structures and forces that lie behind the manifest appearances of everyday life (Hebdige 1979: 6–7) – much like punk culture did before it. These are revealed when such commodities and their meanings are shown to be socially constructed by relations of power buttressed by law. Until then, copyright law continues to enforce a paradigm of control according to which "everything in everyday life is dependent on the representation which the bourgeoisie *has and makes us have* of the relations between men and the world" (citing Barthes, original emphasis). Such power inevitably intrudes on the domain of individual liberty and impacts not only our freedom of expression but the "freedom of a person" (Rothman 2010: 49) more generally. The agency and playful labour of vast numbers of citizens continues to be alienated from them even as copyright's mappings of our social culture are increasingly resisted within the Internet's infrastructure of disaggregated control, a social web that cultural studies scholars might refer to ecologically as an "organic society" (Hebdige 1979: 6).

An organic society is one that is alive and *grows* (often symbiotically) not only through production, but also through reproduction and mutation of its cultural core structures, narratives, symbols, and meanings. Digital culture similarly thrives through cross-fertilization, hybridization, and sampling. As other contributors to this volume indicate, with regard to fan fiction (Westcott) and the free circulation of avant-garde art (Goldsmith), for example, the incentive for players in digital contexts is very often simply to maintain an identity, expressively survive, and interrelate in an ecosystem of shared culture. Currently, however, this incentive appears as diametrically opposed to copyright law's need to petrify fixed original works in a particular time, place, and technological medium, unless otherwise authorized by a singular proprietor (Amani 1999a, 1999b). Unless those who champion the public domain for the purpose of ensuring vibrant and sustainable cultural development intercede, the dominance of one species of expressions by artificial (state-supported) structures will throttle the evolution and development of another, not because play, as a form of expression, is inevitably more vulnerable than work, but because, as we have seen, the digital environment in which play thrives has become ever more hostile towards it. In this context, the importance of the right to freedom of expression for sustaining a robust and meaningful cultural life must be reconsidered.

The Constitutional Guarantee of Freedom of Expression in Canada

In 1997, David Fewer called for a more principled and comprehensive approach to copyright regulation by Parliament and the courts, one that was reconcilable with and accountable to constitutional guarantees of freedom of expression in the Charter. Fewer was dismayed at the lack of Canadian judicial consideration of the inherent conflict between copyright and freedom of expression:

> One might presume that litigation under the Canadian *Copyright Act* would attract considerable constitutional scrutiny: freedom of expression and the law of copyright in Canada should not easily coexist. After all, the *Copyright Act* deals exclusively with the manipulation of expression, which enjoys constitutional protection. (1997: 177)

A decade and a half later, we should be even more distressed by the fact that our policy makers continue to ignore this friction even as it has become ever more pronounced in digital environments.

In *Irwin Toy* v. *Quebec* (1989), the majority of the SCC confirmed that there were three main reasons for protecting expressive freedom:

> (1) seeking and attaining the truth is an inherently good activity; (2) participation in social and political decision-making is to be fostered and encouraged; and (3) the diversity in forms of individual self-fulfillment and human flourishing ought to be cultivated. (para. 976)

The SCC's position was that "activity is expressive if it attempts to convey meaning" (para. 968). Peter Hogg (1992) explains that "this broad definition has been supported by a willing acceptance of the broadest rationale for the protection of expression – the realization of individual self-fulfilment – as well as the Court's view that the Charter should be given a generous interpretation" (1992: 963). While copyright has certain inbuilt limits to extending protections – such as the doctrine of originality, the fixation requirement, the concept of protectable "works," and the distinction between idea and expression, referred to above – the Charter has no requirement of novelty or originality for the purpose of recognizing and defending expressive practice.

There is a good argument to be made that copyright and freedom of expression are compatable and reinforcing because copyright is not a right but a privilege (Boyle 2003) designed to invite expression and bestowed as a matter of cultural policy (Vaidhyanathan 2001). The federal authority to create copyright law is provided under the division of powers in section 92 of the Constitution Act of 1867 and so copyright is borne from federal statute. Freedom of expression, on the other hand, is guaranteed by the Charter under section 2(b), which asserts: "Everyone has the ... freedom of thought, belief, opinion and expression, including freedom of the press and other media of communication." It is therefore a legal imperative that section 2(b) rights be given priority when in conflict with copyright law, unless justified by section 1 of the Charter (as a reasonable limit prescribed by law that can be demonstrably justified in a free and democratic society). The reluctance to confront section 2(b) of the Charter in copyright cases may stem from a practical preference by lawyers and judges to endorse copyright law's internal limits over an external one of such significance and consequence. Charter litigation demands fresh expertise and poses new costs, delays, and dangers. This reluctance may also be part of a more general tendency to narrow the construction of available defences (Fewer 1997: 212). Others have suggested that courts are loath to go beyond copyright doctrine unless these internal limits are wholly ineffectual (Reynolds 2006: 184). Nonetheless, Charter rights are part of the supreme law of the land and although Charter concerns and implications may be to some degree addressed by copyright's internal limits and exceptions, it is clear that where the issue of freedom of expression is raised, an exhaustive Charter analysis is necessary (Fewer 1997: 212–35). Still, such an inquiry is exceptional rather than ordinary.

Another interpretive obstacle that may have delayed such claims is the principle in s. 32(1) that the Charter only applies to public parties, which would not appear at first glance to extend scrutiny to private litigants in copyright disputes. The SCC has established, however, that "in the context of civil litigation involving only private parties, the Charter will apply to the common law only to the extent that the common law is found inconsistent with Charter values" (*Hill* v. *Church of Scientology Toronto*, para. 95). Moreover, as Fewer (1997) observes, the Supremacy Clause (s. 52) of the Constitution Act, 1982 does not differentiate when instructing that "any law inconsistent with the provisions of the Constitution is, to the extent of the inconsistency, of no force or effect" (212). Thus, Fewer contends, "any law – including the common law – that is inconsistent with the Charter should therefore fall under some degree of scrutiny" (213). The government action requirement for raising a Charter defence is readily met where there is the potential for criminal prosecution as is the case for copyright infringement. The SCC has also been sympathetic to Charter claims "where individuals exercise statutorily conferred powers" and "but for the *Copyright Act* – an act of Parliament – the defendant would not be brought before the court to defend his or her expressive activities" (214–15).

Rather than assume that the Charter is redundant because of existing internal copyright limits and safeguards such as the defence of fair dealing, we must acknowledge and embrace Charter compliance as a check on copyright's public reach. Charter analysis is a principled method for reconciling rights of expression with allegations of infringement, providing some normative content for the user's rights side of the social balance that copyright is meant to accomplish. Decisions by the judiciary in copyright cases, and the process by which they are reached, are also subject to Charter review: "the Supreme Court has embraced the reasoning that, after all, court orders are little more than the state's imposition of its will upon private citizens" (216). Fewer's conclusion merits repeating: "Defendants asserting expressive values who are faced with crippling court-ordered injunctions or damages or orders of delivery, could challenge those court-ordered remedies – or at least the court's choice of remedy – as infringing freedom of expression" (217).

Nonetheless, most defendants have neither incentive nor resources to prolong litigation when confronted with scales of justice clearly skewed in favour of copyright owners (Lessig 2004, Coombe 1998, Gaylor 2008). Although public interest in copyright's prohibitions on freedom of expression is increasing, defendants appear to settle or pay the licensing fees requested by the plaintiffs, rather than add further litigation costs and procedural complications by raising a constitutional defence. Perhaps they also recognize that judges have historically been and likely will continue to be cautious with Charter rights in copyright cases because the wholesale privileging of copyrights over expressive works might be found offensive to constitutional guarantees of freedom of expression. This seems especially arguable given the SCC's expansive interpretations of freedom of expression.

In *Irwin Toy*, for instance, the SCC acknowledged that breaking the law (e.g., by illegally parking a car) can be a constitutionally protected expression under section 2(b) of the Charter, if it is done with an expressive purpose – for example, in protest of parking regulations (para. 969). If the act of copying can be considered an act of constitutionally protected expression, then the criminality of the large community of infringers is entirely defensible; one might even say that it is to be encouraged (Gaylor 2008). Are such defiant acts simple vigilantism or might they be seen as an indirect form of constitutional advocacy? As Penalver and Katyal (2009) argue, the acts of "scofflaws" often provoke us to consider the extent to which positive laws accord with our more fundamental values. This raises the possibility of evoking a constitutional challenge against the federal regime itself. Such an action would demand that a court "draw a line embodied by the fair dealing defence" (Fewer 1997: 216), between those kind of takings from the universe of expression that are appropriate and in the public interest and those that are infringing appropriations, allowing for substantial, but permissible takings. In short, such Charter litigation "argues that the [Copyright] Act gets the line wrong" (216).

Whether copied in substantial or insubstantial part, expression that creates and conveys meaning constitutes a legitimate exercise of freedom of expression. The remedies, common law doctrines, and defences of copyright must therefore be interpreted in full compliance with section 2(b) of the Charter. As long as copyright cases refrain from directly engaging the constitutional issue of freedom of expression as central to any finding of copyright infringement, the internal limits of copyright doctrines such as originality, the idea/expression dichotomy, the concept of substantial taking, and fair dealing are, for better or worse, the more immediate safeguards for our constitutional expressive freedoms and the only means we have to ensure that copyright retains any sense of balance. We can only hope that more judgments respecting freedom of expression to limit copyright owners' exclusive rights will eventually mitigate the censorious climate developing in digital environments.

In this latest context, we are collectively witnessing copyright law's full maturation, As many critics have noted, copyright evolved from a tool of state censorship to a tool of private censorship (Lessig 2004,

Moore 2003, Vaver 2006), and it is increasingly a means of eliciting self-censorship against the uncertain exercise of IP enforcement (Sunder 1996). When aggregated, the costs of copyright litigation, the financial vulnerability of defendants, and the understandable propensity to settle rather than engage in legal struggle all militate to turn copyright into a predatory tool of cultural censorship (see also Knopf 2006a). For example, Matt Groening, the creator of *The Simpsons* was amenable to the incidental use of his work in a documentary film to make a critical cultural commentary, but Fox, which held the rights, demanded $10,000 for use of the relevant 4.5 second clip. As Larry Lessig (2004) tells the story, although the critical use of the clip without any permission or payment of royalty would almost certainly be a fair one, the filmmaker was unable to proceed because the production company's errors and omissions insurance required prior clearance of any and all copyright-protected materials (95–8). "Working on a shoestring," the filmmaker could not reasonably make a fair use argument at the end of the industrial process when release deadlines loom, tempers are short, and budgets overextended (98–9). If this is the case under US flexible fair use provisions, such tendencies are only exacerbated in jurisdictions like Canada with strict fair dealing exemptions.

The rhetoric of "copyright wars" may be helpful for emphasizing high stakes with winners, losers, and resource disparities; however, it also serves to underplay the real impact of these cultural wars on the public and social interest (Hughes 1999). It is still not taken for granted that intellectual properties have a cultural life – that they are dialogic forms borne by a social communicative process of creative meaning making in which the consumption and reproduction of existing cultural forms is an integral part of all cultural production (Boon, this volume; Coombe 1991, 1998) and vital social values placed on community (Craig 2006). Copyright in an expressive work rarely recognizes its personal meanings, social origins, or interpersonal value. Increasingly, copyright privileges are shaped only to ensure the commercial exploitation of expressive works after these have been created. Ask any author alienated from her work (as nearly all authors seeking dissemination of their work are likely to be, once they assign their copyright to their commercial publishers), and she will tell you that even if she supports your derivative creations as forms of expressive freedom, her publishers leave her no room to bless your play. Where copyright is only deemed valuable in a market context – a limited system of commodity exchange – the social nature of expressive work is denied, and it is linked to a dominant and inadequate conceptual articulation of property as a form of exclusion rather than relation (Carpenter, Katyal, and Riley 2009; Craig, Turcotte, and Coombe 2011). This feature of copyright is perhaps most troubling in digital environments, where dialogic social play is an integral and critical feature of cultural growth and development (Reynolds 2006, Corneliussen and Rettberg 2008, Coombe, Herman, and Kaye 2006).

I Fought the Law, so Who Won?

The expansion of the universe of expressions that copyright regimes ideally seek to promote is highly valued in free and democratic societies, and it is constitutionally protected activity in Canada, regardless of whether or not the expressions in question constitute copyrightable work. Basic principles of constitutional jurisprudence support Fewer's observation that copyright as a mere property interest is an example of "economic rights that do not also evoke values enshrined in freedom of expression" and thus does not command Charter rights in its own right (1997: 222). The integrity of this position is further supported by the desired policy objectives of the copyright regime itself, which promises to enable and ensure a greater amount of publicly available, intrinsically valued expression (McCutcheon 2008). When copyright law ceases to do this, and fair dealing does not function to enable a greater amount of publicly available, intrinsically valued expression, it loses its legitimacy and its claims upon us.

If freedom of expression as a practice is to flourish, we need the freedom to access, use, and learn from the cultural contributions of others in the public sphere, which, in digital environments, inevitably demands their reproduction. Copyright owners now seek to further obstruct these exchanges in digital environments with pay-per-use and complex one-click licensing agreements supported by the threat and costs of litigation. Insofar as such practices gain the benefit of legal protection, copyright will continue to be used to further circumscribe the expressive freedom of others, coercively eliciting permission where none may be required by law. As we have seen, copyright may also censor those who are too poor to pay or otherwise disenfranchised from defending their dealings, however fair these might be. The emerging culture of copyright is thus entirely a culture of exclusive proprietary rights, rather than one that entails duties of any kind (Vaver 2006). If *CCH* belatedly recognized the rights of users under Canadian law, the case did little to advance copyright holders' duties or encourage a field of respect for dialogue and communicative cultural exchange. To counter this development, we must embrace our freedoms of expression as part of a rights framework that legitimates a wider range of reproductive activities as acts of cultural fair dealing. Money talks, but justice should be more widely affordable. How copyright law adapts to such social justice issues may be the most significant indicator for its prognosis in the twenty-first century.

2 From the Right to Copy to Practices of Copying

MARCUS BOON

The copy shop in Toronto where I have had course packages made for a number of years was busted recently, and the books used to make the copies, along with the copied packages (coursepacks) themselves, were confiscated. The store's owner gave me the number of Access Copyright, the organization responsible for punishing this enterprise. When I called the number and spoke to one of the agents there, I was informed that the copy shop apparently lacked a licence to make coursepacks and that in the future I should only frequent copy shops that hold such licences. My books were shipped back to me, along with a list of legitimate copy shops, whose owners responded in an understandably cautious and suspicious way when I contacted them to check that they were, indeed, Access Copyright licensed. After many phone calls, requests for information, and the like, a copy shop near York University reluctantly produced my coursepacks, at a price approximately four times higher than before. And so, in planning the next semester's courses, I decided to use the York University bookstore, with its six-week turnaround time, high prices, and extraordinary restrictions on the types and quantities of materials that I am permitted to teach.

This was something of a rude awakening for someone who had just finished writing a book called *In Praise of Copying* (2010). In this book, I argue that debates about the legal framing of copying within a system of property rights miss the universal nature of processes of imitation and copying – processes that are constitutive of the very possibility of being human, of inhabiting the world, and of positing the existence of subject and object and other core framings of our situation. Although I have been broadly sympathetic to the liberal critique of existing intellectual property (IP) law as it is embodied in recent works such as

Lawrence Lessig's *Free Culture: How Big Media Uses Technology and the Law to Lock Down Culture and Control Creativity* (2004) and James Boyle's *The Public Domain: Enclosing the Commons of the Mind* (2008), I feel that such critiques accept the capitalist system as it currently stands, and that they propose modifications of IP law that basically support the expansion of that system and its needs to exploit creative labour, the entrepreneurship of ideas, and so on. If those seeking a "free culture" could posit the freedom of culture only in terms of the existing system, then how free could such culture really be? Furthermore, it seems to me that the actual practices of copying that are found on peer-to-peer (P2P) networks, in the promiscuous exchange of ideas, sounds, languages, and bodies in carnivals, dance halls, art events, and other such contemporary spaces are poorly described by the discourses of entrepreneurship or creative labour and point towards a freedom that is joyful and that does not depend on the law.

My story is hardly unusual, just another minor skirmish in the IP wars, yet very revealing of the situation regarding copying in Canada at the turn of the twenty-first century. The distribution of learning materials within the educational system was considered exceptional even before the birth of copyright law with the Statute of Anne in Britain in 1710. For example, specific provisions were made for the legal deposit of copies of all published works in the libraries of the great European universities such as Oxford, dating back to 1610 (Partridge 1938). In certain countries, such as the United States, a fair use exception to copyright has protected scholars who need to make copies of texts for research or study, but education has increasingly fallen within the domain of the marketplace, where such learning materials are today considered private property, which requires permission in order that access be granted, and a corresponding fee levied for use. The more restrictive fair dealing exception in Canadian law offers even weaker protection to scholars and researchers, and in the corporate Canadian university of today, the interpretation and enactment of IP laws, which would previously have been carried out by law agencies directly acting on behalf of the nation state, are today increasingly enacted by private organizations such as Access Copyright that are funded by and act as proxies for the publishing industry. Indeed, it is striking that in both newspaper coverage of coursepack busts and Access Copyright's own press releases, which routinely describe unlicensed copying of coursepacks as "robbery" or "piracy," there is rarely, if ever, mention of the existence of a fair dealing and/or fair use exception (see, e.g., Kenyon Wallace in the *Toronto Star*, 10 Jan. 2009, and Kagedan and Legault in the *Varsity*, 19 Oct. 2009, as well as the corresponding Access Copyright press release from 15 Oct. 2009).

Access Copyright, formerly known as Cancopy, has its origin in a provision of the Canadian law that allows for "collectives" to administer permissions and fees on behalf of a wide range of copyright holders. To quote from the organization's website: "Since 1988, Access Copyright has been meeting the needs of businesses, educators, governments, and other organizations across Canada with our innovative copyright licensing solutions. Our licences give content users immediate, legal access to the copyright protected materials they need to copy from to get their jobs done, while ensuring that creators and publishers are fairly compensated when their works are copied" (Access Copyright). This apparently straightforward and reasonable statement of "what we do" condenses a good deal of the ideology of intellectual property under late capitalism, a discourse of meeting needs, providing solutions, of access, getting jobs done, and of course, fair compensation for all.

The term "fair dealing" is a transposition from the British copyright law of 1911 to the original Canadian Copyright Act of 1921, and the word "fair" itself has a long and complicated history, moving between its traditional senses of beautiful and virtuous to a more particular legal/economic meaning in the eighteenth century, when the term "fair dealing" is first found. It is also worth noting that the word "deal" originates in medieval times, and originally described a process of sharing and distribution, before it took on a more specifically trade-related meaning in the Renaissance.

The term "fair" participates in the rhetoric of impartiality that supported British imperialism as well as capitalist ethics – after the inaugural act of violence with which one imposes a system, one seeks only fair play, that is, behaviour that accepts the newly imposed norms. According to the discourse that this word is a part of, getting something without paying for it is "unfair," and the idea that the poor (e.g., students or users of public libraries) have the same right to access the archive of publicly disseminated works as those who are rich is also "unfair." In the present context, we might, conversely, offer an alternative definition of "fair" by saying that a progressive and just society allows the free circulation of materials required for the education of its citizens, both in libraries and in the classroom, and that such circulation, in order to be "fair," should not be subject to permissions, royalties, seizure, or arbitrary limits on the number of chapters of a book that can be copied. The fact that copy shops offering reprographic services make a profit in facilitating research and study should not distract us from the real issue here: that the fair compensation which Access Copyright pursues puts the private profit of individuals and corporations before the needs of educators, students, and society as a whole – and that this is, in fact, unfair.

Having said this, I know that not every student will buy her or his coursepack from the university bookstore. Some will make their own photocopy of it, or scan and distribute it as a PDF file. Who knows, maybe they will write the texts out by hand, in their class notes, or otherwise? Certainly, some students will share a single copy. Others, deterred by the high price, won't bother to buy or read it at all. Still others will download PDFs of the course texts they have found by searching for them online, or they will use Google Books to "preview" the texts, or (as at least one of my students has done) they will skip the readings in favour of general synopses found on Wikipedia or some other website. It is even remotely possible that one or two might visit the university library and find the texts there. The proliferation of copies continues "asymmetrically," regardless of the wishes of regulators or, for that matter, legal producers. I now get official coursepacks made, but students still find ways around buying them – even though in this situation I obey the law.

We must ask: can there be such a thing as free copying without a profound confrontation with the law? Is this not another instance of the battle between the post-structuralist Deleuzians and Derrideans and structuralists such as Zizek and Badiou? The former affirm the dissolution of hegemonic structures within universal rhizomatic processes of playful assemblage and disassemblage that can only momentarily be held within the illusory framings of discourse, ideology, law, and structure, while the latter insist on the reality of the symbolic structures of law and the necessity of recognizing and confronting such structures in order to enact changes that cannot easily be appropriated back into an otherwise unchallenged logic of capital.

Copying is always already a crucial aspect of our ability to articulate ourselves. Language functions mimetically, and therefore, discourse, ideology, self-expression, and community are also mimetic. The same is true for the university. As Kate Eichhorn (2006) has argued in her study of copy shops around the University of Toronto, historically the university has always – since its origins in medieval times – relied on those who provide copying services, whether legal or not (555).

Put simply: there is no university without copying, since the university's mandate is itself disseminative mimesis. Yet, the universality of copying has been framed in quite specific ways within modernity, usually by obscuring the active constitutive presence of mimesis in discourses, identities, structures, and institutions in order to naturalize them. At the same time, modernity offers the spectacle of a series of abjected, overdetermined, scapegoated mimetic threats that always appear to come from the outside, at the margins, threatening to contaminate and infect that pure, copy-free world of originals we are told we inhabit. Such threats include the foreigner as the non-human, inauthentic Other who pretends to be like us; the feminine as the hysterical, irrational, duplicitous, seductive power of the false; the drug as the simulacrum of pleasure and happiness that leads to ruin; the counterfeiter, the pirate, the mafia as those who infiltrate legitimate economies with illegitimate, fake products. Girard (1987) has analysed many of these phenomena in his work on mimesis, but it was Lacoue-Labarthe (1989) who pointed out that more often than not, the scapegoat is mimesis, that is, the copy itself.

Could we actually live in a world without mimesis? For Locke and Marx, appropriation is constitutive of being in the world through labour or sensuous activity; for Hegel, property and ownership of self are the basis of society (Zeilinger 2009, chapter 1). Both appropriation in general and ownership as a particular form of appropriation are mimetic in that they bestow a particular name on something that identifies and frames it. The named, labelled, identified form (including that of the subject, i.e., ourselves) is always already a copy. The various trajectories of twentieth-century philosophy and theory, from Bataille, Heidegger, Beauvoir, and the Frankfurt School through to Foucault, Derrida, Butler, and Spivak have taken apart the residual overdeterminations of mimesis that were already fully articulated by Plato. These texts contain powerful critiques of intellectual property and the struggle to articulate a different basis for understanding identity, action, and community – but with a few exceptions (Coombe 1998, Wark 2004), this aspect of critical theory has not been fully developed. The core issue that they address is that of a universal flux – a chaosmos, in Buddhist terms, universal impermanence and interdependence. Mimesis, in the Platonic sense, articulates the desire to fix this flux permanently, but it could equally be understood as the radiant, ever-shifting flux "itself" in its infinite transformations and appearances.

The proliferation of copies that is happening in contemporary IP struggles is multivalent: Of course, one has little relish for the fact that mafias in various countries make MP3s available on the cheap. Enforcers of copyright, however, whether overzealous publishers, authors' estates, or state law enforcement organizations are often equally difficult to admire. Yet, this "war" over intellectual property, the endless examples of conflict over the right to copy that fill the press and academic journals and conferences devoted to the topic, even the example of my own struggles with which I framed this chapter – are they not a distraction from the omnipresence of mimesis? By limiting our analysis of copying to a circumscribed set of situations, we risk obscuring something much more troubling and powerful – which, nevertheless, asserts itself in every controversy concerning intellectual property. Mimesis is "the accursed share" that Bataille and Hurley (1988) wrote of – that force or quality of the universe that exceeds us in every way, yet impels us to act, to respond, to frame. Or does it? It is possible, if very challenging, to think beyond or through the frameworks of appropriation that support concepts of property, intellectual or otherwise, towards a "depropriated" subject and object. Indeed, I argue that various traditional cultures, notably for my own work those associated with Buddhism, are built around an ethics and practice that, while often falling sadly short in actually existing Buddhist societies, nevertheless, articulates a vision of a universe and collectivity that actively engages and works with mimesis while abandoning all notions of property at their illusory roots.

It sometimes seems that we live impossibly far from any such utopian vision of equality, justice, and community and that we should, therefore, limit any discussion to modifications of the existing legal structure. But, again, I must insist that something decisive is left out in such an analysis. The legal domains in which copying is framed are themselves mimetic structures. Law as institution, as intervention, as structure, exists in order to place limits on ubiquitous, omnipresent mimetic transformation. Copying occurs inside and outside of these domains, as well as in the act of constructing boundaries and definitions that produce the inside and an outside themselves. For example, Access Copyright's "Captain Copyright" campaign against "illegal" copying used text that had been copied from public domain materials without attribution (see "Captain Copyright" on the Access Copyright website). Without doubt, there is a question regarding how the boundaries that establish law are constructed, what counts as inside or outside, as legitimate and illegitimate, as original and copy, matters. And yet, the persistence of copying points to something else.

What a copy *is* depends on how property and rights, which have particular histories, are defined, and on the community that defines or does not define them. What the Internet offers us is not so much new forms of economy, production, and exchange (although the open source movement has certainly made efforts in those directions), but the opportunity to render visible once more the instability of all the terms and structures that hold together existing IP regimes, and to point to the madness of modern, capitalist framings of property. In this way, contemporary struggles concerned with IP rights link up to a broad range of modern critiques of property, intellectual or otherwise, from the work of critical theorists listed above to the artistic avant-gardes, to folk cultures – traditional, subcultural, and otherwise – to the agendas of explicitly political groups from the communists to Gandhi to anarchists, to the feminist critique of identity and objecthood.

I believe it is a mistake to assume, as most liberal critiques of existing IP law do, that intellectual property and property qua property, physical or otherwise, should be treated as separate subjects. Although there are differences between physical and intellectual property, the problem, at least at the level of contemporary legal-political discourse, is property, intellectual or otherwise, and the systems and structures that govern property. Indeed, what if all property was actually "intellectual property," in other words, a conceptual fabrication or work of imagination rather than a fact? Within the discourse of property and rights, fair use and the public domain are crippled concepts unless they include, for example, the right to cross national borders (fair use of land), or access to food, hospitals, medicine, and education (all of which have been to different degrees parts of public domains at one time or another). One possible and provisional answer to many of the problems that plague humanity today, particularly those predicated on scarcity, is simply to *make more copies* and distribute them freely – as in the story of Jesus and the feeding of the five thousand. From a more fundamental perspective, this could already be considered a gesture in the direction of depropriation.

However, is the core issue concerning intellectual property really that of the "right to copy"? It will be argued that if we give up talking about rights, and the structures that guarantee them, we are left in Hobbes' state of nature, the kind of chaos in which the worst predators, those who are able to most aggressively appropriate, would dominate. Thus, Hegel (1967) spoke of right as fundamental to the constitution of a person and a progressive society (37ff.). But a human being is not just a "bundle of rights," to use the legal expression. A bundle is already a montage, a little package of chaos, and that montage consists of a cloud of transforming repetitions, whose direction, insofar as it is conscious, is a matter of practice. A full analysis of right as it relates to imitation is beyond the scope of this essay. Nevertheless, it is possible to think of copying outside of right and ownership, through conceiving of copying as a practice, or rather a multitude of practices. More importantly, not only is it possible to think this way, but historically, many communities actually have done so. That practice and right are different is indicated by the many stories of great folk artists and masters, whether they were musicians, yogis, warriors, or lovers who stole their knowledge from official sources in order to teach it to others. Practice is highly mimetic, eminently transportable, and belongs to no one, despite all dogma to the contrary. It is a matter of value and competence, rather than right. One does not need to own in order to practice. If anything, a practice owns us, reshapes and reconfigures us, and inserts us in a dynamic collectivity. Practice has its own ethics – and this ethics is worked out in the configuration of practice itself, and in relation to other practices and practitioners.

The concept of practice is oddly underdeveloped within Western philosophical tradition, despite being central to the major modern ruptures of this tradition, which formed the corpus of critical theory and the artistic avant-gardes. Copying as practice is also what sustains many folk communities, from traditional societies through punk and hip hop to whatever is today labelled "subculture." A particular practice of copying also sustains various forms of capitalist economy. The impasse of the avant-gardes can be seen in the Situationist call for the creation of "new situations," which has produced a vast accumulation of gestures that are contained in the huge bubble of the gallery and museum system. Subcultures, however, have developed powerful practices, notably in the fields of music, style, and community, which burst forth as "temporary autonomous zones," to use Hakim Bey's (1991) phrase, but which are either appropriated into the existing hegemonic mainstream or safely bracketed at the margins of society. I generally agree with Hardt and Negri's (2000, 2004, 2009) formulation of the multitude against empire, which articulates a new vision of a common wealth, but what is strikingly absent in their work is any sense of a positive content to revolutionary communities other than "resistance."

We need a reinvigorated, critical concept of practice in cultural and political theory – but more importantly, we need to recognize the way that practices of copying are continually being negotiated and evolving in marginal communities today, in response to a global political and economic system that exploits them, but also autonomously, joyfully, as ends in themselves. Yes, the factory worker in Shenzhen, the *Cumbiero* in Buenos Aires, the rapper in Angola, the student at the copy shop in Toronto need to understand their commonality and the possibility of collective action. The struggle to affirm the most valuable, most enriching forms of practice can lead us beyond the modern formulations of right, property, ownership, and copyright. This struggle can and does begin with the most trivial everyday incidents – the price of an academic coursepack, the right to use a Disney character in a story published on the Internet, the availability of cheap, fake designer bags. In each case, it is the absurd overdetermination and enforcement of an unjust law that illuminates for ordinary citizens the reality of the existing regime. Conversely, every unjust legal intervention draws attention to the trivial but inexorable freedom that underlies our ability to act as individuals and communities in everyday life, and invites us to investigate, familiarize ourselves with it, and realize it, as individuals and communities, *in practice*.

3 The Canadian Public Domain: What, Where, and to What End?

CARYS J. CRAIG

A place like home, where, when you go there, they have to take you in and let you dance.

David Lange, "Recognizing the Public Domain"

What and Where Is the Public Domain?

What is the Canadian "public domain"? The short answer is that the public domain – like almost everything else in intellectual property (IP) law – is a metaphor. What does "the public domain" mean, then? This question, too, is difficult to answer: it means whatever we want it to mean. Far from being either trite or obtuse, this answer reveals the fundamental role of the public domain in IP policy: it represents a political concept that has been quite deliberately loaded, over the past decades, with sufficient normative significance and rhetorical force to be effectively employed in critical response to the rhetoric of property that drives the IP-expansionist agenda.

In this essay, I offer an overview of the many important contributions that have been made in this deliberate effort to substantiate and politicize the public domain concept. I provide some concrete definitions of the public domain in the copyright context, identify ongoing sources of debate in the literature, and highlight significant voices in public domain discourse. Ultimately, I suggest that the public domain is necessarily protean, and that this is the source of its power. Rather than asking, What is the public domain?, we should ask ourselves what we need it to be. For my part, I believe we need a public domain that reflects and protects the dialogic processes of culture in the face of increasingly restrictive IP structures. And so, in response to the question, Where is the public domain?, we might say that the public domain is both nowhere and everywhere: nowhere, because it is best understood as metaphor and not as a metaphysical territory or geographically separate preserve; everywhere, because the public domain is wherever people create and communicate (Cohen 2006: 157).

Recognizing the Public Domain

The existence of the public domain can be traced back to the beginning of copyright law in the sense that the limited time accorded to the author's right effectively brought it into being (see Rose 2003: 76; Patterson and Lindberg 1991: 29–31; Deazley 2006: 108–9). As Mark Rose (2003) notes, however, we must distinguish between "the fact of the public domain" and "the discourse of the public domain," that is, "the construction of a legal language to talk about public rights in writings" (87). The term "public domain" is a relatively recent entrant into common law copyright discourse, appearing only in the late nineteenth century (Ginsburg 2006: 637). The "affirmative discourse" of the public domain – which seeks to render it "a positive and prominent part of the social and cultural landscape" (Rose 2003: 87) and to ascribe to it an expanding normative role in IP policy – is an even more recent phenomenon, the origin of which is widely attributed to David Lange's seminal 1981 essay "Recognizing the Public Domain" (Boyle 2003: 59). In response to the emergence of new "publicity rights" in the US courts, Lange (1981) cautioned against the ad hoc proliferation of "property-equivalent theories" (158) and called for such emergent IP interests to be offset by an "equally deliberate recognition of individual rights in the public domain" (147).

The extent to which Lange's call has been heeded by copyright scholars in recent years is attributable, in large part, to the disruption of this apparent equilibrium in the face of the digital revolution (e.g., Lessig 2006: 56). As copyright law has struggled to adjust to the realities of a shifting cultural environment in which new technologies breed new modes of productivity, consumption, and exchange, the public domain has, indeed, been "pressed into service" (Lange 1981: 466). Perhaps Edward Samuels was correct in his insistence, in 1993, that it was already "a little late in the game to be developing a 'theory of the public domain'" (182), but he was also right to imagine that those who find themselves continually arguing for limitations on the expanding scope of intellectual property may come to need a rallying cry (150).

In Canada, the cry has remained faint and distant – until now. Typically, references to the public domain in Canadian jurisprudence have been rare and uninspired, and the prevailing assumption is that the public domain is no more than IP's leftovers, the crumbs that remain once its appetite is satisfied. Teresa Scassa (2007b) is right to observe that, thus constituted and constructed only in the negative, Canada's public domain is "a fragile thing" (348) whose scope can be expanded or shrunk by either legislative enactment or judicial interpretation. Perhaps our complacency in this regard reflects the absence of any radical change in the form or substance of our copyright law since 1924 (Wilkinson 2003: 31). If so, the time for complacency is over, and the rallying must begin: with copyright reform looming and the expansionist agenda dominating political discourse, Canada sorely needs a positive account of the public domain.

Fortunately, the Supreme Court of Canada laid the groundwork for renewed interest in the public domain in its important ruling in *Théberge* v. *Galerie d'Art du Petit Champlain Inc.* (2002). Justice Binnie, writing for the majority, implied a dynamic role for the public domain in the newly articulated "copyright balance" (para. 30) when he wrote, "Excessive control by holders of copyrights and other forms of intellectual property may unduly limit the ability of the public domain to incorporate and embellish creative innovation in the long-term interest of society as a whole, or create practical obstacles to property utilization" (para. 32). Thereafter, the unanimous Court in *CCH Canadian Ltd.* et al. v. *Law Society of Upper Canada* (2004) expressly acknowledged "society's interest in maintaining a robust public domain that could help foster future creative innovation" (para. 23). Incorporate, embellish, utilize, create, and innovate; the vision of the public domain that has thus emerged from Canadian jurisprudence appears to be one of a vibrant cultural space that facilitates exchange and transformation, inspiration, and innovation, and thereby serves the public interest. But, if the goal of a robust public domain is to survive the next round of legislative reform, its shape and scope are in dire need of both definition and deference.

The Core of the Public Domain

The term "public domain" is most commonly and least controversially used to describe the sphere in which contents are free from copyright or other IP rights. No one individual can claim any better right than any other to use or control intangible expression in the unowned public domain (Deazley 2006: 107). In the spectrum of definitional approaches to the public domain, this one is overtly – perhaps overly – legalistic, but indubitably accurate. Perhaps the most typical example of material in this domain is that of a work whose protection has expired, or a work not deserving of protection because it fails to meet the legally prescribed requirements. Works thus devoid of IP protection belong in what Pamela Samuelson (2006) calls the "core" of the public domain (151).

As Jessica Litman (1990) reminds us, however, the class of works not subject to protection is perhaps "the least significant portion of the public domain" (974). Also within the "core" of the public domain are "those aspects of copyrighted works that copyright does not protect" (ibid.). The line between public and private should, therefore, be conceptualized as a divide internal to the work; it traverses the work, separating protectable from non-protectable elements. Consider copyright's foundational idea-expression dichotomy: ideas, concepts, and theories are excluded from copyright's protective sphere and belong to the public domain – only the expression of those ideas is copyrightable and may be subject to private control. As Justice Learned Hand explained in *Nichols* v. *Universal Picture Corporation* (1930), because ideas or generalized abstractions are beyond the purview of copyright, the author's right will not cover "everything that might be drawn" from a work; its content always belongs, to some extent, to the public domain (para. 12).

Similarly, systems and methods belong in the public domain notwithstanding that the description or illustration of a system or method may be protectable expression. As Lord Justice Davey explained in *Hollinrake* v. *Truswell* (1894), "No doubt one may have copyright in the description of an art: but, having described it, you give it to the public for their use" (para. 428). Facts, information, and data are non-copyrightable and remain in the public domain, although the selection or arrangement of data may be protected as original expression as affirmed in *CCH* (2004, para. 22). Finally, where there is only one or a limited number of ways in which to express an idea, system, or fact, even expression may continue to reside in the public domain in order to ensure that the unprotectable elements are not indirectly subject to private control (*Delrina Corp.* v. *Triolet Systems Inc.*, 2002, para. 52). Even this legalistic definition reveals the inevitable indeterminacy of the public domain, and the extent to which its boundaries resist concretization. Copyright's doctrines are simple enough to state, but their practical application is often complex, context-specific, and therefore, inherently unpredictable. It is easy enough to say that ideas belong in the public domain, but far harder to delineate the contours of expression and the point in a series of abstractions at which protection runs out.

As Deazley (2006) concedes, "it will always remain impossible to determine with accuracy, at any given time, that which is public domain and that which is not" (131). The doctrinal line between public and private will shift over time and with circumstances, not to mention by jurisdiction (Samuelson 2006: 148; Wilkinson 2003: 28–9). This indeterminacy only underscores the value of contemplating the public domain: it reminds us of the indeterminacy of copyright itself, its dissimilarity to traditional property, and the risks that accompany its reification (Deazley 2006: 131–2).

Contested Contiguous Terrains

Once we reject an absolutist conception of the public domain as containing only those works devoid of protection, the definitional boundaries of the public domain become increasingly contentious. A recurring controversy is whether particular uses of protected works that do not require permission by virtue of exemptions or limitations can themselves be conceptualized as lying within the public domain. To the extent that the public and the proprietary are regarded as separate and distinct realms, it may seem nonsensical to describe a statutorily permitted use as somehow rendering the protected work public domain material in a specific instance. For example, Teresa Scassa (2007b), who defines the Canadian public domain as "that which cannot be owned under copyright" (354), insists that the ability to make limited uses of protected works in certain contexts is "a use that is different in character from the use of public domain materials … in which copyright have expired. Fair dealing operates more like a compulsory licence – the copyright owner is obliged to tolerate certain uses of their copyright protected work in specified contexts" (ibid.).

Samuelson's map of the public domain similarly characterizes the public domain as consisting only of "information resources free from intellectual property rights" (2003: 151; 2006: 102–3). She acknowledges the existence of "a penumbra of privileged uses under fair use, experimental use, and other copyright rules that permit unlicensed uses and sharing of information to take place" that are "outside the public domain in theory, but seemingly inside in effect" (2003: 149) and depicts these permitted uses as occupying "contiguous terrain" to the public domain (151).

An alternative definitional approach, however, focuses on uses as opposed to works (or parts of works) as its relevant unit of analysis. Thus, Yochai Benkler (1999) describes the public domain as "the range of uses of information that any person is privileged to make absent individualized facts that make a particular use by a particular person unprivileged" (362). Information in the public domain is, therefore, information "whose use, absent special reasons to think otherwise, is permissible to anyone" (361–2). In other words, fair use of protected works is within the public domain. Deazley (2006) also takes a use-based approach, stating, "If the institution of copyright necessitates permission before use, then the public domain allows for use without the need for permission" (107). The public domain, thus, contains any use for which permission is not required, including use of an insubstantial part of a work; any statutorily permitted uses such as fair dealing and specified exceptions for educational institutions, libraries, archives, and museums, for example; and any judicially established limitations on copyright owners' right to control use of the work, such as a use in the "public interest."

According to Scassa (2007b), the definitional approach that defines all permitted uses as within the public domain "should be a fairly marginal perspective, particularly in the Canadian context, where permitted uses are, for the most part, very narrowly framed and very context specific" (353). Nonetheless, she notes that this approach appears to have been endorsed by the Supreme Court of Canada in *Théberge*, when Justice Binnie wrote, in obiter, that the exceptions to copyright infringement enumerated in the Copyright Act "seek to protect the public domain in traditional ways such as fair dealing for the purpose of criticism or review and to add new protections to reflect new technology" (*Théberge* para. 32). In my opinion, this was not an unintentional "over-statement" by the Court (Scassa 2007b: 354), but an important conclusion that follows from the Court's statement of copyright's purpose, and its depiction of the public domain. If copyright is to promote "the encouragement and dissemination of works of the arts and intellect," and the public domain is to "incorporate and embellish creative innovation," then the latter must be understood as a domain of free use and unrestrained creativity. Regarded in this way, the fair dealing doctrine is an essential part of a robust public domain. When the Supreme

Court went on to endorse a vision of fair dealing as a "user right," it completed this picture (*CCH* para. 12). As Drassinower (2008) explains, "the conceptual and terminological shift in *CCH* from fair dealing as an exception to fair dealing as a user right evidences an orientation bent upon undoing the systematic exclusion of the public domain ... Under this view, the public domain is irretrievably central to copyright law" (202).

A further controversy simmering at the definitional margins of the public domain is the place of open source (OS) and free software movements and initiatives such as the Creative Commons (CC) – a non-profit umbrella organization, under which a network of actors are loosely associated in what has been characterized as a social movement. In the OS model, the source code of computer software is made available to the public; however, the use or modification of the code is subject to the terms of the applicable licence, which typically obliges the licensee to make downstream code and derivative works publicly available, and to impose the same terms on subsequent licensees. In other words, it is only by virtue of the existence and consistent assertion of IP rights that the OS system can operate (see Schellekens 2006: 309–10). Similarly, the CC movement seeks to promote the sharing and reuse of informational works through an innovative use of traditional IP and contract law. According to its website, the organization seeks to define "the spectrum of possibilities between full copyright – all rights reserved – and the public domain – no rights reserved." It uses an automated licensing platform that enables authors to easily share their works under more generous terms, with the objective of restoring "balance, compromise, and moderation" to the copyright system. Like OS, CC is therefore "completely dependent upon a proprietary regime and derives its force from its existence" (Elkin-Koren 2006: 325).

Samuelson's map, again, places OS software in the territory "adjacent" to the public domain (2003: 151). Samuelson explains that OS software and CC-licensed content are not public domain in the sense of being unencumbered by IP rights, as these rights are the very source of authority for the licence terms under which this content is made widely available (2006: 123; Boyle 2003: 65). Scassa (2007b) agrees that including such works within the public domain is "a stretch," since copyright is being asserted, "albeit in a user-friendly way" (353). Other commentators, however, have argued or simply assumed that these innovative attempts to reclaim proprietary constructs for the purpose of public dissemination and use are essentially public domain projects (e.g, Bollier

2002: 14; Merges 2004: 190–3). This position clearly departs from "the old dividing line ... between the realm of property and the realm of the free," and assumes a new divide, perhaps between "the realm of individual control and the realm of distributed creation, management and enterprise" (Boyle 2003: 66). OS and CC content is deemed to be at least functionally equivalent to public domain material because it furthers the goals of wide dissemination and use. Whether such materials are included in the definition of the public domain will depend on whether that definition is drawn on legalistic, political, or aspirational lines. But, as Samuelson (2006) notes, "even those who might question whether contractually constructed commons should be included in a definition of public domain would likely agree that such commons promote public domain values" (124).

Legal Realism for the Public Domain

This lack of definitional clarity may appear to be symptomatic of an inherent weakness in the concept of the public domain: if we cannot agree upon the contents and scope of the public domain, then must we concede that it is simply "too slippery, too imprecise to warrant any coherent and detailed consideration" (Deazley 2006: 105)? On the contrary, perhaps it is exactly because of this definitional ambiguity that the public domain concept is so potentially useful in the political struggle over copyright law and its limits.

As James Boyle (2003) explains, how we choose to define the substance and scope of the public domain "depends on why we care about the public domain, on what vision of freedom or creativity we think the public domain stands for, and what danger it protects against. The public domain will change its shape according to the hopes it embodies, the fears it tries to lay to rest, and the implicit vision of creativity on which it rests. There is not one public domain, but many" (62). The recognition of multiple public domains may present some risk of confusion or miscommunication (Samuelson 2006: 103, 164–5), but it also promises a richer discussion, for it requires us to consider and acknowledge the political purpose motivating our definitional approach. This is legal realism for the public domain (Boyle 2003: 67): the public domain is revealed to be "a social-legal construct" whose purpose is "to organize our thoughts, to serve as a 'short cut,' to denote a mindset, a view, a perception" (Samuelson 2006: 145). Rather than engaging in definitional quandaries, our energies can be spent articulating political goals and exploring the legal and practical tools that may enable their attainment.

Samuelson (2006) responded to Boyle's (2003) acceptance of many purposively drawn public domains by attempting to identify the multiple versions appearing in the literature, and to organize them into conceptual categories. She identified thirteen versions in all, from the negatively drawn "information artifacts wholly free from intellectual property rights" to the "contractually constructed information commons"; from the "constitutionally mandated public domain" to the "privatizable public domain"; and from "broadly usable information resources" to the "unpublished public domain." Ultimately, Samuelson proposed three thematically coherent definitional clusters: those concerned with the legal status of information resources; those focused on freedoms to use information resources; and those that stress the accessibility of information resources (2006: 145–9). Thus, for example, the public domain of IP-free information resources belongs in the first cluster; the domain of broadly usable information resources, as well as privileged uses of IP-protected works, clusters around the question of freedom to use; and definitions that focus on the scientific "commons" or the undisclosed public domain cluster around the theme of public accessibility.

From this clustering process, Samuelson (2006) draws lessons for public domain theorizing. First, we can see that the most robust public domains are those that are free of IP encumbrances while also being widely accessible to the public (150). Second, we can more readily acknowledge that the public domain may be best understood as a continuum of legal states on a spectrum that ranges between information resources subject to the most restrictive legal encumbrances (IP rights, contractual limits, and technological protection measures) and the least restrictive (free of IP rights, and subject to positive – even constitutional – rights of public access and use). Guided by different concerns, different commentators will draw the line for their public domain at different points on the spectrum. Fundamentally, this reveals the need for a nuanced and complex discourse around a pragmatic public domain concept that moves beyond a simple public/private dichotomy.

At the outset of this essay, my claim that the public domain means "whatever we want it to mean" implied that it should be capable of holding back the tide of intellectual property expansion. It should now be clear that form follows function (Boyle 2003: 61). We need the public domain to be capable of many functions in the performance of its political role: "as a building block for the creation of new knowledge, and as an enabler of competitive imitation, follow-on creation, free or low-cost access to information, public access to cultural heritage, education, self-expression and autonomy, various governmental functions, or deliberative democracy" (Samuelson 2006:158–9). In what follows, I highlight some critical contributions to the public domain discourse with a view to supporting a dynamic formulation that situates the public domain in the context of creative processes and cultural participation, and therefore, at the heart of copyright policy.

Towards a Dynamic Public Domain of Creative Use

A legalistic definition of the public domain limited to IP-free information resources risks depicting it as nothing more than "the other side of the coin of copyright [that] is best defined in negative terms" (Krasilovsky 1967: 205). The public domain may then be seen as "undeserving of protection" (Litman 1990: 967), or, worse, it may not be seen at all, and become "the invisible Other" (Boyle 2003: 69). If the public domain is regarded as little more than "a virtual wasteland of undeserving detritus" (Samuelson 2003: 147), then the prevailing assumption will be that anything of value within that realm ought to receive the recognition of propertization. After all, as Jane Ginsburg (2006) has noted, even the common expression "to fall into the public domain" pointedly evokes "the devastation of a fall from grace" (668), suggesting a sense of both loss and waste inherent in depropertization (Cohen 2006: 134).

Julie Cohen (2006) describes a "cultural stewardship model" of the public domain, adherents to which regard ownership as the prerequisite of productive management (134). From this, it follows that "passage into the public domain should occur only after the productive life of a cultural good has ended, and is to be mourned, not celebrated" (Samuelson 2003: 147). Conceptualized negatively, the public domain is situated "outside" of copyright; it is "systematically excluded" (Drassinower 2008: 202) from copyright law and largely deprived of normative significance. As Lange (2003) observes, this is one of the "least useful or persuasive notions" of the public domain, because it fails to attribute to the public domain "an affirmative existence of its own" (473). It has no political capacity to counter the excesses of propertization, because its contents are always susceptible to the privatization rationale.

Juxtaposed with this cultural stewardship model is what Cohen (2006) calls the "conservancy model" (133–4). So-called conservancy theorists are concerned with ensuring the growth of the public domain and its protection against threatened incursions. Lange (2003), who arguably spearheaded the conservancy model, thus appealed for the recognition of the public domain as a "place of sanctuary for individual creative expression" that confers "affirmative protection against the forces of private appropriation" (466). This public domain is not merely the obverse of intellectual property, but a matter of public entitlement that must be conceptualized in positive, indeed, political terms.

The emergence of an affirmative public domain discourse has been closely tied to the critical reconceptualization of original authorship in copyright scholarship. In 1990, Jessica Litman's important contribution to the development of a theory of the public domain drew the link between the fiction of originality and the function of the public domain. The role and relevance attributed to the public domain in copyright law were shown to be intricately connected to the notion of creativity as origination that it assumes. Litman (1990) argued that authorship is not a process of original creation out of nothing but, rather, involves the absorption and recombination of raw materials encountered in preexisting works (998); it is, therefore, only by virtue of the public domain concept that copyright can function in spite of its fallacies. She explains: "The public domain rescues us from this dilemma … It furnishes a crucial device to an otherwise unworkable system by reserving the raw material of authorship to the commons, thus leaving the raw material available for other authors to use" (1023). From this perspective, the public domain is essential to the processes of authorship, and therefore central to a copyright system whose objective is to encourage authors to create.

Building on this insight, several copyright scholars critically examined the "romantic author" who occupied the protagonist's role in copyright discourse, and revealed the significance of "author reasoning" in the diminution and marginalization of the public domain (Boyle 2003: 51; see also Boyle 1996, Jaszi 1991). Stripped of his romance and the fiction of original creation, the author was revealed to be dependent on others' work for inspiration and material, and the public domain was hailed to be the intellectual commons from which he or she must draw. Even this picture of the public domain, however, may be thought to lack the vibrancy and dynamism that conservancy advocates increasingly hope to capture. The problem, perhaps, is the manner in which the organizing metaphor posits the public domain as a discrete preserve, for all purposes notionally equivalent to a geographical space in which the public freely roams. An increasingly complex understanding of the cultural and cumulative processes of creativity suggests a vision of the public domain without such static boundaries. In 2003, Lange argued that the metaphor of place is no longer – and probably never was – sufficient to describe the public domain from the perspective of creativity and a better metaphor was status: "Imagine the public domain as a status that arises from the exercise of the creative imagination ... a status independently and affirmatively recognized in law ... omnipresent, portable, and defining" (474).

It is this public domain *status*, according to Lange (2003), that will allow us to more clearly understand the protection that exercises of the creative imagination require, and so to deploy the public domain against the encroachments of intellectual property upon creative activity (476). Thus, for example, fair use would be an aspect of the public domain and any creative appropriation presumptively privileged (479–81). This conception of public domain as status is founded on a recognition of the creative process as a vital aspect of our citizenship and human experience; the role of the public domain is to secure our innate aspirations "to think and to imagine, to remember and appropriate, to play and to create" (483).

Sharing Lange's perception of the public domain as vital to creativity and, in turn, of creativity as a social phenomenon vital to the self-actualization of the situated author, Cohen (2006) appeals to a conception of the public domain guided by "a sociology of creativity" rooted in "the day-to-day realities of creative practice" (146). Pointing to the socially embedded nature of the creative process, she similarly takes issue with the implications of the public domain metaphor. Drawing connections between copyright's "public domain" and that of US land law, Cohen shows how our chosen metaphor complicates the political task of copyright's public domain advocates and appeals to "a different type of spatial metaphor" that more accurately reflects the realities of creative practices (137): namely, the "cultural landscape." According to this model, public entitlements to access, engage with, and borrow from the cultural landscape cannot be contained within an ontologically separate entity called the public domain. Rather than reifying this domain, we should reformulate it to reflect a cultural commons that is distributed and disaggregated (166), dynamic and relational

(158). The cultural landscape is not defined by ownership but by the experience and participation of the creators who draw on its resources, and the public domain, as "a distributed property of social space" (124), is part of that landscape. This reformulation shifts our attention back to the public's relationship with cultural resources and the social reality of creative borrowing, thereby bringing into relief the impact of copyright on creative practice, and the necessary limits of commodification.

Finally, Michael Birnhack (2006) is similarly concerned with creativity as a relational and communicative enterprise, with "a crucial role in personal self-development, learning, experience, imagining, speaking with others, creating new works for the benefit of ourselves and wider circles, starting from the immediate interlocutor and up to the entire community" (60). The public domain is central to this deliberative enterprise because "it is where knowledge is created and where it lies awaiting new interpretations, new applications and new meanings" (ibid.). Birnhack, therefore, envisages the public domain as human entitlement equivalent in nature, purpose, and importance to the freedom of speech. Once again, a vision of authorship as discursive participation, as opposed to simple origination, necessitates a rich conception of the public domain in which participants can join in and build on existing works, but also reuse and reproduce works in a way that changes their meaning (85). Because copyright, as a form of cultural control, interferes with exchange in the communicative sphere, Birnhack's democratic (indeed, constitutional) account of copyright demands that it does so with the aim and result of improving of the quality of public discourse and generating a better – richer and more diverse – public domain.

Samuelson (2006) includes the work of Lange, Cohen, and Birnhack in a cluster focused on the freedom to use information resources even when works embodying these resources are protected by IP rights (146). She goes on to laud the public domains articulated by them as "among the most imaginative and inspiring public domains in the literature," submitting that "from their work, readers should take away a more dynamic and vibrant sense of the role of public domains in creative work and public discourse" (167). In my opinion, it is in this dynamic vision of the public domain – as central to the creative and communicative practices that define our sense of self and society – that we see the potential power of the public domain concept to shape copyright policy in the digital era, from the inside out.

A Public Domain Discourse for Canada

This is a critical moment in Canadian cultural life. New networked technologies present unprecedented opportunities for creative expression, critical engagement, and participation in public discourse. But, as the editors of and contributors to this volume remind us, these technologies are subject to social regulation and cultural controls, often in the form of proprietary regimes that allocate rights of exclusivity over information resources and so restrict their creation, circulation, and management. Copyright law, in particular, has arrived at a crossroads where it suddenly seems that a choice must be made between maximizing the potential of the digital revolution and reinforcing the norms of the analogue world. Thankfully, this is a false dilemma: copyright policy contains within it the norms and aspirations that not only permit but necessitate the development of a robust public domain in which citizens freely participate – a domain made more open, accessible, democratic, and vital by the advances of network technologies.

The copyright system should be regarded as one element of a larger cultural and social policy aimed at encouraging the process of cultural exchange that new technologies facilitate. The economic and other incentives that copyright offers to creators of original expression are meant to encourage a participatory and interactive society, and to further the social goods that flow through public dialogue. Copyright's purpose is to create opportunities for people to speak, to develop relationships of communication between author and audience, and to fashion conditions that might cultivate a higher quality of expression (Craig 2006). The public domain that is irreducibly central to the copyright system (Drassinower 2008: 202) protects the cultural space in which this happens.

In Canada, there is some cause to be optimistic. The Supreme Court has already sketched a picture of a robust public domain that can "incorporate and embellish creative innovation in the long-term interest of society as a whole" (*Théberge* para. 32) and "help foster future creative innovation" (para. 23). In *Robertson* v. *Thomson Corp.* (2006), Justice Abella considered copyright's capacity to "keep pace with technological developments to foster intellectual, artistic and cultural creativity" and stated that, in facing the challenges of regulation in this context, "the public benefits of this digital universe should be kept prominently in view" (para. 79). Citing Michael Geist, the minority judgment continues, "The Internet and new technologies have unleashed a remarkable array of new creativity, empowering millions of individuals to do more than just consume our culture, instead enabling them to actively and meaningfully participate in it" (ibid.). Such statements seem to hold promise of a copyright system that respects and reflects the transformative possibilities of new technologies, rather than resisting and constraining the emerging cultural practices that these technologies permit.

This promise, however, is increasingly remote; so, too, is the vision of the public domain that is essential to such a system. The existing sketch must be filled in with firm strokes or risk erasure. Threats to the Canadian public domain are too many and too varied to canvass here, but it is worth mentioning a few that are pertinent to the copyright reform process currently under way. In addition to the legal, economic, and transactional obstacles of IP, the value of the public domain is subject to the physical and technological barriers that can prevent access to even IP-free information resources. In order to occupy its central role in cultural practices, the public domain must be practically accessible to creative actors; but, rather than protecting the rights of the public to access and use resources in the public domain, proposed reforms move to protect the right to lock up these resources. Acts permitted in relation to owned content – users' rights to read, listen, research, study, criticize, transform – can be prevented by the use of technological protection measures, and they could potentially be rendered unlawful by anti-circumvention provisions.

Where copyright and technological barriers do not suffice, the norms of contract law can step in to further limit users' activities; generic "click-through" contracts place still more restrictions on the public's enjoyment of resources in the cultural landscape, effectively supplanting so-called user rights and the public domain. Rather than attempting to protect the public domain against these incursions, proposed legislation makes explicit the priority of contractual obligations. Even proposed additions to statutory exceptions for users, educational institutions, libraries, and museums are so narrowly drawn and subject to such rigorous provisos that they are more indicative of a constriction and marginalization of the public domain than its protection. Moreover, it is important to bear in mind not only the potential application of a revised copyright law, but also the *perception* of increased regulation and criminalization that these legal reforms generate. As Deazley (2006) reminds us, "in practice, the manner in which [the public domain] functions is bound up in individual perceptions of the way in which people can or cannot use those cultural products to which they have access" (118).

In the rush to respond to the "challenges" of the digital age, copyright reforms threaten to reduce the shape and operation of the public domain in the name of furthering copyright's policy goals. This fails to reflect the centrality of the public domain to copyright and broader cultural policy. But, if perception and practice are intertwined and mutually supportive, then each presents its own opportunities for resistance. Practically, the dynamic fair dealing practices explored in this volume support and expand the Canadian public domain; but, in terms of perception, these practices must be complemented by the affirmative understanding of the public domain canvassed here – one that recognizes it as a source of public entitlement, and a vital part of our cultural landscape.

Conclusion

The ownership and control of information resources is one of the most important forms of power in contemporary society (Boyle 1997: 87). Digital technologies, therefore, have the potential to alter and subvert power structures by changing the ways in which we access, engage with, and participate in the creation of these resources. By the same token, IP laws have the capacity to shore up existing power structures and limit creative practices by enforcing and expanding traditional proprietary norms in the digital environment. Boyle (2003) has argued that we are in the midst of a "second enclosure movement" where the commons of facts, ideas, and other previously unprotectable subject matters is being enclosed by an IP system that assumes that more property is better (40). The expansion of intellectual property is not only formal but also practical. In a networked society, digital reproduction blurs the lines between communication, storage, recreation, and reproduction, such that "the reach of the rights has been expanded at the same moment that their practical effect has been transformed" (40). In response to this threat, he called for a new form of "environmentalism" for the Net: a unifying idea that can add a moral overtone to our discussion about intellectual property and the public domain; an insistence that there are larger structural reasons for our failure to preserve the public domain; a rallying cry that brings together the voices that disparately protest the gradual chipping away of the public domain. The concept of the public domain may be posited in multiple and overlapping ways, but it, nonetheless, has the power to help us "to reimagine creation, innovation, and speech on a global network" (74).

In Canadian legal discourse, the public domain has typically been mentioned, if at all, only in passing, as though its meaning were self-evident. Presumably, the operating assumption has been that the public domain is no more and no less than that to which IP rights do not attach. I hope that this essay has shown the public domain to be a far more nuanced, compelling, contested, and potentially useful concept than this inattention would suggest. Conceptualized as a vibrant, dynamic, and shifting space in which citizens freely engage in communicative and creative activities, the public domain takes on a positive dimension and a political power. This power can be harnessed to challenge the expansion of IP and its paradigms of control and exclusivity in our networked society.

4 Dynamic Fair Dealing with Orphan Works: Lessons from "Real" Property

REN BUCHOLZ

The discourse of copyright overflows with colourful imagery meant to illustrate, define, and inflame. Teenagers who download music without authorization become "pirates," and that label justifies all manner of harsh punishments. Decades ago, the movie industry told the US Congress that the videocassette recorder (VCR) was to the American filmmaker what "the Boston strangler is to the woman home alone" (Valenti 1982). In more recent times, the US Congress scheduled hearings on file sharing, organized crime, and terrorism (Gross 2003). A less bombastic but more persistent metaphor is the characterization of cultural goods as intellectual "property" (IP). This last image is at the heart of copyright's modern expansion, but its accuracy has been heavily contested for the past three decades (Easterbrook 1990, Gordon 1989, Lemley 2005). How faithfully do we rely on real property metaphors in the management of IP, and where do those metaphors fail? Imagine the following two scenarios.

In the first scenario, a new ice cream scoop sits on an empty sidewalk. No initials are carved on the handle, no clues about its provenance are visible. It appears, in all respects, to be ownerless. But, it is also a handsome ice cream scoop, so you put it in your pocket and bring it home. Provided that you make a reasonable effort to find its true owner – for example, post a flyer announcing "FOUND, LOST ICE CREAM SCOOP, CALL FOR DETAILS" on a nearby lamp post – your legal obligations regarding the object are extinguished. The scoop is yours to use until the true owner emerges, and even then, you would simply have to return the item.

In the second scenario, a poem, typed on a sheet of paper, sits on the same sidewalk. It is similarly anonymous. It is also an amazing piece of writing, and you are instantly taken with its verve and metre. At home, you google its key phrases and make inquiries at the Canadian Poetry Association, but its author eludes you. You even run an advertisement in *Canadian Literature* that reproduces the entire poem and begs readers to send any information they might have on its origins. You get your wish a few weeks later. A letter arrives from the lost author's lawyer, informing you that a civil lawsuit for copyright infringement is being filed. You are amazed to learn that you may have to pay statutory damages in the amount of $20,000.

As these examples suggest, a clear point of dissonance between physical property – a term used here to denote both "personal" and "real" property – and IP can be seen in the wildly different ways that each regime deals with missing owners. The law of physical property has long favoured policies that encourage the efficient use of resources (see, e.g., Rose 1985: 159). Most Western legal systems give broad allowances to people who find productive uses for land and goods that are abandoned, lost, or neglected. A number of modernizations in the real property system, like comprehensive title registration databases and statutory guidance for adverse possessors, have helped bring the law of physical property into correspondence with its theoretical justifications. The realm of IP, however, has been comparatively bereft of similar reforms. Copyright, in particular, seems to have parted ways with many values that inform traditional property jurisprudence. Almost universally, copyrighted works whose authors are unlocatable – commonly known as "orphan works" – are unexploited by their true owners but untouchable by would-be users. Tragically, this has contributed to a situation where broad swathes of our cultural commons lie fallow (Boyle 2008).

Given the prevalence of physical property metaphors in the realm of IP, this essay suggests that the personal property concept of the "lawful finder" – sketched in the scenario of the lost ice cream scoop and discussed further below – can usefully be applied to the IP problem of orphan works. The resulting concept of a "creative finder" could be incorporated into Canada's fair dealing provisions, and help bring copyright law back into alignment with the values that animate the larger property system.

The Problem: Lost Authors and Orphan Works

Copyright policy is meant to strike a balance between the social benefits of encouraging creative production and the need to fairly remunerate creators. This typically takes the form of a time-limited monopoly on certain uses of the work, exceptions to that monopoly for some unauthorized uses, and the eventual passing of the work to the public domain once its copyright protection has expired. During a work's term of protection, unauthorized users must turn to the fair dealing provisions of the Copyright Act or the emerging common law principle of user rights (D'Agostino 2008) in order to avoid significant liability for copyright infringement. This structure is designed to encourage a would-be user to ensure that her use is fair, or to seek permission from the copyright holder.

But, what happens when a potential user cannot locate the copyright holder? Over time, copyright holders become harder to locate: companies go out of business, addresses change, authors die. Moreover, there is no longer a centralized directory that links copyright holders to their works. In the past, copyright protection was contingent upon an author's willingness to meet certain formal registration requirements, like mailing a nominal fee and registration information to a central repository. The result of these so-called formalities was a relatively complete picture of which works enjoyed copyright protection and who their owners were. Would-be users could check to see if a work was still covered by copyright and open a dialogue with its owners. However, while similar registration systems were being considered for real property, the law of copyright regressed, doing away with formalities altogether; see Berne Convention, Article 5(2).

Without formalities or any other method of centralizing information about copyright holders, uncertainty runs rampant. The crippling effect of uncertainty can be seen in the real property context, where a clouded title means that "no one [will] make any productive use of the land because there is little incentive to plant when there is no reasonable assurance that one will be in possession of the land at harvest time" (Mossman and Flanagan 2004: 100). Rational people – and their mathematically inclined insurers – are unlikely to use a copyrighted work unless the rights holder can be located. Orphan works, therefore, exist in a limbo where uncertainty prevents their productive use. Works with unknown authors lie in a limbo in that they are neither protected, and thereby available through licence, nor unprotected and available as part of the public domain. To make matters worse, an author may be unlocatable or non-responsive for different reasons, and each reason may create different legal conditions. For example, queries to the last known author may go unanswered, but there is no way to know if the author received the correspondence and has decided to remain silent for strategic reasons, if the correspondence was never received, or if the author has previously placed the work in the public domain or otherwise formally ceded her legal rights (Khong 2007).

In the world of intangible property, this uncertainty is particularly troubling because a large proportion of our cultural heritage is not being efficiently used. Data from the United States indicates that fully 97.7 per cent of books and 93.2 per cent of movies published between 1927 and 1946 are out of print (Lemley et al. 2003). It is difficult to determine the proportion of those works that have been "orphaned" in the formal sense, but it seems reasonable that *some* of those works are unexploited because their owners have disappeared. This is unacceptable, as the materials in question comprise our recent cultural history. We can learn from that material; we can alloy it with our own work to make something new. Without a mechanism for allowing those works to be used, they will simply lie fallow for the decades until their copyright expires.

Compared with other countries (Breakthrough Films 2004, n6), Canada has a reasonably sophisticated method for dealing with this problem. Section 77 of the Copyright Act allows a potential user to petition the Copyright Board for a licence to exploit an orphan work. However, this regime still falls short. First, it requires a would-be user to make an application to an administrative board, which takes both time and money. The result is that this process scales poorly, especially when compared with the potentially vast number of orphan works in existence. Second, because each licence is granted on the facts particular to that application, no rules of general applicability are generated for future users. Without rules of precedent that order the civil and criminal judicial processes, each would-be user must reinvent the wheel at the Copyright Board. Third, the Copyright Board's policy of holding licence fees in escrow for authors who may never reappear is both arbitrary and wasteful. Such requirements limit the number of people who can use the work, while tying up funds that could be better used elsewhere. As outlined below, codifying the common law's approach to lost personal property and applying it to intellectual property could reduce these transaction costs.

Personal Property and Lawful Finders

At common law, a finder is a person who is in possession of property, but who is not its true owner. The lawful finder has a better title claim to the property than anyone save the true owner (*Armory* v. *Delamirie*

1722). This title comes with a burden, however: a finder is obliged to make reasonable efforts to locate the owner (*Parker* v. *British Airways Board* 1982). The doctrine of the lawful finder is designed to balance the rights of the owner against the desire to promote efficient use of property. Could this framework be expanded to the "creative finder" in order to address copyright law's orphan works problem? Before delving into this investigation, it is important to note two caveats. First, as mentioned above, many commentators rightfully distinguish between the disparate historical and philosophical foundations for the various forms of physical and intellectual property. This essay is not an endorsement of blindly transposing physical property doctrines to intellectual property, or vice versa. Second, however, I submit that applying a doctrine outside of its native context can help interrogate the wisdom of both its traditional and novel applications. The following thought experiment illustrates how far copyright law has drifted away from both its original purpose and traditional property values.

Intellectual Property and Creative Finders?

How would the doctrine of the lawful finder map onto the creative finder? First, a creative finder should have an obligation to determine whether an owner is truly "lost." She might fulfil this duty by contacting the relevant rights collecting society, as many section 77 applicants do. If the owner has failed to register with a group whose sole purpose is to facilitate the commercial exploitation of their work, it would be reasonable to infer that the owner is out of the picture. Drawing inspiration from a finder of personal property, she might also post an advertisement in an appropriate publication (*Bridges* v. *Hawkesworth* 1851). It would not be enough to inquire at the last known address of the rights holder and equate silence with absence, however. As the US Copyright Office (2006) noted in its consideration of orphan works, there are many reasons why a copyright holder might not respond to a request for permission. A proper approach might be, therefore, to require a good faith effort to locate a missing author, plus an affidavit that the last known contact information for an author is no longer valid or reasonably determinable.

Second, we have to ask which party is most analogous to a "true owner." In the context of copyright, there is often a distinction between the author of a work and the rights holder of a work. For the purpose of the initial search, treating the rights holder as the true owner would be the least disruptive choice; she or he already has legally recognized title to the work, and circumventing that title would needlessly complicate matters. However, if the rights holder cannot be located, but the author *is* available, should the creative finder be obligated to seek permission from the naked author? I submit that such a requirement would not reflect the legal reality of the author's position. Instead, requiring the creative finder to provide notification to the author might be an equitable solution, especially if it signals that the author might be able to resume productive use of her work as well.

Third, how would a creative finder show "possession" in the sense contemplated by the law of personal property? In the physical property context, "One who 'finds' a lost chattel in the sense of becoming aware of its presence, but who does no more, is not a 'finder' for this purpose and does not, as such, acquire any rights" (*Parker* at 1009). Instead, the common law recognizes possession after the possessor commits a "clear act" that brings the property within her control, and manifests an intention to possess (Rose 1985: 97). Applied to copyright, these principles suggest that simply becoming aware of a work's orphan status would not be enough to create a property interest. Instead, some kind of affirmative, productive use should be a requirement for a creative finder.

This requirement exposes one of the fundamental differences between physical and intellectual property. How can a person show exclusive possession of a work that might exist in multiple locations around the world? In keeping with the personal property values of clarity and intention to possess, perhaps the creative finder would approximate meeting this requirement by notifying the Copyright Board of the work's status and her intention to use it. If the Board maintained a public directory of such notices, it would serve the dual purpose of providing public notice to the rights holder community while building a record of newly adopted orphan works. Moreover, this would fit with Rose's idea that possession requires communication, the goal of which is to notify "the audience composed of all others who might be interested" in the property (Rose 1985: 159). Ironically, in accordance with its Article 5(2), the Berne Convention's ban on formalities would not bar this requirement because the creative finder is not an "author" whose copyright hinges on registration. The requirement for a clear act might also support the cultural practice of using abandoned work, which is itself a virtue.

Perhaps most importantly, what would the nature of the creative finder's right be? After the limitation period has expired, a lawful finder of personal property gains absolute title to the chattel, including the right to exclude others. Does this suggest that a creative finder would acquire an exclusive right to exploit the work, effectively donning the mantle of the true owner? Again, the distinct features of physical and intellectual property complicate the exercise. Intellectual goods are not rivalrous, meaning one person's enjoyment of the work does nothing to reduce another person's ability to enjoy it at the same time. Therefore, the exclusivity that springs naturally from having care and control of personal property has been artificially reproduced in the world of copyright. By arming copyright holders with devastating statutory damages – see section 38(1) of the Copyright Act – that can be deployed against unauthorized users, copyright law attempts to restrict the unregulated flow of cultural goods. This artificial scarcity is often viewed as a "necessary evil" (Gordon 1989: 1344), and I do not propose to recapitulate that evil in the world of the creative finder. Instead, I submit that a non-exclusive right to use, coupled with protection from damages, would be adequate to encourage use while not unduly introducing new thickets of rights. This lack of exclusivity would have the added benefit of elegantly dealing with the lawful finder concepts of occupiers and joint finders; if other parties have a competing claim to the orphan work, their use of it is both allowed and encouraged within the parameters outlined above.

A New Role for Formalities?

It is hard to overstate how much the problem of orphan works is exacerbated by the lack of formalities. Without a centralized record of who authored a work, it becomes infinitely more difficult to establish its current owner, the terms under which it is licensed, and the steps necessary to secure permission for new uses. Such a system for clearing permission before use is even more crucial because, to date, we have refused to apply ameliorating physical doctrines after a cultural work is used. Moreover, everyone benefits from formalities because they produce clarity and facilitate dialogue.

Digital technology makes it easier than ever to find and distribute all kinds of cultural goods, but it also simplifies the management formalities. In 1971, when they were formally abolished in the Paris text of the Berne Convention, formalities were dismissed as overly onerous. Indeed, when dealing with paper records, stamps, and manual data entry, the prospect of keeping track of owners of works would have been daunting. Recent technical developments could be enlisted to ease the burden on both parties. For example, if the Internet Archive can maintain multiple, iterated copies of the entire Internet in its "Wayback Machine," certainly we can keep a current list of who recorded which pop song or wrote which novel. There is no question that our ability to maintain large databases has skyrocketed in the past forty years.

Even more fascinating are the ways that a comprehensive database of cultural works could be searched by the creative finder to determine whether a particular work has an owner. Audio fingerprinting technology allows a computer program to "listen" to mere seconds of a song, then report whether it matches any of the millions of tracks stored in its database (Stone and Helft 2007). Similar services exist for text (Jesdanun 2007) and video (Bradbury 2007). Copyright holders intent on stopping infringement are the typical users of these systems, but they would be of equal or greater use to someone who wants to identify the owner of an orphan work. We have the tools ready at hand to collect our cultural heritage, digitize it, and sift through it efficiently. Our failure to do so only ensures that fewer people will use orphan works – and that more authors will remain estranged from their creations.

Conclusion

In sum, the concept of the creative finder is best described as requiring a double discovery. The first step is finding that a work is an orphan; the second is finding a productive use for that work and notifying the rest of the world. As a reward, the lawful finder would gain a non-exclusive right to exploit the work in question. In this instance, applying a personal property doctrine to intellectual property illustrates a reasonable alternative to copyright's long departure from accepted property values.

We should no more punish the industrious creative finder than we would a lawful finder of personal property who discharges her duties. Notwithstanding the differences between personal and intellectual property, the core values that animate each policy should be similar. The concept of the creative finder is informed by goals that (should) undergird all property law: promoting efficient uses, fighting economic waste, rewarding creativity, and encouraging the development of rich public resources. Combined with a more sensible approach to formalities and the use of digital technology in their management, the creative finder could help find much-needed homes for orphan works.

5 Publicly Funded, Then Locked Away: The Work of the Canadian Broadcasting Corporation

KYLE ASQUITH

Overregulation stifles creativity. It smothers innovation. It gives dinosaurs a veto over the future.

Lawrence Lessig, *Free Culture*

But if public broadcasting is to play a significant role in the commons, it must insulate programming decisions from both politics and an ever-growing commercial orientation.

Jeff Chester, *Digital Destiny*

Canadian citizens, artists, activists, and scholars often call for new intellectual property (IP) regimes that foster innovation and creativity, privilege the public domain, recognize the dialogic connection between creators and users in the digital age, and highlight creator and user rights over punitive punishments (Geist 2005). With a viable public domain that meaningfully responds to what the public needs from this sphere (see Craig, this volume), and an approach that frames the notion of fair dealing as a user right rather than an exception or defence, Canada's digital media landscape could be a cultural commons where citizens are in a constant dialogue, engaged, and simultaneously creators and users (Drassinower 2005: 466). This discourse, one of citizenry, common space, creativity, culture, and dialogue, is not unique to Canadian copyright debates in recent years; rather, much of this rhetoric has been used for decades to define and justify the purpose of Canadian public broadcasting. From the emergence of radio in the 1920s through the countless Standing Committee reports and political speeches on public broadcasting that followed, similar values have been invoked repeatedly: the simultaneous rights of audiences and producers, creativity, innovation, accessibility, and a desire for a common sphere that fosters critical national dialogue (Peers 1969: 440).

Whereas public broadcasting ideals should overlap nicely with goals of the free culture movement (see Lessig 2004) or the values of "copyleft," this chapter explores how the Canadian Broadcasting Corporation's content ownership practices are inconsistent with these goals and values. When discussing how the CBC seeks to police its intellectual property at the expense of protecting the public good, we are not necessarily looking at how archaic IP laws impact Canadians. Instead, we can spotlight how institutional policy and institutionalized ways of thinking shackle Canadian creators and users.

Publicly Funded, Then Locked Away: CBC Radio One's *The Contrarians*

Jesse Brown, a Toronto humourist, journalist, and producer, created and hosted *The Contrarians* on CBC Radio One in the summer of 2007. The program introduced unpopular and sometimes uncomfortable ideas. With special guests and interviews, Brown would introduce a contrarian position (thesis), provide the alternative argument (antithesis), and eventually arrive at some kind of conclusion (synthesis). The series was playful – one *Contrarian* episode suggested that copyright law should be abolished, while another episode was based on the suggestion that hip hop is the greatest cultural form of the century – and Brown certainly had fun introducing positions that he did not necessarily support. The purpose of the program was to demonstrate that no unpopular idea is so extreme, controversial, or counter-intuitive that we should avoid thinking it through before casting it aside. Its goal was never to sway an audience, only to challenge thought orthodoxy and demonstrate the value of lively debate.

The flavours of "thought orthodoxy" Brown selected to challenge were deliberate. In fact, *The Contrarians* subtlety challenged a certain kind of CBC orthodoxy. One *Contrarians* episode, for example, questioned the positive connotations associated with a Canadian identity. Perhaps a bigger attack on the institutional culture of the CBC was the contrarian position that suggested, "multiculturalism doesn't work … we only eat each other's sandwiches." This thesis on multiculturalism was taken up in Brown's pilot episode. Incidentally, the CBC executives who green-lit the series were very enthusiastic about his playful stance on multiculturalism – in fact, they encouraged him to be edgier and to go further. Brown was, understandably, pleased with the enthusiasm of CBC programmers.

The level of freedom Brown enjoyed at the start of the project disappeared once the summer series ended. Although he was able to posit, in one episode, that copyright should be abolished, after the summer ended Brown quickly learned that the CBC takes its role as a copyright holder very seriously. Like many freelancers, Brown maintains a personal online portfolio, and at one point, he included several excerpts from *The Contrarians* on his website. This site was never promoted to listeners, and was certainly not intended as an archive of CBC content or a pirate channel to deliver Radio One programming. Nevertheless, CBC management quickly contacted Brown to remind him that his contract prevented him from posting show material on the website. The CBC's takedown request was puzzling. Although the CBC certainly had the right to enforce its contracts, what exactly the CBC had to gain from Brown removing the content was unclear. At the time of the request, the series was over, and as far as Brown was told, management had no intentions of re-airing or repurposing it, nor was CBC Radio One archiving the series in any publicly accessible way. *The Contrarians* aired at a time when the CBC was just beginning to dip its toes into podcasting. Only a few programs were permanently archived as podcasts, and given the limited nature of the summer series, Brown could not convince the broadcaster to archive *The Contrarians* online.

The frustration Brown experienced in not being able to showcase his work in an online portfolio, however, seems relatively minor when compared with the larger issue here: publicly funded media content is being locked away from the citizens whose tax dollars funded the program in the first instance and who are, therefore, in significant ways its producers. The CBC clearly has a problem with content circulating beyond its immediate control, even when this circulation benefits Canadians. In the months following the show, Brown received dozens of requests from listeners for copies of the show. Numerous teachers contacted Brown, asking for episodes to use as teaching resources on topics including copyright law, multiculturalism, and feminism. As it turned out, *The Contrarians* furnished a useful aid for debating teams, who have also been in touch with Brown requesting episodes. Brown's hands were tied. Given his experience posting samples on his personal website, Brown could not personally distribute episodes of *The Contrarians* – a troubling situation considering both the nature of the show and the CBC's ostensible purpose in fostering a national cultural commons. The requests Brown received were arguably consistent both with fair dealing and what public broadcasting *should* be aiming to encourage: the spreading of ideas, particularly to help educators and students, and hence, to further dialogue, critical thought, and creativity.

For a show like *The Contrarians*, the CBC owns everything: the name, the interviews, and the episodes. CBC contracts even require a producer to waive his moral rights, so that Brown cannot even protect the integrity of *The Contrarians*. In sum, Brown's CBC contract not only stopped him from posting a clip of *The Contrarians*, but also prevented him from having any control over his own creative work – including what happened to that work after the series aired. Yet, the CBC's overzealous content ownership rights, enforced via contract, did not originally bother Brown. He envisioned himself working for the public and offering a public service. CBC Radio One does not carry advertising, and it is, therefore, almost entirely funded by parliamentary allocations. As such, Brown was comfortable reducing his creative labour to a "service" – as opposed to "producing a show." Perhaps no one other than the Canadians who fund, listen to, and enjoy public radio should be understood to "own" this show. If Brown is comfortable with the fact that he does not own his CBC-produced work, he is nonetheless uncomfortable with having this work locked away from the public, especially when the CBC is unlikely to be harmed (financially or otherwise) should it allow teachers, students, and other citizens to benefit from these old episodes.

A Larger Trend Emerges: www.CBC.ca and iCopyright

Brown's experience with *The Contrarians* is not an isolated incident for Canada's public broadcaster. In early 2010, the CBC website implemented the controversial iCopyright "instant licensing" system that created uproar among many Canadians. Significantly, this move suggested that the CBC has an institutional bias towards an interpretation of copyright more consistent with the perspective of an American entertainment conglomerate than an institution envisioned to protect the public interest and to foster a Canadian cultural commons. An American firm, iCopyright offers a supposedly "intelligent copyright" payment system that has been adopted by several major institutions including, notably, the Associated Press. Briefly stated, iCopyright instantly creates licences that permit users to make copies of and otherwise redistribute website content. Visitors who click the "licence" link at the top of an article can purchase the rights to display the full article on their website or blog for a monthly fee of $250. The standard "print" and "email" article tools are also connected with the iCopyright system; users can make five free printouts, or purchase the right to print additional copies.

At best, this licensing system is wholly unnecessary. Although promoted by iCopyright as a way to clarify to users what they can and cannot do with online content, there are already legal frameworks in place – namely, fair dealing provisions – that allow users to quote from materials, and in some cases reproduce them entirely, for purposes of news reporting, study, research, and criticism. If the CBC feels that users are confused about how they can or cannot use cbc.ca materials, an explanation of *user's rights* would be a more appropriate response by a public institution than a perplexing licensing system that speaks only to the CBC's rights as the copyright holder.

At worst, by placing significant, costly, and at times confusing restrictions on how online CBC productions may be shared, iCopyright flies directly in the face of CBC's public service mandate. The new www.CBC.ca implementation goes against the spirit of fair dealing, the capacities of the Internet, and the objectives of public broadcasting. The system of iCopyright is designed to extract commercial value from the standard "Article Tools" options – for example, print, email, or share on a multitude of social network sites – generally seen on the vast majority of online news services. The iCopyright service fills a market niche, serving content providers who are obsessed with return on investments and paranoid that they are losing revenue by allowing users to send articles to their friends. Making this point explicitly, an iCopyright white paper declares that "each article tool should be a sampling stand with a cash register waiting to ring up a sale for the customer who wants more than a free sample" (iCopyright Inc. 2009: 3). Finally, as a method to enforce the licences, iCopyright advertises rewards of up to $1,000,000 for reporting "piracy." By electing to align itself with an organization like iCopyright, the CBC appears to be adopting a position with regard to content ownership and copyright policing that is remarkably similar to that of the American entertainment industry.

Canadian legal scholars, bloggers, and journalists (including Jesse Brown) criticized the CBC's adoption of the iCopyright licensing system, noting that it is a distinctly American interpretation of copyright created by an American company. Similarly, critics pointed out that as

Canadians we fund and, hence, should have certain implicit rights to the content produced by the CBC. Licence fees upwards of $250 per month are astronomically high for a publicly funded content provider. On a positive note, within a matter of days, the CBC acknowledged the criticisms and opened up dialogue on the CBC's official blog (http://cbcrcblog.com/), reassuring its audience that not much had changed. Users were still welcome to quote from cbc.ca works in blog posts, and spread content via social networking sites, just as they were before the new licensing system. Although the CBC acknowledged the public confusion, it did not go so far as to terminate the iCopyright features. Critics wondered why, if "not a lot has changed," the CBC needed to bother with this service. There is a parallel here to Brown's encounter after *The Contrarians* program ended; if the CBC had little to gain by keeping the show locked away from listeners and educators, then why would it pursue Brown to remove all excerpts from his website? Once again, we have a situation where users have something to lose from the CBC's ardent policing of its copyrights, but whether the CBC has anything to gain is questionable.

Imagining a Different Public Media Future

A simple but compelling argument can be made that publicly funded media content should be publicly licensed and generally publicly available for use. Throughout the history of Canadian public broadcasting, the CBC has been positioned as a protector of the public interest, national identity, and cultural sovereignty (Standing Committee on Canadian Heritage 2003: 177). Sequestering content or making Canadians pay hefty licences to use it are ineffective ways to achieve such lofty goals. By the same token, overzealously protecting content appears to go against the CBC's mandate, as detailed by Canada's 1991 Broadcasting Act, which states in section 3(m)(vii) that CBC programming "must be made available throughout Canada by the most appropriate and efficient means and as resources become available for that purpose."

Part of serving the public interest involves ensuring that all content is properly and publicly archived – and the resources are now available to do this. In this sense, the CBC's online offerings may be contrasted to the National Film Board of Canada's much-praised NFB.ca "Screening Room," launched in 2009. Visitors from around the world can watch a selection of 1,500 (and quickly growing) high-quality, publicly funded Canadian productions, online, for free. Each video offers a "share it" shortcut that allows users to embed the video in a blog, website, or share it through a variety of social media tools. The NFB even offers an iPhone application. To be fair, the CBC is aware of the benefits and efficiency of digital distribution. The CBC's online presence is extensive, and, compared with many private broadcasters, CBC Radio has been on the leading edge of podcasting. But, as the case of *The Contrarians* shows us, despite a strong online presence, content is falling through the cracks. Worse still, as the case of iCopyright illustrates, the CBC is frequently policing its rights as a content owner without considering whether Canadians should have inherent rights to the content.

Compared with a private broadcaster, the CBC has less to lose and can afford to stick its head out on the digital line: the CBC does have to answer to the Heritage Minister and to Parliament, but CBC management does not have to answer to shareholders and CBC Radio executives do not even have to answer to advertisers. Furthermore, the CBC has an institutional history of taking risks, innovating, and connecting with Canadians in new ways. The institution revolutionized radio in the late 1960s by debuting shows like *As It Happens*. A "call-out" show, *As It Happens* was intended to stir up dialogue across the country and to offer a "meeting place for public debate and cultural exchange in Canada" (Standing Committee on Canadian Heritage 2003: 191). The public broadcaster has always pushed the envelope, and in many ways has been well *ahead* of the free culture movement of the past decade. Public broadcasting is fundamentally about providing content *for free* in an effort to provoke critical dialogue, to entertain, and even to inspire others to create; public broadcasting should contribute to a greater Canadian cultural commons. Given its mandate, funding source, and history, the CBC is well equipped to set the bar for Canadian broadcasting – and, historically, it has in some instances.

Over the past two decades, however, as technology has opened up new options to reach Canadians in innovative ways, the CBC has started to behave more and more like a paranoid private entertainment conglomerate, interested in the bottom line, and in control over content. A user's right to content, especially content he or she helped to fund, is marginalized among these increasingly more commercial priorities. This is not wholly surprising given the political climate. Supporters of the CBC recommend stable, long-term funding to allow the public broadcaster to take risks and better serve audiences (Standing Committee on Canadian Heritage 2003: 217). Instead, the CBC has been in crisis since the 1990s, subject to budget cut after budget cut, and consistently placed in a position of having to justify its very existence to Parliament. These macro-political forces leave the CBC with few options other than a more commercialized business model and an emphasis on meeting short-term budgetary goals. Accordingly, in early 2009, amid some of the most significant job cuts in CBC history, rumours circulated that the CBC might open up Radio One and Radio Two to commercial advertisements (Friends of Canadian Broadcasting 2009), presumably to curb the costs of keeping content available. Archiving material properly does require time, skill, and resources. As Chester (2007) cautions, "while the Internet has an endless source of such non-profit information, it is important to make such content readily accessible and easily locatable" (196). Simply making content available is only half of the battle; making content available in an accessible, useful, non-proprietary, and publicly licensed system is another story. Properly indexing and tagging this content is powerful but costly. The commercialized decision makers at the CBC might ask, "What return do we see on this investment?"

There are, indeed, internal – or institutional – politics at play. There is no caricatured, conniving mastermind to blame in this story. There is no recording industry president aiming to alienate producers from their work or divorce Canadian citizens from the content they help to fund. As Brown's experience illustrates, the interests of CBC workers are often consistent with the interests of CBC listeners; unlike some other debates over intellectual property, this is not an adversarial situation where user rights face off against, or must be balanced against, the rights of creators. Creators of CBC's works, like Brown, have an important place in promoting and protecting the public interest because they are members of the same publics. The CBC is equipped with staff, producers, and managers with progressive ideas when it comes to the distribution of digital content. These workers, however, deal with a larger institutional hierarchy and culture. It is through institutionalized biases that CBC management may have trouble deciphering the difference between reproduction, distribution (e.g., Brown's home page), and infringement. Through fair dealing provisions, however, copyright law has the potential to distinguish simple reproduction from infringement although the CBC's deeply embedded corporate culture may lack an understanding of this nuance.

Whether we take the case of the CBC requesting Brown to take down excerpts from *The Contrarians* from his personal website, or the more recent implementation of iCopyright on CBC.ca, the public broadcaster is clearly taking a narrow interpretation of its IP rights and applying these rights in a manner that is consistent with the interests of American recording and motion picture industries. Fair dealing provisions may permit users to reproduce CBC.ca pieces, even entire articles, but the use of iCopyright demonstrates a flawed understanding of fair dealing. The CBC appears to have a corporate bias towards protecting content as a means to protect direct revenue and indirect equity through tight control of the CBC "brand." This attitude is inconsistent with the public broadcaster's mandate of serving the public interest and creating a common cultural space for national dialogue. It is worth reiterating that public broadcasting in Canada, from the earliest days of radio, has been premised on resisting commercial influence and giving away content for the greater cultural good. This attitude of prioritizing protection and permissions is also, as other contributors have noted (Amani, this volume) inconsistent with the nature of communications and social practice in digital media landscapes. Finally, it would seem that the CBC has little to lose by providing a wealth of content online or in allowing users greater freedom in terms of how they can (re)use this content. *The Contrarians* run was over when Brown received a takedown request from the CBC, and the iCopyright licensing system is unlikely to turn into a major revenue source or solve the broadcaster's financial woes.

How can the CBC alter its philosophy? One way to move the CBC beyond its current mentality would be the adoption of some kind of public media "Bill of Rights." This is something Brown suggests to ensure all publicly funded media content is, at minimum, easily accessible to all Canadians. This Bill of Rights could plainly state that Canadians own the CBC content that they fund, and motivate the CBC to make all content publicly accessible. This public media Bill of Rights could also be adapted for other kinds of publicly supported media, like the NFB or Telefilm movies, and television programs supported by the Canadian Television Fund. However, because television shows and films are often supported through a combination of public and private funds, forcing producers to make their work publicly accessible, publicly licensed, or even part of the public domain becomes more complicated. Such a move would need to frame issues of content ownership in a positive way – a focus on user rights would need to replace the CBC's current fixation with licences, permissions, and punishments.

Pushing this argument further, the Bill of Rights could require the use of Creative Commons (CC) licensing as a way to give Canadians greater control over their public media. CC licensing would provide the

CBC with a flexible way to determine what content can be shared and the conditions under which it can be redistributed. In other words, the CC system could do many of the allegedly "instant" and "flexible" things iCopyright licensing claims to take care of, without the need to contract with an American company, sacrifice public service ideals, or antagonize a large number of Canadians. Adopting a CC licensing system for CBC.ca material could set the CBC free from its costly, narrow-minded, and heavy-handed approach to copyright protection; provide an opportunity to recognize the value of spreading content (instead of sequestering it); and, thus, connect the spirit of public broadcasting with the spirit of the Internet as a networked common space. The "rights" to CBC content could lie in the hands of the many, rather than a singular controlling broadcaster. This would require a fundamental change in CBC corporate philosophy, but – unlike other private broadcasters or private news organizations – the CBC actually does have the freedom to make such a daring move.

Ensuring that CBC content is publicly accessible and licensed is an objective for which the public broadcaster should strive. An even gutsier move – and one Brown also champions – would be to make public media content, or at least all public radio content, part of the public domain. *As It Happens* debuted over forty years ago on Radio One as an innovative and edgy way to create public dialogue. What better way to create a dialogue and sense of community among Canadians than tossing content out into the public domain, and allowing users to use it, break it down, and rebuild it into something new. Putting content into the public domain might even help the CBC deal with its dwindling human and financial resources. As noted, there are challenges in properly organizing, indexing, and tagging material – it takes time and money. Instead of attempting to do this in-house, the CBC could send the raw material out into the commons and allow eager users to develop their own ways of organizing and indexing it in socially and historically meaningful ways. A new partnership between CBC Radio and Canadians might thus be born. Despite chronic budget challenges, a bright digital future for the CBC is not unrealistic. The CBC is already a leader in some aspects of digital distribution. With a bigger push, the public broadcaster could continue to set and raise the bar, putting pressure on private broadcasters to keep up with the CBC's contributions not only to public service and public dialogue, but also to the public domain.

6 Resisting Enclosure: Licences, Authorship, and the Commons

JOHN W. MAXWELL

The eminent Harvard Law School professor Yochai Benkler wrote, in 1999, that "we are in the midst of an enclosure movement in our information environment" (354). Benkler's metaphor invokes the land enclosure movement of the sixteenth to eighteenth centuries – in which formerly open (and, colloquially, "common") fields in Britain were fenced and divided among private landholders. The metaphor is, as James Boyle (2003) notes, "too succulent to resist" by contemporary intellectual property (IP) commentators. In his article on this second enclosure movement, Boyle teases the metaphor out into its various threads:

> The critics and proponents of enclosure are locked in battle, hurling at each other incommensurable claims about innovation, efficiency, traditional values, the boundaries of the market, the saving of lives, the loss of familiar liberties. Once again, opposition to enclosure is portrayed as economically illiterate; the beneficiaries of enclosure telling us that an expansion of property rights is needed in order to fuel progress. (41)

In early modern Britain, the enclosures fenced off commonly used grazing lands. But our contemporary notion of the "commons" has been shaped in response to the enclosure movement: a reflection on a local political and economic milieu brought into sharp relief by the imposition of enforced property laws. The ensuing debates over land enclosures pitted the goods brought about by encouraging private investment in and improvement of private land against the traditional good of access to common pastureland as a public resource. Since then, the discursive and even legal entity of the commons has been employed to make a variety of political and economic points – not least of which was Garrett Hardin's now-infamous 1968 article, "Tragedy of the Commons." The terms we use to talk about such issues are themselves products of the playing out of these debates. Similarly, the invocation of an intellectual, cultural, or "creative" commons is a response to the imposition of formerly non-existent or non-obvious property rights on new realms of our intellectual and cultural landscape. We are learning the new vocabulary as we go, as the law, economics, and day-to-day practices of the digital age shift under massive technological change.

A notable case in point is the recent shift of the domain of copyright law from its original role as state regulation of industrial printing – a means of ensuring fair competition – to its contemporary application in the fine control of individuals' *use* of creative works. The Internet makes *every act* an act of copying; this is the nature of digital media. As the technical foundations upon which copyright has traditionally rested shift significantly from industrial manufacturing to personal and peer-to-peer (P2P) engagement, individual uses begin to have real effects on existing business models. As such, representatives from affected industries have not surprisingly taken various steps to extend the reach of IP protection into the digital realm, in the pursuit of stronger laws – and in construction of higher fences: the "technological protection measures" of contemporary legislation.

Boyle's (2003) historicizing of this second enclosure movement is in large part in the service of the *public domain*, itself a concept invoked and reified in discursive response to the growth of copyright legislation and jurisprudence. Beyond the *negative* definition of the public domain (consisting simply of those works for which the copyright term has expired), the *positive* conception of the public domain as something of considered value, deserving of public, and even constitutional protection, dates to as late as 1966 in the United States (58). Boyle is co-founder of something called the "Institute for the Study of the Public Domain" and, as such, is part of a larger movement to articulate the broader positive value to society of such a commons. In a rhetorical move drawn directly from the rise of the environmental movement, he notes, "Like the environment, the public domain must be 'invented' before it is saved" (ibid.).

Indeed, now is the time to take the public domain seriously (see Carys Craig, this volume). This broad conception of an intellectual or cultural "ecology" is not entirely new – such existing legal constructs as "fair dealing" and the American "fair use" have been long recognized for the balancing role they play in a larger ecology (in which copyright plays a dominant part). Fair dealing has been defined as a set of exemptions to the restrictions already coded in copyright law. As rights holders have sought greater and more detailed articulations of their legal protections, it is also necessary to define cases and scenarios that mark their reasonable limits. While the public domain has been invoked to cover those areas of human expression where copyright protection is not or is no longer justifiable, fair dealing defences and fair use exemptions address those *contexts* in which copyright-protected works ought to be accessible without requiring formal clearance. The canonical examples of research, private study, criticism, review, and news reporting all make more or less unproblematic sense when considered thus.

The trouble, as Lawrence Lessig (2004) has taken pains to elaborate, is that there is a general movement in copyright reform towards greater and greater articulations of the reach of copyright protection – especially into the digital realm – at the expense of the sorts of public access previously thought of as "fair." Hence, we see the invocation of the "enclosure" metaphor and the rise of a number of strategies to resist encroachment of stronger property laws and to develop alternative frameworks for understanding and articulating these issues. However, these tend to be rearguard tactics as opposed to coherent strategic action, which is not surprising given the scope and scale of forces mobilized to maximize copyright protection.

There are a variety of tactical approaches to resisting further enclosure that might be seen to fall into two basic camps. The first is action on the level of copyright legislation and jurisprudence; this includes efforts to lobby for more liberal copyright laws, efforts to expand the scope of fair dealing, and/or to pursue these causes in court. The now famous *CCH Canadian Limited* v. *Law Society of Upper Canada* (2004) case offers a notable example, helpfully expanding the discourse around how fair dealing can and, indeed, ought to be interpreted. The second approach is to promote more explicit articulation of *user's rights* in licence agreements between the rights holder and end users. This approach arises from the groundbreaking work of the Free Software Foundation in the 1980s (see Stallmann 1985), and is now perhaps more popularly recognized in the widespread promotion of Creative Commons (CC) licences. Such approaches are, typically, said to be layered on top of existing copyright legislation, which has the ironic effect of presenting a rather conservative appeal to the original conception of copyright, while seeking more radical articulations of use and licence.

Negotiating "Gridlock"

The broad public appeal of such movements towards liberalization responds to a growing spectre of what is often referred to as copyright maximalism. Michael Heller's popular book, *The Gridlock Economy* (2008), outlines the dangers of too much enclosure – a "tragedy of the anticommons" in which the problem of too many rights holders prevents effective action because of the spiralling costs of negotiating and arranging rights clearance. Heller's examples are largely drawn from dramatic and widely recognized legal minefields: biomedical patent negotiation, real estate development, and wireless spectrum regulation. Documentary filmmakers, too, have often complained about the difficulties of navigating such a permissions landscape (see Zeilinger and Horwatt, this volume; Knopf 2006a). The basic point is broadly applicable to the role of copyright in our contemporary intellectual and cultural landscape. Given a dense fabric of properties and property rights, we face a chilling effect on use and reuse owing to the high transaction costs of rights clearances.

As the landscape of intellectual property becomes more explicitly articulated and monitored, we begin to see culture more as a matrix of restrictions and licences than ever before. Lessig (2004) notes that we have moved from a world in which the vast majority of the uses of cultural works were unregulated to a world in which almost all uses are regulated in one way or another, with exemptions like fair use – and open licences – providing only a thin layer of public access. He lays out three realms of control: "In real space, then, the possible uses of a book are divided into three sorts: (1) unregulated uses, (2) regulated uses, and (3) regulated uses that are nonetheless deemed 'fair' regardless of the copyright owner's view" (143). Historically, he argues, the first category of unregulated uses was dominant: we were utterly free to read a book, write in its margins, give it to a friend, use it as a doorstop, and so on. The formally regulated realm applied primarily to the activities of printers and such industrial enterprises, and the "fair" exemptions operated as a reasonable and practical limit on the regulated uses. But, with the advent of the Internet and digital media, where every act is an act of copying, "uses that before were presumptively unregulated are now presumptively regulated" (143). In the world we now live in, practically all uses of digital, networked cultural content are potentially regulated, with only a thin layer of explicit exemptions. All works now have a formal legal rights status, even those sitting openly on the World

Wide Web, and even those released under an open licence. We are increasingly in a position of being forced to consider where any particular use falls vis-à-vis that legal status. This is to note that the gridlock scenario applies both where "all rights are reserved," but also in an open environment such as that promoted by the CC movement.

The danger is that we are headed towards a "total information awareness" model of IP rights, a world in which every piece of intellectual and cultural material is explicitly owned and licensed and/or marketed, with increasingly hefty and complex requirements for rights discovery, clearance, and marketing; even in the case of so-called free culture and open access movements. Consider the predicament of the Science Commons project, which promotes open access to research data sets in the name of making scientific endeavours both more efficient and more broadly accessible. Director John Wilbanks (2008) describes a potential gridlock scenario in the sciences, even in the context of open data licences, simply because of the basic need to declare rights and attribution information at every level:

> In a world of database integration and federation, attribution can easily cascade into a burden for scientists if a category error is made. Would a scientist need to attribute 40,000 data depositors in the event of a query across 40,000 data sets? ... Indeed, failing to give attribution to all 40,000 sources could be the basis for a copyright infringement suit at worst, and at best, imposes a significant transaction cost on the scientist using the data. (3)

Even in an open project like the Science Commons, where freedom of use and openness of information and technologies are central norms, the problem of formal rights status and proliferation of legal terms threatens the entire endeavour. The response of the Science Commons, under Wilbanks' direction, was to champion the "public domain as first recourse" (2008: 5) instead of open licences for data sets. Interestingly, the Creatuve Commons has responded with a new "licence" which can be used as a "waiver" or an "assertion" of public domain status.

One Ring to Rule Them All

Many believe that the problems of transaction costs and related gridlock effects can be solved by digital media itself; an all-encompassing database listing the ownership, licensing, and market terms of all works will make it quick and easy to look up and determine the status of any particular work. Such a master database would let everyone know the status of everything, and would thus be invaluable in day-to-day digital transactions. Users searching for free or open-licensed works would be able to locate what they want, while those interested in pursuing rights clearance in a more commercial context would have a one-stop shopping opportunity. There already exist various private (and "public") initiatives to create such a master database or rights clearing house. It is worthwhile for us to consider some of these carefully.

In 2002, the Department of Canadian Heritage announced the Electronic Copyright Fund, a $2.7 million initiative aimed at the development of "online copyright licensing systems." The funds would allow Access Copyright, its French-language counterpart, and a third party, RightsMarket, to create a master catalogue of rights. Access Copyright, the English Canadian agency that provides copyright licensing for photocopying and related institutional uses, is almost by definition enclosure oriented. Access Copyright already maintains a large voluntary database of works and encourages creators and publishers to register so that they can receive royalties "whenever we find your works copied under one of our licences" (Access Copyright website). Access Copyright's role in distributing royalties from widespread institutional photocopying is by now a commonplace, and today the organization has its sights set on the online world, with the possibility of making its registry much more comprehensive. More recently, Access Copyright and Creative Commons Canada announced a similar registry of works in the public domain: "There is currently no one place where information about the public domain is collected. The registry will make published works in the Canadian public domain easily identifiable and accessible in an online catalogue" (Access Copyright 2006). While no royalties would presumably be collected or paid for public domain works, such a registry clearly strengthens Access Copyright's position of omniscience. In a digitally mediated economy, those who control the *obligatory passage points* (Callon 1986) of rights discovery and negotiation are in considerable positions of power. But, of course, Access Copyright is but a small player in the game of omniscience. There is a much larger project, which threatens to completely overshadow such initiatives.

The canonical example of such a master database is Google and its Book Search Program. In the Amended Settlement Agreement of November 2009, there are provisions for a "Book Rights Registry" and "Unclaimed Works Fiduciary," somewhat at arm's length from Google itself, which would play the role of master rights database. As Google's ambition, and probably practical reach is to index every book ever published (as well as every website), it is reasonable to see such a registry as the beginnings of a master rights index of all textual works – every text in the world. Google is not alone. The Open Content Alliance (OCA), a "permanent archive of digitized work" set up by a consortium of organizations – including Yahoo, Microsoft, and the Internet Archive – in response to the unilateral agenda of Google's book-scanning endeavour, distinguishes itself from the Google project in its *openness* – the OCA's collection will be non-proprietary and "free to read" (OCA FAQ). But it, too, represents an attempt to create a comprehensive index of rights information, an index that we would be required to consult at every turn. As one critic of the project, Kalev Leetaru (2008) wrote:

> To determine the rights status of any particular work, a user must follow the link in both the Digitizing Sponsor and Book Contributor metadata fields to view the rights restrictions enforced by the two organizations … Hence, the burden falls to the user to read and legally interpret the rights statements of both entities before being able to determine the rights status of any particular work and whether a particular usage would be permitted.

The burden, of course, may not ultimately fall to the user, but to an agency which would take care of the rights navigation and negotiation on the user's behalf – in the interests of streamlining the whole business, making it simpler and more efficient. We should not be comforted by such a scenario.

Even the Creative Commons itself – taken to its logical conclusion – relies on the assumption that there is some queryable source that is the final word on what one can and cannot use in a particular situation. The Creative Commons forswears any ambition to *create* such a registry, but in the large, the universe of CC-licensed works – and especially the relationship of that set of works to the larger copyrighted world – practically presupposes such an index, although it may conceivably operate in decentralized fashion. The Creative Commons FAQ defers to the notion of the "Semantic Web" (Berners-Lee, Hendler, and Lassila 2001) to solve the practical problem; that the declarations made in metadata form an aggregate database, queryable at all times. And even more local- and commons-oriented initiatives are oriented to such a *telos*.

Here is the question that arises: if everything – even the so-called free and open works – is subject to some listing in a rights and access database, then *how free is free*? We do not appear to enjoy our freedom to the same degree as with the "unregulated uses" Lessig recalls from our pre-digital history. To extend Boyle's "enclosure" analogy somewhat, despite the existence of free and open-licensed materials, everything is still fenced in. Some of the fenced-in plots may display a notice that says, "You are free to graze your cattle here," but the fences themselves are an integral – perhaps *the* significant – feature of the landscape. Lessig goes on to challenge us, asking if this is, indeed, the kind of world we want to live in – a world, he writes in his essay "For the Love of Culture," in which "every bit, every published word, could be licensed. It is the opposite of the old slogan about nuclear power: every bit gets metered, because metering is so cheap" (2010: 27).

Considering the Role of Authorship in the "Commons"

How we have come to this point relies, in large part, on deeply embedded assumptions about authors and authorship. For copyright is not solely an industrial regulation; the ideological and moral foundations of such IP laws are tied up in the Enlightenment's conception of the author and the inseparability of the author and his work. Most explicitly, this is captured in the continental *droit d'auteur* notion, but centrality and inalienability of the author is invoked and evoked repeatedly in the Anglo-American tradition (in Canadian law, the connection between author and work is formally protected in the "moral rights" described in section 14.1 of the Canadian Copyright Act).

The "public domain," in the quotidian sense as the *shadow* cast by the lamp of copyright illustrates the centrality of authorship nicely: works in the public domain are either formally "authorless" or those whose authors have been *divorced* (by death and time) from their rights to the work. The public domain has come to rest on a severance of the assumed connection between author and work. It is that *abnormal* part of the landscape where the fences are down and the grass unmown; the land nobody loves. As such, the public domain has proved of little use in efforts to resist enclosure. Nearly all of the significant free-licensing strategies – starting from the Free Software Foundation's copyleft approach (GNU General Public License; Stallman 1985) – have rejected the public domain and, instead, chosen to build "free" and "open" and "public" access on a foundation of copyright. There are, however, differing effects achieved by the various strategies. It is instructive to examine copyleft – especially the GNU General Public License (GPL), the

Creative Commons, and more restrictive licences to see how differently they render the relationship between authorship and legal control.

Where the public domain assumes, literally, the "death of the author," the Creative Commons shows him alive and kicking, making "attribution" the most fundamental of the CC licence components, the sole non-optional item. CC licences are customizable in a variety of ways; a licensor can restrict the user's rights to redistribute commercially ("nc" or *non-commercial*) or to modify ("nd" or no-derivatives), or to require that modified works inherit the same licence terms as the original ("sa" or share-alike, itself a copyleft approach). But, the "by" line remains the core of the CC licence; to relinquish this is simply to consign one's work to the public domain. In this version of the teleological argument, if there is a licence, there must necessarily be a licensor, although there are in practice a variety of ways of treating the attribution portion of a CC licence: in someone else's name, or pseudonymously, or even anonymously (see Wikipedia's anonymity). This rhetorical centrality of the attribution component has significant implications for the Creative Commons. In putting attribution first, the Creative Commons assumes a modern, author-centric world of "creative" genius. This may put it rhetorically at odds with the very idea of a commons. David Berry and Gilles Moss (2005) note:

> As a result, the Creative Commons network provides only a simulacrum of a commons. It is a *commons without commonality.* Under the name of the commons, we actually have a privatised, individuated and dispersed collection of objects and resources that subsist in a technical-legal space of confusing and differential legal restrictions, ownership rights and permissions. The Creative Commons network might enable sharing of culture goods and resources amongst possessive individuals and groups. But these goods are neither really shared in common, nor owned in common, nor accountable to the common itself. It is left to the whims of private individuals and groups to permit reuse.

In contrast, the "copyleft" approach taken by the GNU GPL – and the CC's share-alike licence provision – puts authorship second to the licence itself (and the public commons that is effected), and in doing so, makes a much more radical statement. Copyleft licences establish an irrevocable state of public access to licensed works. All uses, including modifications and derivative works, are subject to the original licensing terms, and are thus permanently "free." The effect is a different kind of "death of the author" – the author is legally required at the outset, since only the author has the right to license the work in the first place; but once licensed, the author becomes effectively invisible from a rights standpoint. The work's own licence terms are *self-sufficient*, and the design of the licence prevents the work from ever being effectively relicensed or revoked (FSF FAQ). It is this self-governing move that gives the GNU licence its apparently scary anti-commercial aura.

Copyleft thus achieves a different kind of "commons" than most of the CC licences. Without consigning works to the post-copyright afterlife of the public domain, copyleft effectively establishes an intellectual commons, a domain of free public access and use. Most of the CC licences, while invoking a "commons" in name, fall short of this by preserving the controlling right of the author. The fences remain the salient feature of the landscape, regardless of the "free-for-all" licence on any given plot. What difference does this make, though? Arguably, the attribution-centric approach of the Creative Commons has been enormously successful. As of June 2010, the photo-sharing site Flickr.com reported over 145 million CC-licensed photos. While this certainly has implications for stock agency businesses, and while Flickr-sourced photos now commonly adorn everything from Powerpoint presentations to wedding invitations, we should still ask whether Flickr consitutes a commons in any meaningful sense. To be more precise, the largest category of CC-licensed Flickr photos (over 44 million images) invokes both the "non-commercial" and "no-derivatives" options.

By comparison, Wikipedia is a collaborative project that looks much more like a working commons: by mandating a core copyleft licence for all contributions – originally the GNU Free Documentation License, but since June of 2009 the GPL-like CC-SA (share-alike) licence – the project has ensured that all contributions are unencumbered by property rights restrictions. Although individual, fine-grained contributions and edits – located not so much within a particular article as within a revision history – may be (at least pseudonymously) attributed if the contributor takes the trouble to register and log in, the vast majority of contributions have been de facto anonymous (Anthony, Smith, and Williamson 2007).

In practice, Wikipedia's authorship is almost entirely effaced – something that has invited heaps of scorn from those critics who hold authorship to be central to trustworthiness (e.g., McHenry 2004). But those criticisms, dramatic though they may be, do not make so much as a dent in the popularity and sheer usefulness – not to mention general accuracy – of Wikipedia. This is an example of a successful creative project that is simply not about authors; rather, the success of Wikipedia may even be despite authors, as the complete absence of fences encourages the incremental, often casual contribution of an indeterminate number of indeterminately interested people. This is the *opposite* of gridlock; it is an environment that actively encourages contributions on a variety of levels.

Wikipedia has presumably inherited its tradition of anonymous contribution from its underlying software architecture. The original WikiWikiWeb (Portland Pattern Repository), in existence since 1995, was created as a means of collecting descriptions of software design patterns (Cunningham and Venners 2003) and simply had no means of user registration or login. Since the user community it served was originally quite small, and a good deal of the spirit of this community was centred around the elaboration of a collaborative process of agile software development (see Beck 2000), the WikiWikiWeb simply put the issue of authorship and rights *second* to the production of the community, relying when pressed on the assumed goodwill and mutual respect of participants and on vague references to "fair use." Far short of a policy, an appeal to the *virtue* of "EgolessWiki" is referenced in several places in the work.

Even more intriguingly, the WikiWikiWeb discourse maintains a distinction between "ThreadMode" and "DocumentMode," where:

> DocumentMode is when a Wiki contribution is written in the third person and left unsigned. The piece of text is community property; it may have multiple and changing authors as it is updated to reflect the community consensus. This is in contrast to ThreadMode, comments which are usually signed and in the first person, and rarely edited by people other than the one who signed them. (Portland Pattern Repository: DocumentMode)

ThreadMode, "a form of discussion where our community holds a conversation," encourages contributors to "sign" their comments. It is interesting to note that in this distinction, attributions of authorship are seen to have value where there is controversy, where there is no agreed-upon consensus, but lose that value once general agreement has been achieved. Here we find echoes of the history of scholarly communication. Guédon (2001) noted that the seventeenth-century *Philosophical Transactions of the Royal Society of London* played the role of formal "register" of intellectual work, allowing for the extended, written *conversation* of scholars responding to one another's work. This function was not the same thing as copyright – indeed, it preceded copyright by at least forty-five years. Guédon tells us that the function of *Philosophical Transactions* was to establish "intellectual *paternity* rights" rather than property rights. Property rights only became important when printers' and publishers' interests began to be negotiated.

More generally, science and the academy, which have long legitimized themselves by appealing to the public good, have traditionally relied on an *unbundling* of authorship and property rights. Far from tying authorship to reproduction and usage rights, science and scholarship have flourished by making the latter as open as practically possible, while retaining attribution as a means of organizing and recognizing the community of participants. Science Commons John Wilbanks (2008) notes that this allows for a degree of localized convention: "Requesting behavior, such as citation, through norms and terms of use rather than as a legal requirement based on copyright or contracts, allows for different scientific disciplines to develop different norms for citation" (5). In this context, Wilbanks' warnings of the dangers of overapplication of attribution do make a radical break with established practice; they serve to show how scholarship need not be a slave to IP regimes. Even when the ideals of such a regime are openness and access, the architecture of the regime may lead to unanticipated constraint, so it is our responsibility to pay attention not only to the licence terms, but also to the infrastructure upon which the licence relies. Let us pay attention to the fences, not just the land they enclose.

Dealing "Fairly"

Fairness is surely a concept that is justified and rationalized locally, with respect to actual practice, and with reference to the various axes upon which a given situation turns. Fairness may not actually be capturable in a definitive, encompassing (statutory) statement, neither of exception nor of privilege. The anthropologist and Creative Commons adviser Christopher Kelty (2004) has noted that finely attuned cultural sensibilities cannot be captured entirely in law; rather, functional laws often need to be loose enough for actual communities to interpret and apply in consideration of the local situation. Kelty argues that at some point, the legal side must "punt to culture," thereby granting to communities of practice some scope in the judgment of what is and is not possible: "Rather than make more law, or call in the police, the license *strategy* relies on 'culture' to fill in the gaps with people's own understandings of what is right and wrong, beyond the law" (553). We have any number of examples of distinct communities of practice: in the norms of organized academic disciplines, in both their productive research communities and their pedagogical facets. We see online peer production communities of practice from Flickr.com to free software and from the WikiWikiWeb to its massively scaled-up offspring, Wikipedia – and now, it appears, in a codified form for the Science Commons (Science Commons 2007). It is arguable that practices such as P2P file sharing may reveal "local" norms and customs that are worthy of such consideration. These community understandings of the "logic of practice" operate in addition to (and, clearly, sometimes even trumping) the copyright legislation and jurisprudence.

In academia and in most organized contexts, we operate with a set of expectations that guide our practical activities and judgments. Those expectations and local conventions ought to be the foundation for legal articulations of rights and licences in a world where copyright concerns the everyday actions of millions of citizens. In such a scenario, "fair" dealing would be the starting point of the law, rather than its after-the-fact exception. Wilbanks (2008) appeals to a sense of goodwill: "If we abandon the idea of the 'bad actor' and the concomitant requirement to constantly pursue and prosecute, we can articulate methods that reward the good actor – the person who obeys the norms" (8). Such an approach requires that we abandon all-in-one approaches, both in attempts to comprehensively rationalize who owns what and under what terms, and to more perfectly delineate exceptions to the rules. What is missing from a great deal of the debate about copyright in the twenty-first century is the question Lessig asks: what kind of world do we want to live in? But, where Lessig's target is the ill-conceived Google Book Settlement – which seeks to do the right thing by all the wrong means – there is surely an opportunity at hand to think about copyright, fair dealing, and the public domain in a way that does justice to the world our children and grandchildren will inherit. This is a world, I dearly hope, where everything isn't nailed down, indexed, and registered to infinity; where there is still a good deal of fair "play" in our systems of commerce, cultural exchange, art, and expression. Where there is still room for local interpretation, on-the-fly navigation, and creative negotiation, there is still room to breathe.

7 Weaving an Open Web: Innovation and Ethics in the Virtual Commons

ELIOT CHE

Sharing software ... is as old as computers, just as sharing recipes is as old as cooking.

Richard Stallman, *Free Software, Free Society*

The concept of openness is nothing new to modern computing. During the advent of mainframes in the period after the Second World War, software was distributed by means of source code printed on paper, whereby a programmer would manually input the code into the device, line by line. However, the rise of commercial applications for computing brought with it new types of non-technical (end) users and business models focused on maintaining control over the ways in which software was made. Today, two general approaches to software computing exist alongside one another: the closed source (CS) model, which maintains a degree of secrecy and proprietary right over source code, providing only an end product to users; and the open source (OS) model, which makes available the application source code to enable collaboration and knowledge sharing among developers and communities interested in technological change.

The re-emergence of openness is interdependent with the rise of the Internet and the World Wide Web – much of the server and infrastructure of the Internet is based on OS technologies. Moreover, the rising popularity of Web-based content management systems (CMSs) such as Drupal and WordPress is pushing the parameters of the debate further into public consciousness, prompting the everyday user to make decisions about CS and OS models when launching a new blog, extending a business online, or building a community forum. Providing a look into the state of open source, as such, this chapter seeks to cover extensive ground. After briefly appraising how copyright and proprietary models came to drive the development of OS approaches embodied by a moral economy of openness and an ethic of fair dealing, I focus on the open Web – a term used to describe the collection of OS technologies and techniques that form an integral part of an increasingly ubiquitous online experience. In particular, I examine the maturation of CMSs and their role in pushing forward new conceptions of innovation and ethics through a discussion of technologies and techniques such as peer review and modularization, and concepts such as communities of practice, recursive publics, and cultural usability. In Canada, OS activity remains low, even though the country ranks high in terms of Internet penetration (Baker and Douglas 2009). As the government of Canada and several sectors of the economy and society begin to consider implementing new online technologies, it is necessary to consider successes of open source and the open Web, as well as components and approaches that remain works in progress. Although recent high profile projects such as Mozilla's Firefox have helped bring OS computing and development into the spotlight, its future remains unsettled and its implications remain unclear.

Opening the Web: Successes of Open Source

Infrastructural technologies offer far more value when shared than when used in isolation.

Nicholas Carr, "IT Doesn't Matter"

The concept of OS software finds its contemporary origin in a clash of ideologies – between the commercialization of software and the free exchange of information and cooperation. In the early 1980s, a shift towards commercial, CS software brought with it new limits to collaboration and knowledge sharing for large communities of independent developers, including academic research departments. In what was previously an open domain, uncertainties and ambiguities surfaced over the legality of sharing what could now be considered proprietary technologies. This tension, compounded by the widespread emergence of personal computing, set off a series of events discussed throughout this volume that would lead to what we understand today as the OS movement.

At the 1997 Linux Congress, Eric Raymond drew critical attention to the dynamic practice among a growing community of developers of dealing openly and fairly in collaboratory projects. Raymond's pivotal essay, *The Cathedral and the Bazaar* (1997), compared two different models of software development: the traditional "Cathedral" model, where source code development is restricted to an exclusive group of developers; and the emerging "Bazaar" model, based on an open community of developers from across the Internet working on source code that is continually and freely distributed (see Raymond 1998b). This moment marked a (re)discovered awareness of the potential embedded within open models of development, and helped bring about a new period in software engineering and computer culture. For example, it led to the open sourcing of the Netscape browser, which would eventually become Mozilla Firefox, as well as the coining of the phrase "open source," which was previously known as "free software."

The turn of the millennium saw the rise of new software technologies focused on online content creation, information sharing, and collaboration – sometimes referred to as "Web 2.0" (DiNucci 1999). Open source contributed to this evolution conceptually, in that software developers and entrepreneurs invoked ideas of collaboration and an ethic of fair access and free information exchange in the wake of the OS movement's heightened visibility and demonstrated ability to build communities based on voluntarism. The first online social networks were created. OS's technical contribution to the new Web was not only in forming part of the infrastructural foundation, but also in playing a vital role in pushing the Web forward with the engineering of new technologies for the production of knowledge and online collaboration, such as Drupal, WordPress, and MediaWiki. Previously, contributions to the visible body of the Web required an intimate knowledge of code and a certain degree of expertise in computer programming. As access to the Internet became more widespread, Web-based content management tools were developed to fill the gap between content creators without the adequate technical expertise and those well versed in programming languages and network protocols.

For example, in 2001, Dries Buytaert produced an online message board system that would quickly come to be extended by a large community of developers into a full-fledged CMS called Drupal. Today, Drupal ranks among one of the most widely used OS CMSs. Acting as a graphical user interface to enable the creation of content in a fashion similar to how one would produce a word processing document (e.g., in Microsoft Word or OpenOffice), Web-based CMSs do not require the traditional level of technical programming knowledge previously required for creating, updating, or maintaining Web pages. This degree of accessibility upholds an ethic of openness and fair access, extending the capacity for the production and dissemination of knowledge to new demographics and expanding the reach of open source.

OS CMSs such as Drupal, wiki software like MediaWiki and its implementation as Wikipedia, as well as browser platforms released under OS licences such as Mozilla Firefox are part of what I suggest we call the "open Web." The history of the open Web is part of the most recent history of open source, denoting an expanded scale of accessibility and representing a movement towards an increasingly user-centred experience, as opposed to the traditional approach focused predominantly on the developer and programmer. The technical and conceptual achievements of open source are long-standing and have not changed significantly in the past decade. However, the advent of new software projects directed towards an open Web, which have come to be influential due to the immense expansion of the Internet, allows us to evaluate some of the activity in the OS domain from a fresh perspective, and to explore the ways in which OS communities are sustained. Through this lens, the successes of open source can be described in terms of potentials, stemming from three features characteristic of the approach: increased reliability and security due to peer review, active communities of collaboration, and modularization employed to mitigate the complexity of a considerable number of people participating in large projects; not discussed here are the low cost of entry and the total cost of ownership – see Wheeler (2007) and, for an opposing perspective, Driver (2008).

The transparency of code in OS software enables and promotes expanded prospects for peer review and, consequently, an ethic of fair dealing. In this sense, making an application's source code widely available can result in improved reliability and stability. Peer review is not limited to the discovery of functionality defects (or "bugs"), but also works to bring forward possible improvements and foster consistency in implementation, often according to design standards established by the developer community or larger governance organizations. The adherence to "best practices" in combination with the availability of source code ensures that the software can be maintained without the participation of the original developer. Thus, when defects or flaws are discovered, the response time and availability of developers to repair OS software can be shorter than that of CS counterparts. Because much of the interaction involved in peer review occurs via the Internet in open forums and list-serves, the referee function in weighing contributions is able to limit some of the social contextual factors, or at least provide transparency in making visible whose contributions carry weight and why (Weber 2006). The peer review capacity of OS technologies also facilitates security and privacy auditing. Although both OS and CS developers often make claims to providing secure systems, the OS approach enables third parties to verifiably identify and evaluate potential security problems. In-depth and widespread code-level auditing by third parties is an alternative to the problematic approach of relying on the secrecy of source code to achieve or maintain "security through obscurity" (e.g., Diffie 2003).

The availability and accessibility of source code also enables active community and entrepreneurial participation for development and support. Because the code is available to the public, organizations using open source can adapt their software as institutional or individual needs change. Development flexibility to customize the application, and freedom from vendor lock-in provide a multitude of alternative sources for support if the original development company ends its software engineering operations. This flexibility and freedom effectively enhance and extend the life of the software product, and are critical in making possible the collaboration resulting from the capacity to share code combined with the increasing ubiquity of the Internet. The development of proprietary software, with a limited number of employees, has difficulty committing itself to the increased workload that often accompanies improvements or new feature sets. Thus, according to Johnson (2006), employees are frequently hesitant to offer suggestions for enriching the software product; in marked contrast, the voluntary nature of most OS projects indicates that ideas are more freely shared since "an agent voluntarily supplying labor to an OS project cannot be compelled to work beyond his natural inclination" (478). The ethic of openness and a practice of dealing fairly to accommodate various degrees of ability and engagement, therefore, work to produce technologies that are both flexible for developers and appealing to large numbers and types of people.

The contribution of fresh ideas and the production of new development goals inevitably increases the complexity of a project. During the dot com bubble, there were suggestions that the Internet and open source would render managing this complexity unnecessary, enabling the formation of "episodic communities on demand … virtual organizations that come together frictionlessly for a particular task and then redistribute to the next task just as smoothly" (Kelly 1998, cited in Weber

2004: 171; also Tapscott et al. 2000). However, standard arguments contending that formal organizational structures necessarily arise out of increased complexity have proven to be more accurate. Large OS projects follow along these lines and generally have three types of participants: users, who are not involved with the development of the software, but who may ask and answer questions in online forums; contributors, who provide bug reports, patches, tutorials, or documentation to complement the work of the core development team; and committers, the core developers who also act as gatekeepers in determining what code is implemented into the body of the software. Within this general framework there are subgroups that form a degree of modularization, in the same way that a large program works by calling on other smaller independent modules. As such, the organization of people in a large OS project has come to reflect the structure of the software project itself.

Such structures are largely based on the approach adopted by older OS projects such as Linux, and partly explain how the OS community, a dispersed group of developers possessing varying degrees of ability and availability, can come together to create a complex product. Modularization, a large active community of potential auditors and a preponderance of voluntarism follow closely along the design principles laid out in Jean Lave and Etienne Wenger's concept of "communities of practice" that call for an allowance of different levels of participation (see Lave and Wenger 1991, Wenger et al. 2002). This concept describes a long-standing process whereby people who share interests come together, and by sharing information and experience acquire expertise and knowledge fundamental to the formation of a communal identity. Beyond simply producing software, the OS model of development "also produces the interacting system of knowing, learning, and doing that organizes the community and its relations with other communities" (Tuomi 2007). This type of system is described by Chris Kelty (2008) through the development of the concept of the "recursive public"; defined as publics that are "constituted by a shared concern for maintaining the means of association through which they come together as a public" (28), recursive publics are concerned with moral-technical order – with hardware, software, networks, and protocols that are conceptually interdependent with codes of conduct and the organization of economy and society. The recursivity of the OS movement is illustrated in recent attempts by Canadian OS software creators, Web developers, and advocates to mobilize social networks and to make, maintain, and modify OS technologies in lobbying for the procurement and implementation of open source in government. As Kelty notes, "They argue *about* technology, but they also argue *through* it. They express ideas, but they also express *infrastructures* through which ideas can be expressed (and circulated) in new ways" (29, original emphasis).

Thus, while the general structure of large OS projects has seemingly come to mimic traditional commercial software organizational practices, the significant difference is that it has done so *because of* a dispersed community from across the Internet consisting mainly of volunteers who increasingly feel a sense of membership the more they participate – with a level of recursivity and transparency, a degree of openness and fair dealing not present in the world of commercial software engineering. Steven Weber (2004) argues that transparency in open source is a key component in the longevity and resilience of the community and its projects, since it "makes transparent the pressures [e.g., of demands for new features, or deadlines] and the costs of not meeting them, thus pressing trade-offs out into the open where developers are forced to deal with them in a self-conscious way" (174). Openness and transparency, peer review and recursivity, and the knowledge production and identity formation that occur as projects play out are central to answering the question of how OS communities hold together.

A Tangled Web? Usability and Open Source as a Work in Progress

Good programmers know what to write. Great ones know what to rewrite (and reuse).

Eric Raymond, *The Cathedral and the Bazaar*

As both physical and virtual globalization continue to expand, politics and sociality, particularly in the Canadian social imaginary, are increasingly concerned with the tension between cultural diversity and social inclusion. The open Web and broader OS communities, constituted largely by an ethic of openness and a culture of fair dealing, must therefore, critically engage with questions of sociopolitical scale as OS technologies reach new demographic sectors such as local arts groups or various levels of government. Openness, and more significantly the ethic of fair dealing are constitutive but not necessarily a foregone conclusion in the evolution of open source. Although the organizational structures of many OS projects are conducive to software production and community development, the open Web poses new questions as open source expands into these new demographic territories.

OS projects, for example, have often been criticized for overlooking non-expert users and the corresponding necessity of considering interface psychology (Raymond 1999c, Nichols and Twidale 2007) to consider user experience. In addition, as the OS communities of users and programmers expand, the roles of culture and sociality in relation to openness and fair access are increasingly called into question. Thus, the remainder of this chapter focuses on usability, a particular critique of OS development that comes in various forms, some of which are being addressed by open Web communities such as Drupal and WordPress, and some of which have yet to be taken up. Although there are numerous researchers studying traditional forms of usability (Nielsen 1993, Nichols et al. 2001, Fennell 2008, Wells 2008), what follows is a brief analysis of two more recent types: cultural usability, a recent stream of human-computer interaction (HCI) studies that expands the scope of usability research by examining the impact of cultural (understood as nationality-based) background; and what we might call "social usability," in order to account for the expanded scale of new open Web technologies.

Emerging questions of cultural usability highlight that current forms of localization and internationalization in open Web technologies are insufficient. Localization and internationalization (numeronymically identified as L10n and i18n, respectively) are terms used to describe the process by which products or services are adapted to particular languages or regional differences. As of this writing, Drupal employs L10n and i18n synonymously with language translation, mainly from English to various other languages. However, the error of assuming that usability is understood similarly across cultures with only minute differences in terminology has consequences for the expansion of the OS technologies and the growth of the OS movement. For example, Drupal conducted usability studies in 2008 at the University of Minnesota and the University of Baltimore. In each study, the classification of individual participants was highly technical, centred primarily on the participants' past experience in using CMSs.

Such methodologies are in accord with the conventionall HCI axiom that "usability must be considered a universal phenomenon in order for HCI to move forward as a science" (Clemmensen 2009). However, studies in social psychology (e.g., Chua et al. 2005) indicate marked differences in perception based on cultural background. For example, Miyamoto and colleagues (2006) found that "people of Western culture tend to engage in context-independent cognitive processes and to perceive and think about the environment in an analytic way," while "people of East Asian culture tend to engage in context-dependent cognitive processes and to perceive and think about the environment in a holistic way" (113). One user's focus on salient foreground objects contrasted with another user's focus on context has important implications for open Web and OS communities that seek to expand membership into new demographic constituencies. Maintaining a culture of fair dealing and openness in the OS community, particularly given Canada's diverse population, demands that open Web developers consider culture in the conceptualization and production of communications technologies.

Future usability studies conducted for OS CMSs might also consider factors other than age, employment, and technical experience. Studies might use techniques beyond those of eye-tracking, verbal feedback, or written response. For example, researchers have identified areas of study in non-verbal behaviour, such as kinesics (body language) or paralinguistics (vocal cues such as pitch, tone, and modulation), and applied these concepts to usability testing (Yammiyavar et al. 2008). Usability studies might also be performed in partnership with other research centres around the world to build a more inclusive recursive public that can speak to and engage with a diversity of cultures – or to address our predisposition towards clustering and "engage with difference" (Weinberger 2009).

Thus, while the OS development community has been successful in limiting the impact of some social contextual factors (e.g., Weber 2006), thereby engaging with difference, dealing openly and fairly requires asking questions about ethics: which social, cultural, or contextual factors matter and which ones do not? Is it relevant that two developers coding a program come from different parts of the world, one from North America and one from South East Asia? Does it matter that, if the government of Canada adopts Drupal for its public Web presence, users may be Canadian citizens from China, Somalia, or First Nations communities? Addressing such questions requires expanding the scope of what is currently understood by open Web developers as usability, localization, and internationalization.

A variant of cultural usability is what we might call "social usability." Apart from national or regional culture, studies in cultural psychology indicate that there are historically developed ways of thinking embedded in the everyday use of computers and other interactive products by individuals and small groups (Clemmensen 2009; also Vatrapu and Suthers 2007, Sun 2004). Thus, the open Web community can grow its membership more effectively by considering what kinds of modules, designs, or architectures might better incorporate the demands of these types of potential users or developers. This process is not, drawing on Clemmensen (2009), a matter of choosing either evolutionism or relativism. Rather, it is about accommodating the world of peoples and communities in an open and fair manner in determining what is universal, and what is mutable. In what ways are small groups distinctive, and how do they (want to) communicate or publish information and produce knowledge? Archiving content that is, for example, highly performative in nature such as oral histories or traditional knowledges requires and involves more than simple digitization and record keeping. As the Artmob project (see introduction, this volume) and other chapters in this volume indicate, techniques of archiving are themselves acts of creativity. In terms of the present chapter, a necessity for open Web recursive publics is to embrace both diversity and inclusivity. Drupal has been successful in appealing to, among others, non-governmental organizations and creative arts groups. Sustaining the momentum of this aspect of the OS movement, and maintaining openness and an ethic of fair dealing as core and constitutive components of such a recursive public, requires further dialogue about and research on cultural and social usability.

Conclusion

Modern computing has come a long way since the era of electromechanical mainframes and the invention of the integrated circuit; and the principle of openness has persisted in a sometimes tenuous partnership. In accounting for the contemporary origins of open source computing and the growth of the open Web, and appraising some of their successes and works in progress, this essay has covered a great deal of ground. However, it has illustrated a wide-ranging trajectory of open source in order to better understand and describe the current state of the movement, wherein copyright, innovation, and ethics interact in a much larger whole. A political economy of openness is emerging, from smartphones to social networks. As the community extends its reach to new types of users and new kinds of software, peer review, active communities of practice, and modular strategies remain at the core of the OS approach. And although new users and new software reawaken variations of old critiques, OS projects are making progress and have many opportunities for improving the diverse forms of usability. Addressing such concerns is not only critical to driving forward the dynamic practices of openness in cultures of fair dealing, but will also play an instrumental role in helping a recursive public consisting of researchers, developers, and users understand and mobilize within the increasingly complex intersections of technology and society.

8 "This Content Is Not Available in Your Region": Geoblocking Culture in Canada

IRA WAGMAN AND PETER URQUHART

For many people engaged in activities on the Internet, from the most committed users to casual surfers, the fact that cyberspace is no longer an open frontier is hardly breaking news. Sometimes this is as clear as day; in recent years, we have seen that in places like China, Iran, or Myanmar, the Internet can be turned off with a flick of the switch, forcing dissidents who want to get the word out to circumvent state censorship by employing tactics intended to mask a user's location. In democratic countries like Canada, the situation is far less serious – the fencing off of the Internet is much more subtle. The very speed of one's service, however, is often dependent on the time of day, a phenomenon that the industry and those invested in debates about "net neutrality" refer to as "throttling." Here, the Internet is not switched off, but rather subject to a series of delays, like traffic jams. In other cases, the problem is not a matter of speed but of place. Depending on where you are, websites may be accessible or restricted from view. This reveals one of the Internet's central tensions, between a technological system widely perceived as permissive and one widely seen as restrictive. As many have pointed out, this is a prominent motif of most media systems throughout history. Except for the most technologically savvy, the nature of that tension (between the Internet's openness and its closure), and the extent to which people must "deal," or negotiate between the two tendencies, depends on where you surf.

To illustrate, we take up the example of geoblocking, the practice of denying access to a Web address on account of the Internet protocol (Ip) address of your computer. With an Ip address that indicates you are in Canada, access to a range of services, such as the music site Pandora, the video streaming service Hulu.com, and the websites of individual television programs or networks, are restricted from view. Typically, users accessing these sites from Canada are reminded of the power of place when they are notified either that the content is "not available in your region" or that there are places in cyberspace – namely, Canadian broadcasters – where one can access the content legally.

The reasons for the geoblocking of online content have to do with questions of intellectual property (IP) and copyright. Generally, geoblocking occurs when rights to distribute a given work in Canada have not been determined or when those rights specifically indicate that Canadians can only see the content with the show's Canadian partner. There are other cases, where systems of artist compensation – royalties – have yet to be determined. Overall, such practices of geoblocking are hardly restricted to Canadians. In many cases, such as trying to access coverage of the Olympics on Canadian television channels, Americans experience cyber-reciprocity, as many sites offering Canadian content are screened from view. Indeed, the same is true for computer users worldwide, whenever they are hoping to access content from beyond their borders. As Tama Leaver (2008) has explained, Australians attempting to access webisodes of programs like *Doctor Who* or *Battlestar Galactica* are met with the same message of being "out of region."

There are, however, other reasons for sites to be geoblocked. People surfing the Web at workplaces and public wi-fi hotspots may discover that certain websites – such as Facebook – are blocked by corporate software. Here, geoblocking may occur in the name of productivity or for purposes of public relations, to protect organizations from embarrassing material leaking onto the Web. In Montreal's Bibliothèque Nationale, where a portion of this essay was written, an attempt to access one of the author's fantasy baseball teams was blocked, as sites categorized as "gaming" by the institution's filtering software were blocked from view. The logic here may be legal in nature; even as libraries rebrand themselves as hubs for seekers of information, every institution needs to protect itself from lawsuits responding to problematic activities occurring on its wireless connection.

For many, the blocking or slowing down of the Internet is a source of frustration, because cyberspace is imagined to be *placeless* and *instantaneous*, a zone where one can access anything from anywhere at any time. Such blocking also frustrates the possibility for audiences to experience the full effect of what Henry Jenkins (2006) calls "transmedia storytelling," where narratives of media texts like television's *Heroes* or the film *The Matrix* are spread across different media platforms.

However, from the ads that offer links to Toronto Blue Jays tickets down the side of one's Facebook page, or the redirection to google.ca when the .com address is entered into a Web browser, the fact remains that *where* you access the Internet says a lot about *what kind* of Internet you experience.

Although we acknowledge the seriousness posed by copyright laws that threaten to further restrict what can and cannot be done online, we argue that a broader consideration of geoblocking is also necessary. For us, the example of geoblocking is not just a *legal* problem, nor is it simply part of the "myth" offered by every new technology (e.g., Quail 2009). Rather, we suggest here that geoblocking also has a *cultural* component. In what follows, we suggest that flows of material culture have been blocked, delayed, or interrupted in the name of other causes beyond intellectual property or copyright. Denying users access to content, for transformative or other reasons, has been the rule and not the exception in the development of national and global media systems, and those arguments have as much to do with *territory* and sovereignty – as well as bordered national economic protectionism – as they have to do with *rights*. Contending with place and with conditions that delay a user's desire for immediate gratification in what is supposed to be a "placeless" Internet promising instant happiness should be a key factor in the development of a "dynamic" code of fair dealing.

This chapter, therefore, will move some distance from the conventional, strict, meaning of fair dealing and will invoke what we call the various "deals" media consumers are offered, the relative "fairness" of those deals, and explore how media consumers through their concrete actions "deal" with the conditions they are presented with. In an effort to begin reconceptualizing the current narrow definition of the concept of fair dealing, we invoke these analogies – and the specific historical examples we cite along the way – to demonstrate that by thinking differently about the concept, we might find new avenues into the critical tensions that surround fair dealing as it is currently understood.

In 2007, the thirteen-minute film *Hotel Chevalier* was created by director Wes Anderson to serve as the prologue to the feature-length release *The Darjeeling Limited*, which was due to be released later that year. The film was first presented at the Venice Film Festival, and was then shown in theatres in the United States and Canada. For a brief period of time, the film also streamed for free on iTunes, Apple's online store. However, in Canada, the film was unavailable. Accessing iTunes from a Canadian IP address returned a message informing users that "this content is not available in your region," as the film's producers had not yet negotiated the Canadian rights with Apple to distribute the film (*National Post Online*, 9 Oct. 2007).

The distance between the content that we want and its availability in Canada seems to be a prevalent feature of the Canadian Internet experience. Canadians are especially aware of this when it comes to some of the latest devices. The Amazon e-book reader Kindle, for example, was still unavailable to Canadians months after its launch in the United States, as the retailer worked with domestic industry representatives to sort out how Canadian artists and publishers would be compensated for e-books. In another celebrated example, Canadians had to wait for Rogers and other telecommunications companies to bring iPhones to the national market. For those with a stronger sense of history, this is but a case of déjà vu – the Canadian experience with emergent media technologies has almost always come with a delay. The American radio system, for example, which was dominated by the networks, was well in place by the end of the 1920s, long before Canadians had their own networks. The same is true for television: Canadians living near the US border who owned antennas were able to pick up US television for years, before a distinctly Canadian system was set up. Those not living close enough to the American border had to wait for the establishment of national broadcasters.

It would be silly to suggest that the case of *Hotel Chevalier* or the other examples described above amount to what in a digital age is called a "denial of service." In the context of many such examples, even to say that something has been "blocked" may be a misnomer. In the case of *Hotel Chevalier*, those interested likely found a number of ways around the block, either by using software like BitTorrent to get access to the film, by asking friends in the United States to burn a copy and send it to them via the mail, or even simply by waiting until the film came out on DVD and watching both films on their home entertainment systems. In other cases, users take advantage of software or websites that are intended to mask the user's Ip address.

Sometimes, this action can be accidental. Until recently, a Canadian using the security application HotSpot Shield would have discovered, for example, that the scrambled Ip address this software provides is an American one, granting users access to websites otherwise forbidden to users located in Canada. The blogosphere abounds with public advice to the frustrated blocked user, detailing how to use such devices to circumvent geoblocking attempts that are characterized, variously, as a simple annoyance or even as a breach of one's human rights (e.g., Newman 2009). In many ways, this too is an old story about the unintended consequences of technological innovation; a few years before Canadians had access to television, a December 1949 article in the *CBC Times* told the story of how one of the company's employees picked up two twenty-minute segments of *The Milton Berle Show*, broadcast from a television station in Pittsburgh, thanks to a fluke signal that was intended for Pennsylvania, but instead ended up in the Halifax area (*CBC Times*, 4–10 Dec. 1949).

To a degree, it emerges that old forms of media have always been used, and are still being used to transport forbidden new media content. In another sense, examples such as that of *Hotel Chevalier* can best be described as characterized by delayed gratification, one in which Canadians can *see* and *hear* about the latest device, software, or program while surfing the Internet, listening to radio, or watching television, but have to deal with the fact that their *access* to this content has almost never been seamless – unless, as in the case of HotSpot Shield, a user camouflaged his or her geographical location. The "work-around procedure" for some such problems can even be quaintly old-fashioned: Canadian Apple Macintosh computer users wishing to order the upgrade to the "Snow Leopard" operating system, upon finding out that the California-based website won't allow them the privilege that American Apple customers enjoy, were told by the support staff that the solution is to download a PDF order form, fill it out with *a pen*, put it in *an envelope*, affix sufficient postage, and *mail* it to California. In this case, the "block" has nothing to do with "rights," but is simply a mistake, according to the company. Yet, it remains another quotidian example of the nationally specific delayed gratification experienced by the Canadian media consumer.

Let us consider geoblocking beyond its connection with IP rights, and towards its connection with blocking in the name of territory. Considered in this way, we see that the geoblocking of mediated texts is the rule, rather than the exception, and that Canadians are routinely teased with cultural materials only to find that they are unable to access them because of where they are. For example, Canadians watch advertisements for contests or game shows they cannot enter. On a more local level, many contests open to Canadians are not open to residents of Quebec. The issue here is legal more than cultural; many contests which operate in Quebec have to be registered with the Regie des alcools, des courses, et des jeux. On the website of Canada's A-Channel, the broadcaster's parent company, Bell Globemedia explains that "following the procedural steps imposed by the Régie requires a longer lead time, which we do not always have, and which our co-sponsors may be unwilling to extend" (A-Channel FAQ). We have known Canadians or heard stories about professional athletes playing for Canadian teams who travelled to the United States specifically to buy breakfast cereals or snack foods unavailable for sale in Canada (e.g., Farber 1990). What is at issue here is likely nothing more than the geographical limits of profitable distribution. While this situation may seem to stretch the analogies we are making with geoblocking, we would point out that product launches for products like Doritos in new national territories can have legal and cultural implications in addition to economic ones, just as geoblocking does. Specificities of brand positioning against new local competitors and even product packaging alterations (e.g., using French, in Canada) are just two of the factors we would point to.

For media channels such as television, geoblocking is evident in the means of reception. After the proliferation of satellite dishes, which were able to pick up hundreds of channels that broadcast without commercials during the 1980s and 1990s, program providers such as HBO began encrypting their signals, creating a robust black market for descramblers that viewers needed in order to regain access (Attallah 1996: 271). The same is true in the case of movies. Consumers from Asia or the Middle East purchase VHS cassettes encoded in the PAL format, while Canadians and Americans use cassettes using the incompatible NTSC format. Digital video discs, or DVDs, also come equipped with region encoding, intended to limit where a film can be played. It is interesting to note the presence of VHS players equipped with both NTSC and PAL formats, or of DVD players that will play discs from different regions, regardless of their encoding. Acknowledging their presence, we also note the relative scarcity of them in homes and the marketplace, at least as compared with the huge variety and majority adoption of region-specific players. Once again, the work-around procedure here – the acquisition of a multiregion player – comes with added effort and cost in a manner analogous to taking the trouble to mask one's Ip address in order to watch streamed video content on Hulu.com.

Even technologies intended to encourage placeless communication have geographical limitations. Canadians are well aware that many toll-free numbers for things as diverse as magazine subscriptions, catalogue shopping, customer service, or party lines are inaccessible to those dialing from Canada. On the one hand, Canadians are exposed to a torrent of American culture; on the other hand, access to that culture can often be elusive. Although these examples of "blocking" exist for legal or technical reasons, there have also been many, many moves in Canada to limit access to cultural texts on cultural grounds. One might argue that a major feature of Canadian cultural policies has been to block, or perhaps interrupt, flows of culture coming from other places in the name of a broader, national purpose. The significant defensive side of the history of Canadian cultural policy is one in which, in the service of the nationalist project of "making space" for "our voices," access to foreign media of many kinds has been blocked and in many others limited or delayed so that certain kinds of content can be filtered out and others – notably, the Canadian content – can be added in. Canadians have Food Network Canada not only for rights reasons, but in order to satisfy requirements laid down by broadcast regulators that ensure television stations are owned by Canadians, show a prescribed amount of Canadian content, and contribute to Canada's independent production industry. We characterize these policies as "defensive" because of their stated aim to "protect" Canadian from undue foreign – chiefly American, of course – influence. Arguably, most Canadian cultural policy shares this defensive motivation.

One small, but powerful, feature of Canadian television policy allows major broadcasters the right to simulcast television programs airing on US channels and replace the accompanying commercial advertisements with those aimed at Canadian and local markets. Canadians are usually reminded of this policy towards the end of January, when the commercials for the Super Bowl are replaced by a small number of Canadian ads for furniture retailers, beer companies, or promotional spots for programs airing on the Canadian broadcaster. Simultaneous substitution interrupts American television flows in the name of broader industrial ends (e.g., supporting the advertising industry, providing a revenue stream for the broadcaster) as well as cultural objectives (e.g., rerouting industry revenues into funds that support domestic production). The effort and expense of the work-around procedure for those Canadians wishing to participate in the now international spectacle of the much-anticipated Super Bowl ads (i.e., the real, American, ones) – acquiring a satellite dish, or watching the game at a bar that has one – *is* an available option, but one that is taken up by few Canadians other than those with a *particular* interest in consuming this blocked media.

Canada's infamous magazine policy, that replaces American versions of magazines with Canadian versions incorporating some Canadian content, provides another prominent example of an interruption undertaken due to geography, and that has, broadly, cultural goals. Just as in the case of simulcast, the economic policy objective here is closely tied to the cultural goal of making space for the Canadian magazine "voices" by providing them a larger possible revenue source through limiting advertisements in American magazines. The "split-run" magazine saga in Canada is one that has gone on for decades, and though it has been seen by American governments as an economically protective trade practice – a view shared by rulings from both the General Agreementon Tariffs and Trade and the World Trade Organization – it is an issue consistently framed in Canada in cultural terms. In fact, as outlined in Keith Acheson and Christopher Maule's (2001) analysis of the trade implications of the split-run issue, "immediately after the [WTO's dispute resolution] panel's report was released, a front page story in Toronto's *Globe and Mail*, arguably English-Canada's most influential newspaper, quoted a senior federal official as stating that the US position 'is just classic 19th Century white man's burden – they've got to bring us their ways and their language. They'll only be happy when we have drive-by shootings or something'" (3). This histrionic response from a federal official is illustrative of the sort of cultural nationalist passions enflamed by debates over blocking Canadians' access to foreign media. What is striking about these and other measures that perform a similar function is that many members of artistic and scholarly communities see such blocking as a necessary function of a cultural policy intended to ensure the survival of national cultural industries, and to ensure robust opportunities for cultural expression for Canadians.

During a recent round of hearings of the Canadian Radio-television and Telecommunications Commission examining whether (and to what extent) the CRTC should get involved in regulating the content of the Internet, some creator groups went to great lengths to explain that methods such as Deep Packet Inspection could be used to prioritize Canadian material or to slow down foreign material, and might serve in the national interest. From an industrial perspective, such stances are entirely reasonable, because they reflect the fact that revenue models for new media remain an unknown quantity. At the same time, however, such measures also reflect the tension between creators and consumers that are exacerbated by new media technologies and platforms, from digital cameras to YouTube. Here, the delay may be felt on an individual basis; however, the effect on the domestic cultural industries is seen by many – both within and outside these industries – as being of national importance.

Conclusion

The examples outlined here raise important questions about the arrangements or "deals" that have made such developments in geoblocking possible. The question of fairness, both of the "deal" and "having to deal," is a topic that runs throughout our discussion here. Although they pertain to the Canadian case, this is hardly a distinctly Canadian phenomenon; nevertheless, the porous boundaries in which cultural works are seen but yet not purchased, or heard but yet not available, have historically given the Canadian case its distinctive shape.

If ideas around geoblocking, and the apparent political power afforded to copyright problems and issues of net neutrality testifies to anything here, it is to the incredible resonance of the powerful rhetoric surrounding new technologies – particularly the Internet – which posits that "information wants to be free." Historians of technology, as well as communication and media studies scholars will easily confirm that this, too, is a very old story, one that dates back at least to the age of electricity's initial popularization, where technological progress appeared to break open the shackles that theretofore kept information and those charged with holding onto or dispersing it in chains.

We suggest that within this context, two issues have been largely ignored – issues that both policy makers and those who create cultural works must contend with. First, we must gain a stronger appreciation about how such "deals" have significantly structured the ways in which Canadians experience mediated texts, both in the contemporary case and historically. We also need a more rigorous and robust analytical vocabulary to make sense of how Canadians access, consume, and transform cultural works in the digital age. This entails much more critical consideration of the rhetorical claims to borderlessness and instantaneousness, values that are inherent in the discourse around electronic media, and serious attention to the significant history of means by which such values have been continually offset by policies intended to block access on the basis of geography.

9 Net Neutrality and the Threat to Open Cultural Expression

STEVE ANDERSON

When Vancouver-based RainCity Studios wanted to create a suite of innovative online services, they did not need to ask Internet service providers (ISPs) for permission, they simply set up shop online. Likewise, when the new, Toronto-based global independent news organization TheREALnews wanted to experiment with real-time online debate formats, they did not need to pay expensive distribution costs, they just began streaming their content. The open Internet is a communications platform that supports social, economic, and cultural innovation. It entails both a low barrier to technological innovation and open circulation of culture. The open Internet was designed to offer a "level playing field" for all users, where ISPs respect the core principle that preserves the integrity of an open network, known as "network neutrality." Net neutrality stipulates that ISPs do not manipulate or interfere with online content or traffic, thereby helping ensure that the Internet remains a neutral, non-discriminatory space. Essentially, net neutrality is a telecommunications policy principle that secures the Internet as an open space and protects our ability to direct our own online activities.

Since at least early 2008, some Canadian ISPs began moving away from operating their networks based on net neutrality principles. By taking control of Internet traffic, dominant ISPs can potentially profit from charging for priority Internet distribution, while also deflating competition from independent cultural producers and other competitors who use the open Internet to cheaply distribute their content. ISPs can potentially act as online traffic "gatekeepers" because the Internet infrastructure is owned and controlled largely by a few telecommunications corporations with limited public accountability.

Until recently, the regulator of telecommunications in Canada, the Canadian Radio-television and Telecommunications Commission, has had an increasingly hands-off approach with the industry. While the reaction to the shift away from net neutrality has not been as swift or as strong here in Canada as it has been in the United States, the "traffic management" activities of ISPs have not gone without protest. A diverse array of civil society organizations, labour groups, businesses, and individuals are intervening in the policy process, calling for an open, neutral Internet. Recent traffic management decisions by the CRTC suggest that this collection of social actors can effectively coalesce into a force that can override the financial wherewithal and political savoir-faire of the dominant ISPs. Whether or not the positive momentum on the side of open Internet defenders can lead to binding legislation or even enforcement of the CRTC guidelines remains to be seen.

Digital Fiefdoms

In both the United States and Canada, much of the infrastructure used to develop the Internet resides in corporate hands. However, the Internet initially took shape as a public project, owned and operated cooperatively by government agencies and university departments. Jeffrey MacKie-Mason and Hal Varian (1992) describe the early Internet in the United States as a publicly owned "backbone connecting together a group of regional networks" (1). Today, the full architecture of the Internet contains a myriad of physical spaces and elements that help give it shape including the "backbone," "last mile," "middle mile," "point of presence," and "Internet exchange points." The two main elements of Internet infrastructure are the "backbone" and the "last mile" of the network. The "backbone" is the very fast network, comprised mostly of fibre cable that connects all of the global regional networks. It is "maintained through a complex set of interconnection (peering) arrangements amongst the world's largest Internet Service Provider networks" (Weitzner 2006: 13). The "last mile," the piece of wire (or other data transportation method) that connects a user to the Internet, is the space that is contested in the net neutrality debate.

One way to understand how the last mile has become such a contested space in the United States is to look at how AT&T has transitioned from a tightly regulated national monopoly telecommunications provider to a giant, relatively unregulated, ISP. In 1971, the US *Federal Communications Commission (FCC)* ordered AT&T to allow competitors to use the telephone network for data services without interference (Daggett 2007: 3). Furthermore, since AT&T owned the network, it was also not allowed to offer data service itself as this would result in an unfair advantage. Common carriage rules, the public backbone, and the 1984 AT&T forced divesture, continued to facilitate a relatively competitive and innovative market of Internet services during the 1980s (Daggett 2007). In the 1990s, the Telecommunications Act and other regulatory changes set the stage for the consolidation of the ISPs (Mowery and Simcoe 2000: 21). Today, in most US markets, citizens are faced with a duopoly in broadband service, and some communities do not even have two choices (Turner 2007). Liberated from the pressures of a competitive market, and gradually freed from public interest regulations (as detailed below), ISPs are now in a position to limit access to the open Internet, against the wishes of their customers.

Comparing the similarities and differences between the last mile deployment in the United States and in Canada reveals that privatization can take very different forms and manifest at differing speeds. In the US ISP industry, a national regulated monopoly became a competitive market, which later transformed to the uncompetitive oligopoly that exists today. Canada experienced a somewhat similar trajectory with Bell Canada and other large telecommunications companies; however, the early Canadian Internet also saw a vibrant, at times publicly funded, community-network sector, as well as several public provincial networks.

Before the deregulation of Internet service in Canada, community networks numbered as high as thirty-five, with over 250,000 members across Canada (Gutstein 1999: 260). These Internet providers were "non-profit, locally based, locally controlled, and locally owned … networks that provide access to community resources and other information" (ibid.). Community networks relied primarily on government grants geared towards providing Internet service to those who could not otherwise receive it. Unfortunately, lack of a supportive regulatory policy coupled with a lack of sustainable revenue prevented most community networks from keeping up with technological developments.

Unlike the United States, several provinces in Canada used public telecommunications networks for Internet provision. In the early twentieth century, the provincial governments of Manitoba, Saskatchewan, and Alberta were each spurred to create their own telephone companies, partially in reaction to Bell's aggressive, predatory, and monopolistic practices (Babe 1995: 190). The Manitoba Telephone System (MTS),

Saskatchewan Telecommunication (SaskTel), and Alberta Government Telephones (AGT) services continued to be primarily publicly owned by their respective provincial governments until the early 1990s, when all but SaskTel began to be privatized (see Babe 1990). AGT became Telus Communications in 1990, and is now one of the largest ISPs and cell phone carriers in Canada (see Heritage Community Foundation 2004). By 1997, MTS, too, was privatized (MacKinnon 2007: 1). Only SaskTel continues to be owned by a provincial Crown corporation, providing service to rural communities that are deemed unprofitable to private corporations, and adding revenues to the public treasury – $783 million between 1987 and 2001 (Swift 2003: 103). Although SaskTel maintains competitive services, the ruling provincial Saskatchewan Party notably announced it would review Crown corporations for possible privatization after taking office.

The Canadian telecommunications industry changed drastically throughout the 1990s. Independent ISPs were on defence against big telecommunications companies that wanted access to the Internet service market. The independent ISPs argued that big telecommunications companies should not be allowed to take over the market, because they controlled access to the local networks and could thus exploit their monopoly position. Bell argued that there was plenty of competition in the market, and that ISPs in the United States were successfully bundling services without negative effect (see Winseck 1998), an assertion that the CRTC accepted. In 1995, Bell and Telus withdrew the basic network service on which the independent ISPs relied, and introduced another service that was 300 per cent more expensive (Winseck 1998: 297).

Prior to the withdrawal of reasonable network service by Bell and Telus, many small, independent providers kept the ISP sector very competitive. Large cities like Vancouver supported fifteen to twenty ISPs – this was a period of rapid growth, about 10 per cent per month (Winseck 1998: 297). As a result of the CRTC's failure to block the large corporations' abuse of their monopoly position, most Canadians now have two or fewer Internet service providers to choose from.

The Origins of Net Neutrality

Largely free from the obligations of public service or market competition, the dominant ISPs are attempting to pull away from the principle of net neutrality. Net neutrality protects our ability to direct online activities according to our preferences, openly share material, and consume culture, but in turn, requires that a network move data in a non-discriminatory manner based on the demands and desires of Internet users. Without net neutrality, ISPs are free to control the speed of Web content based on its source, ownership, or destination. Without organized protest, the result could be a much more centralized communications system.

Net neutrality is a principle based on historic "common carrier" telecommunications regulation, which stipulated that telecommunications networks provide "neutral" access to communications infrastructure – a mandate that net neutrality seeks to apply to Internet-based communications and publishing. Common carrier regulations were initially applied to the railway, and stipulated that owners and operators could not discriminate against cargo based on its owner or destination, thus creating a level playing field for cargo companies. The common carrier rules were later applied, if inconsistently, to telegraph and telephone networks and now form the core principles of preserving the free and open Internet.

Canadian common carrier rules, too, were born out of early railway legislation (see Barratt and Shade 2007). Laws specified that the "obligation was on the owner of the network to ensure that data was treated equally, as well as to make available their network to other networks" (Barratt and Shade 2007: 296). Canadian common carrier rules also have roots in the early twentieth century, when telegraph companies were network service providers somewhat similar to current ISPs. Because of a lack of industry regulation and oversight, news services depended on the two existing telegraph companies for distribution. The telegraph companies were also involved in the provision of news, and they were able to charge punitively high rates to rivals and, sometimes, refuse service. The leading telegraph corporation at the time argued that rates charged for its services were not within legitimate regulator territory (Babe 1990). The Canadian telegraph regulator at the time, the Board of Railway Commission, rejected these claims, and the telegraph companies were then compelled to treat all news services equally. Later, the BRC prohibited Bell from denying network interconnection to third parties (competing companies). During this period of strong public interest regulation, the number of telecommunications providers went from about 600 to 1,695 (Winseck 1998: 132).

There are clear ebbs and flows in the preceding Canadian communications regulation history, but a high point can be found in one of the first statements from the CRTC after assuming authority for telecommunications regulation in 1976:

> the principle of "just and reasonable" rates is neither narrow nor a static concept. As our society has evolved, the idea of what is just and reasonable has also changed ... Indeed, the commission views this principle in the widest possible terms, and considers itself obliged to continually review the level and structure of carrier rates to ensure that telecommunications services are fully responsive to the public interest. (CRTC 1976: 3, cited in Winseck 1998: 193)

Bell tried to dodge this CRTC oversight by arguing that carriage was not within the purview of the CRTC. The CRTC forcefully disagreed. In a conflict between mobile communications equipment manufactures and Bell, the CRTC was wary of the "system integrity" arguments used by Bell, concluding that refusing network connectivity related to Bell's disinterest in real competition and thus was "unjust and discriminatory."

In part due to multinational trade agreements and a more market-oriented regulation approach at the CRTC, this orientation towards assertive public service regulation had faded substantially by the mid-1980s. One of the most important decisions came in 1999, when the CRTC decided against regulating Internet service provision, opening the door to possible traffic shaping etc. by ISPs. Canada does, however, still has some government policy that follows the logic of net neutrality. Section 27(2) of the Telecom Act, for example, states:

> No Canadian carrier shall, in relation to the provision of a telecommunications service or the charging of a rate for it, *unjustly discriminate or give an undue or unreasonable preference* toward any person, including itself, or subject any person to an undue or unreasonable disadvantage. (emphasis added)

Although this section of the Act provides a point of leverage for public interest groups, by itself it does little to keep the Internet open if the CRTC fails to acknowledge and enforce the clear statement above.

Recently, many disturbing discordances with net neutrality have been reported in Canada. According to Michael Geist (2007), large ISPs already have a "history of blocking access to contentious content (Telus), limiting bandwidth for alternative content delivery channels

(Rogers), and raising the prospect of levying fees for priority content delivery" (para. 9). During the Telus employees strike in 2005, the corporation blocked access to a website run by striking Telus employees called "Voices for Change," and at least 766 other websites (Barrett 2005, para. 5). Rogers and Bell have also admitted to limiting peer-to-peer (P2P) applications. In response to customer concerns, Bell recently admitted that they "are now using 'Internet Traffic Management' to restrict applications that are using a large portion of bandwidth during peak hours. Some of the applications that are included are the following: BitTorrent, Gnutella, Limewire, Kazaa" (Forum Administrator 2007, para. 13). Rogers recently went so far as to forcibly display its own message on top of websites being viewed by its customers, thus imposing messages onto Internet users' online travels. In response to public outcry, Rogers vice-president of communications Taanta Gupta said, "We're trying different things, and we'll test customer response" (cited in CBC News 2007).

A Movement for Open Media

In 2006, a US coalition of consumer and public interest groups calling itself the "SavetheInternet.com Coalition" launched a campaign to protect net neutrality. This coalition eventually grew to comprise 850 groups, including the National Religious Broadcasters, the Service Employees International Union, the American Library Association, Educause, Gun Owners of America, Future of Music Coalition, Parents Television Council, and the American Civil Liberties Union. The grassroots groundswell of activity that grew out of this coalition led to an unprecedented 1.5 million Americans contacting their representatives and urging them to support net neutrality (Save the Internet 2007, para. 1).

On 28 December 2006, AT&T officials agreed to adhere to network neutrality provisions as part of their $85 billion merger with BellSouth. SavetheInternet.com dubbed the AT&T agreement as "A Victory We Can Hang Our Hats On" (Scott 2006, para. 1). The AT&T clause provides a verifiable definition of net neutrality that public interest groups can use to maintain net neutrality in other contexts, and to achieve further policy gains. In early 2008, another important step was made when FCC Chairman Kevin Martin announced that he was "ready, willing, and able" to take action against practices violating net neutrality (Burrows and Kharif 2008, para. 4). What's more, on 1 August 2008, the FCC put forth an "enforcement order" that requires Comcast to stop blocking content and publicly disclose its methods for managing Internet traffic (FreePress 2008). The election of Barack Obama has enabled further gains for Internet openness advocates. Soon after taking office in 2009, President Obama signed an economic stimulus bill dedicating $7.2 billion to get fast, affordable, neutral Internet to the nearly half of US homes that do not already have it (Reardon 2009). He stipulated that telecom companies receiving money through his broadband stimulus package must adhere to net neutrality principles and appointed a known net neutrality supporter, Julius Genachowski, as the FCC chairman. On 21 September 2009, Genachowski made a bold move in favour of net neutrality by adding two principles to the four existing FCC net neutrality principles, announcing the FCC's intention to make the six principles into official and enforceable rules (Anderson 2009). If that weren't enough, he also called for the rules to apply to wireless Internet services as well. Applying openness rules to wireless is an important move because mobile devices are expected to become an increasingly common and important Internet access point.

Although the open Internet movement in Canada has been slower to assemble, net neutrality has been hotly debated both in the press and in Parliament, and the CRTC took up the issue in a public hearing in July 2009. A string of events early in 2008 sparked the movement for an open Internet in Canada. In March 2008, an all-party Committee on Canadian Heritage report recommended the CRTC create rules guaranteeing net neutrality (Standing Committee on Canadian Heritage 2003). Soon after, the net neutrality debate was fully ignited when it was revealed that Bell Canada's "throttling" of traffic was significantly limiting people's ability to view the CBC's hit show *Canada's Next Great Prime Minister*. In effect, Bell's throttling was limiting CBC's ability to fulfil its mandate to serve Canadians using the most "appropriate and efficient means." Weeks later, it was revealed that Bell Canada was also throttling traffic passing through its network from third-party independent ISPs (their competitors).

Shortly after the throttling was revealed, the Canadian Association of Internet Providers (CAIP) demanded that the CRTC put an end to throttling of third-party traffic. The CAIP raised a number of concerns with Bell's traffic-shaping practices. By providing third-party businesses with limited Internet service, Bell could limit competition in the market. The CAIP described the quality of service as "degraded beyond recognition" (Copeland 2008: 2). On 20 November, the CRTC ruled that Bell could continue to throttle independent ISPs using its network. The

CRTC's ruling in the CAIP proceeding limits competing ISPs from offering differential services, like providing access to the open Internet.

The conspicuous activities of Bell Canada and other dominant ISPs sparked a national movement and the launch of a diverse "SaveOurNet.ca coalition" consisting of public interest groups, labour, businesses, and individuals. In the months preceding the events detailed above, the SaveOurNet.ca coalition began providing information about the issue of net neutrality, rallied the public to support the CAIP submission, and helped organize a net neutrality rally on Parliament Hill in May 2008. Following these demonstrations, both New Democratic Party and Liberal members of Parliament put forth private member's bills in support of net neutrality. Providing further evidence that the open Internet movement had gained traction, Konrad von Finckenstein, chairman of the CRTC, made a speech on 17 June to the 2008 Canadian Telecom Summit, where he said with respect to net neutrality: "Fundamental issues of technology, economics, competition, access and freedom of speech are all involved … it is one of the polarizing issues of the day. It will have to be addressed and debated by all of us" (para. 40).

Whereas the CRTC's 20 November CAIP decision appeared to be a setback for Internet openness, in hindsight it may have been more of an attempt by the CRTC to buy more time to make more concrete decisions regarding net neutrality. The CRTC announced a "Traffic Management" hearing for 9 July 2009 at the same time as the CAIP decision. The Traffic Management hearing would raise the same issues raised at the CAIP hearing, but in a more compressive way. For open Internet advocates, the Traffic Management hearing provided a focal point and sufficient time to put together movement building and policy intervention strategies. In 2009, four cities held SaveOurNet.ca "Open Internet Town Hall" events, and over twelve thousand citizen comments calling for net neutrality were sent to the CRTC. Formal submissions sent to the CRTC in favour of net neutrality included consumer groups (Public Interest Advocacy Centre), labour (National Union of Public and General Employees), cultural groups (Alliance of Canadian Cinema, Television and Radio Artists), and domestic and international businesses (Zip.ca, Open Internet Coalition). OpenMedia.ca (then called CDM) and the Canadian Internet Policy and Public Interest Clinic (CIPPIC) made a submission including support from one of the original architects of the Internet, Dr. David Reed of MIT, and network experts Dr. Andrew Odlyzko of the Minnesota Internet Traffic Studies (MINTS) project, and Bill St. Arnaud, chief research officer for CANARIE Inc.,

Canada's Advanced Internet Development Organization. At the 9 July 2009 hearing, David Fewer, acting director at CIPPIC, and I joined the Internet experts to make a well-received presentation before the CRTC.

On 22 October 2009, the CRTC issued its ruling concerning traffic management, choosing to adopt new traffic management guidelines resembling some of the rules put forth by CIPPIC/OpenMedia.ca, the Open Internet Coalition, and others. The traffic management rule is a huge milestone in the effort to keep Canada's Internet open; however, several ISPs continue discriminatory traffic-throttling practices. The CRTC guidelines put the onus on citizens to file complaints and to prove that ISPs are "unjustly" throttling traffic as defined by the guidelines. Furthermore, while political support for net neutrality has grown rapidly, there is still no indication that a net neutrality law is imminent. Consequently, it is imperative for open Internet advocates to maintain pressure on the CRTC, and for elected officials to ensure that Internet traffic is treated equally. Net neutrality supporters will need to push the CRTC to enforce its own traffic management guidelines by either submitting formal traffic management complaints or by convincing Industry Minister Tony Clement to mandate regular compliance audits of ISP traffic management practices.

Conclusion

The impetus of big telecommunications companies to undemocratically control access to the infrastructure of digital networks is an ever-present threat. Large Internet service providers not only control the physical Internet wires, but also they are now using that power to change the very properties of the Internet. When two companies dominate a market, as they do in most Canadian and US markets, those companies are able to regulate the service towards their own financial interests. In the long term, the most important element of physical Internet governance is ownership. The push to abandon net neutrality did not surface out of a social vacuum; rather, its appearance corresponds with the rising centralized corporate ownership of the physical infrastructure of the Internet and associated relational forces. With or without enforceable net neutrality rules, Internet service providers still maintain monopolistic control of the Internet, and thus have the monopoly profits to invest in further lobbying. Taking back our communications system will mean creating a plurality of ISP ownership types with public/municipal and community/non-profit ISPs as pillars. As one community Internet activist aptly put it, "the only reason they are able to shape bandwidth is because they own the infrastructure. If the community owns the infrastructure, that's how you're going to get net neutrality" (telephone interview, 24 Feb. 2008). Net neutrality regulation is a pivotal battle for democratic communication, but it is not a panacea for concentrated telecommunications power. The movement for an open Internet will first need to secure net neutrality, but will ultimately only sustain that victory by reinstating some kind of public Internet service regime.

10 Copyright and Access to Media for People with Perceptual Disabilities

J.P. UDO AND DEBORAH FELS

When accessing entertainment media, individuals who are blind or have low vision (B/LV) and those who are deaf or hard of hearing (D/HOH) face significant barriers, as they are partially or completely unable to access the visual or sound stimuli presented. Closed captioning (CC) and audio description (AD) are two sets of practices and processes that are being used to improve access to entertainment experiences for these users groups. CC endeavours to provide a verbatim translation of dialogue and important sound stimuli for individuals who are D/HOH, whereas audio description aims to provide individuals who are B/LV with spoken descriptions of important visual stimuli presented to the audience. CC and AD are generally seen as an access strategy developed to make pre-recorded media such as television or film more accessible.

The addition of CC and or AD to media raises some issues, especially when considering the interests of the copyright holders versus individuals who are B/LV or D/HOH. While the copyright holders have the legal right to ensure that others do not infringe upon their intellectual property (IP), individuals who are B/LV or D/HOH require access to alternative formats and means of accessing it. As such, the Canadian Copyright Act ensures lawful access to these alternative means through the enactment of exemptions for people with disabilities. However, these exemptions use language and terminology that is often misunderstood or misinterpreted by the public at large. This situation is further exacerbated as numerous tools designed to allow amateurs to CC and/or AD content for themselves or for others enable users to post CC or AD online. Although the CC or AD track may become public domain because it is posted online, the original content is not. A CC or AD track must be somehow associated with the original content (usually through coordination of time code) in order for it to be rendered accessible to the D/HOH or B/LV audiences. Reconciling these differences is a complicated task that copyright legislation has yet to adequately address.

In this chapter, we outline how the Canadian Copyright Act accounts for accessibility for television, film, and the Internet by making specific exemptions for individuals with perceptual disabilities. Specifically, we focus on the applicability of these exemptions to the entertainment experiences of individuals who are B/LV and D/HOH. As well, we introduce and evaluate the various dissemination strategies used by governing bodies, legislators, and the public at large to encourage content creators and, in some cases, members of their audiences, to create entertainment experiences that include CC and AD. Finally, we propose an alternative director-centric strategy that gives the content creator the skills and knowledge required to produce CC and AD that is a seamless extension of their vision.

Conventional Practices and Processes for Creating CC and AD

The conventional and generally accepted process for CC or AD begins when the broadcaster or producing studio sends a copy of the master tape to a third-party accessibility vendor or to an in-house captioning department. For AD, a team of individuals, often consisting of a describer and an audio production or technical expert, creates a description script, records and edits the description track, balancing for volume levels and timing, mixes it with the main program audio, and then submits it to the production studio or broadcaster (WGBH Educational Foundation, n.d.). For CC, often an electronic script is available for the captionist, who is responsible for adding, subtracting, and adapting information so that viewers understand what is occurring onscreen. The caption data are then encoded onto the program's video (WGBH Educational Foundation, n.d.). For a description of the technical encoding processes see WGHB NCAM (n.d.).

Although AD of streaming video is virtually non-existent, several broadcasters and re-broadcasters are taking steps to make their streaming media accessible to D/HOH by giving users the ability to activate and deactivate CC as part of their player interfaces. Hulu.com and YouTube.com, streaming media sites, allow users to search specifically for content that is captioned or caption files that are available for various pieces of content. Software such as Quicktime or Microsoft's Media

Player gives users the option of having captions automatically play when they are available.

The technical aspects of going from broadcast television to streaming video has proven to be complex, as the encoding process for CC on television is entirely different online. The CC file associated with a piece of media will be readable by broadcast television receivers while that same file will be unintelligible to an online player, as it is not configured to read it. With respect to creating, hosting, and playing online captions, questions inevitably arise regarding ownership of the captions and caption file and how they are associated with the original content for which the captions are produced.

The Canadian Copyright Act and Its Applicability to Multimedia and CC and AD Users

The Copyright Act defines copyright as applicable to original literary, dramatic, musical, and artistic works. Harris (2001) explains that although the legislation does not use the term "audiovisual materials," its scope extends to their use. She holds that audiovisual materials are protected in that they are "expressed by any process analogous to cinematography" (R.S., c. C-30, s. 1.) which, she argues, "does not require that the work be made on film (with a negative) or on magnetic tape" (p. 65). Since cinematographs fall under dramatic works within the Copyright Act, so too, does audiovisual material. The Canadian Intellectual Property Office seems to agree, citing dramatic works as "films, videos, plays, screen plays and scripts" (CIPO 2005: 19).

The Copyright Act ensures that creators of original literary, dramatic, musical, and artistic works are given credit for their contribution and complete control over the production or reproduction of it. If the copyright holder wishes to allow another individual to use his or her work, the act informs the copyright holder of his or her rights and responsibilities. Hence, the Act protects the interests of the copyright holder and, many argue, caters to their needs above those of users. Litman (2006) maintains that copyright law needs to be clear and take into account the needs of the user and not just the copyright holder: "If the public is to play by copyright rules, then those rules must be designed with the public's interests in mind" (72). To determine the needs of the public, a diverse set of groups should be consulted which includes individuals with disabilities.

However, for the purposes of this chapter, we have limited the scope of our discussion to understanding what individuals who are B/LV or D/HoH can do to make their entertainment experiences accessible without infringing on copyright. Under the Copyright Act, sight (B/LV) and hearing (D/HoH) are considered "perceptual disabilities" pursuant to section 1:

> "Perceptual disability" means a disability that prevents or inhibits a person from reading or hearing a … work in its original format, and includes such a disability resulting from: (a) severe or total impairment of sight or hearing or the inability to focus or move one's eyes, (b) the inability to hold or manipulate a book, or (c) an impairment relating to comprehension.

It is commonly assumed that the needs of individuals with disabilities fall under the fair dealing exception; however, this is not the case. There are many other exemptions within the Copyright Act, and those that accommodate the needs of individuals with disabilities are separate and distinct.

These exemptions do not specify or even provide examples of "formats specifically designed for persons with a perceptual disability" and thus leave the reader to infer that CC and AD would be legitimate formats that apply specifically to individuals who are D/HoH and B/LV. The Canadian Copyright Act does allow a person or non-profit agency to create an accessible copy, yet only at the request of an individual who is disabled and solely for enjoyment by that individual. It does not, however, seem efficient or effective to rely on requests to make programming accessible and then insist that the accessible copy is for the sole enjoyment of the requesting individual. Several approaches, conventional and newly developed, are available to increase the quality and quantity of CC and AD available on television and online. These approaches tend to support the spirit of the exemptions outlined in Canada but do not rely on the request of CC and AD users as required in Canadian law.

Approaches to Disseminating Media with CC and AD: Legislative Approaches

Within Canada, the Canadian Radio-television Telecommunications Commission requires broadcasters to offer programming that is accessible to individuals who are D/HoH and B/LV (CRTC 2007). In 1995, the CRTC set out its original requirements for the inclusion of CC in broadcast television programming. After consulting with broadcasters and special interest groups, the original CC requirements were as follows: broadcasters earning more than $10 million annually were required to CC 100 per cent of local news and 90 per cent of all programming, while smaller broadcasters were encouraged to achieve similar levels of captioning (CRTC 1995). In 2001, the CRTC made CC a condition of licence renewal for English-language broadcasters. The most recent decision requires all broadcasters to caption 100 per cent of their programs (CTRC 2007: 54).

As of 2007, the CRTC requires over-the-air broadcasters (CTV, Global, CHUM) to provide four hours of audio description, 50 per cent of which must be original content (CRTC 2007: 246). Specialty channels are initially required to offer a minimum of two hours in their first year and, by their third year of operation, three hours of audio described. In addition, broadcasters must upgrade their equipment to ensure that they are able to offer AD services. If a broadcaster is interested in buying a program, it is required to buy the AD version when available. The CRTC also approved licences for three accessibility-centric channels. Two of these channels are newspaper-reading services: VoicePrint (English language) and La Magnétothèque (French language). The third is The Accessible Channel which features programming that is 100 per cent accessible to individuals who are B/LV or D/HoH. The Accessible Channel provides AD and CC using an open format, meaning that it is heard and seen by all users and does not require special activation. The channel operates twenty-four hours a day and must be carried by all satellites and cable distributors with more than two thousand subscribers (CRTC 2007: 246).

Access to audiovisual media on the Internet would have existed under the scope of regulations overseen by the CRTC had it chosen to disregard the "barrage of submissions from media organizations imploring it to refrain from establishing new regulations" (Geist 2002: 223–4). Many problems have resulted from this decision, not the least of which is the question of who, how, and when media can be used within this unregulated playground. Without regulation, it is not surprising that the creation of CC and AD on the Web has failed to find widespread adoption, seen as a voluntary but costly initiative rather than one that promotes cultural and social equality.

Standards Approach

Several organizations have produced standards of practice as a means of addressing the quality and quantity of accessibility initiatives. Internationally, there are numerous standards that address the needs of individuals with disabilities. For example, the DAISY Consortium (2005) has written an international standard for the creation of digital and talking books. The standards of the World Wide Web Consortium (W3C) were written as guidelines "to lead the World Wide Web to its full potential ... [and to] ensure long-term growth for the Web" (W3C, n.d.). Through the Web Accessibility Initiative, the W3C has published the Web Content Accessibility Guidelines V2.0 (2008). In these guidelines, specifically Guidelines 1.1 and 1.2, a minimum recommendation is that text alternatives be provided for all non-text content and that CC and AD be provided for all pre-recorded audio and video materials that are not made as alternatives for textual materials.

Nationally, the Canadian Association of Broadcasters (CAB 2008) developed a standard set of practices for closed captioning on English-language television. There are four main tenets of the CAB's captioning standard: accuracy; responsibility to preserve the meaning and intent of the television program; consistency; and clarity – remain as close to the original intention of the program as possible, including the identification of who is speaking. The standard goes on to further define how to accomplish these four objectives for closed, open, and real-time captioning scenarios. However, very few specific details are provided. AD, being the younger of the two main access technologies, has not been subjected to such extensive standardization work as CC.

What is of concern in using guidelines to generate CC or AD is that all content is then presented using the same style. In its original form, however, media appear in many different styles, often reflecting the norms of a genre or the preferences of the creative team. CC and AD may require creative styles that allow them to match the style of the original content rather than being forced to be different and distinct in order to meet a particular standard.

Do-It-Yourself Approach

Audio description was provided long before the advent of specialized technology. Snyder (2007) believes that AD, as an ad hoc access strategy, has existed since the invention of human language, since language allows people to describe what is occurring around them. In theatres, the cinema, and at home, this ad hoc strategy continues to be used today. Despite technological advancements, friends and family often act as informal describers, whispering improvised descriptions of onstage or onscreen action to individuals who are B/LV. Moreover, there are at least twenty-five different amateur captioning tools, not including those for professional captioning of television and film content, that are available for use online or for download for a wide range of caption applications (e.g., for Flash videos, for use on Macs, PCs, or Linux machines, for webcasting, etc.). For example, YouTube (n.d.) has created a simple user interface that allows users to create subtitles and captions for media they upload. In addition, there are caption databases that have caption files for many shows (see, e.g., www.opensubtitles.org/en, www.sub-titles.net and mysubtitles.com). The popularity of amateur language subtitling online may have influenced the rise in popularity of amateur CC, an area that has yet to be addressed in the literature. In the education field, teacher-generated captioning has been a popular practice for language learning and for providing access to video materials for students (Robin 2007). For example, Caption It Yourself (n.d.) advocates for a do-it-yourself approach, particularly for online materials. They provide guidelines and resources for teachers and others who would like to caption their materials.

Caption files that are produced and uploaded to caption sites by amateur and educational captionists could be considered illegal in the same way that fansub anime subtitles are, when captions for a piece of content are already available (see Hatcher 2005 for an explanation of the legality of fansub anime subtitling practices). However, much of the cultural material released on the Internet, including film and television, is not captioned, thus, it seems unreasonable not to exempt these from findings of infringement, if their use enables members of a disadvantaged minority to have greater access to cultural goods. Certainly, a dealing should be considered "fair" if it enables an underserved segment of the public to have access to a work that would not otherwise be accessible to it. Unlike subtitled anime, moreover, caption files are usually shared as independent files, and players combine a recognized caption format with a playable and associated piece of video content. Sharing licensed media containing amateur captions, in an open caption format, is not the typical method of delivery or operation of caption files.

Researchers have begun to assess the feasibility of facilitating amateur AD, outlining the processes and practices of the amateur audio describer and seeking to assess the quality of the final product. For example, Branje et al. (2006) showed that amateur describers or those who have never performed AD before were able to learn and apply description techniques to an episode of a television show. Participants created and recorded their descriptions using a software tool called LiveDescribe, and with as little as one hour of training and practice, several of the amateur describers produced AD that was later rated as entertaining by individuals who are B/LV. While the project is hosted by a university and is thus able to operate under certain provisions of the Canadian Copyright Act, users are encouraged to deploy media located within the public domain and available via websites such as http://archive.org/index.php. However, there are some individuals who have audio-described material that is copyrighted. Even then, the wiki (see http://www.livedescribe.com/wiki/browse.php) does not host the media, only the description tracks that the user then downloads, combines, and plays with a purchased copy of the original content.

While copyright issues may have yet to be explored for amateur AD, the more serious implications pertain to moral rights where creators have the right to maintain the integrity of their work and prevent its alteration. Audio description, by its very nature, must change the presentation and prominence of the information contained in a cultural product because there is neither time nor space for a complete description of all the visual information contained in a work. The quality, style, and accuracy of amateur captions might pose moral rights issues. Amateur AD leaves decisions regarding what to describe and how to describe it in the hands of creators and publishers. The representation of content to B/LV audiences or consumers of AD is wholly contained in a newly created audio track. This newly created track also becomes copyrighted material in its own right, and issues may arise with respect to how it can be used or deployed (e.g., language translation or combined and copied with pirated versions of the original video/audio content).

An Alternative Universally Designed Approach

To abide by the tenets of universal design theory, the design of a product or service needs to not only consider the inclusion of as many potential users and uses as possible but also do so from conception (Erlandson 2007). Control over the creation and adaptation of the design should, therefore, fall under the purview of the original designer. Conventional CC and AD processes do not meet these requirements, because the works are never created under the supervision of the director or members of a creative team (Udo and Fels 2009b, 2010b). CC and AD are adaptive processes, since they are "tacked on" after the production of a television show or film is completed and created by a third party not affiliated with the content creators. For CC and AD to abide by the principals of universal design, they must be considered and created under supervision of the director as well as accurately translate audio stimuli through visual or other means and vice versa. We suggest that using universal design theory combined with standard production processes that are well established in the television and film industry, a new model of accessible content production can be derived. That is, considerations for CC and AD can be generated during the production process rather than after it.

An example of this technique is discussed in Fels et al. (2006a, 2006b), who report on the development of an alternative AD strategy for the television show, *Odd Job Jack,* shown on the Comedy Network, which followed this approach. The scriptwriter, director, and sound team were involved in creating and producing the AD. The creative team decided that a first-person narrative approach would be the best way to convey the visual comedy that was presented onscreen. The main character, Jack, provides a first-person oral account of the important visual constructs in the episode. The authors have also used this director-centric strategy for live events and theatrical productions (Udo and Fels 2009a, 2009b, 2010a).

Similarly, captioning is a means through which to create an entertainment experience that is entertaining for individuals who do not speak American Sign Language and who rely on or prefer to use CC. The captions used on www.deafplanet.com, for example, are unconventional, because the content creation team experiments with the use of different fonts and font sizes as well as colour and caption positioning. The content creation teams of deafplanet.com and *Odd Job Jack* seem to indicate that their creative needs were not adequately represented through the use of traditional third-party service vendors. As such, they were interested in exploring an alternative set of practices and processes that gave them creative control over captioning and AD, respectively. Interestingly, this approach may serve to address not only the needs of content creators, but those of their audience, by decreasing reliance on the narrow exemptions within the Copyright Act provided for individuals who are D/HOH and B/LV.

Conclusion

There are no simple answers to the issues of providing access to copyrighted material for people who are deaf/hard of hearing or are blind/low vision; however, the exemption clauses provide some opportunity to address them. Because there is little creative or business incentive to motivate a model of universal access practices among the content creation, production, or distribution channels, regulatory and legal systems are needed to ensure that there is fair and just access for all citizens. However, the Internet is not and will likely not be regulated to the same extent as broadcast television or film distribution, and regulations regarding access requirements do not apply, although copyright legislation still does. As a result, the providers of content and "the public" are being asked to make their online materials more accessible in accordance with standards or good practice, but this still involves efforts that are primarily voluntary. Amateur content producers and unpaid or amateur captionists and describers are taking on the tasks of providing access to either their own or other's content and making it available online to those with disabilities. The challenge then becomes finding ways to accomplish access that respects and recognizes the original work and its creators while also making it accessible to a legitimate and important audience, those with perceptual disabilities. Quality control and decisions regarding fair dealing are currently left in the hands of the amateur captionist and describer who arguably bear too large a burden.

If, on the other hand, content creators, producers, and distributors were to ensure that their content is accessible regardless of distribution venues, the need for legislative exemptions and more robust fair dealing provisions would become irrelevant and unnecessary, and quality control and copyright could remain wholly with copyright holders. There would be no issue of how to synchronize secondary-source captioning and description with the original audio/visual material. New business models as well as standards or best practices models could also be developed to ensure that inclusive practices are viable and sustainable and reach larger audiences. The principle and practice of providing fair access to cultural content for people with sensory disabilities is wholly within reach.

11 If You're Asking, It's Not Fair Dealing: Animating Canadian Copyright Issues in a "Read-Write" Classroom

MATT SOAR

Instructors and students in the humanities and fine arts are currently confronted by a peculiar paradox: we have access to a bewildering and ever-expanding range of on- and off-line digital tools to assist in the realization of our creative ideas, but this is often overshadowed by a pervasive and well-founded culture of fear with respect to copyright. In my own field – communication studies – this experience manifests as an uncertainty shared by instructors, teaching/research assistants, and students on at least three fronts: the existing media we quote or incorporate into exercises and assignments; our creative and personal work; and the distribution and protection of the work we produce. These concerns are quite aside from a familiar, long-standing anxiety over what media (and how much of it) we can actually show in the classroom as part of our teaching about media.

Outside the academy, the ongoing "computerization of culture" (Manovich 2001) has much to do with the creation of a general sense of uncertainty and anxiety about dealing with media. The seemingly inexorable consolidation of media ownership across the developed world, the increasing prevalence of digital locks (digital rights management) and traffic shaping, plus the aggressive prosecution and/or persecution of alleged copyright infringers by corporate lawyers are all challenging the few things we thought we understood about how digital networks functioned.

Inside the academy, we can add additional factors to this list. Some have to do with the shifting divisions between fields of study, such as the emergence of the digital humanities, and the reification of "interdisciplinarity" (successor to the previous decade's vacuous yet magic keyword: "excellence"), and the relative novelty of research/creation grants. Others have to do with the technologization of faculty.

There is now a latent expectation that new faculty members will arrive with sufficiently developed technical skills to be able to create course blogs, research websites, or online archives, or that they will develop many of these skills as part and parcel of their research programs, regardless of their area of intellectual specialization. The consolidation and expansion of undergraduate communication studies programs with substantial production-oriented courses in their curricula and the emergence of graduate programs offering practice-based alternatives to theses and dissertations increase such demands, and present unforseen scenarios. We also have to face new questions about the archivability and sustainability of digital research. Many of us make unhesitating promises to granting agencies that an integral outcome of our research projects and funded conferences will be a website or a DVD (or both), as well as articles or books.

With this complex of factors in mind, I would like to reflect on the opportunities and fears associated with the problems of media making as a pedagogical activity involving faculty and students in the humanities. Given the present volume's focus on "dynamic" fair dealing, I locate this discussion within a web of shifting and emerging tensions. Not the least of these is the burden of copyright per se, and the very few exceptions that Canadian educators "enjoy" under the tentative provisions of fair dealing (and its more expansive American cousin, fair use). In addition, we must take into account the conservative and self-protective undercurrents of educational administrations; the political and creative necessity of constantly testing the boundaries of what is "allowed" (i.e., according to university regulations, or in law, or via rumour and anecdote); and the willingness of students to engage in critical – even transgressive – media practices, tied to the formal imperative that they engage in productions worthy of inclusion in their portfolios and resumes.

Context: A Production House Built on Fair Use

From 1997 to 2002, while studying for my PhD in communication at the University of Massachusetts–Amherst, I also worked for the Media Education Foundation (www.mediaed.org) as a graphic designer and video producer. The MEF is a non-profit video production company dedicated to creating and distributing classroom documentaries on media issues. Over the past eighteen years, the MEF has worked with many leading figures in the arena of media and cultural criticism, including Noam Chomsky, Susan Douglas, Stuart Hall, bell hooks, Jean Kilbourne, Naomi Klein, Robert W. McChesney, Edward Said, and Janet Wasko. Many of MEF's most successful videos address problematic representations of race, ethnicity, gender, and sexuality in TV shows, advertising, videogames, news, and cinema.

This experience was also my first formal encounter with making media under the terms of fair use. Indeed, the very existence of the MEF, which was founded in 1991 by Sut Jhally, a professor of communication at the University of Massacussetts–Amherst, is entirely predicated on fair use as a legally defensible (as opposed to a legally protected) position. As Jhally (n.d.) has recalled, the whole enterprise started quite by accident. In the 1980s, he began collecting recorded excerpts of various media, especially music videos, with a view to playing them in his large lecture courses for the purposes of analysis and critique. He then cut together multiple examples to make a short classroom video on the problematic portrayal of women in music videos, which he repeatedly edited and tested out in the classroom. The result was a controversial piece called *Dreamworlds* (Jhally 1991), which he then started duplicating in VHS format to distribute to other scholars and teachers.

In what has since become a rather predictable scenario, Jhally received a cease-and-desist letter from MTV's lawyers claiming copyright infringement and demanding that he retrieve and destroy all copies of the tape. These kinds of letters have become ubiquitous, and are often spurious at best, as the evidence accumulated by the Chilling Effects Clearinghouse (www.chillingeffects.org) makes clear. Jhally refused to comply, citing fair use, and MTV ultimately backed off. By mutual agreement with his university, Jhally went on to establish the MEF as an entirely separate entity. With a catalogue currently running to over seventy video titles, the MEF has continued to critique the media by quoting liberally from its output, all under the auspices of fair use. Although my chief responsibility at the MEF was to design their annual catalogue, flyers, videoboxes, and interstitials, I did produce and co-direct *Behind the Screens: Hollywood Goes Hypercommercial* (Soar 2000), a video about product placement, merchandising, and tie-ins in the movies (see www.brandhype.org). It is comprised solely of footage taken from the movies, interspersed with talking heads, and we did not seek permission for a single movie excerpt. (As many of us now know, if you're asking, it's not fair use.)

It is worth reminding ourselves that, in the pre-DVD, pre-TiVo, pre–World Wide Web milieu of the mid-1980s to mid-1990s, teachers were routinely obliged to record whatever media they wanted for purposes of study and critique via their own VHS machines as it was aired. Failing that, it was necessary to badger colleagues in the hopes that someone else happened to record it, or to attempt to purchase tapes after the fact, directly from the broadcasters. Although the technologies have changed, the culture of fear that we live with today was clearly very active twenty years ago. Indeed, it seems many people have always shied away from recording television shows or ads, let alone playing them back in the classroom. And not much seems to have changed in academic publishing, to take another, related example: we're still chasing up permissions for media images to support our scholarly articles because the journal or press concerned isn't sure enough about its rights, or, more bluntly, is frightened of being sued. Important exceptions remain, which, given their image-heavy critiques, would simply not have been feasible without fair use. Key examples in the realm of visual culture include Goffman (1979), Williamson (1978), and Gross et al. (2003).

Copyright as Cause Célèbre

Timeshift to October 2008, when copyright, intellectual property (IP), fair use, and fair dealing have become the wildly improbable causes célèbre of artists, musicians, academics, and librarians. I am attending the premiere of *RiP!: A Remix Manifesto* (Gaylor, 2008), an award-winning, feature-length documentary directed by Montreal-based filmmaker Brett Gaylor. *RiP!* (working title, *The Basement Tapes*) has been screened at multiple festivals, in theatres, and on television stations across the world. It is now available for viewing in HD, for free, on the National Film Board's website. The film, produced by EyeSteelFilm and the NFB, offers a highly polemical view of contemporary copyright law in the United States and Canada, including interviews with activists such as sound artist Mark Hosler of Negativland, Standford law professor Lawrence Lessig, and musician and former Brazilian Minister of Culture Gilberto Gil. In the film, Gaylor deploys a faux-naïve, first-person narrative to explore questions about the limits of copyright as it relates to music sampling, focusing on his "favourite artist" Girl Talk. Appropriately enough, Girl Talk, aka minor mash-up star and likable exhibitionist Gregg Gillis, has a well-deserved reputation for creating eminently danceable tunes on his laptop, by recycling some of the catchiest and kitschiest pop hooks of the past twenty years. While some of this work has been released through a record label called (wait for it) Illegal Art, Gillis is best known on the club circuit for his wild live shows. Strapping on his laptop like an electric guitar, or diving headlong into the crowd, Gillis brings fresh meaning to the notion of nerd chic.

Although I have a vested interest in copyright issues, my main reason for attending the premiere was to see the final cut of a film that includes sections of an animation made by my first-year students. I had not even heard of Girl Talk when, a year earlier, I had invited Gaylor to talk about his Open Source Cinema Project (OSCP) with the students in my Intermedia I course. For my regular unit on copyright, I would usually begin with a guest lecture by my colleague Nancy Marrelli, Concordia University archivist emerita, on the history of copyright law in Canada. After that I'd move on to an extended discussion of alternatives, chiefly the Creative Commons (CC), and illuminate these ideas with contemporary "real-world" examples, such as the case brought by the Associated Press against graphic designer and provocateur Shepard Fairey, creator of an iconic Obama poster called "HOPE," for which Fairey used an AP photograph as source material, without permission.

Case Study: Girl Talk Rotoscoped!

After much discussion, planning, and patient bureaucratic shepherding by the faculty, the fall of 2007 saw the launch of a new undergraduate curriculum in my department. An entirely new feature of this curriculum was the introduction of the department's fourth production stream, called Intermedia, which I had a significant role in developing. Its three new courses (introduction, intermediate, and advanced) were conceived as a complement to long-established offerings in film, video, and sound. The goal was never simply to provide "digital media" courses, or to teach Web design, or "computers." Rather, we sought to open up a critical and creative space in which students and faculty could together explore many of the hybrid and liminal media practices that have come to the fore in recent years.

The first-year course, which I have taught twice a year over the past six years, has necessarily been a work in progress. In 2008–09, we routinely addressed a variety of issues and ideas relating to residual and "new" media, including basic critical/creative explorations of photography and sequential storytelling, graphic design and editorial illustration, interactivity, database narratives, usability, and copyright. Given the size of the class (60–65 students, on average) and a strategic need to have the students develop their collaborative production skills, most exercises and assignments at this point were conducted in pairs or small teams. I had always wanted to adapt a filmmaking exercise I encountered several years earlier to the digital realm, and finally hit on the notion of using Adobe's Flash – which we already had in the lab – to animate over a previously shot and edited video.

Year on year, Flash is hands down the most desired, yet enigmatic, software application for my first-year students. It is a ubiquitous program for creating interactive, primarily Web-based, media. For those who've ever tried using it, however, it's notoriously difficult to learn, partly because of a slew of maddeningly counter-intuitive features and functions. Making good-looking work can also be tricky, as the students often discover. Substantially interactive works require that they learn how to program inside the application, using a native coding environment called ActionScript, which has itself gone through at least three major transformations. Using Flash for animation work meant that the students would become familiar with the application's interface and some of its quirks (e.g., work files being distinct from published files; incompatibilities between versions) while avoiding ActionScript. It would also be an opportunity to develop non-trivial work with immediate, gratifying results, while more or less subverting the program's chief function. All we needed were source videos over which we could animate.

The approach I conceived was this: the short video would be divided up between all the students, with each one animating just a few seconds. The animation technique we deployed, called "rotoscoping," involved digitally drawing over the video frame by frame, and in this case removing the video entirely once the animation process was complete. Traditional rotoscoping can be seen in the fluid movements of Snow White in Walt Disney's *Snow White and the Seven Dwarves* (1937); more recently, digital rotoscoping has been used to create entire movies, such as *Waking Life* (2001) and *A Scanner Darkly* (2006).

RiP!: A Remix Manifesto began life as an attempt to create a collaborative documentary on music sampling using Web-based social networking tools. At Gaylor's appropriately named Open Source Cinema Project website, visitors were invited to help write the script, shoot or download appropriate footage, then edit and upload the results. After he'd presented the OSCP to my class, I asked Gaylor if he might have some appropriate footage for my students to rotoscope. Gaylor offered me a three-minute video of Girl Talk in concert. It was a superbly shot and assembled montage of various live performances edited to a single pre-recorded mash-up, including his sublime track "Bounce That," which samples everything from Stevie Wonder to The Breeders. Gaylor had his own motives: what would an animated remix of a video of a remix artist's performance look like, and how might it contribute to the argument he was developing for his documentary? Once we'd figured out the logistics, my students – all sixty-four of them (ably supported by two teaching assistants, senior intermedia students Daniel Laurin and Kennetha Story) – began rotoscoping individual sections of approximately two to three seconds each (at 12 frames per second, this amounted to around 30–40 separate digital drawings per student). The process took four weeks, and each time the class met, we would review the progress made.

Since our students generally don't have fine arts backgrounds, the quality of their individual contributions was highly variable, as were the techniques (line, colour, movement) they deployed. That said, the rough-and-ready feel of mash-ups in general, and the driving beats of the track itself, ensured that the piece hung together. Once *RiP!: A Remix Manifesto* was finished, we posted the completed animation on the OSCP website. Another copy (dubbed *Girl Talk – Bounce That – Best Fan Video Ever*) found its way onto YouTube. What happened next took us all by surprise: our work was soon picked up by Pitchfork, the highly influential online music magazine – as one student Facebooked excitedly, "We've been Pitchforked!" – and multiple blogs (e.g., Drawn, Gawker), and the number of hits on OSCP and YouTube began climbing rapidly. As of July 2012, the copy posted on YouTube in late 2007 had been viewed nearly two million times.

Why so much attention, so much Internet traffic? One could fairly claim that, out of context, the animation simply became just another trivial meme – a pleasurable, if inane, diversion akin to viral videos of celebrities behaving badly, babies biting their brothers, performing cats, and disoriented, post-dentist kids. Certainly, some of the thousand or so comments it has so far received on YouTube suggest as much, for example, "cool ass video," "love this!" Others simply reference the artist or the sampling, for example, "What song does the first beat come from?" or "I think the 1.38 sample is 'Ma Cherie Amour' by Stevie Wonder." A few acknowledge the context in which the video was produced, as described in the associated information panel on YouTube and in the titles and credits before and after the animation: "yeh that was good made me think alot about copyright and how it controls us girl talk is a hero of copyright breaking"; "Love this! I'm totally going to use it for a video dance bday party I have coming up. Love the idea of open source cinema ... That is the way things should be. I'm tired the big record companies trying to lock down youtube. [sic]"

We also know that mash-ups can be anything but inane: *The Lord of the Rings* (2001) reimagined as a parable about capitalist hegemony; Buffy from *Buffy the Vampire Slayer* (1997–2003) confronting the creepy Edward Cullen of *Twilight* (2008) when he enters "her" bedroom uninvited; Mel Gibson "arguing" with Christian Bale in a mutual display of extreme machismo. Subtitle mash-ups of *Der Untergang* (aka *Downfall*) (2004), the German drama that follows the last days of Hitler's reign, run the full gamut, from uncannily incisive to irredeemably inane.

Reflections

Viral success aside, the degree to which this animation has contributed to ongoing debates about copyright, if at all, remains to be seen. That the piece was ultimately featured in *RiP!* as an example of public, grassroots participation in remix culture was certainly validating for the students, the teaching assistants, and for me. Girl Talk has been described more than once as "a lawsuit waiting to happen," which makes one wonder if the same can be said about derivative works (like ours) drawing on his sample-based music, or even the documentary itself. I imagine this issue was not front-of-mind when my university's house organ, *Now* (formerly *Concordia Journal*), covered the story favourably (Herland 2008), and the university's PR people posted yet another copy of the animation on their YouTube Channel (almost 6,000 views) – without permission.

It's also worth pausing to think about the nature of our classroom remixes. The favourite examples cited in works by (predominantly male) authors such as Cory Doctorow, Michael Geist, Lawrence Lessig, or Kembrew McLeod often refer to a single medium: audio tracks sampled and remixed; video footage appropriated and recut. With our projects, the derivation is an entirely new interpretive "layer" of visuals; in three out of four projects, the original source video has been completely removed (the exception, *RoboProfessor*, was specifically performed and shot with a view to being animated over by us). The legality of this kind of creative work is precisely what was being fought over in the United States, between Shepard Fairey's Obama poster and the Associated Press.

I do not want to suggest that my experience with this assignment is typical or, indeed, particularly illuminating in terms of a broader debate about the (over)reach of contemporary copyright law. That said, it has been highly instructive for me and my students, since the animation assignment – which I've now used three more times since *Girl Talk Rotoscoped: Steamboat Mickey* (winter 2008, with sound design by Owen Chapman); *RoboProfessor* (fall 2008, featuring a performance by Kembrew McLeod, in service of *Copyright Criminals*, the 2009 documentary he made with Benjamin Franzen); and *The Poem of the Transparent Girl*, (winter 2009, using a performance shot in Brazil by the OSCP) – offers direct, creative engagement with a pressing issue that is already having profound consequences for them as a generation "criminalized" for its "Read-Write" activities. Lessig (2008) defines a Read/Write culture as one in which "ordinary citizens … add to the culture they read by creating and re-creating the culture around them"; in contrast, a Read/Only culture is "less practiced in performance, or amateur creativity, and more comfortable … with simple consumption" (28). Criminalization occurs regardless of whether or not users acknowledge it or identify with this characterization. Even being asked simply to make an informed, collective decision about which CC licence to choose for a class project, for example, a self-produced e-zine on Montreal culture, can lead to a more engaged discussion about copyright than might otherwise be possible.

In broader terms, online engagement and activism around copyright issues are vital to the development of enlightened policy initiatives, especially amid the current flood of rather regressive proposals. The Conservative governments' Bill C-32, and other, more recent initiatives, have been criticized (Doctorow 2010, Geist 2010b) as a problematic retread of the US Digital Millennium Copyright Act (DMCA), specifically around the issue of digital locks. It made for especially surprising reading as it followed in the wake of an unprecedented period of public consultation (http://ic.gc.ca/eic/site/008.nsf/eng/home), which was overwhelmingly in favour of regulations that did not merely appear to mimic the provisions of the DMCA. Meanwhile, the minister responsible for the Bill, James Moore, recently argued that people who oppose his proposal are "radical extremists" (Singleton 2010) who simply don't want any copyright at all. Proof, indeed, that we need more, not less, public involvement in these debates.

In Closing

Classroom media productions serve to augment or problematize the key theories and concepts set out in the curriculum. This is less a matter of supplementing intellectual explorations by "making stuff"; rather, the two activities can be made to work iteratively and symbiotically. Further, having the whole class work together on one production assignment can reap many benefits. Students are inevitably inspired by what some of their peers produce from week to week with exactly the same tools and parameters, and the collaboration also becomes more than the sum of its parts.

The dynamism of fair dealing, if not its very existence, depends on a willingness to occupy the notional space it offers, and to continually test its boundaries; to challenge the culture of fear and the associated chilling effect on creativity; and, to recognize that the classroom is as good a place as any to do so. The history of the Media Education Foundation reminds us that many of these issues are not new; further, while the university administration protected itself by requiring that the MEF become an independent entity, the MEF has yet to be sued for copyright infringement.

12 Hacking Education: How Openness and Sharing Can Transform Learning

ALEC V. COUROS

A key to transformation is for the teaching profession to establish innovation networks that capture the spirit and culture of hackers – the passion, the can-do, collective sharing.

David Hargreaves, *Working Laterally*

Open source software communities are one of the most successful – and least understood – examples of high performance collaboration and community-building on the Internet today. Other types of communities could benefit enormously from understanding how open source communities work.

Eugene Kim, *An Introduction to Open Source Communities*

In January 2008, I led a graduate-level educational technology course at the University of Regina titled "Social Media and Open Education." The course was developed, designed, and facilitated using primarily free, open source (OS), and social tools. More significantly, the course was taught using open pedagogies, teaching methods inspired by the OS movement. As a result, the context for learning was an engaging series of experiences where students freely interacted with educators and theorists from across the globe. Students redefined boundaries for learning, as they were encouraged to build online learning networks and to collaboratively explore, negotiate, and create authentic social connections and content. This essay outlines the philosophies that inspired the course, describes several pedagogical methods, and offers insight into the importance of openness and sharing in educational communities.

Philosophy of Openness

My views on learning fundamentally shifted in July 1999. It was a month of transition for me as I changed my city of residence (Saskatoon to Regina), moved to a new position in higher education, defended my M.Ed. thesis, and began my doctoral work. Most importantly, I stumbled upon (literally found an abandoned copy in the photocopy room) Eric Raymond's *The Cathedral and the Bazaar* (1997). I knew very little about Linux and OS software previous to this discovery, but through Raymond's thesis, I was able to draw important parallels between the worlds of software developers and educators.

The Cathedral and the Bazaar contrasts two different software development models. The first approach, labelled the cathedral method, reflects a structured, systematic, and hierarchical process where software source code is held privately and made available only to an exclusive group of software developers at specific intervals of time. The second approach, labelled the bazaar method, describes a process in which software code is developed in full view of the public (i.e., the Internet) by an ad hoc group of developers bound only by weak ties. The latter approach has gained prominence in software development communities (see Che, this volume), and is an important factor for the successful, sustained development of complex software projects such as Linux distributions (e.g., Ubuntu, SuSe, Mandriva), Web browsers (e.g., Firefox, Camino, Flock), and productivity software (e.g., Open Office, AbiWord).

The success of OS software could not have been achieved by merely modifying types, frequencies, and boundaries for collaboration. Arguably, one of the most important factors that stimulated collaboration in these communities was the development of the GNU General Public License (GPL) by Richard Stallman. The GNU GPL, an evolved instance of the first copyleft licence, ensures particular software freedoms: the right to free distribution, the right to modify code, and the assurance that modified software remains free under copyleft provisions. In simplified terms, the GPL ensured that the work of the community would be developed within the commons: free to use, free to modify, and free to distribute. This mechanism ensured that work done by community members would remain in the community, would benefit the community, and could not be exploited by any individual or group for profit.

Shortly after the introduction of OS methodologies in software communities, some educators began to draw parallels to these collaborative processes within their own contexts. Notably, in 1998, David Wiley, who coined the term "open content," developed "copyleft" licences for educational materials (Grossman 1998). Wiley's Open Publication License (OPL) was developed in consultation with the aforementioned software pioneers, Eric Raymond and Richard Stallman. Although copyleft licences in education took several years to gain recognition, the concept of open content gained a greater public profile with projects such as MIT's OpenCourseWare initiative, the Creative Commons (CC), and the OER (Open Educational Resources) Commons. The momentum of collaboration espoused by software communities began to challenge structures and processes within educational communities.

In 2003, I began a two-year study focused on collaboration and sharing in such educational communities. I targeted individuals, found nationally and internationally, who had been influenced by OS communities and had integrated these collaborative influences into their own educational contexts. Through this research, I defined "the open movement" as:

> an informal, worldwide phenomenon characterized by the tendency of individuals and groups to work, collaborate and publish in ways that favour accessibility, sharing, transparency and interoperability. Advocates of openness value the democratization of knowledge construction and dissemination, and are critical of knowledge controlling structures. (Couros 2008)

Several participants in this study, individually and collectively, attempted to find ways to bring these philosophies into their teaching practice. At first there were technical barriers for collaboration and sharing in a wider educational community (e.g., tools not available or not yet mature); however, with the popularization of Web 2.0, participants found there were now many simple ways to create, share, and collaborate (e.g., blogs, wikis, podcasts). Participants of the study who had been influenced by the philosophies of the open movement were now able to bring the spirit of these ideals into their classrooms.

From the data I gathered, I was able to diagram some of the profound changes occurring with this group of educators as emerging technologies helped enact their philosophies around sharing and collaboration (see Figures 12.1 and 12.2). Several participants moved from the "typical

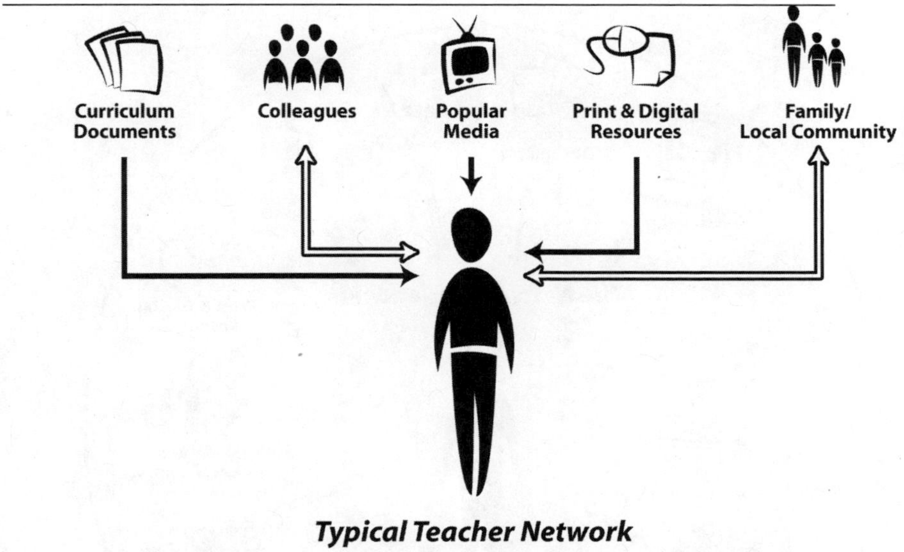

Figure 12.1. The typical teacher network.

teacher network," a generally passive mode of knowledge construction, to becoming the more active, "networked teacher" (Couros 2008).

This latter model positions the individual, in the midst of an abundance of tools, as a connected learner who frequently collaborates and shares with other practitioners and theorists through distributed networks of practice. It was this discovered transformation that I hoped to replicate through the facilitation of "Social Media and Open Education." It was hoped that participants in the course would develop online personal learning networks, deconstruct what it means to be open and connected, and evaluate the implications for educational practice.

The Course

In the summer of 2007, work began on the development of "Open, Connected, Social." I received a Technology Enhanced Learning (government) grant to develop the course and had access to a group of competent instructional designers and media developers at the University of Regina's Centre for Academic Technologies. However, in the hope of disrupting the entire design process, I opted instead to hire high school

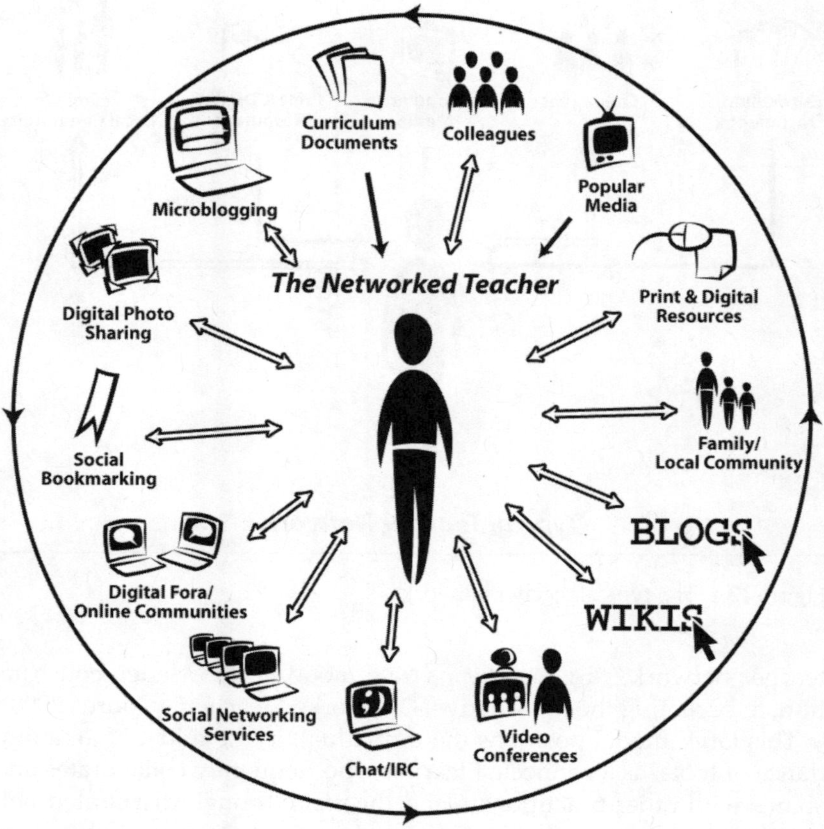

Figure 12.2. The networked teacher model.

teacher Rob Wall, one of the participants from the previously mentioned study. I made this choice for two key reasons. First, I wanted to follow a process of design that would be accessible to educators not equipped with institutionally provided technical support. In other words, I wanted to prove that teachers using publicly available tools could build good online courses. Second, I wanted to work with someone who had experienced the transformation observed in the study, someone who also believed in the importance of collaboration, sharing, and openness. As we began work on the course, we quickly made a number of techno-pedagogical decisions that would determine our direction and, ultimately, the shape of the learning experience. Here are some of the key decisions, each with a brief rationale.

Avoid Walled Gardens

The desired learning experience in an online course is directly related to the structure of the learning environment. In other words, the architecture of the learning environment directly affects how individuals and groups learn, and what educational experiences may be possible. In several planning meetings, Rob and I contemplated the desired learning experiences and what types of technical and social environments would best support these. For this course, we outright rejected WebCT (BlackBoard) as it is proprietary/commercial software and because it is designed to create only closed learning communities (walled gardens). Although we highly recommend Moodle as an OS content management system (CMS) and for its strong community support, it was also rejected for this project as we felt it would not create the transparent community we desired. Social network services like Ning and Elgg proved worthy candidates, but again, these were rejected because of our desire for greater transparency. We chose, instead, a hosted wiki service, as it was free, easy to use, and easy to modify (for developers and participants), transparent, did not require a login, and could freely integrate dozens of other Web 2.0 tools as necessary.

Allow for Dynamic Content Development

Online courses typically feature a large amount of predetermined content for students to absorb. In "Open, Connected, Social," course content was developed dynamically, "on the fly," through the adoption of several process. First, ten prominent individuals from the field of educational technology (e.g., professors, teachers, administrators) were invited to join in conversations with our students. These synchronous sessions were recorded in various formats (e.g., video, audio, transcripts), were available for viewing on various devices (e.g., computers, iPods), and content was released under the CC licences. Students who could not attend these live sessions could experience the content in their own time. In addition, students were encouraged to visit the online spaces of these guests, and in most cases, the conversations continued well after the sessions, and in some cases, beyond the course itself. Second, students worked collaboratively on a wiki project (a course requirement). In effect, students built the course curriculum, recommended course readings (via a Delicious tag), and created text and audio/visual tutorials (using screencasting tools) for shared understanding. Third, students spontaneously chose topics for study based on current events in the subject area. For example, several students became interested in exploring the Internet-based virtual world *Second Life* and its implications for education. Through various online social connections, we were quickly able to arrange a sophisticated, guided tour where class participants were immersed in the application.

Focus on Building Social Capital

In the early stages of course development, it became clear that the traditional role of the professor, as the fount of knowledge, would prove antithetical in this course that focused on sociality and openness. Rather than providing content to students, it was decided that the focus would be on assisting students in forming sustainable personal learning networks, or more specifically, social capital – described by Cohen and Prusak (2001) as "the stock of active connections among people: the trust, mutual understanding, and shared values and behaviours that bind the members of human networks and communities to make cooperative action possible" (98). Students blogged regularly in their own spaces. And, rather than attempting to respond to each post with my own thoughts, I looked to my own social network and asked those individuals I felt had an educated opinion or relevant experience in each topic to respond personally to student posts. Often, these responses evolved into more frequent interactions among participants as students began to build authentic, professional connections that persisted well beyond the last day of the course. In other words, I leveraged my own social capital and network connections to help others build sustainable connections with other educators and theorists. My role as an educator was most importantly a connector and network builder versus the more traditional content expert.

Create the Context for Distributed, Sustained Personal Learning

Through careful assignment design and the choice of tools, the course fostered the development of distributed learning while students developed lasting, personal learning networks. Although the course wiki provided centralized details regarding course events, assignments, readings, and an archive of synchronous sessions, individual student blogs were key to navigating and documenting personal learning. Through their blogs, students developed personalized learning spaces that could exist after the course had ended. Had we chosen to use a tool like WebCT, much of the student content that had been developed would have ceased to exist at the end of the semester. Most importantly, the course was designed so that learning could occur anywhere within the network, on the course wiki, on student blogs, or throughout any of the spaces in between. This helped students deeply foster an understanding of on-demand, anywhere, anytime, professional development and the serendipitous nature of networked learning.

Open Access to All Interested

The most radical component of this course proved also to be one of the most effective. For the first month of the course, for lack of better options, we experimented with two proprietary Web-conferencing tools, Adobe Connect and Elluminate, to host our synchronous sessions with our guests. We experienced bandwidth issues with Adobe Connect when in large groups. And, while Elluminate seemed more stable, we found its user interface to be dated and non-intuitive. However, the bigger issues we perceived with both tools was that they were expensive, proprietary, licensed by a finite number of seats, and thus created the walled garden effect that we were determined to avoid. Luckily, through consultation with our network, we soon discovered a free, live video streaming tool called Ustream. Although the tool was not designed for education, we were able to hack it for our purposes. Due to the demand (our course was becoming quite popular), we opened up the synchronous sessions to our network, and on many occasions, non-registered participants outnumbered registered participants. Not only did the free tool work better than those tools we paid for, it helped us achieve a greater level of open access to the course – access to the live lectures themselves. Since the first offering in 2008, I have run "Social Media and Open Education" for three additional semesters. The concept of the course has largely remained the same; however, emerging social tools and a greater public understanding of social networking have allowed for greater innovation and advanced pedagogical strategies. The most important recent innovations include the introduction of new digital tools.

Student Introductory Videos

In the first course offering, students who developed a transparent, digital persona more easily formed meaningful, personal learning networks. One of the important activities in this progression was the creation of introductory "about me" videos. These artefacts were produced in various ways, ranging from the "talking head" webcam approach to narrated slideshows. For those students who desired greater anonymity, tools like Xtranormal were used to mask one's true identity through the projection of an animated figure. In all cases, these videos served to introduce a desired persona to other networked educators, to share basic career information (e.g., Grade 7 teacher, arts educator), to provide learning goals and assets, and to provide a point of reference for relationship building.

Microblogging

The increasing popularity of Twitter and other microblogging services has proven to be one of the most important developments for the viability of personal learning networks as an educational strategy. As an instructor, I have deliberately developed a high-profile Twitter identity that has had great implications for my practice. Through Twitter, I have been able to highlight and share student work, greatly increase "outsider" participation in course events, significantly increase readership of student blogs, connect students to educational expertise, and assist in the development of distributed learning networks by students. Microblogging has made it possible to greatly amplify the original course strategies, and offers altogether new affordances towards networked learning.

"Teach Us Something"

There are many instructional tools freely available to educators and students. Digital video is now much easier to produce and screencasting has become popular. A YouTube search with the keywords "instruction" or "how to" will produce a list of thousands of videos developed solely to provide instruction for learning any skill imaginable. In the third offering of the course, I invited students and others to "teach us something" through the production of five-minute microlectures. Dozens of such lectures were created and shared, all under copyleft licences. These artefacts covered a wide range of topics, and students were exposed to and collectively developed many innovative instructional strategies inspired by digital and social affordances.

Aggregated Content

Through feedback from students, it was found that one of the most difficult aspects of learning in a networked environment is managing the continuous, distributed information flow. Fortunately, many free tools and strategies were found to aid in this process. For instance, the use of Google Reader bundles allowed for the collection and easy subscription to student blogs, relevant information feeds, and course-specific sites. More importantly, the use of shared tagging made it possible for students and others to track course information flow through sites like Google, Summize (Twitter search), Flickr, YouTube, and others. Tagging was vital to affording learners the ability to produce work in a variety of media spaces and being able to track and manage all course-related content.

Conclusion: Towards the Concept of Open Teaching

As I work to deconstruct the course and examine the pedagogical and philosophical decisions that guided the experience, the concept of open teaching begins to emerge. Through a thorough review of the literature, I did not discover an existing course with similar methodologies that had been previously offered. In sharing this experience, I offer the following definition and key characteristics of what I define as open teaching. Open teaching is the facilitation and development of learning experiences that are open, transparent, collaborative, and social. Open teachers are advocates of a free and open knowledge society, and they support their students in the critical consumption, production, connection, and synthesis of knowledge. Open teaching may include some or all of the following activities:

- Advocacy and use of free and/or OS tools and software wherever possible and beneficial to student learning
- Integration of open content and media in teaching and learning
- Advocacy of open content licences for student content production
- Facilitation of student understanding regarding copyright law (e.g., fair use/fair dealing)

- Facilitation of student personal learning networks for collaboration
- Modelling of openness, transparency, and responsible copyright/ copyleft use and licensing.

The concept of open teaching may not be agreeable to all educators. Certainly, these characteristics can be viewed as representing deep personal philosophies and assumptions regarding the ownership of knowledge, the freedoms and rights of creators and consumers, and the preference towards a connected knowledge society. However, I feel that if anything, acknowledging how distant we still are from the vision of the open teacher can begin a relevant discussion on ever-changing views of knowledge in education and society.

The facilitation and development of "Open, Connected, Social" and the study leading up to its inception are, without a doubt, the most significant events of my educational life. Not only have I gained new understandings of teaching and learning, I now better comprehend the changing structures and relationships of knowledge within our greater society. I once again defer to Eric Raymond (1998a) as he describes hacker culture as a true semblance of a gift culture: "Gift away cultures are adaptations not to scarcity but to abundance … Abundance makes command relationships difficult to sustain and exchange relationships an almost pointless game. In gift cultures, social status is determined not by what you control but by what you give" (n.p.). From a knowledge perspective, we have clearly moved into this abundance society. Students no longer complain about not being able to find enough information. Rather, they struggle to make sense of the data, or voice their lack of the necessary skills and tools to filter the incoming stream. In this state of information exasperation, the existing rules and conditions for the ownership of knowledge are no longer logical or beneficial. The tools and strategies we have used in the past do not suffice in helping students make sense of the world.

If education is to be successful in this new landscape, we need to revisit pedagogy and current structures of content and software licensing. The reform of both pedagogy and policy, through a lens of openness and connectivity, will better enable our students to become successful navigators of our changing educational environment. Through careful reform, students will gain the skills necessary to become critical consumers and producers of information in our knowledge economy, and they will become connectors and developers of their own, highly personalized learning environments.

PART B

Mediations

13 Open Access Publishing and Academic Research

ROWLAND LORIMER

The Roots of Open Access

The scoundrel, thief, probable spy, and publisher Robert Maxwell (Bower 1988: 222, 310; Prokesch 2008; Thomas and Dillion 2002) could well be credited with setting in motion a transformation of scientific, medical, and technical (STM) journal publishing from a service industry to a vastly profitable enterprise (Bower 1988: 77–87; Haines 1988: 169–79). Maxwell played this role by becoming a sales agent for German scientific journals in the aftermath of the Second World War (Bower 1988: 40). So great was the demand for access to German science of the time that Maxwell discovered that (almost) no price was too great to ask. By the time the Germans were granted the right to regain control over their own business, Maxwell had founded his own scientific journal-publishing operation, Pergamon, and was busily flying to science and chemistry conferences around the world, finding research leaders in opening fields, and setting them up as editors of journals that he then sold, for tidy sums, to research libraries (78–86).

Little research has been undertaken into Maxwell's exact role, the roles of other publishers, and even the publishing activities of discipline-based associations. The evidence (see Chase 2002, Tananbaum 2003) is that other publishers followed in Maxwell's footsteps. Certainly, statistics on the "serials pricing crisis" (Krillidou 2004; Thatcher, n.d.) suggest that since STM journal prices rose consistently, well beyond the consumer price index, and public companies such as Elsevier regularly reported profits in certain activities of well over 20 per cent. The price record also suggests that there was no serious competition mounted based on providing fair value for money. Of the pattern of price increases that extends up to the 1970s, only a fraction can be attributed to expanding page counts, suggesting that Maxwell was only the first to recognize the inelasticity of demand for scientific journals related to price. This was the beginning of an understanding of the value of information, and the notion of an information economy (OECD 2002).

Until recently, the overpricing of journals was limited to STM journals and professional fields such as law and engineering. It was never a particular problem in the social sciences and humanities (SSH) where publishers did not have the confidence to test demand elasticity by continuous, substantial price increases. But the prices of STM journals did not leave SSH information production untouched. They clearly affected the social sciences and humanities by robbing library budgets of their ability to purchase SSH journals and monographs. More recently, commercial SSH journal publishers appear to be following tentatively in the pricing footsteps of the STM journal publishers, although I know of no systematic data collected on the subject.

Continuous cries for reform by research librarians largely went unheeded by the academic community until they became fairly strident in the mid-1990s. The lack of concern in the scientific community seemed to be accountable to a sense of the esteem in which scientists thought their work should be held, combined with the notion that since publishing was not science, it should be of no concern to scientists. Yet, two groups of scientists saw things differently. One was the computer scientists, one of whom, Vincent Cerf, developed the idea of the Internet in 1973, which came to fruition ten years later. The other group was the high-energy physicists, who were quite dependent on the timely and complete circulation of research findings. Building on Cerf's work, on Christmas day in 1990, the world was introduced to the World Wide Web by CERN (Conseil Européen pour la Recherche Nucléaire, or European Council for Nuclear Research) fellow, Tim Berners-Lee (CERN 2007). Less than a year later, Paul Ginsparg, another physicist/computer scientist, set up a preprint server in Los Alamos to allow his colleagues to deposit their yet-to-be-published research results for all to see and review. These developments presented a way of circumventing the ransom being demanded by the STM journal publishers for the final preparation and circulation of scientific information.

By 1994, a range of academics was beginning to experiment with what were then called electronic journals, journals that had no print existence. Not long after, facing a lack of reader interest in the new medium, a few print journals, such as the *Canadian Journal of Communication* began making html versions of their articles available online. Throughout the 1980s and 1990s, the STM journal publishers held their ground against a growing concern in the academic community over continuous price increases above the consumer price index. They also held it in the context of a growing awareness of the value of intellectual property and a growing assertion of creators' rights (see Charter of Rights for Creators, Government of Canada 2003), particularly in the realms of both patents and copyright. Finally, they held it against a background of dramatic changes in information technology.

Rights-Holders' Rights, the Public Interest, and Technological Alternatives

In the world of knowledge production and dissemination, the simultaneous development of both copyright and technological facilitation of information exchange resulted in the same contradictions that exist in music downloading and file sharing. One might even claim that the tension between these parallel developments in production and access reflect an element that has been understood from the beginnings of copyright law: the need to balance the interests of rights holders (creators and publishers) and users. The dwindling purchases of offprints by authors to circulate their articles, replaced at first by photocopying, and then by digital file exchange, presented challenges to publishers' claims to copyright. Where copyright had once facilitated the flow of research in the print world by helping to create an orderly marketplace, in the face of new technologies, it was beginning to operate as a bottleneck to the circulation of ideas.

Part of the stance of STM journal publishers involved their claiming to add considerable value to the preparation of articles. But as Willinsky (2004) has reported, obtaining a reliable estimate of the actual costs of journal production was fairly impossible. Estimates varied widely, and it was not until 2003 that an estimate for Canadian SSH journals was provided (Lorimer and Lindsay 2004). In face of a lack of information and the dubious claims of the commercial publishers of the cost of their value additions, Willinsky set out to create a low-cost alternative to journal production. Unknown to him at the time, he (and others) worked in parallel with the commercial journal publishers. Each developed efficient, paperless, Web-based systems for complete automated submission, management, and publication of research and scholarship.

A Changing Discourse

It could reasonably be claimed that the STM journal publishers' intransigence with respect to high journal prices, their increasing assertions of copyright, along with their tradition of requiring scholars and researchers to assign their rights to journals (bolstered by no less an authority than the *Chicago Manual of Style*), led to the development of open access (OA). No doubt these factors played a role, but there were other pertinent dynamics including the presence of technological potential, and the awakening of the academic world to the main dynamic and purpose of scholarly journal publishing. It was and is the production and circulation of research produced with public funds, by publicly paid employees, largely employed in public institutions. Like Luther, many in the academic community began to ask whether an institutional mediator was necessary to direct interaction with this wisdom and insight. Why not, they asked, open access completely to the bible of all research findings, once they passed the rigours of peer review? With this proposal nailed to the door of commercial journal publishing, and with technology having evolved to transform publishing into a truer public good than was the case with print publishing – in the sense that the good is not destroyed by its consumption but lives on infinitely no matter how much or little it is consumed – the need for subscriptions as a market mechanism to determine who should gain access to research and scholarship almost vanished. The unsolved issue was first-copy costs.

The discourse of concern surrounding STM journals shifted from reasonable pricing to the laying of plans by the academic community to redesign and reassert control over its formalized communications system. Against the background of the Internet, the Web, and Ginsparg's preprint server, the academic community began to reinvent scholarly publishing, rallying around "open access," a term that captures the primary responsibility and role of scholarly and research journal publishing, that is, knowledge dissemination. But what, exactly, is open access?

Open Access Publishing

As blogger Peter Suber (2006) points out in a thorough review of the subject, the meaning of open access derives from three statements crafted at meetings in Budapest (Feb. 2002), Bethesda, Maryland (Apr. 2003), and Berlin (Oct. 2003). Suber notes that OA literature is digital and can be found online, but what characterizes it is "free availability and unrestricted use": the absence of both price barriers (subscriptions and fees) and permission barriers (copyright and licensing restrictions). Each OA provider decides which permission barriers it will remove, but there is an overall consensus that following the tenets of fair dealing or fair use, and removing price barriers, is insufficient.

The point of open access is to make what would come under fair dealing the rule, rather than a legal exception. Indeed, open access wants a wide swath of uses to be recognized as entirely legitimate. Given that researchers are producing reports of their research with the purpose of having such reports disseminated as widely as possible, and they are doing so without expectation of recompense, open access is much truer to that purpose than is subscription-based (print) publishing. OA advocates call only for recognition of the author (the date of publication can also be important is some fields), and in some cases the impermissibility of commercial exploitation without compensation. As Suber (2006) states it, the purpose of open access's various conditions is to "block plagiarism, misrepresentation, and sometimes commercial re-use, and authorize all the uses required by legitimate scholarship, including those required by the technologies that facilitate online scholarly research" (n.p.). Open access is a significant idea, and is advancing the discourse on research dissemination well beyond quibbling about price, but many such ideas die ignoble deaths. Has it had any effect on practice?

Significant Developments in Open Access Publishing

Perhaps the most noteworthy developments have been in physics and in the biological sciences and medicine, where the research and research communications system has been severely compromised by sponsorship and an ever-increasing control over research studies by the pharmaceutical industry (Willinsky et al. 2007: 599). While OA initiatives do not directly address the distortion of findings based on their funding body, they do represent a significant effort in encouraging the wide and free dissemination of scientific and medical information.

Founded in 2002, the US-based PubMed Central is a digital repository for biomedical and life sciences journals that meet PMC's editorial standards (focusing on research and peer review, even though the term "peer review" is not mentioned). Journals may voluntarily deposit their entire archive of contents up to the most recent or, if they have a moving wall of access, the archives to that point. The advantage to the journals of doing so is both further exposure to potential users and the advantage of having all contents in a common format in a single depository. These include "searching, manipulation, and cross-linking of the complete collection … [and the] integrate[ion of] the literature with a variety of other information resources such as sequence databases and other factual databases that are available to scientists, clinicians and everyone else interested in the life sciences" (PubMed Central).

The British BioMed Central differs fundamentally from PMC in that it is "an independent publishing house committed to providing immediate open access to peer-reviewed biomedical research. BMC's website adds that it "is committed to maintaining high standards through full and stringent peer review [and] … offers a wide variety of journals [197 currently] and other services" (BioMed Central, n.d.). The services to which BMC refers include commissioned reviews and a literature evaluation service. The Public Library of Science is a less ambitious undertaking. PLoS fills a gap for the United States between PMC as a repository or archive, and BMC, as OA publishers. PLoS is a non-profit organization of scientists and physicians committed to making the world's scientific and medical literature a public resource. It is an OA publisher that deposits its journals with PMC.

In Canada, in science journal publishing, efforts have been more subdued, partly because science journal publishing is relatively small. The National Research Council Press publishes sixteen journals. In its policy statements it requires authors to assign copyright, if they have it, to the NRC. It does not have an access policy but, in practice, the contents of all of its journals are made freely available to all Canadians and sold by subscription outside Canada (National Research Council, n.d.). Not to be left behind, the physicists have come up with their own, innovative plan called $SCOAP^3$ (Sponsoring Consortium for Open Access Publishing in Particle Physics). The physicists are calling for explicit funding of peer review and other editorial services by libraries and research institutions rather than by implicitly funding such functions through subscriptions. The plan is for funds now paid out in subscriptions to be redirected to $SCOAP^3$. The role of $SCOAP^3$ will be to determine the appropriate contributions to be made by each country based on the number of relevant articles published, to negotiate with publishers the price of peer-review services, based on a tendering process, and to provide funds to journals to cover their costs. In turn, all journals will be open access. Given the very real possibility of full cooperation by the 20,000 to 30,000 high-energy physicists around the world, and support from major institutions, the project has a reasonable chance of succeeding (Mele 2008).

The SCOAP^3 proposal addresses quite a significant problem that other plans lack. To some degree, the initiatives discussed in this chapter prior to the SCOAP^3 proposal are competitive with the commercial publishers. Their vulnerability is that they must draw money from grants and producers. In certain fields, this makes them vulnerable to political vagaries. For example, while research funding may be sufficient to cover such expenses in science in the developed world, in developing economies and in the social sciences and humanities, relying upon continuous, adequate, and likely, increasing grant funding, is probably less rather than more reliable than the current market-based system. SCOAP^3 addresses this vulnerability by creating a worldwide system and effectively obliging libraries and research agencies to contribute or deny their researchers publication opportunities. It has the added value of placing the financial burden on those who can afford it, and on those who benefit from it most.

The United States has addressed the issue of obligatory contributions to research dissemination in the health sciences through law. Division G, Title II, s. 218 of PL 110–161 (Consolidated Appropriations Act 2008) states that all investigators funded by the US National Institutes of Health must submit an electronic version of their final, peer-reviewed manuscripts to PubMed Central upon acceptance for publication, to be made publicly available no later than twelve months after publication. The Canadian Institutes of Health Research has a policy similar to the US law. On 4 September 2007, the CIHR announced that grant recipients now must ensure that their peer-reviewed publications are freely accessible through the publisher's website (Option 1), or an online repository as soon as possible, and in any event within six months of publication (Option 2). Under Option 2, grant recipients must archive the final peer-reviewed full-text manuscripts immediately upon publication in a digital archive like PubMed Central. This policy does not currently apply to book chapters, reports, monographs, editorials, or conference proceedings (CIHR 2007).

Prestigious institutions such as Harvard Law School and the Stanford Faculty of Education have put in place complementary policies endorsing the use of institutional repositories (IRs) – archives of the research carried on by members of a particular institution. They are complementary to other OA policies because they exert institutionally based moral or legal suasion on researchers to ensure that their work is publicly available within a reasonable time period. They also serve the interests of institutions by documenting the contributions they make to the greater good. However, as other OA archives become established, they become somewhat redundant; whether this is useful or not is an open question. A researcher is less likely to seek research at a particular institution than within a discipline-based database. Yet, research articles are used for a variety of ends and are found using a variety of search behaviours. As well, search engines can find an appropriately tagged article anywhere. Thus, the redundancy may be a net positive.

Open Access Publishing in the Social Sciences and Humanities

Most interesting, and prior to the developments in physics, are initial steps towards a $SCOAP^3$-type system taken in Canada by the Aid to Journals program of the Social Sciences and Humanities Research Council. SSHRC provides partial support to Canadian SSH journals – $850 per article – provided that they are not-for-profit and Canadian-owned and -run entities. SSHRC has also adopted open access in principle, even though it is having some difficulty implementing it in practice.

What is missing from SSHRC's actions is full funding so that all qualified journals can go open access. That, too, is almost functionally in place but, from the point of view of a full commitment to open access, structurally flawed. Two puzzle pieces deserve mention. The first is a journal-hosting initiative called Synergies. Funded by the Canada Foundation for Innovation, Synergies utilizes the library and information technology (IT) infrastructures of a number of Canadian universities to create a decentralized repository for commonly formatted articles, together with a centralized search facility like PubMed Central's. It has funds to develop value-added tools for researchers and, with a stroke of a funding or policy pen, could become an OA repository. The second piece of the puzzle is an organization called the Canadian Research Knowledge Network. The CRKN is a consortium of Canadian libraries with a mandate to acquire SSH content on behalf of its members. Conceived in the context of a subscription-based system, it has negotiated acquisition of electronic archives of Canadian and foreign materials that include few English-language SSH journals. Setting that peculiarity aside, CRKN could readily evolve into a partnership with SSHRC to provide full funding so that all Canadian SSH journals could become open access. Two elements stand in the way. First is the desire of a number of Canadian SSH journals to maintain their print copies, based in part on their reluctance to lose their earned income. Second is the embarrassing fact that Canadian SSH journals are subsidized outside Canada, mainly by substantial numbers of subscriptions from US research libraries (as much or more than 50% of earned income). They are also subsidized by other foreign purchasers, but to a much smaller extent (about 10%). Were open access to take hold in the United States in SSH journals, this income subsidy would most likely disappear. But it would be replaced by open access by Canadian researchers to US-based SSH journals, and thus the diminution or disappearance of the need of Canadian libraries to make journal purchases.

This review of the Canadian SSH journal scene makes obvious a missing discussion of developments in SSH journal publishing worldwide. Understanding that scene is somewhat more difficult than understanding the STM journal scene, because there are an abundance of new, online only, OA journals, and many journals moving to add an online version to their print operations. These projects exist alongside a number of larger integrative projects such as JSTOR, Highwire Press, and Project Muse. In overview, there appears to be sufficient momentum towards establishing open access as a principle for research dissemination to make it work. The foundational transition principle is this: currently, funding for the management of peer review, editorial and production services, and the dissemination of research is provided by research agency–based support and subscription-based "market" income directed to not-for-profit and for-profit print and online publishing. Funding comes almost entirely from within the academic community. Were the same, or even slightly less funding available for peer review and editorial services, then far more effective dissemination through open access could occur. Access would be universal and it would be without price barriers. The drawback: print journals would be unfunded; however, journals could continue selling print subscriptions, if they so wished and could afford it.

Self-Archiving and Green and Gold Open Access

This discussion would be incomplete without mention of self-archiving and the "green" and "gold" routes to open access. Self-archiving has been championed by such researchers as Stevan Harnad (2001), who, in face of commercial journals restricting the circulation of research, advocates that researchers take it upon themselves to upload their submitted articles onto the Web, provide them with a digital object identifier (DOI) and metadata to conform with the Open Access Initiative Protocol for Metadata Harvesting (OAI-PMH). This method, when it is acted on at the time of submission of the work for publication, has been dubbed the "green" route to open access. A second route, the "gold" route, has the publisher making the final version immediately publicly accessible. Like repositories, "green" open access constitutes redundant or parallel publishing and the natural site for works self-archived are either personal websites or IRs (or both).

There are several copyright issues that arise in the evolution to open access. First, most journal publishers ask that researchers assign the copyright for their article to the journal. An assignation of rights is generally perceived to be a total transfer of copyright. An alternative would be for an author to grant an exclusive, time-limited licence to a journal publisher, combined with a perpetual non-exclusive right to continue making the work available in its published form. The copyright that is assigned, most often, is to the work as edited and laid out by the journal publisher. It is arguable that the submitted work is a different work, in part, because copyright protects the fixed expression of an idea rather than the idea itself. Thus, especially if an author lodged the submitted version in a repository prior to or on submission, there would be grounds for claiming a maintenance of copyright in that work as opposed to the work published by the journal. This is the position taken by the NIH, which allows the author to make the work public through PubMed Central, independent of what the journal does with its version of the work. Again, a combined exclusive and non-exclusive licence would be akin to a "gold" rather than a "green" route to open access.

Meta-level Publishing

If the research community is determined to take back control of journal publishing, where does this leave the commercial publishers? In any production process, there is a value chain. The value chain in research journal publishing became clearly visible in an examination of a series of developments beginning in February 2008, when Canada's law schools engaged in a public quarrel with Reed Elsevier's LexisNexis Quicklaw legal service. Through spokesman Patrick Monahan, Osgoode Law School's dean, the law schools objected to the intention of Quicklaw to charge Canadian law schools $50 per student for access to the Quicklaw service ("Bar Talk"). This charge was to be levied notwithstanding that the database on which the Quicklaw service operates was developed by professors and students over the years.

In subsequent discussion (Patrick Monahan, personal communication, 5 Mar. 2008), it transpired that there was a parallel public service by the name of CanLII operated by the Federation of Law Societies of Canada. The opinion of the lawyers, subsequently confirmed by other lawyers, was that Quicklaw added so much value to its service that CanLII was not competitive for the use of lawyers in court cases. Nor was it very likely that CanLII had ambitions to attempt to compete. After this event and the revelation of how Quicklaw had been able to secure itself in the market, the activities of Reed Elsevier in another arena came to light. For years, the dominant indexer for scholarly journal publications has been Thomson Reuters' ISI Web of Knowledge, basically a citation index with numerous add-on features. The one element that is both a strength and a weakness is that ISI is selective in the journals it includes: most are science, few are SSH journals.

Reed Elsevier has decided to compete with ISI and has developed a competitive citation database called Scopus that it claims is "the largest abstract and citation database of research literature and quality web sources accessing 15,000 peer reviews journals and 33 million abstracts" (Scopus, n.d.). Here, again, Reed Elsevier is creating a value-added product to secure a marketplace position in meta-publishing.

A final initiative: In a presentation to the ELPUB 2008 conference, Anita de Waard, an employee-researcher of Elsevier Labs also appointed to the Department of Information and Computing Sciences at the University of Utrecht, talked about her research in codifying scientific research or, in her words, "establishing a new format for the scientific research article" (de Waard and Kircz 2008: 234). At the simplest level, it was a scheme for mining relevant data from scientific articles. In two areas, physics and computing science, she and her co-investigator had been working on the concept of modular documents, "content elements that can exist and be published independently" but "linked by meaningful relation" (ibid.). She also reported on an XML encyclopedia in pharmacology, a semantic data integration project, and the nature of rhetoric in biology. Two outstanding findings are sufficient to the purpose here. The first is that research articles do not report facts. Rather, they report "claims" and the consensus of the community determines their status as facts. Second, in scientific articles (in biology) there exists science and narrative, both necessary for the communication of research results. However, good science does not guarantee good narrative nor vice versa.

This research, combined with the development and implementation of Scopus, and the already existing dynamics of scholarly and research communication, including the vastness of the existing literature and its fast expansion, plot the future of commercial activity in research communication. Commercial publishers are well positioned to comply with the SCOAP^3 model of providing publishing services on a competitive basis. While maintaining a basic publishing service operation at normal profit levels rather than reaping excess profits, they can concentrate on developing value-added services that demand considerable investment, thereby minimizing competition, and features that will provide well-endowed researchers with competitive advantage. If they are consistent with their prior behaviour, they may even abandon the field of journal publishing to scholars and concentrate on the creation of value-added information products in academe and beyond, for which they will charge tidy sums.

Where does that leave open access and the role of researchers in the communication of research? The research community must also start planning to add its own value-added services if it does not want to end up like most primary producers who barely survive financially while others in the supply chain benefit handsomely.

14 Open Access Mandates and the Fair Dealing Button

ARTHUR SALE, MARC COUTURE, ELOY RODRIGUES, LESLIE CARR, AND STEVAN HARNAD

Introduction and Initial Motivation

Many disciplines have had a long history of distributing research findings by mail, even before the scholarly journal appeared. In a few fields, such as high-energy physics and computer science, preprints used to be systematically mailed to a set of collaborating universities even before refereeing and publication (Goldschmidt-Clermont 2002, Postel and Reynolds 1985). In these and many other disciplines, however, researchers would also mail a postcard to the author after publication to request a reprint of the published, refereed paper for research use. The author would then mail to the requester either a publisher-supplied reprint, or if such were unavailable, a photocopy of the published article or of its accepted final draft. This practice was commonplace and accepted, explicitly or tacitly, by the journal publishers. It is at least half a century old (Bratt 1937, Garfield 1972).

Starting in the early 1980s, as the Internet began to transform the world of scientific and scholarly communication, researchers turned to using email in place of mail for the same purpose. Copies were sent as eprints, saving time, printing costs, and postage. Soon, journals began to list their authors' email addresses to facilitate enquiries directed to the author. The scholarly community began to operate even more in a coordinated, collaborative fashion. With the growth of the Internet and of researchers' institutional home pages, and with them the mounting demand for free online access to refereed research, known as open access (OA), it became apparent that authors' institutional repositories (IRs) could make both requesting and providing eprints much easier and more efficient. The obvious and optimal option was for eprints to be deposited in their author's IR and immediately made open access, so that anyone on the Web could find and download them whenever they wished (Harnad 1995).

For articles published in the majority of journals, this soon became possible in principle, because their publishers had endorsed this OA self-archiving by their authors immediately upon publication (SHERPA RoMEO). The remaining journals, however, either endorsed only the self-archiving of the unrefereed preprint, or imposed an embargo of six months, twelve months, or more before their authors could make their refereed final drafts open access, or did not endorse OA self-archiving at all. Thus was born what would later be variously called the "request-a-copy" button, the "email eprint request" button, the "fair dealing" button, the "fair use" button, etc. The button appears on an IR page describing the metadata for a refereed article whose full text is deposited in the IR as closed access rather than open access. The button then makes it possible for would-be readers to request that the author email the eprint to them for individual research purposes under the provisions of fair dealing in the world's copyright acts.

History of the Development

The motivation for adding the button to the EPrints Institutional Repository software (Tansley and Harnad 2000, Sponsler and Van de Velde 2001) was to provide authors with an alternative way of providing access on an individual request basis, to papers that they had deposited in their IR as closed access rather than open access (Hitchcock 2006). In addition, the button was conceived as a further incentive for institutions and funders to adopt mandates requiring IR deposit of all refereed journal articles.

This statement needs explanation. Although authors could already have been making at least 63 per cent of their annual articles open access immediately upon publication with the publisher's approval, only 15 per cent were actually being deposited. Institutions and funders accordingly began adopting deposit mandates (see ROARMAP; Sale 2006a, 2006b, 2006c, 2006d), but because 37 per cent of journals did not endorse immediate OA self-archiving, the mandates (known as "delayed-deposit mandates") were weakened to allow deposit to be delayed as long as the publisher chose to embargo open access. Moreover, in the case of authors whose publishers could not be persuaded to accept an author addendum to the copyright agreement that would explicitly sanction OA self-archiving, these delayed-deposit mandates had to allow waivers whereby authors could opt out of depositing. It is here that the button is potentially useful and perhaps sees its greatest importance, for another kind of mandate is possible – the immediate deposit/optional access (IDOA) mandate (Harnad 2006), also called the "dual deposit/release strategy" (Suber 2006). The idea is that once all refereed final drafts, without exception, are being deposited in the author's or fundee's IR immediately upon acceptance, whether in closed access or open access, the button can immediately begin to allow users to request and authors to provide individual access to closed access papers.

The button also allows institutions and funders to strengthen author-addendum/opt-out mandates (such as Harvard's; see ROARMAP) that require the author to negotiate reuse rights with the publisher. Although it is true that an author addendum would retain authors' self-archiving rights as well as certain reuse rights, such mandates must always allow opt-out waivers by authors who are either unsuccessful in getting their publishers to adopt the author addendum or who do not elect to try. IDOA, in contrast, mandates immediate exception-free deposit regardless of whether the author opts out of negotiating the author addendum. Whatever its subsequent access fate, every born-digital object (the final accepted draft of an article) is captured by the institution in its records at the point in time that is the natural milestone in the author's workflow (official acceptance for publication), which is also the optimal time to begin providing access (Swan and Carr 2008). The button can then provide "almost open access" for closed access deposits under "fair dealing." For these reasons, the button was developed for the EPrints software in 2006 by one of the present co-authors (LC; Hitchcock 2006) and then replicated in DSpace by another co-author (ER; Rodrigues 2006).

How Does the Button Work?

As previously described, the button appears alongside the metadata of articles deposited as closed access (see Figure 14.1). Note that the following figures are simulated screenshots derived from a French-language Canadian repository running EPrints software (Archipel, at l'Université du Québec à Montréal).

If users click on the "request a copy" button (action 1), they see a form page that asks them to enter their email address (action 2) accompanied by a generic statement of the fair dealing conditions (in this example, according to Canadian copyright law; D'Agostino 2008) and a statement that the document is to be used according to these conditions. A click

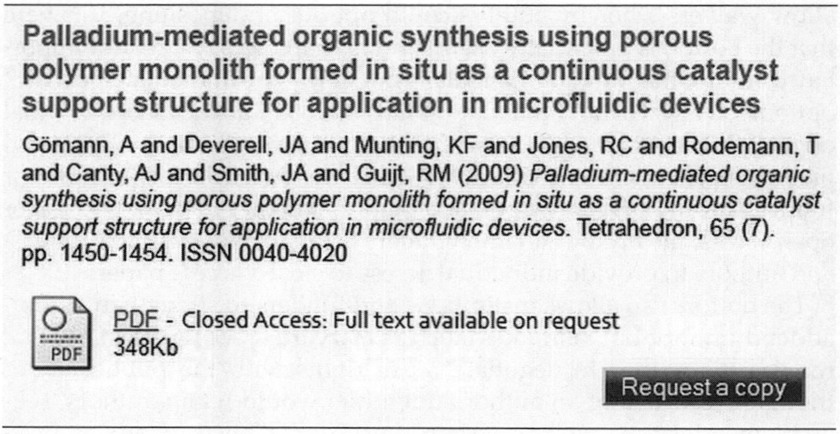

Figure 14.1. The fair dealing button as the viewer sees it.

on a second "request a copy" button (action 3) indicates assent and completes the transaction. Normally, a following page acknowledges the request (see Figure 14.2).

Behind the scenes, the repository looks up the depositing author of the article and sends an email requesting the author to authorize the release of an electronic copy to the requester. Note that the requester need never see or know the author's email address; nor does any crawler, thus reducing spam. The author receives the email and is presented with two one-click alternatives: approve the request or deny it. The author can also choose to ignore the email. If the author approves the request, an electronic copy of the article is automatically emailed to the person who requested it. If denied, a short email to that effect is sent.

A few implementation details have been glossed over in the above description, such as how to identify the responsible author, what happens when the author has left the university, and what happens when the work is in two or more parts. These are minor problems for the repository software and management to handle, not the person making the request or the approving author.

Legal and Policy Considerations

Copyright is a real concern among repository managers as well as researchers. Researchers are fearful of what they do not know, or do not

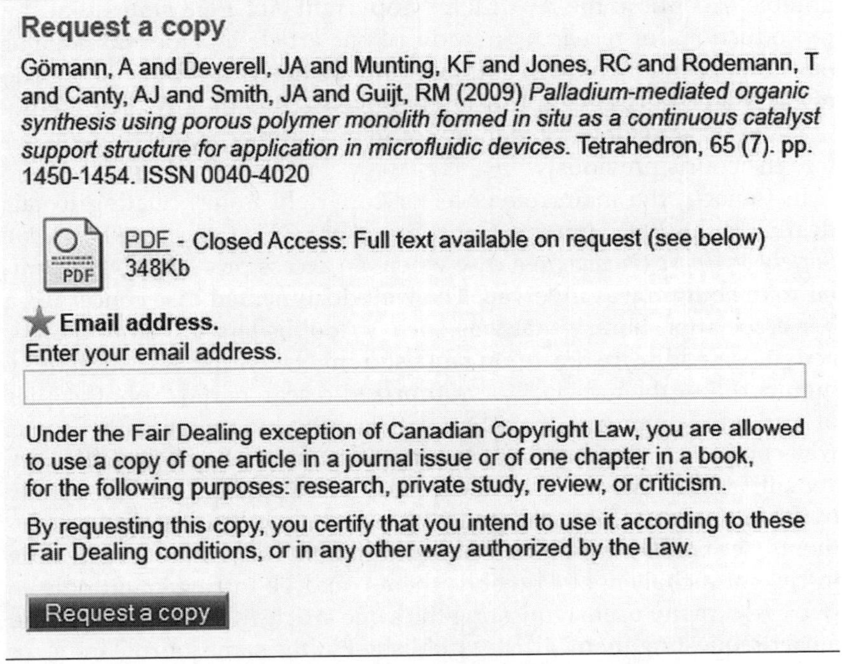

Figure 14.2. The request page as the viewer sees it.

understand. It is thus useful to clarify the legal status of the button and its uses. Closed access is usually chosen because the publisher, who has required the assignment of copyright or an exclusive licence, has invoked consequential rights to forbid self-archiving or to impose an embargo period. The policies of such publishers normally imply that sending even a single copy of the article is illegal unless explicitly authorized by the publisher.

What these policies usually do not mention is that the fair use and fair dealing provisions (or exceptions) of the various national copyright acts make this act legal if it satisfies certain criteria and if it is done for one of a few specific purposes, most of them common to all these jurisdictions: research, study, criticism, and news reporting. What must be realized, however, is that in all jurisdictions, fair use and fair dealing provisions are notoriously imprecise. In particular, legislators and courts have been reluctant to specify quantitative norms as to the amount of dealing that could maintain fairness. (Australia is a notable exception: the Australian Copyright Act 1968 states that the reproduction, for research or study, of one article in a journal issue or one chapter in a book will automatically be deemed fair dealing.) The result is a case-by-case approach that makes difficult any firm prediction about a situation not identical or highly similar to one brought before the courts previously.

In Canada, the main reference for copyright issues relating to fair dealing is the 2004 Supreme Court judgment *CCH Canadian Ltd.* v. *Law Society of Upper Canada*, in a case where an access procedure very similar to the button was involved. The well-documented case concerned a bar association library that was sued by publishers for, among other activities, sending by fax upon request from "lawyer[s], law student[s], member[s] of the judiciary or authorized researcher[s]," photocopies of various documents, including articles; the judgment, in this case, was completely favourable to the bar association. Replacing "fax" by "email," which is a very small step, one sees that the reported scarcity of the button's use, as compared with direct downloading of OA documents (see below), would be a strong argument in favour of fair dealing in case of a challenge. Arguably, there could be infringement only in two cases: many users requesting the same article in a short period, and a user requesting many articles published in the same journal issue, or many chapters in a single book (e.g., a collective work). An interesting statement, in the same Canadian Supreme Court judgment, is that "research must be given a large and liberal interpretation in order to ensure that users' rights are not unduly constrained, and is not limited to non-commercial or private contexts" (para. 51). Another relevant part of the judgment concerns the Bar Association Access Policy, which played an important role in the Court's decision. The policy enumerates the types of works and portion thereof that can be sent to requesters, and provides for an annual review process of potentially infringing requests. As the Court concluded, "The [library] Access Policy and its safeguards weigh in favour of finding that the dealings were fair … This policy provides reasonable safeguards that the materials are being used for the purpose of research and private study" (para. 66).

The first part of this policy suggests that it would be advisable for IR managers to (1) display clear statements on the IR website about what should – and shouldn't – be downloaded, both in the case of open access and closed access, and (2) to explain the risk of unfair use in the email-generating page associated with the button and in the emails themselves (see Figure 14.3).

From: Archipel [mailto:archipel-admin@uqam.ca]

Sent: 28 Jan. 2007 16:18

To: Gömann, Anissa

Subject: Archipel: Request for "Palladium-mediated organic synthesis using porous polymer monolith formed in situ as a continuous catalyst support structure for application in microfluidic devices"

This document has been requested by requester@someplace.ca for the purpose of research, private study, criticism or news reporting, or for another use allowed by the Law. Please can you respond.

Gömann, Anissa et al. (2009). Palladium-mediated organic synthesis using porous polymer monolith formed in situ as a continuous catalyst support structure for application in microfluidic devices. *Tetrahedron*, 65(7): 1450-1454.

<http://www.archipel.uqam.ca/00/>

Note. Accepting a large number of requests for the same document in a short period, or requests for more than one article in the same journal issue or more than one chapter in a book may result in copyright infringement.

Click here to send the requested document.

<http://www.archipel.uqam.ca/perl/users/respond_doc?eprintid=00&email=requester@someplace.ca&action=accept>

Click here to reject the request.

<http://www.archipel.uqam.ca/perl/users/respond_doc?eprintid=00&email=requester@someplace.ca&action=reject>

Archipel
http://www.archipel.uqam.ca
archipel-admin@uqam.ca

Figure 14.3. The authorization email sent to the author following a user request.

As to the second part of the policy, one could envision an automated monitoring of potentially unfair dealings. For example, one could try to detect an abnormally high rate of (accepted) requests for a single article. One could also try to detect successive requests, by the same user, of many articles in the same journal issue or many chapters in the same book. In both cases, the goal would not be to block these possibly infringing uses, but to inform or remind the author that acceptance of such requests could constitute an infringement of copyright. This is one lesson from the Canadian Supreme Court judgment, which overthrew the lower Court of Appeal decision in which fair dealing was not deemed proven because no one could guarantee that all the material provided was used in a "fair dealing manner." As the Supreme Court explained, it was not the Law Society's duty to prove that the requested materials were used according to the society's posted fair dealing practices.

The Immediate Deposit/Optional Access Mandate

The button is derived from the fair dealing provisions of the various copyright acts around the world and has long-standing publisher acceptance. It extends the capability of acquiring a copy of the closed access deposit even to researchers in disciplines where reprint requests were rare. Moreover, although in the terminology of the US National Information Standards Organization (NISO) the deposit is just the "accepted manuscript" rather than the "version of record" (VoR), this is a minor difference for users who would otherwise have no access at all. The bibliographical metadata of the canonical VoR are, in any case, available if the work needs to be cited.

The most important factor driving the implementation and spread of the button is the immediate-deposit/optional-access mandate. Previously, making the world's refereed research accessible entailed trying to persuade publishers to approve self-archiving of the author's accepted manuscript. It was assumed that deposit could only be mandated in cases formally approved by the publisher, because deposit was conflated with OA setting. With the button, deposit is separated from access setting, and the mandate only governs deposit and its timing. Institutions can require their authors to deposit all final drafts, without exception. The button allows authors to provide "almost open access" to articles on an individual request-by-request basis, so that for the would-be reader, almost open access is still free but involves a delay in receiving the eprint requested, and a risk that it might not be provided.

IDOA plus the button make the universal adoption of deposit mandates both legal and useful.

It is hard to overstate the potential importance of this simple practical technical development. Mandatory deposit of *all* accepted manuscripts can now be required by *all* universities, research centres, and grant-giving bodies worldwide. However, the implications of this new possibility have not yet been fully realized, let alone exploited. At the time of writing, only 101 institutional and departmental mandates and forty-two funder mandates have been registered with the global mandate directory ROARMAP.

The Mandatory Background

In the Web era, the optimal way for authors to make eprints of their published, peer-reviewed journal articles accessible is through their institutional repositories. For the authors of articles published in the 37 per cent of journals that have either not endorsed making such OA deposits, or have stipulated an embargo of six to twelve months or longer, IDOA still makes it possible to capture the author's born-digital accepted manuscript at the time of acceptance. A variety of options then open up.

First, it is now possible to enter an embargo expiry date in the repository at deposit time, after which the article automatically becomes open access without further intervention. This is efficient for both the author and the repository manager. Second, the button enables researchers worldwide to request the closed access articles. This "almost open access" preserves the central aim that the world's research should be open to any researcher, free of charge. What it lacks is immediacy and certainty, in that the copy is not delivered immediately, and there is also the possibility that an author might ignore the request, not approve it for some reason, or not receive it. For these reasons, use of the fair dealing button cannot be regarded as full open access, but it comes close.

The terms of existing OA mandates vary significantly. Some specify deposit in a subject repository, some in an institutional repository. Some insist that their contract with the researcher predates and limits any contracts that the researcher may make with a publisher and, hence, overrides all such later contracts. Some offer funding for upfront OA fees where they exist (e.g., some OA journals). The momentum for open access has altered the attitude and tactics of publishers: realizing that progress towards open access is unstoppable, many publishers have endorsed "green" OA self-archiving of the accepted manuscript by their authors. Some converted to OA publishing, making their own online version-of-record open access. Some also began to offer hybrid models. In a hybrid model, the journal is still toll-restricted to subscribers during an embargo period, but authors can buy immediate OA rights for their individual article for a fee. Regardless of the price and value of such a purchase, it illustrates that the scholarly publishing industry is in the middle of inexorable change and is adapting to the challenges of the Internet.

Although not all research is funded by grants, across all fields most research is produced by universities or research centres. This is why institutional mandates are even more important than funder mandates. Moreover, the optimal locus of deposit for both kinds of mandates is the author's own IR. The IRs are all compliant with the Open Access Initiative (OAI), and hence, interoperable. This means that harvesting and aggregating IR metadata for seamless joint search and retrieval is feasible; several examples of such central harvesters exist at the national level (Australian Research Online) and the global level (Citeseer, Base, and OAIster).

Take-up and Usage

Research on the fair dealing button is only just commencing, since it has not been in use for long. In what follows, it should be noted that common search engines return an OA full-text page as a higher-ranking item than its metadata page, so most views of OA items go to that page. Only if the item is closed access will the metadata page appear near the top of the ranking, where the viewer can see the button. However, in gateways like Base and OAIster, which harvest only metadata, the metadata page will be presented as the norm and the only version. The data summarized in Table 14.1 are from three IDOA-mandated institutions: the University of Southampton, the University of Stirling, and the Universidade do Minho. The approval success rate varies from 27 per cent to 60 per cent. Very few requests are actively denied. The majority of unapproved requests are probably due to non-receipt of the email or uncertainty regarding the legal status of the request; some repositories report author fatigue in dealing with requests to be a factor.

Putting the Button into Perspective

Given the significant number of button requests that are ignored or lost, one might be tempted to assume that it has not worked. However, this

Table 14.1 Responses to Requests in Three University-Based Repositories (%)

Author Responses	University of Southampton[a] (UK)	University of Stirling[b] (UK)	Universidade do Minho[c] (Portugal)
Approved	47	60	27
Ignored/ unanswered	53	37	72
Rejected/denied	< 1	3	1

[a] Aug. 2008 to Jan. 2010.
[b] Apr. 2009 to Jan. 2010.
[c] Jan. to Dec. 2009.

is not true. The principal impact of the button has been to enable the adoption of institutional IDOA mandates. Deposit is mandated immediately without legal constraints, with the button serving to assist authors interested in the dissemination of their articles. To put this into context, data from two universities with long-standing mandates are presented in Table 14.2, showing that the button applies to 5 per cent to 7 per cent of the deposited articles, but without it, all the other OA articles might be missing.

Summary

The fair dealing button has facilitated the adoption of immediate deposit/optional access mandates around the world, and in this it has had a sizeable impact. The growth in these mandates creates the climate for universal open access for all researchers, something that all researchers want for their own publications. That is why they give the rights in their articles away for free in the first place (Lawrence 2001; Swan 2006; Harnad et al. 2008, 2009; Hitchcock 2010). Even more importantly, IDOA mandates coupled with the button take the publisher completely out of the loop insofar as the adoption of and compliance with a deposit mandate is concerned: publishers have no say over whether or when a deposit is made in an institutional database; they only have a say in whether or when the deposit is made open access or closed access, possibly embargoed until a designated date.

The IDOA mandate and the button divide and conquer. All hesitations about whether and when a university, research centre, or funder can mandate deposit itself are rendered irrelevant. The button provides "almost open access" for embargoed content, and also for permanently

Table 14.2 Closed Access in Two University Repositories

Articles	University of Southampton[a] (UK)	Universidade do Minho (Portugal)
Total	7,864	7,515
Closed access	551 (7%)	353 (5%)

[a] Since 2001.

closed access content. Immediate deposit can be universally mandated by all funders, all universities, and all research centres: there is no remaining need to worry about the legality of adopting a mandate at all, nor any need to allow opt-outs, waivers, or delayed deposit, because obligatory deposit is separated from the optional OA setting, with the fair dealing button bridging the gap for those who cannot provide open access immediately. Researchers from all disciplines can be confident that the couple of clicks required to give a fellow researcher access to their closed access article is legal – and fair.

15 The Evolution of Cultural Heritage Ethics via Human Rights Norms

ROSEMARY J. COOMBE AND NICOLE AYLWIN

The rights of peoples with respect to cultural heritage goods pose new and pressing challenges in terms of balancing the exercise of intellectual properties with individual freedoms of creativity, collective rights, and international human rights obligations. Digital technologies heighten anxieties around cultural appropriation because they enable the reproduction and publication of cultural forms at unprecedented speeds (Burri-Nenova 2008). If, as Michael Brown (2005) argues, digitization has accelerated the social decontextualization of cultural objects, it has also increased awareness of the exploitation of cultural heritage resources. Digitization has further enhanced political consciousness about the injuries these practices may effect, while fostering new initiatives for managing and sharing cultural heritage resources in a politically sensitive manner (Coombe 2009). Digital communications also afford new opportunities for communities to benefit from new uses for traditional cultural expressions that promote sustainable development (Antons 2008; Burri-Nenova 2008, 2009; Sahlfeld 2008).

In light of the increased spread and availability of digital technology, issues of cultural appropriation have received new scrutiny. The tendency to treat all cultural forms in digital media ecology as mere "information" enables everyone to access and make use of cultural goods – assuming we overlook the "digital divide." Nonetheless, it is important to recognize that when creativity involves a practice described as appropriation, an assertion is being made that a text has been moved or removed from its authorizing context, or that it has, in some other significant sense, been taken (Meurer and Coombe 2009). In some cases, this decontextualization may be deliberately and critically intended – to challenge the fields of meanings in which the object properly figures, to assert an alternative ownership over it, and/or to consider the importance of other realms of connotation in which it might signify. Other allegations of appropriation may occur when a cultural text is understood to have been *improperly* recontextualized to the harm of those who have serious attachments to its positioning in specific worlds of social meaning. In this chapter, we deal primarily with those forms of appropriation that effect injury to groups, primarily because of the power relations at work in digital environments that enable old inequities to be perpetuated in new ways.

As a representative example of this latter type of appropriation, anthropologist Steven Feld (2004) traces the sampling of a Solomon Islands Baegu lullaby by world music producers who earned handsome profits from their derivative work without compensating the singer or her community. Such appropriations are enabled by legal interpretations of oral tradition that invisibly transform the status of "signifying that which is vocally communal to signifying that which belongs to no one in particular" (74). Unless we know more about the social and cultural significance of such songs, however, we cannot deem such appropriations to be harmful nor characterize such takings as unethical. The status of ethno-musicological recordings as informational goods is also questioned by Coleman and Coombe (2009), who, as a moral philosopher and legal theorist, respectively, demonstrate that in certain Indigenous societies, music fulfils functions beyond those of expression or entertainment, and serves performatively – as a legal mechanism to transfer property rights and responsibilities. The categorization of such recordings as informational goods ignores the customary legal functions of the songs they register to the potential injury of a community and may even potentially affect the legal recognition of its territories. Both the "free sampling" of these recordings and restrictions of access to the work of a people's ancestors – by virtue of intellectual property (IP) protections held in the recordings themselves – serve to perpetuate histories of colonial subjection, in which Indigenous culture was both targeted for eradication in community life and "salvaged" for the edification (and enrichment) of others. These studies suggest that both global IP regimes *and* the prevailing ethos and ethics of a universal digital cultural commons may provide insufficient recognition for community rights and interests.

Most of the essays in this volume assume that we need to understand the digital use of cultural goods – including protected intellectual property – as creative activity that actively produces our cultural heritage. Rather than the passive appreciation of a field of static works, then, cultural heritage is the result of a dynamic, expressive, and productive practice of dialogue. This approach is consonant with an international movement to revalue cultural diversity and reconceptualize heritage values. However, this global revaluation of heritage also situates such cultural activities in the normative field of human rights. This has a number of implications for our ethical orientations when we share cultural forms in digital environments. When we consider our cultural activities with the copyright-protected goods of others as a matter of cultural rights, new freedoms come into view, but so do new responsibilities. In other words, although access and participation rights have become a major part of contemporary rhetoric about expressive liberties, we also need to acknowledge the necessity of respect for the cultural properties and heritage interests of others.

Cultural Heritage and Human Rights: New Relationships and Challenges

Cultural rights have authoritative origins in the 1948 United Nations Declaration of Human Rights (Silverman and Ruggles 2007, Arzipe 2010), specifically in Article 27, which specifies both that (1) "everyone has the right freely to participate in the cultural life of the community, to enjoy the arts and to share in scientific advancement and its benefits," and that (2) "everyone has the right to the protection of the moral and material interests resulting from any scientific, literary or artistic production of which he is the author." The text simultaneously recognizes both individual rights to participate in the cultural life of a community and private rights to benefit from the creation of cultural goods, which means that proprietary rights that wholly exclude others from all use of works would rarely qualify. As a human right, an author's material and moral interests carry weight. However, corporate exercises of IP rights that wholly prohibit the use of cultural objects – and, therefore, prevent cultural expression, participation, and the public enjoyment of the arts – do not. Digital technologies clearly enable new forms of access to cultural works and participation in cultural life, so exercises of intellectual property that constitute the simple trumping and trampling of those rights in the name of corporate profit should have little normative purchase. Cultural rights also address the interests and needs of collectivities, particularly minority groups and Indigenous peoples, whose rights with respect to cultural goods bear a distinctive relationship to their dignity, autonomy, and potential self-determination.

Contemporary debates about the extension of IP rights and the endangerment of the public domain, however, have largely ignored questions of cultural rights (Coombe 2005, 2006). Perhaps this is because the most publicized IP activists operate within US legal traditions, where the cure for ever-greater expansion of copyright monopolies is a combination of a robust jurisprudence of "fair use" and strong constitutional protection for freedom of speech. At the same time, they rightly lament the lack of certainty that such principles provide to the average user of cultural works (e.g., Boyle 1996, 2008; Lessig 2001, 2004; McLeod 2001, 2007; Vaidhyanathan 2001, 2004). It should be clear that in Canada we lack this strong jurisprudential foundation, along with any legitimated recognition of the constitutional dimensions and limits to copyright (Amani, this volume; Reynolds 2006). We do, however, have distinct international obligations to respect social, economic, and cultural rights, to which we give, at least nominally, greater allegiance than does our southern neighbour. The International Covenant on Social, Economic, and Cultural Rights, for example, alludes to rights of intellectual property as means to serve specific ends (protecting an author's moral and material interests), and arguably IP should be so limited. Moreover, as human rights, intellectual properties should be governed by the overarching human rights obligation to identify and take specific measures to improve the position of the most vulnerable and disadvantaged groups in society.

The assumption that there is or should be a singular or unitary public domain of cultural materials does not acknowledge the interests of ethnic minorities and Indigenous peoples and their distinctive histories (Hardison 2006, Graham and McJohn 2005, Brown 2003). These include long periods of forced assimilation, prohibitions on Indigenous cultural practices, and the appropriation of cultural forms by majority groups under situations of internal colonialism, where heritage may be the basis of group identity and an integral resource for the continued survival of a people and their self-determination. Indigenous heritage has often been seen as de facto public domain material (Nicholas, this volume); appropriations are often justified by enduring colonial narratives that place Indigenous culture in the past with little regard for its importance as "living culture" (Aylwin, this volume). But, as Bowrey and Anderson (2009) argue, the assertion of a cultural commons is a political act that serves particular interests and ignores others, leaving existing relations of power intact and ignoring the disparate means that groups have to represent themselves in public fora.

Movements to enhance human rights have been instrumental in opening up spaces for non-state actors such as NGOs and advocacy groups to draw attention to the plight of Indigenous peoples, questioning the modern relationship between the state and the individual as the primary vector of rights violations and providing new opportunities to acknowledge social collectivities as rights-bearing subjects (Anaya 2004). Two major international human rights covenants, the International Labour Organization Convention No. 169, adopted in 1989, and the 2007 Declaration of the Rights of Indigenous Peoples, for example, reiterate as principles of international human rights that Indigenous communities have some measure of control over their cultural heritage (Ahmed, Aylwin, and Coombe 2009).

International human rights norms demand a special sensitivity to the rights of minorities and Indigenous peoples, whose cultural rights have often been violated through a long history of sanctioned state initiatives designed to forcibly assimilate minorities and to catalogue their allegedly "dying" cultures (Nicholas, this volume). Recently, however, international policy has recognized that Indigenous and minority heritages are not remainders of the past, but dynamic and ongoing reservoirs of knowledge, practices, innovations, and expressions invaluable for maintaining the interlinked goods of cultural and biological diversity while providing the basis for sustainable development. The World Intellectual Property Organization (WIPO), for example, has accepted the need to reach out to "new beneficiaries" and acknowledged the need to find new means to recognize, maintain, and protect traditional cultural expressions (TCEs) if the global IP system is to retain legitimacy (Graber and Burri-Nenova 2008). Although rarely framed as such, these efforts involve the elaboration of cultural rights principles.

Many of WIPO's draft legislative provisions (the Provisions) for the protection of TCEs – internationally negotiated over the past decade – are designed to recognize that the cultural heritage of Indigenous peoples and other cultural communities has inherent value, and provides people with culturally meaningful resources that can be used to meet community social needs and promote development guided by community aspirations. They aim to prevent misappropriations and misuse of heritage that might damage the integrity of community identity:

> Protection should respond to the traditional character of TCEs/EoF [expressions of folklore], namely their collective, communal and inter-generational character; their relationship to a community's cultural and social identity and integrity, beliefs, spirituality and values; their often being vehicles for religious and cultural expression; and their constantly evolving character within a community. (WIPO 2010)

The Provisions draw upon legal principles such as copyright, moral rights, performance rights, unfair competition, trademark, certification and collective marks, fiduciary obligation, and the prevention of consumer confusion; they are balanced by familiar IP exemptions. Some dimensions of these new proposals to provide protection for TCEs outline exclusive rights that may allow communities to use their TCEs as the basis of economic development strategies (Art. 2, Art. 4). They also provide means to insist upon fair compensation and recognition of source and/or to insist that researchers and corporations follow local customary protocols (Art. 4). In some limited instances, communities are enabled to prevent the use of especially significant TCEs by others who may use them in ways that are contrary to a community's aspirations and cultural identity (Art. 3). Ultimately, the guiding principles of the Provisions rest on a renewed valuation of cultural distinction; they are designed to promote respect for traditional cultures and the intergenerational character of heritage (Coombe 2009). This may be read as an indication that WIPO is gaining awareness that IP rights need to be shaped in such a way that they respect the principles of cultural rights enshrined in the international human rights framework.

These developments should not be interpreted to suggest that Indigenous peoples have no interest in sharing their knowledge, or that the concept of the commons is necessarily alien to their needs. Indeed, there have been various initiatives to create commons of traditional knowledge as well as proposals for using open source (OS) software models to manage traditional knowledge. As early as 2005, it was suggested that despite their seemingly disparate interests, open knowledge advocates and traditional knowledge rights advocates might both agree on the need for a "some rights reserved" model for sharing cultural materials in digital environments (Kansa et al. 2005), in order to prevent undesirable forms of unfair exploitation that might detract from community abilities to share resources in the future. Building upon the voluntary licensing tools pioneered by the Creative Commons (CC), originating communities could impose their own restrictions on how cultural content was used. In this way, it might be possible to avoid both exclusive private rights and a universalizing public domain that fails to consider local needs and values:

> As Creative Commons has demonstrated, enhancing communication requires recognition of the motivations and interests of content creators. By extension, recognition of the motivation and interests of researchers and members of indigenous communities must be a priority. In the case of traditional knowledge and field sciences, we must similarly explore how to facilitate negotiations that reconcile the needs and interests of all the diverse stakeholders. It is only by considering these diverse perspectives and interests that we can hope to build communication frameworks that encourage both greater respect for multiple claims of ownership and enhanced openness, sharing, and creative use of information. (Kansa et al. 2005: 292)

Recently, for example, a group of elders, traditional knowledge practitioners, and legal activists met in South Africa to devise the principles of a Traditional Knowledge Commons (that drew upon values expressed by traditional healers in Rajasthan) and to develop a biocultural community protocol to govern access to traditional knowledge. Such protocols are charters "developed as a result of a consultative process within a community that outlines the community's core cultural and spiritual values and customary laws relating to their traditional knowledge and resources" (Abrell 2010: 7). They outline terms and conditions of access and are "used to emphasize the central importance of the interdependence of traditional knowledge, biodiversity, land, cultural values and customary laws to the holistic worldview of many indigenous communities" (7).

Recognizing that many Indigenous and local communities conceptualize their relationships to their knowledge and heritage as involving not only rights but also customary responsibilities and obligations to peoples, territories, and ecosystems, activists argue that any mechanisms to "protect" knowledge or to share it must take customary law into account as a fundamental matter of human rights (8). A Traditional Knowledge Commons based on the online use of general public licences for non-commercial use of knowledge and cultural expressions has also been proposed by indigenist advocates as a means of creating a more sustainable knowledge commons based on conditions of mutual recognition and respect (Christen 2012).

Digital communications will not fulfil *all* needs for knowledge transfer and exchange between communities. From a cultural rights perspective, it might be just as valuable to enable and support cross-cultural exchanges that enable traditional healers to share their knowledge as it might be to build online databases, especially given the tacit, embodied, and sociological dimensions of much traditional medicinal knowledge. Still, the endeavour to imagine new means for practitioners of traditional knowledge to communicate and exchange information online in a fashion that respects and communicates their values has produced many initiatives. The Honey Bee Network, for example, involves documenting agricultural innovations and traditional practices among communities in seventy-five countries, in order to enable local communities to share their knowledge for the enhancement of community security and sustainable development (http://www.sristi.org/hbnew/index.php). Such initiatives are concomitant with new valuations of cultural heritage and evolving legal recognitions of cultural rights.

Cultural Rights and Heritage Interests

The management of cultural heritage properties is one area in which cultural rights are increasingly recognized in practice. Canada has historically played a key role in the work of UNESCO – the UN body responsible for preparing and interpreting international normative principles and instruments with regard to cultural heritage – and has recently ratified the International Convention on the Protection and Promotion of the Diversity of Cultural Expressions, which links the management of cultural heritage to respect for cultural difference and the promotion of diversity (Aylwin, this volume). During the 1980s, international debates about the meaning and value of cultural heritage were positioned within larger deliberations about the relationship between culture and development. In 1987, the United Nations launched its World Decade for Cultural Development (1987–1997), adopting a more anthropological view of culture as a way of life and a form of social organization (Blake 2009: 48). This new definition reinforced the idea that cultural heritage could not be restricted to historical sites and monuments, but also needed to include oral tradition and expressive culture (Blake 2009). In 1995, at the UNESCO General Conference, the World Commission on Culture and Development solidified this new perspective in its report *Our Creative Diversity*, by highlighting that heritage is made up of more than monuments and historical sites, and that both tangible and intangible cultural heritage are key to "ensuring the flourishing of human existence" (Arzipe 2010: 32).

Claims to heritage have since become central to the collective struggles of many marginalized peoples, who see culture as a concept to be used reflexively when engaging with state institutions or non-governmental organizations. The purposes of this reflexive use include asserting identity, demanding greater inclusion in political life, local autonomy, and control over resources, and also enabling the search for new forms of engagement with (and resistance to) global markets (Coombe 2009). Cultural distinction has gained new international purchase as a valuable social, political, and economic resource (Yúdice 2003, Rao and Walton 2004, Comaroff and Comaroff 2009). As marginalized communities attempt to regain control over their cultural heritage, cultural rights have been vehicles for the pursuit of political claims. Cultural claims now figure in struggles for political autonomy, legal entitlements to territory and other resources, and designs for alternative forms of development (Coombe 2011a, 2011b; Marrie 2009; Robbins and Stamatopolou 2004).

Claims by groups that seek the acknowledgment of their cultural distinction have too often been characterized as an expression of an inherent or universal need for recognition. This has the effect of siphoning off the political context in which such claims are made, and separates them from the more pressing economic disadvantages that marginalized peoples often face (Holder 2008, Fraser 2000). Conceiving of struggles over the recognition of difference narrowly, as a form of mere identity politics, may have the effect of minimizing political and economic interests that may be central to them, such as the assertion of self-determination and the redistribution of material resources (Jung 2003, 2008).

New forms of cultural heritage preservation are being negotiated to meet political and economic needs. Archaeologists, cultural resource managers, and museum curators, among others, have come to understand that the management of heritage is crucial to contemporary political movements of decolonization that redefine relationships between the modern state and resident minorities (Coombe 2009: 399). New and creative uses of intellectual properties, particularly in the area of digital heritage management, have allowed Indigenous groups to limit inappropriate use of heritage while building goodwill between various stakeholders. One such project is the Mukurtu Archive, an archiving tool that uses OS software designed by an Indigenous community to dictate how their cultural goods are circulated, accessed, and viewed, based on rules consistent with their own customary cultural protocols (Christen 2012, n.d.). In similar fashion, the Indigenous Knowledge and Resource Management in Northern Australia project created a digital Indigenous knowledge archive that gave Indigenous researchers the primary role in developing protocols for database structures. As Verran (2009) suggests, this meant that Indigenous property rights were protected in a way that facilitated intergenerational transmission of knowledge, relinking people and places, clans and territories, a process crucial to Indigenous territorial entitlement and political self-determination.

Canada is no stranger to efforts of rethinking cultural heritage management with the goal of giving effect to cultural rights principles. The country boasts a progressive museum movement that recognizes the needs of diverse communities, is sensitive to the politics of multiculturalism, and promotes intercultural dialogue (Houtman 2009). The University of British Columbia's Museum of Anthropology, for example, is a world leader in collaborative practices. Its former director, Michael Ames, critiqued traditional museum practices and called "for their democratization in favour of the under-represented people of the world," championing the rights of all peoples to tell their stories and curate their own exhibitions (Mayer and Shelton 2010: 11). It is now widely acknowledged that the museum is "a performative space in which to develop new practices that meet the ethical, political and representational challenges posed by pluralism" (Phillips 2005: 89). To further this recognition, from 2005 to 2010 the Museum undertook a massive restructuring of its institutional, space, and presentation policies in order to better recognize Indigenous stakeholders and the continuing rights of descendant communities with respect to the cultural materials held in the Museum's collections. In the *Management of Culturally Sensitive Material* policy statement, the Museum affirms its commitment to the values and beliefs of the cultures it represents:

> We know that our collections contain items which are important to the originating communities, and whose placement and care within the museum continue to affect the values and beliefs of those communities. The museum recognizes that these objects have a non-material side embodying cultural rights, values, knowledge, and ideas which are not owned or possessed by the museum, but are retained by the originating communities. (Cited in Laszlo 2006: 304)

Digital communications enable museums to give greater effect to rights principles. Museum restructuring has included the development of the Reciprocal Research Network, an online research community that allows geographically dispersed users, including international museums holding Northwest Coast collections, and First Nation elders, artists, families, and researchers to share knowledge about the history and significance of cultural artefacts as research partners (Rowley et al. 2010). They hope that respect for cultural heritage rights will be achieved by new and potentially more intercultural and dialogic strategies in a digitally connected world. For the first time, through activities that Houtman (2009) has described as "virtual repatriation," communities striving to reclaim lost cultural histories and families tracing their ancestry have access to cultural heritage held in distant museums (12). Moreover, museum archives are attempting to develop new protocols that balance the competing needs of different members of the public, recognizing that users and those peoples represented in the holdings may have distinctive interests:

> Many of the ethnographic materials we house are considered by First Nations communities to be cultural property and to contain cultural copyrights that are retained by the peoples depicted. The case of images that portray ceremonial rituals and objects that are not intended to be seen by the uninitiated provides a good place to illustrate a number of the points under discussion and to begin to look at practical steps that the Museum of Anthropology archives has taken to improve the way it administers ethnographic records. We have consulted with First Nations groups about which of our records contain culturally sensitive images. Thumbnails of those images have subsequently been removed from our finding aids, with a note indicating what was removed and why. For the time being these images are restricted to all but members of the communities depicted. Currently, we have no protocols in place to handle requests from others to view these restricted images, but are in the process of setting up partnerships with communities to determine answers to questions of access and control of this type of material. (Laszlo 2006: 305)

The use of the term "cultural copyright" by this museum administration suggests that the logic of *both* IP and cultural rights now informs archivists' understanding of the collective heritage interests of stakeholder groups. Although archivists might be expected to encourage and promote the greatest possible use of the records in their care, they are also required to give attention to issues of privacy, confidentiality, and preservation, mandates that have been interpreted to accommodate the cultural and spiritual concerns of groups for whom certain cultural materials have historical significance as markers of their identity as a people. This is not to restrict access to materials simply because some groups might find them offensive, but rather to restrict only the circulation of images that have important sacred and ritual properties to specific communities, a process that will involve continual dialogue and collaboration.

In projects such as these museum initiatives, new forms of negotiated proprietary claims and relationships contribute to an emerging form of cultural rights dialogue. International instruments addressing the rights of Indigenous peoples – the most significant of which is the Declaration on the Rights of Indigenous Peoples (the Declaration) – have fundamentally altered the international consensus on the scope and meaning of cultural rights (Holder 2008). Prior to the negotiation of the Declaration (a 20-year process), international law largely objectified culture. Cultural rights protected heritage practices and cultural identifications only to the extent that these could be fixed as static symbols subject to state cultural recognition. This served to emphasize rights of access, preservation, and use (17), rather than material domains where communities have authority and political voice (12). As culture has come to be regarded as an activity and resource, however, its political and economic dimensions have come to the fore, putting new emphasis on community security, economic stability, and sustainable development. More and more, cultural rights claims have enabled groups to achieve control over significant material resources (Robbins and Stamatopolou 2004) and have heightened their stakes in fields of cultural representation.

Cultural rights now are broadly conceived to incorporate protections for minority communities, and to enable them to develop their capacities to engage with their cultural heritage in meaningful ways. Their recognition has prompted new forms of respectful, mutually beneficial negotiation between parties. New technologies make access to and the sharing of intangible heritage virtually effortless, but the dialogue and deliberations necessary to use digitalization to achieve greater respect and recognition between communities, and a more equitable share of political and economic benefits, are still works in progress.

16 Indigenous Cultural Heritage in the Age of Technological Reproducibility: Towards a Postcolonial Ethic of the Public Domain

GEORGE NICHOLAS

In *The Past Is a Foreign Country* (1985), David Lowenthal explored the degree to which objects, architectural motifs, and other manifestations of the past permeate the present. He concluded that contemporary Western society – from clothing styles to architecture to art and literature – is largely composed of elements derived from other times and places. Our access to cultures, both foreign and ancient, is the culmination of centuries of archaeological and historical inquiry, now facilitated by the ease of worldwide travel and electronic communication; never before has there been such ease of access to world cultural heritage.

The idea that we are the product of everything and everyone that has come before us fuels the notion that society does (and, indeed, should) benefit from mutually shared ideas and information, a position promoted by the open access (OA) and access to knowledge (A2K) movements, and by individual scholars (e.g., Boyle 1996, Lessig 2001, Young 2008). New reproductive technologies and cultural borrowing have inspired creativity, such as perpetuating ancient stories through new media (e.g., the retelling of Homer's *Iliad* in the 2000 film *O Brother, Where Art Thou?*) or the development of new music genres (e.g., David Byrne and Brian Eno's use of sampled voices in their 1981 *My Life in the Bush of Ghosts*). Yet, the benefits to society of such creativity are tempered by the need to reward the efforts of those whose research or creative efforts have produced new products. In Western law, protection of intellectual property is based on property values and "rights," ownership is based on individual rights, and infringement results in economic loss. Protection is available through such means as copyrights, patents, trademarks, and trade secrecy law. Each protects very specific types of intellectual property. Generally, the legal protection these afford the products of creativity is limited to a set number of years, subject to renewal, after which the work becomes part of the public domain, where it can prompt new opportunities for creativity. The result is a set of laws and social norms that seek to protect the best interests of society.

Within a cross-cultural context, this situation changes appreciably. Western society has for centuries turned to the cultural heritage of Indigenous peoples worldwide as a source for inspiration for stories, art, architecture, and such. This is certainly evident across North America, where traces of the first peoples of the land can be found in tribal names for sports teams, rock art designs on clothing, and use of sweat lodges in New Age religious practices, to name but three examples (for a more comprehensive list, see Brown 2003). Often, these borrowings are justified as an appreciation of the great "vanished race," or by the assumption that such things are "of the past" and, therefore, fall within the public domain. For First Nations peoples, however, these appropriations of their heritage amount to the unauthorized use of items and expressions that are still important within their culture.

In this essay, I challenge the notion of Indigenous heritage as being de facto public domain, identify some of the harms or costs that inappropriate use of their heritage has on First Nations and other Indigenous peoples, and then discuss the need for developing a postcolonial research ethic that will facilitate or encourage fair dealing in digital realms as well as more broadly. I illustrate the latter through a Canadian-based international research effort, the Intellectual Property Issues in Cultural Heritage (IPinCH) Project.

Why Indigenous Heritage Is Not Public Domain

In Canada and the United States, it takes very little effort to find things Aboriginal. Images, place names, traditional designs and art, words and phrases, music, religious practices, traditional knowledge, and other elements of Indigenous cultural traditions are found virtually everywhere. Western society has become a voracious consumer of First Nations culture: images of supernatural beings have been transformed into posters, tea towels, and refrigerator magnets; the *inukshuk* (standing stone figures) of the Arctic have become the logo of the 2010 Olympics; and baskets, blankets, masks, and other items fetch astounding prices at auction.

Representations of Native Americans (both of the north and of the south) and of other vestiges of their culture have been ubiquitous in

North America for a very long time. Already in the seventeenth century, Europeans were becoming familiar with the peoples of eastern North America through the drawings of John White. In the nineteenth century, drawings gave way to paintings and photographs. In Canada, the paintings of Emily Carr, influenced by Picasso, Matisse, and the European Primitivism movement, popularized the totem poles, masks, and other elements of the Kwakwaka'wakw (Kwakiutl) culture. Soon after motion pictures became popular, Curtis' film of the Kwakiutl, *In the Land of the Head Hunters* (1914, retitled *In the Land of the War Canoes* in 1974), and Robert Flaherty's *Nanook of the North* (1922), both set in Canada, turned film viewers into surrogate ethnographers, veiling the fact that both films were highly subjective portrayals of Native societies that had been artificially restored, for the purpose of filming, to their "pristine"' (i.e., pre-Contact) state. Ultimately, it was Hollywood films that solidified, perhaps more than any other medium, the image of Native Americans in the public's mind.

Both the audience for and influence of these images has increased with each technological advance in information exchange. From newspaper accounts and early sketches to mainstream cinema and the Internet, access to images and information about Native Americans has risen exponentially in the past five hundred years, to the point where it is so embedded in Western culture as to be treated as public domain. Since this interest focuses on Native American cultures as they were – or at least as they were imagined to be – in the past, they further separate First Nations from their culture.

Viewing cultural heritage as something "of the past" is problematic for several reasons. First, it often reduces heritage to the level of "quaintness," and turns respect into curiosity or academic interest. Second, considering cultural heritage as "part of the land," not "of a people" separates living descendant communities from their past, which, in turn, becomes national patrimony. Thus, the 2010 Winter Olympics turned the *inukshuk* into a symbol of all of Canada, rather than of the Inuit. The failure of Canada to recognize heritage as "living culture" (see also Aylwin, this volume), has, arguably, contributed to the idea that Indigenous heritage is part of a Canadian public domain.

What's the Harm?

Without question, cultural borrowings may enrich people's lives, as they are generally educational and illuminate the diversity of human lifeways; they can be playful (such as the B-52s' use of ethnographic film clips in the music video *Roam*), and, occasionally, very creative, such as Aboriginal artist Brian Jungen's transformation of Nike basketball shoes into Northwest Coast masks (see Jungen and Augaitis 2005), or the retelling of traditional Indonesian stories through *wayang kulit* (shadow puppets) using new media (Norcott 2010). So why, then, are Indigenous peoples and other descendant groups concerned about how their cultural heritage is used by others?

Cultural heritage consists of both tangible and intangible elements, of ideas and their material expressions. In Western society, these are considered separately; in fact, Western society is filled with many dichotomies (such as male/female, nature/culture, natural/supernatural, and so on) that neatly categorize the world and everything in it. In addition, the passage of time is here viewed as linear. Many Indigenous societies, however, may function differently. There may be more than two genders; time may be viewed as cyclical; and there may be no perceived distinction between the tangible and intangible elements of cultural heritage. Thus, many Indigenous peoples perceive their world as one in which material objects are more than just things, and in which ancestral spirits are part of *this* existence, rather than of some other realm.

These differences have profound implications that go far towards explaining the intense concerns of First Nations peoples facing the seemingly trivial appropriation and commodification of elements of their culture. Thus, archaeological sites may not only be places where artefacts of ancient activities are found, but where ancestral beings still reside. The same holds true, for example, for carved stone bowls and figurines found in British Columbia, which are treated by some First Nations communities as actual beings, rather than representations (e.g., the remains of *T'xwelats*, an ancient shaman turned to stone, was repatriated to the Sto:lo Nation in 2006). Likewise, pictographs (paintings on rock surfaces) are not simply historical documents to be studied or appreciated for their anthropological or artistic values, but reflections of a possibly still active world view and spiritual interactions. Indeed, First Nations peoples often express concern for the well-being of archaeologists, because they may be encountering formidable, sometimes dangerous powers. Clearly, to then have the images of rock art or stone figurines used in advertisements, wine bottle labels, or t-shirt designs may be troublesome.

With this in mind, it is evident that fundamental cultural differences between Western and Indigenous societies persist even after centuries of colonial impact. As is illustrated in recent Indigenous resistance to the public domain and in some of the newer legal literature on public domain and commons, these differences are often manifest in notions of property (see Belder 2007, Bowrey and Anderson 2009, Graham and McJohn 2005, and Hardison 2006). Within First Nations societies, there may be no distinction between tangible cultural property and intellectual property (IP). Protection of Indigenous property is situated in customary law and culture, and it is based on social relations and responsibilities: ownership of information or objects may be communal. Infringement of property rights may result in cultural, spiritual, and economic loss (for details, see Nicholas and Hollowell 2007).

Technological Reproducibility

New technologies may further increase threats to traditional knowledge and intellectual property, especially by providing access to images and information from places never visited. Rock art is one example. Images painted of ochre or pecked into the rock surface are expressions of belief systems or other aspects of ancient cultural systems and knowledge. Originally, they could be viewed in only one place, often a location endowed with special qualities, and frequently geographically isolated or inaccessible to the uninitiated. With the advent of photography, however, the images are not only removed from their original geographical and cultural contexts, thereby destroying their uniqueness (see Berger 1972: 19), but also made available to the general public; see Hollowell and Nicholas (2008) for a discussion of this breach of privacy.

In his seminal essay, "The Work of Art in the Age of Mechanical Reproduction" (1936), Walter Benjamin explored the transformation of art by photography, and anticipated some of the challenges we today face as it becomes increasingly easier not only to access and share information, images, and music, but also to manipulate or reconfigure them. New technologies create artistic freedom while also creating new challenges to the meaning and, indeed, ownership of things.

The ability to reproduce objects that Indigenous peoples (or members of other descendant communities) still consider their property or otherwise important to them, significantly increases opportunities for cultural appropriation and commodification. Even after IP issues are sorted out in one realm (e.g., photocopying, music downloads), they thus emerge elsewhere as a result of new media (e.g., podcasts), new technologies (e.g., 3-D printers), and previously unanticipated uses (e.g., see Graber and Burri-Nenova 2008, Gosseries et al. 2008, Luong 2010). A considerable lag between concerns raised and solutions enacted is the result, and Indigenous peoples generally have much fewer means of recourse when their cultural heritage is being appropriated and commodified through use of new technologies (Riley 2004).

As I've sketched out here, so much of what matters the most to Indigenous communities is not protected by patents, copyrights, and similar means because of its nature or age. How, then, can Indigenous peoples protect those aspects of their heritage that are essential to their cultural identity and well-being? The appropriation, commodification, or otherwise unwelcomed and inappropriate use of Indigenous cultural heritage is widespread, and involves both intellectual and material property (Brown 2003, 2005; Nicholas and Bannister 2004). However, we need to be cautious about making assumptions of what constitutes appropriate use. For example, many Indigenous peoples see the Internet and related technologies as a great equalizer or, at least, a suite of new tools and opportunities (see Burri-Nenova 2009, Dyson et al. 2007, Landselius 2006; see also the "Long Road" project and the "Digital Songlines" project). Further still, some First Nations groups may also see certain uses of elements of their cultural heritage as appropriate in commercial ventures, as two cases from British Columbia reveal. The Kamloops Indian Band has incorporated a series of rock art designs in the marquee of a gas station on their reserve, while the logo and wine bottle labels of the Nk'mip Winery consists of a projectile point and a rock art image design (Nk'mip Winery, n.d.). Another example concerns the Saginaw Chippewa Tribe of Michigan, and use of an image from a culturally significant petroglyph panel:

> In February 2008, a tribal member opened a sporting goods store and enquired with the Ziibiwing [Cultural] Center about using the archer as a logo. They were refused, not only on grounds that the image should not be used commercially, but also because the archer's teachings have nothing to do with hunting; instead, he is shooting ancestral knowledge into the future, so that it will be available to the people. (Hollowell and Nicholas 2009b: 152)

What these examples and the earlier discussion reveal is that Indigenous expressions of cultural heritage may be used differently in contexts that reflect cultural pride, political sovereignty, national identity, or commercial initiatives. There are also significant differences in how different Indigenous peoples view and care for their cultural heritage. Whatever the context, a key point is always that each group has the right to venerate, care for, or use its heritage as they see fit, whether or not this agrees with Western expectations. Historically, however, due to the imposition of colonial regimes, Indigenous peoples have often had little, if any, control over many aspects of their heritage. It is for this reason that a postcolonial ethic of the public domain is required regarding the heritage of descendant communities.

Indigenous peoples and other descendant communities have responded to the lack or loss of access to control over their cultural heritage in two basic ways: restrictive and inclusive responses. "Restrictive responses make use of various (legal, social, political) mechanisms for controlling or restricting access to archaeological materials and information" while "inclusive responses include various forms and degrees of consultation, reciprocation, and collaborative practice" (Nicholas and Wylie 2008: 30). Due to the limits of legal protection relative to cultural heritage, restrictive responses generally have little applicability. Also, the results of litigation are expensive, time consuming, and often unsatisfying in the end. Inclusive responses, on the other hand, may be much more effective and satisfying as they address the underlying sources of conflict. I focus the final section of this essay on that approach.

The Need for a New Research Ethic

In the Americas, Australia, Africa, and other settler countries, Indigenous peoples have endured the loss of sovereignty, expropriation of land, and other unimaginable impositions intended either to remove them from the lands entirely or incorporate them into a new social order. Although such events are largely a thing of the past, Indigenous peoples worldwide continue to confront the legacy of scientific colonialism, which is the extraction of knowledge from a source community and its use to create products that benefit others (Nicholas and Hallowell 2007: 60–2). As gatekeepers of knowledge about the past, archaeologists have positioned themselves to become the experts on other people's heritage. This has often come at the subjects' expense, as Native scholar and activist Vine Deloria, Jr. (1971) notes:

> Over the years anthropologists have succeeded in burying Indian communities so completely beneath the mass of irrelevant information that the

> total impact of the scholarly community on Indian people has become one of simply authority. Many Indians have come to parrot the ideas of anthropologists because it appears that the anthropologists know everything about Indian communities. Thus many ideas that pass for Indian thinking are in reality theories originally advanced by anthropologists and echoed by Indian people in an attempt to communicate the real situation. (82)

Beginning in the 1970s, but especially in more recent years, a growing number of anthropologists and archaeologists have been working to improve relationships with Indigenous peoples. One avenue has been efforts to involve members of descendant communities in all aspects of archaeological and cultural heritage protection and management. This "Indigenous archaeology" is "an expression of archaeological theory and practice in which the discipline intersects with Indigenous values, knowledge, practices, ethics, and sensibilities, and through collaborative and community-originated or -directed projects, and related critical perspectives" (Nicholas 2008: 1660). The result is greater representation of Indigenous peoples in archaeology, a broadening of archaeological method and theory, and capacity building within Indigenous communities (Chanthaphonh and Ferguson 2008, Silliman 2008).

A second approach concerns efforts to decolonize the disciplines that have traditionally been involved in the study of Indigenous peoples – archaeology, anthropology, and related enterprises. As Maori scholar Linda Tuhiwai Smith (1999) has stated, "Indigenous peoples have other stories to tell, and would like the history of Western research told from the perspective of the colonized" (2), adding:

> The process of decolonization is more than a deconstruction of Western scholarship, it is an attempt to offer ways of doing indigenous research that contribute primarily to the need for survival of indigenous communities and individuals, enhanced through the past, our stories, local and global, the present, our communities, cultures, languages and social practices. (Ibid.)

However, decolonization is not just shifting the frame of reference, but also it changes the structure of the decision-making process regarding heritage matters, which scholars and scientists have long controlled (on decolonizing the postcolonial discipline of archaeology, see Liebmann and Rizvi 2008, Nicholas and Hollowell 2007, Denzin et al. 2008, Lydon and Rizvi 2010). This unequal power relation has long meant that Indigenous peoples were removed from the processes of collecting, studying, and marketing their culture, and that they generally have not received benefits. Today, many voice this same concern with regard to the dual threat of having their culture both essentialized and treated as though it was in the public domain.

Challenging existing power structures will aid Indigenous peoples by helping to restore at least some degree of control over their culture. It will require researchers to engage in a different type of relationship with members of descendant communities. What is needed are research methods such as participatory-based research (PAR) and the derivative community-based participatory research (CBPR), which promote collaborative, reciprocal relations (Hollowell and Nicholas 2009b, Denzin et al. 2008). Such approaches to postcolonial research ethics can lead us beyond the spectre of scientific colonialism, and promote the fair and equitable exchange of cultural and intellectual property. An ongoing, Canadian-based initiative illustrates this perfectly.

The Intellectual Property Issues in Cultural Heritage project is an international collaboration of over fifty archaeologists, lawyers, anthropologists, museum specialists, ethicists, and other specialists, and twenty-five partnering organizations. It is working to explore and facilitate fair and equitable exchanges of knowledge relating to archaeology (see "IPinCH" for details). IPinCH thus provides a foundation of research, knowledge, and resources to assist scholars, academic institutions, descendant communities, policy makers, and many other stakeholders in negotiating more equitable and successful terms of research and policies through an agenda of community-based research and topical exploration of IP issues. A key component of the project is the development of fifteen case studies that will explore emerging IP-related issues in archaeological or cultural heritage contexts, the means by which they are being addressed or resolved, and the broader implications of these issues and concerns. Each project is developed by community partners with the assistance of IPinCH team members, and employs a CBPR methodology. The communities or organizations involved in these projects identify issues, co-develop case studies, and review results before dissemination. In addition, ethics approval for each project must be obtained from Simon Fraser University's institutional review board, from any other participating university, as well as from the host community. The effect is that although the results do contribute to IPinCH's research agenda, the results of these studies primarily address the community's needs, not the researcher's (Hollowell and Nicholas 2009b: 148).

Some IPinCH community-based initiatives include the creation of a database to record Moriori elder knowledge; sustainable land use practices and heritage landscapes in Rehoku (the Chatham Islands), Aotearoa (New Zealand); and the development of policies and protocols for culturally sensitive intellectual property by the Penobscot Nation, Maine, particularly to guide relations with researchers and external entities. Such IPinCH initiatives are demonstrating that collaborative research projects such as these address community needs and also contribute to the development of new knowledge of value to society.

Not surprisingly, the requisite institutional procedures needed for ethics review and grant transfer agreement approval for such cross-cultural and often international projects can be daunting, as well as frustratingly slow at times. In addition, although there is growing recognition of the importance of collaborative and CBPR research by such organizations as SSHRC, the current Tri-Council Policy statement is a poor fit. As a result of such factors, the amount of work entailed in starting these projects has been more than anticipated, yet this has also provided an important learning experience about the realities of collaborative research for all involved.

Conclusions

We have entered into an age where it is becoming possible to acquire, digitize, disseminate, and store virtually all information in existence. The expectation is that everyone benefits from increased access to information, whether in the sciences, the arts, or entertainment. There are, however, limitations on accessing certain types of information. In the business world, for example, some types of information are proprietary, and justifiably so, since their loss can financially jeopardize the company's success. But what about protecting information or restricting its dissemination and use when it is vital to cultural identity, as is the case with First Nations in Canada and Indigenous peoples elsewhere?

Indigenous peoples seek to protect their cultural and intellectual property, to control the flow of information and materials emanating from their cultural heritage, and to restrict or stop unauthorized and inappropriate use of that heritage. Failing to do so has real social and economic costs for the community. Given that there is limited legal protection for the tangible elements of their heritage, and even less for the intangible ones, the challenge of achieving adequate control and protection is substantial, especially when that heritage is viewed as public domain.

As technology continues to promote and facilitate the flow of information, it appears that this flow has often been away from source communities, with the transformation of cultural capital into social and economic capital (Hollowell and Nicholas 2007). Yet, engaging in respectful dialogue and collaborative initiatives can contribute to an enhanced ethics of decolonization and establish new notions of fair dealing (as Aylwin and Coombe's chapter illustrates). A growing number of anthropologists and archaeologists working with Indigenous heritage have been engaging with digital forms of fair dealing that practises this postcolonial research ethic. Kimberly Christen's project "Mukurtu: An Indigenous Archive and Publishing Tool," is one example – "a digital, standards-based, adaptable archiving tool that emphasizes cultural protocols and provides a means for indigenous knowledge to inform public and private collections" (see Christen 2012). Another is Eric Kansa's "OpenContext" project, an online, open access research data publication venue (see Open Context 2010).

Recognizing that inequities exist in archaeological practice, and that few benefits from that practice have returned to source communities, goes far in revealing why Indigenous peoples have long been wary of archaeologists. The widespread view that Indigenous cultural heritage is part of the cultural landscape, and thus essentially material in the public domain, is a source of injury at the root of much social damage. Addressing the concerns of Indigenous peoples requires recognizing their special – and continuing – relationship with their heritage. Does this mean the end of archaeological research or use of Indigenous motifs and materials? Certainly not. But it does mean that we need to develop new practices. As Kansa et al. (2005) suggest, "the Creative Commons concept of *some rights reserved* ... can be extended into areas where scientific disciplines intersect with traditional knowledge. This model can help build a voluntary framework for negotiating more equitable and open communication between field researchers and diverse stakeholding communities" (285, original emphasis).

Notions of equity, negotiation, collaboration, and fair and appropriate use of heritage goods are central to achieving resolution of outstanding grievances between Indigenous peoples and settler societies. However, it is also important to realize that the new model practices noted in this chapter are not restricted to the realm of Indigenous heritage but have potential currency wherever there are competing interests in or claims to cultural heritage in contemporary societies.

17 Cultural Diversity: A Central Dimension of Canadian Cultural Heritage?

NICOLE AYLWIN

Culture is now internationally recognized as a valuable economic, social, and political resource. Consequently, it has become a terrain on which numerous struggles for rights and recognition take place. The protection of cultural diversity and intangible cultural heritage represent two such sites of struggle, and both issues have prompted intense international debates regarding the nature of cultural goods, the value of "living" cultural heritage, the limits of ownership, and the appropriate role of intellectual property (IP) rights in regulating the flow of cultural goods.

The promotion and protection of cultural diversity is central to Canada's internationally developed cultural policy platform. It would seem self-evident that copyright – including the important exception of fair dealing – would be considered a central aspect of Canada's cultural policy, given that it regulates the reproduction and use of cultural texts (Vaidhyanathan 2001). Yet, copyright is rarely considered to be an integral part of Canada's larger cultural policy framework. Although often cited as a "stimulant" for the "creative economy" (Richard Florida's work is a prime example) and as a means to protect and to promote Canadian cultural industries (particularly audiovisual industries), there is very little consideration of how copyright might function to support a full range of national cultural policy objectives, including federal multiculturalism policy and Canada's international obligations. In other words, Canada's commitment to cultural policy as an economic incentive measure overshadows, when it doesn't wholly obscure, the possibility of using cultural policy to support a greater range of social and cultural objectives.

Canada has been an active player in international debates regarding both cultural diversity and intangible cultural heritage; given Canada's long history of dealing with domestic diversity and heritage concerns, this seems reasonable. However, by focusing on the government's treatment of two recent international legal instruments, the Convention on the Protection and Promotion of the Diversity of Cultural Expressions and the Convention for the Safeguarding of the Intangible Cultural Heritage, I will argue that in spite of Canada's self-declared role as a defender and promoter of international cultural diversity, the narrow focus of Canada's existing cultural policy calls our country's commitment to cultural diversity into question.

An examination of both the context in which cultural diversity became an international concern and Canada's own circumstances during this historical period will allow me to demonstrate that Canada's limited view of culture as pertaining to arts and industry obscures the importance of protecting the "living culture" of minority communities as a means for promoting diversity. Ultimately, I will also suggest that by narrowly framing the protection of cultural diversity as a matter of protecting national economic and cultural interests, the Canadian government ignores the larger human rights commitments around which international cultural policy is developing, and thus hinders our ability to live up to our desired reputation as a global leader promoting cultural diversity.

Protecting Cultural Diversity: An International Concern

The 1990s were characterized by the rapid advancement of new communications technologies and a major shift in many of the policies that regulated these technologies. These changes were particularly acute in the cultural sector where they allowed for non-tangible goods such as culture and cultural knowledge to be more easily circulated and transformed into information. As a result, the economy shifted away from traditional manufacturing practices towards the ownership and trade of information, making culture one of the most valuable forms of economic capital in the global economy (for a longer discussion, see Kundnani 1998). Culture became newly legitimized through the recognition of its exchange value. Once considered predominantly as a non-market entity, culture was transformed into a market-stimulating activity and recast as a resource (Yúdice 2003: 17) to feed innovations that might fuel new demands for symbolic goods.

During this period, the United States began to aggressively pursue a global, neoliberal economic agenda through all available international policy mechanisms. It focused, in particular, on expanding the scope of IP rights (see Drahos 2002) since these serve as the vehicles through which symbolic goods can be commodified and made more economically valuable than traditional tangible goods, because of the continuing royalties or rents such intangible goods may garner. In 1995, the Agreement on the Trade-Related Aspects of Intellectual Property (TRIPS) came into effect after significant international pressure from the United States was placed on both developing and developed countries to sign the agreement (Drahos 2002). To be administered by the World Trade Organization (WTO), TRIPS positioned IP rights (and thus the protection of non-tangible cultural goods) as matters of trade, providing the legal foundation for the neoliberal orthodoxy that cultural goods should be treated the same as any other commodities. As a result of this legally binding agreement, all nation states that were – or wanted to become – members of the world trading community were required to treat culture as a tradable market good, and many countries, less powerful than the United States, were forced to adopt policies and implement laws that were often disadvantageous to their unique national situations (Drahos 2002). Soon after the adoption of TRIPs, many governments realized that fulfilment of their trade obligations prohibited them from protecting national cultural differences and the specificities of the goods produced by their culture industries, such as books, film, and television.

The perceived threat of US cultural imperialism and the possibility of a "global monoculture" loomed large, particularly since TRIPs was only the last in a long line of political and legal strategies that the United States spearheaded in order to expand the reach of copyright protection well beyond its original intent to "encourage creativity, science and democracy" (Vaidhyanathan 2001: 4). As one of the largest exporters of cultural goods, the United States sought to secure its dominance in the international cultural industries by ensuring that the neoliberal "property at all costs" logic (Coombe 2004: 369), which had been used to expand its own domestic copyright protection, became a global standard.

The erosion of national cultural sovereignty became a key concern for many countries, a concern that was only magnified by the speed at which newly valorized cultural assets were being circulated. Many countries felt that their cultural resources were escaping their domestic control (Appadurai 1990) and that cultural diversity itself was, as a consequence, endangered. Under these circumstances, cultural diversity came to be regarded as a scarce resource that nation states needed to protect from the growing hegemony of the international trade regime and rapidly advancing digital communications technologies.

In 1998, the idea for developing a binding international instrument to protect cultural diversity was presented to an international group of state ministers of culture by the then Canadian Minister of Heritage, the Honourable Sheila Copps, and the international community began to consider the possibility of establishing an alternative international legal mechanism that would protect valuable forms of cultural distinction. In 2005, the United Nations Educational, Scientific and Cultural Organization (UNESCO) adopted the Convention on the Protection and Promotion of the Diversity of Cultural Expressions (hereinafter, the Diversity Convention), the first legally binding international instrument designed to globally promote and protect cultural diversity.

The Diversity Convention moved from proposal to ratification in less than a decade – a remarkably quick period in terms of international policy development. In addition to being the first nation state to propose such a convention, and the first signatory to it, Canada was also the most prominent state agent in its conception, development, promotion, and adoption. The country's zealous support for the agreement might be interpreted as an extension of its long-standing sensitivity to US cultural hegemony, a threat that has only been exacerbated by America's dominance in global cultural industries. Indeed, many of Canada's cultural policy decisions, including our flagship cultural policy of multiculturalism, have been motivated by the desire to fend off US cultural domination (Miller et al. 2005, Mackey 1999). By the end of the 1990s, however, Canada found itself surrounded by new allies facing many of the same cultural sovereignty issues that it had been struggling with for years; soon, Canada became a global leader in the global cultural diversity debates, working diligently to protect cultural diversity as a right of national sovereignty. Not coincidently, international support for a legally binding convention to protect intangible cultural heritage was also growing during this same period.

Out of Step: Canadian Cultural Policy and Global Heritage Practice

Intangible cultural heritage (ICH) – which includes "living heritage" practices such as oral traditions, performance art, ceremonies, festival, songs, and dance – are the types of meaningful cultural goods that were considered most threatened by the new information economy and its rapid circulation of intangible commodities (Graber and Burri-Nenova 2008). Cultural diversity has always been implicitly valued in the practices of cultural heritage management and protection (Donders 2008: 7); however, during the late 1990s, the protection of ICH was explicitly acknowledged as integral to the objective of fostering and maintaining cultural diversity because it provided communities with a sense of identity and continuity and fostered human creativity. Although tangible heritage, such as historic buildings, monuments, and "naturally occurring heritage sites" like Stonehenge had been protected since the 1972 Convention Concerning the Protection of the World Cultural and Natural Heritage, "living culture" (i.e., dynamic heritage practices) had not been the subject of a UNESCO declaration or other norm-setting instrument prior to 2003 (Smith and Akagawa 2009: 3). After a ten-year process of negotiations, the Convention for the Safeguarding of the Intangible Cultural Heritage (hereinafter, Intangible Heritage Convention) was adopted in 2003, coming into force in 2006 after being ratified by more than 180 countries.

Ironically, despite its leadership on the cultural diversity front, Canada has not ratified the Intangible Heritage Convention and has shown a remarkably weak commitment to the objectives of international intangible heritage protection. This may be partly explained by a constitutive contradiction in Canada's domestic cultural policies; as cultural planning expert Greg Baeker (2002) suggests, Canadian cultural policy suffers from a "definitional dilemma." Canada, he argues, has abstractly recognized the "anthropological" definition of culture, which defines culture as "a way of life" (183) – a definition that accords with UNESCO's and recognizes cultural practices, artefacts, and tangible and intangible cultural heritage as integral aspects of social life, but one that has had no legal implications or direct policy application. Canadian cultural policy instead remains committed to an "arts and humanities" definition of culture that characterizes culture as artistic and creative expression (184). This characterization emphasizes the authorial nature of culture, and presupposes culture to be a result of individual creative pursuits, resulting in works that are properly disseminated by creative or cultural industries aided by vehicles like copyright insofar as they serve to provide incentives to transform creative expressions into sources of economic capital as commodities that circulate in markets.

Unlike creative expressions, heritage was historically conceived as the common heritage of humankind, or as the inalienable property of a nation (Coombe 2009). As a consequence, heritage protection has been relegated to a less privileged tier of cultural policy, that of conservation (Baeker 2002: 18). Traditionally, copyright had little if any place in heritage protection, because heritage was perceived as having primarily historical value. No single author could reasonably request "rewards" (i.e., copyright protection) for her or his creative contributions to heritage, because heritage, and particularly the traditional heritage of Indigenous peoples, was (and often still is) considered to be part of the public domain (Nicholas, this volume) and was of little consequence to the creative industries, with the possible exception of tourism.

Copyright, in this context, is strictly a means to maximize the profits of the contemporary culture industries, rather than part of a larger cultural policy framework designed to balance economic and social needs. Matters pertaining to the economic growth and returns of the culture industries have thus become the primary focus of Canadian cultural policy, and this focus is now reflected in international cultural policy instruments such as the Diversity Convention. As legal scholar Christoph Beat Graber (2008) notes, the Diversity Convention makes it clear that its focus is on cultural expressions or discrete creative works and that it is designed to address the promotion and protection of diversity in the media marketplace (145). In other words, it is not designed to promote or to protect internal domestic cultural pluralism. Anthropologist Robert Albro (2005) agrees, arguing that the Diversity Convention is preoccupied with the *forms* culture takes, rather than support for the diversity of cultural activities or plurality of minority cultural groups (250).

In making culture synonymous with cultural expressions and cultural expressions synonymous with cultural works and goods, the Diversity Convention allows for diversity to be managed as a type of inventory (Aylwin and Coombe 2008); it acts as a regulatory regime that helps to harmonize culture with market interests. The emphasis on the production, distribution, and dissemination of cultural expressions places the nation state and its culture industries as the subjects and objects in need of protection. Culture, when it is not private property, remains the patrimony of the nation state, and the diversity in need of protection is limited to the diversity between nation states, their cultural industries, and the distinction of the goods they produce. It does not include the social diversity reflected in the cultural life of peoples

(Aylwin and Coombe 2008), namely, the "living culture" valued by the Intangible Heritage Convention and its international activities.

Arguably, the Intangible Heritage Convention has the potential to challenge conventional Western policy discourses with respect to heritage practice. This could be achieved by engaging minority cultural communities such as Indigenous peoples, whose cultural practices have either been excluded from protection or, alternatively, appropriated and marketed by the state and reconstituted as national heritage (Smith and Akagawa 2009, Blake 2009). Canada has long been "guilty" of reconfiguring Indigenous heritage as merely part of Canadian national identity (Mackey 1999). The definitional dilemma through which Canada organizes its cultural policy commitments is emphatically *not* apolitical; it constructs diversity in a way that ensures that the nation state remains the only rights-bearing subject. The right to protect cultural diversity is configured as a national right and, in the process, heritage practices are marginalized from core cultural policies. By sidestepping the challenges posed by the Intangible Heritage Convention's guidelines, which insist that communities be engaged and involved as full stakeholders in the preservation, management, and development of the ICH to serve local social needs (Coombe and Turcotte 2012), Canada skirts the contentious terrain of minority cultural rights and avoids its duty to protect and promote community cultural life.

A Cultural Rights Approach: Linking Cultural Diversity and Heritage Protection?

Despite public complacency about cultural policy, Canada's constitutive contradiction in cultural policy is a violation of its human rights commitments under the United Nations Declaration on Human Rights, the International Covenant on Civil and Political Rights, and the International Covenant on Economic, Social, and Cultural Rights, all of which contain cultural rights provisions. Both the Diversity Convention and the Intangible Heritage Convention are indivisible from this larger human rights framework, and they should, therefore, be interpreted through a human rights lens. This would require active encouragement of national policy practices that promote cultural rights. Unlike some of the earlier human rights declarations and conventions, many of the more recently adopted ones, such as the Diversity Convention and the Intangible Heritage Convention, go beyond the idea of non-discrimination to promote positive protection and promotion of ethnocultural diversity

(Kymlicka 2007: 16). These conventions require nation states not just to abstain from discrimination, but also to actively promote practices that build symbolic, economic, and institutional resources to foster cultural diversity.

In international law, cultural rights include the right to the protection of intellectual creations and the right to benefit from them (often protected through IP rights), the right to cultural participation, the right to develop and foster cultural heritage, and the right to speak one's own language (Albro and Bauer 2005, Symonides 1998). In the past decade, cultural rights have been given more sustained judicial attention (Helfer 2007), and a more substantive understanding of cultural rights has emerged (Coombe 2009). As the economic and social significance of culture and cultural resources increases internationally, more claims for cultural rights are being made as a way to further social justice objectives.

Many such claims focus on cultural heritage because it has become a "polyvalent crossover concept" (Albro, n.d.). Through discourse and practice, cultural heritage is now central to multiple fields of aspiration, including economic and social development as well as the arts and cultural industries (Albro, n.d.). As Rosemary Coombe (2009) notes, cultural heritage has become a revitalized area of cultural property and cultural rights politics precisely because heritage bridges the gap between culture and economy. Cultural identity is often expressed through material manifestations of culture (Silverman and Fairchild Ruggles 2007: 5), and the rights to control material heritage and related intellectual properties are of central significance to Indigenous peoples as they struggle to gain control over the management of their own cultural history and to find new ways to empower their communities. Rights to control cultural resources through legal vehicles like copyright become a new form of social legitimation and a source of political leverage for obtaining the "ear of the state" (Smith 2007: 160).

Cultural rights claims, which can take many forms, are not merely political claims for recognition; they are also "a means of attaining economic and political objectives that cannot be attained more directly" (Robbins and Stamatopolou 2004: 430). They are attempts, in other words, to redress the economic and social inequalities experienced by historically marginalized groups. IP vehicles such as copyright, trademarks, geographical indications, and trade secrets, along with other collective marks, are increasingly becoming a means by which minority communities deny the assumption that their heritage belongs to "humankind" and assert rights to culture and cultural difference. For example, the use of fair trade identification or "traditionally made" certification marks have offered Indigenous communities, in some instances, the ability to use their local physical environment and traditional knowledge practices (or "living heritage" practices) to produce goods that appeal to a niche market of global consumers who wish to consume ethically made products (Coombe and Aylwin 2011). The use of Maori trademarks in New Zealand and certification marks by First Nations groups in Canada are also examples of Indigenous communities using IP rights to capitalize on the symbolic value that authenticity holds in global markets. These strategies may enable Indigenous communities to maintain lifestyles of their own choosing, while also providing material benefits to their communities. Rather than displacing material concerns (Fraser 2005), the use of IP rights as cultural rights vehicles may allow minority communities – long considered the objects of cultural management policies dictated by others – to become recognized participants in a more democratic field of politics.

By emphasizing conservation and ignoring the economic, political, and cultural importance of heritage for supporting and empowering diverse communities, Canada's domestic and international cultural policy ignores the living cultures that actually produce diversity. It also distances the country's cultural policy from the important political dimensions of cultural rights claims made by minority cultural groups that seek to gain recognition through efforts to control their heritage and its properties. This erasure of cultural politics is consistent with historical conceptions of cultural policy as instrumental and value-free (Miller and Yúdice 2002). It is also consistent with the definitional dilemma in Canadian cultural policy, which privileges "consumer sovereignty," or market-ready diversity, over citizenship-related concepts such as cultural rights (Beale 2002) and hides the political and contentious nature of cultural policy, its inalienable tie to human rights, and its relationship to democratic participation and cultural recognition.

Taking a cultural rights approach to diversity means reinserting the political in an effort to recognize minorities and historically marginalized communities as equal participants in the management of their intangible cultural heritage. Protecting and fostering cultural heritage practices is integral to recognizing and promoting alternative cultural identities. A cultural rights approach to diversity and heritage should look to foster intercultural diversity (i.e., the diversity that exists between cultural groups within a nation), rather than focusing solely on the diversity between nation states and their national cultural industries. Taking a cultural rights approach to diversity, therefore, would mean recognizing cultural pluralism as the cornerstone of diversity, thus creating the policy space for cultural heritage debates to become part of a larger politics of recognition and redistribution.

Moving towards Fair Dealing:
Creating Robust Cultural Heritage Practices in Canada

Creating robust heritage practices that foster cultural diversity in Canada will take more than tinkering with policy definitions. In the copyright context, it means considering the rights and claims of cultural source communities to expressions of intangible cultural heritage. A great deal of scholarly and activist attention has been focused on the impact of current copyright practices on users' rights and on the effect of these practices on the cultural industries that rely on the use of creative expressions. Discussions about the relationship between copyright and democratic practices in the media, on the public domain, and on the use and misuse of copyright have also proliferated. Where discussion focuses on producers in the context of the digital domain, the expressive rights of users and the ownership of the fruits of virtual labour are dominant issues; see Lawrence Lessig (2004, 2006) for the controversies around the labour of open source (OS) software writers, and Sara Grimes (this volume) for the use of children's affective labour in online gaming.

All of these discussions, in one way or another, tend to revolve around the contours of fair dealing in the market. Whether we consider fair dealing a user's or a creator's right or duty, or even as a means to enable the creative construction of our cultural heritage (Coombe, Wershler, and Zeilinger, this volume), most debates are concerned with how copyright operates once creative expressions have already been produced and released into the public sphere. There is, however, little consideration for how copyright might be used to foster the conditions for cultural pluralism, to allow for diverse communities to produce a diversity of creative expressions, and to create robust cultural rights practices in Canada.

Copyright, as cultural policy, is intimately related to the human rights of the many minority communities that constitute the diversity of Canada's cultural expressions. The IP-protected works of minority communities are cultural expressions, but as cultural expressions they are also sources of cultural heritage. As citizens, we can no longer afford to assume that cultivating only market-friendly creative goods will foster meaningful cultural pluralism. If Canada is truly going to live up to its historical reputation as a "strongly multicultural" country (Kymlicka 2007), it must consider a new frame for conceptualizing cultural diversity and cultural heritage, one that takes into account the connection between its cultural policies, its human rights obligations, and the importance of cultural rights to diversity. Dealing fairly deserves no less.

Social anthropologist Antonio A. Arantes (a central figure in international cultural heritage negotiations) offers the 1988 Brazilian Constitution as a prime example of how cultural rights, heritage, and diversity can be married in such a way as to reset the policy "frame" that so often constrains heritage and diversity norms and practice. By abandoning the idea of a homogeneous nation in favour of a recognition that national heritage is the product of a diverse population engaged in a diversity of creative pursuits, Brazil's Constitution undermines the idea that culture is the domain of extraordinary elites who produce "art" and creates new spaces for alternative legal claims to culture that are based on affirmations of social difference (Arantes 2007: 292–3). The Constitution of Brazil, thus, does not merely affirm practices of non-discrimination, nor does it seek to "manage" cultural expressions that have been made artificially scarce. Rather, it actively pursues cultural pluralism by promoting diverse cultural practices and recognizing *difference*, not expressions, as the foundation of diversity.

Canada has the tools to reframe its own understanding of cultural diversity in much the same way, but policy makers will need to rethink some of their own assumptions regarding the purpose and subject of cultural policy. First, we would have to replace the idea of intercultural diversity with intracultural diversity and recognize the importance of non-conventional spaces of creative expression, such as the cultural practices of minority groups, and look for ways in which cultural policy tools, like copyright, can contribute to creating the conditions of diversity, rather than merely managing it. Second, civil society actors must continually remind policy makers of both Canada's national commitment to cultural diversity, as expressed through the country's multicultural policy, and its international policy commitments. If federal governments could successfully widen their gaze to include heritage as a legitimate source of cultural creation in their policy mandates, then Canada could actively promote the practices of unique cultural communities that build symbolic, economic, and institutional resources, instead of just preserving the resulting "heritage." In order to do so, however, Canadian policy officials and civil society activists alike must seriously acknowledge that cultural heritage and cultural diversity are linked, and that both are a matter of cultural rights – rights not only to the protection of expression, but also to the recognition of unique cultural identities and access to the symbolic and economic resources needed to maintain them.

Cultural policy is not a bureaucratic apparatus free from political moorings; it has been used historically to divest people of their language, traditions, and cultural heritage. In policies of assimilation, for example, many peoples' cultural identities have been devalued. In the worst cases, such as Canada's historical policies with respect to Aboriginal peoples, people's use of their ancestral languages and their cultural practices have been prohibited through government measures that in hindsight look like forms of cultural genocide (Coleman and Coombe 2009). Yet, cultural policy is also generative; it actively constructs the way in which claims to heritage and for diversity may be forged (Albro, n.d.). As an international framework of cultural policy continues to emerge, Canada will need to re-evaluate the conditions under which it is forging its own norms and practices for dealing fairly with cultural goods. If Canada is really interested in promoting diversity, and if as Canadians we truly want diversity to be "part of our heritage," we need to consider the larger political context of cultural policy – its relationship to identity and community well-being – and recognize that cultural policy is a matter of cultural rights, not simply rights to cultural expressions.

18 Parodists' Rights and Copyright in a Digital Canada

GRAHAM REYNOLDS*

On 29 June 2012, Bill C-11, An Act to Amend the Copyright Act, received royal assent. Among other reforms, this Act expands the fair dealing defence through the addition of three new fair dealing categories, two of which are parody and satire. This legislative reform represents a significant expansion in parodists' rights. This chapter discusses the scope of parodists' rights both under the Copyright Act as it was prior to being amended and under the amended Copyright Act. Specifically, it focuses on the impact of fair dealing on parodists' rights. As the broadest defence to copyright infringement and a user's "right" (*CCH Canadian Ltd. et al.* v. *Law Society of Upper Canada* [2004], para. 48; hereafter, *CCH*), fair dealing has the potential to provide considerable protection for parodists (and, more broadly, persons who engage in acts related to the creation and dissemination of parodies) against claims of copyright infringement.

For the purposes of this chapter, I will refer to the Copyright Act prior to Bill C-11 as the "pre-amendment" Copyright Act (and will make reference to this Act in the past tense). I will refer to the Copyright Act, as amended, as the "amended" Copyright Act (and will make reference to this Act in the present tense). This chapter proceeds in six sections. First, it will discuss different definitional categories of parody. Second, it will argue that acts related to the creation and dissemination of parodies are beneficial to Canadian society. Third, this chapter will discuss parody and prima facie copyright infringement under both the

---

* A version of this article was first published in the *Manitoba Law Journal* as "Necessarily Critical? The Adoption of a Parody Defence to Copyright Infringement in Canada" (2010) 33: 241–2.

pre-amendment and amended Copyright Acts. Fourth, it will set out the broad framework for fair dealing under both the pre-amendment and amended Copyright Acts. Fifth, it will describe how parodists' rights were limited under the pre-amendment Copyright Act by the way in which fair dealing was structured. Sixth, this chapter will discuss the scope of parodists' rights under the amended Copyright Act; in this section, it will be argued that although the addition of parody and satire categories to fair dealing significantly expands parodists' rights in Canada, other reforms enacted in the same piece of legislation pose the risk undermining this grant of additional protection.

Definitional Categories of Parody

At least since the time of Aristotle, parodies have been used to comment, to critique, and to celebrate (Dentith 2000: 10). The earliest parodies were spoken, written, or sung. Later parodies crackled over radio airwaves. With the emergence of film and television, parodies began to be created for and shown on the silver and small screens. Today, many parodies are created and disseminated using networked digital technologies.

Throughout the term's long history, many definitions of parody have been suggested. However, none of these definitions can be seen as authoritative. Simon Dentith (2000) notes that "because of the antiquity of the word parody (it is one of the small but important group of literary-critical terms to have descended from the ancient Greeks), because of the range of different practices to which it alludes, and because of differing national usages, no classification can ever hope to be securely held in place" (6). Although no single definition of parody can be established, three definitional categories of parody can be identified. Under the first category, a parody is seen as a work that imitates or inverts another work in order to critique or subject to ridicule the original work (Gredley and Maniatis 1997: 341). Under the second category, a parody can be seen as a work that imitates or inverts a work (the parodied text) in order to attack either the original work or something else, such as the artist or society. These types of parodies can be referred to as "weapon parodies" or, alternatively, can be described as satire (Spence 1998: 594). The third category of parody encompasses the first two, and is broader still. Definitions falling within the third category of parody do not insist upon criticism. Under this conception of parody, the imitation or inversion of the parodied text can be done for a wide variety of purposes, including criticism, humour, or as an expression of respect or appreciation (Hutcheon 1985: 27; Dentith 2000). I am not taking a position on which definitional category is "correct" (if any): the purpose of this section is to demonstrate both the breadth of conceptions of parody that have been proposed over time and the malleability of this concept. In evaluating the scope of parodists' rights in Canadian copyright law, the extent to which proposed solutions protect these differing definitional categories of parody should be considered.

Benefits of Parody

I have previously argued that the acts of creating and disseminating parodies provide significant benefits to Canadian society. Specifically, I have asserted:

> The creation and distribution of parodies promote the fundamental values underlying the constitutionally protected right to freedom of expression. Through parodies, individuals can progress in their "search for political, artistic and scientific truth," protect their autonomy and self-development, and promote "public participation in the democratic process." (Reynolds, 2010a, citing *RJR Macdonald Inc.* 1995, para. 72)

Well-constructed parodies can skewer a politician's speech, illuminate a work of art for an observer, and give individuals different perspectives through which to question scientific theories; they can help individuals progress in their own self-development by giving them opportunities to question, mock, or demonstrate appreciation for certain works, genres, or events that may be central to those individuals' sense of self; and they can inspire individuals to take part in a democratic culture defined both by political and cultural participation (Balkin 2004: 3–4).

Networked digital technologies give individuals the tools to create parodies and to distribute these parodies to a broad audience. By facilitating both the creation of parodies and their near-instantaneous dissemination to broad audiences, networked digital technologies enhance the societal benefits provided by parodies. As the next section will demonstrate, however, the creation and dissemination of parodies likely prima facie infringes copyright in Canada.

Parody and Prima Facie Copyright Infringement under Both the Pre-amendment and Amended Copyright Acts

Copyright in Canada is frequently referred to as a "creature of statute." That is, the rights and responsibilities of copyright owners and users are set out, exhaustively, in the Copyright Act. The rights of copyright owners with respect to artistic, musical, dramatic, and literary works are outlined in section 3 of the Copyright Act. These rights include the right to reproduce the work, the right to perform the work in public, the right to communicate the work to the public by telecommunication, and the right to authorize any of the copyright owner's exclusive rights. Copyright is prima facie infringed when anyone, without the consent of the copyright owner, does anything that only the copyright owner has the right to do (Copyright Act, s. 27).

Both the creation and distribution of parodies may prima facie infringe the exclusive rights of the person who owns the copyright in the original work. The right most likely to be prima facie infringed in the creation of a parody is the right to reproduce the work. This right may be infringed either where a work has been reproduced in its entirety or where a substantial part of a work has been reproduced. The question of whether a substantial part of a work has been reproduced is determined through both a quantitative and qualitative analysis (*Hager* v. *ECW Press Ltd.* 1998). That is, a parody that reproduces only a small portion of a copyright-protected work could still prima facie infringe the copyright owner's right to reproduce the work if, qualitatively, the portion of the work that is taken is deemed to be a substantial part of the original work.

Parodies generally attempt to evoke, in the mind of the individual experiencing the parody, the original work upon which the parody is based. One way in which many parodies do so is by reproducing the original work's "most distinctive or memorable features" (*Campbell* 1994). In so doing, the original work is made recognizable within the parody (*Campbell* 1994). If a person creates a parody in Canada in which an existing copyright-protected work is made recognizable, there is a strong possibility that a Canadian court – if such a dispute is brought before it by a plaintiff – would hold that, by quoting a work's core elements, this parody reproduces, in a qualitative sense, a substantial part of the original work, thus prima facie infringing the copyright owner's right to reproduce the work. The distribution of parodies may also prima facie infringe rights held by the copyright owner. Specifically, the distribution of parodies may result in the prima facie infringement of the copyright owner's right to communicate the work to the public by telecommunication, the right to authorize any of the copyright owner's rights, and the right to reproduce the work.

All parodists risk being sued for copyright infringement by the owners of copyright-protected works that they set out to parody. As detailed above, because of the structure of Canadian copyright law, there is a strong possibility that parodists (or persons who engage in acts related to the creation or dissemination of parodies) would be found to have prima facie infringed copyright. The question of whether a defence to copyright infringement (specifically fair dealing) might apply to render this conduct non-infringing, under both the pre-amendment and amended Copyright Acts, will be discussed in the next three sections of this chapter.

Fair Dealing

Under Canadian copyright law, once the plaintiff has established a prima facie case of copyright infringement, the burden shifts to the defendant to establish a defence to the infringement. If the defendant can do so, she or he will not be seen as having infringed copyright. The broadest defence to copyright infringement under both the pre-amendment and amended Copyright Acts is fair dealing.

The fair dealing analysis proceeds in three steps. The first step requires a court to determine whether the allegedly infringing act was done for one of the purposes listed in the Copyright Act: research, private study, criticism, review, and news reporting in the pre-amendment Copyright Act; and research, private study, criticism, review, news reporting, parody, satire, and education in the amended Copyright Act. The second step in the fair dealing analysis applies only to acts done for the purpose of criticism, review, or news reporting. In order to be protected by fair dealing, acts done for these purposes must mention the source of the work and the name of the author of the work (if given in the original). The third step in the fair dealing analysis requires the court to determine whether the original work was dealt with fairly. The term "fair" is not defined in the Copyright Act. Whether something is fair "is a question of fact and depends on the facts of each case" (*CCH* para. 52). In assessing whether fairness has been established, the Supreme Court of Canada (SCC) has set out a list of several factors that triers of fact may consider, including the purpose of the dealing (the use being made of the work), the character of the dealing, the amount of the dealing, alternatives to the dealing, the nature of the work, and the effect of the dealing on the work (*CCH* para. 53).

In *CCH Canadian et al.* v. *Law Society of Upper Canada* (2004), McLachlin C.J., writing for the Supreme Court of Canada, described fair dealing as an "integral part of the *Copyright Act*" (para. 48). Whereas fair dealing had been previously portrayed as a limitation on the copyright holder's exclusive rights or as an exception that should be strictly interpreted (see, e.g., *Michelin* para. 63), McLachlin C.J. stated:

> The fair dealing exception, like other exceptions in the *Copyright Act*, is a user's right. In order to maintain the proper balance between the rights of a copyright owner and users' interests, it must not be interpreted restrictively. As Professor Vaver ... has explained ...: "User rights are not just loopholes. Both owner rights and user rights should therefore be given the fair and balanced reading that befits remedial legislation." (para. 48, citing Vaver 2000: 171)

This statement is built on the SCC's decision in *Théberge* v. *Galérie d'Art du Petit Champlain Inc.* (2002), in which Binnie J., writing for the majority, discussed the concept of the "proper balance" between the rights of copyright owners and the public interest. Binnie J. noted:

> The *Copyright Act* is usually presented as a balance between promoting the public interest in the encouragement and dissemination of works of the arts and intellect and obtaining a just reward for the creator ... The proper balance among these and other public policy objectives lies not only in recognizing the creator's rights but in giving due weight to their limited nature. In interpreting the *Copyright Act*, courts should strive to maintain an appropriate balance between these two goals. (paras. 30–1)

Fair dealing, by giving individuals the right to use the copyright-protected expression of others for certain purposes, provided that they do so in a fair manner, plays an important role in helping to maintain the balance between the public interest and the rights of the copyright owner.

Parodists' Rights under the Pre-amendment Copyright Act

This section will discuss the scope of protection for parodists' rights under the pre-amendment Copyright Act. Specifically, it will focus on fair dealing, the broadest defence to copyright infringement under both the pre-amendment and amended Copyright Acts. As will be demonstrated, the way in which fair dealing was structured under the pre-amendment Copyright Act limited the scope of parodists' rights. It is unclear whether, under the pre-amendment Copyright Act, acts related to "weapon parodies" (or satire) would have been protected under fair dealing. As well, many acts related to non-critical parodies would likely not have been protected by fair dealing as it was structured under the pre-amendment Copyright Act.

The pre-amendment Copyright Act set out fair dealing as follows:

s. 29. Fair dealing for the purpose of research or private study does not infringe copyright.
s. 29.1 Fair dealing for the purpose of criticism or review does not infringe copyright if the following are mentioned:
(a) the source; and
(b) if given in the source, the name of the
  (i) author, in the case of a work,
  (ii) performer, in the case of a performer's performance,
  (iii) maker, in the case of a sound recording, or
  (iv) broadcaster, in the case of a communication signal.
s. 29.2 Fair dealing for the purpose of news reporting does not infringe copyright if the following are mentioned:
(a) the source; and
(b) if given in the source, the name of the
  (i) author, in the case of a work,
  (ii) performer, in the case of a performer's performance,
  (iii) maker, in the case of a sound recording, or
  (iv) broadcaster, in the case of a communication signal.

As noted above, the first step in the fair dealing analysis required the court to determine whether the allegedly infringing act was done for one of a number of listed purposes. Under the pre-amendment Copyright Act, these purposes were research, private study, criticism, review, or news reporting. Despite the absence of an explicit parody category, some acts related to the creation and dissemination of parodies could have been seen as falling under one of the listed purposes.

The SCC has stated that research is "not limited to non-commercial or private contexts," and must be "given a large and liberal interpretation in order to ensure that users' rights are not unduly constrained"

(*CCH* para. 51). Acts with respect to parodies done for the purpose of research – for instance, making a copy of a parody as part of the background research for a paper about the parodist, or creating a parody in the context of researching parodies more generally – would have fallen within this category.

Parodies created by individuals in private, and not shared with others, could have been seen as having been created for the purpose of private study. Many parodies created in private, however, are then disseminated publicly online through YouTube, blogs, or other websites. Such an act of public dissemination might have prevented parodists from relying on the private study category of fair dealing (see *Hager* 1998, *Boudreau* 1997, para. 51; but see *Alberta (Education)* 2012, para. 27).

Some acts with respect to parodies may have been seen as having been done for the purpose of news reporting. Acts that would likely have been seen as being encompassed by this fair dealing category included the reproduction of parodies on news programs and the creation of parodies for the purpose of disseminating news in an alternative manner (such as through political cartoons). As well, some acts with respect to parodies could have been seen as having been done for the purpose of review. For instance, a parodist could imitate a certain painting for the purpose of reviewing the painter's entire oeuvre.

Many parodies are critical. Some parodies imitate works in order to critique them or subject them to ridicule. Other parodies imitate or invert works to critique something other than the parodied work itself. Does criticism, in the context of fair dealing, encompass these forms of critique? Courts have held that criticism is not "confined to 'literary composition'" (*Michelin* para. 61). As well, Courts have noted that for the purposes of the fair dealing defence the "object of criticism" (*Hager* 1998) can be the style of the work, the ideas set out in the work, the work's "social or moral implications" (*Fraser Health Authority* 2003), or the "text or composition of a work" (*Hager* 1998). These decisions seem to protect many different types of criticism from claims of copyright infringement.

The first Canadian case to specifically address the issue of whether the fair dealing category of criticism encompasses parody is *Cie Générale des Établissements Michelin-Michelin & Cie* v. *C.A.W.-Canada et al.* (1996). In *Michelin*, the defendant, Canadian Auto Workers union, as part of an organizing campaign occurring in the midst of labour unrest at Michelin Canada's Nova Scotia plants, had created leaflets that featured the plaintiff's corporate mascot Bibendum (the Michelin Tire Man) "broadly smiling ... arms crossed, with his foot raised, seemingly ready to crush underfoot an unsuspecting Michelin worker" (para. 8). The plaintiff, who owned the copyright in Bibendum, sought "damages on the grounds that its intellectual property rights were violated by the defendants" (para. 3). Michelin also sought a permanent injunction to restrain the CAW from "using its trade-marks and copyrights in future organizing drives" (para. 3).

The CAW argued that their version of Bibendum was a parody and, therefore, the defence of fair dealing (under the fair dealing category of criticism) should apply to render their conduct non-infringing (para. 49). Teitelbaum J. rejected the CAW's argument, stating that under the Copyright Act, "criticism" is not synonymous with parody (para. 42). In rejecting the CAW's argument, Teitelbaum J. adopted a narrow view of criticism, stating that criticism, for the purposes of the fair dealing defence, "requires analysis and judgment of a work that sheds light on the original" (para. 66). This definition of "criticism" privileges the view of criticism as an exercise through which excerpts of a work are presented and dissected through analysis. It rejects those types of criticism, such as parody, that do not fit this narrow definition.

Teitelbaum J.'s decision was grounded in the belief that "exceptions to copyright infringement should be strictly interpreted" (*Michelin* para. 63). In *CCH*, the SCC overruled this approach, stating, as noted above, that the fair dealing defence is a user's right (*CCH* para. 12), not simply a defence or an exception (para. 48). As such, it "must not be interpreted restrictively" (para. 48). As noted previously, mandated by the SCC to give a "large and liberal interpretation" to the categories of fair dealing, courts that heard cases subsequent to the decision in *CCH* could have accepted that the category of "criticism" was broad enough to encompass other types of criticism, such as critical parodies or satire. Some commentators have suggested that courts might adopt such an approach (see D'Agostino 2008, Crowne-Mohammed 2009). Given the incorporation of a separate parody category within fair dealing in the amended Copyright Act, however, it is unlikely that future defendants will need to rely on the argument that the fair dealing category of criticism includes critical parodies.

Other issues that could have arisen had the Copyright Act not been amended to include a separate parody category within fair dealing relate to the question of whether courts would have found that works functioning as "weapon parodies" or satire would be encompassed within the category of "criticism" for fair dealing purposes and to the question of the extent of protection that non-critical parodies would have received under fair dealing. Not all conceptions of parody insist on criticism. Under some conceptions of parody, the imitation or inversion of the parodied text can be done for non-critical purposes, including humour or homage. These types of parodies, as they are not critical, would not have received protection under the fair dealing defence category of criticism (see Reynolds 2010a).

In the context of the pre-amendment Copyright Act, the second step in the fair dealing analysis could also have posed difficulties for persons engaging in acts related to the creation and dissemination of parodies that sought to rely on fair dealing as a defence to claims of copyright infringement. The second step in the fair dealing analysis applied only to works created for the purpose of criticism, review, or news reporting. To be protected by fair dealing, parodies created for the purpose of criticism, review, or news reporting needed to have mentioned the source of the work and the name of the author of the work. As mentioned above, under the pre-amendment Copyright Act, many acts related to parodies could have been seen as having been done for the purpose of criticism. Acts related to these parodies would thus have had to cite the source of the work and the work's author in order to satisfy the fair dealing requirements.

While the requirement to cite the source of the work and the work's creator is not an issue for many types of works (papers written by academics, for instance), the nature of parodies – in which the source work is evoked in the mind of the individual experiencing the parody – means that few parodies explicitly reference the source work. The source (at least in effective parodies) is implicitly known to the listener or viewer. However, given that under the pre-amendment Copyright Act, acts related to the creation and dissemination of parodies might only have been protected under the fair dealing category of criticism, and given that parodies created for the purpose of criticism needed to mention the source of the work and the name of the author of the work in order to satisfy this step of the fair dealing analysis, parodists might have been required (should they have wished to avail themselves of fair dealing) to artificially insert the source of the work and the name of the author into their parody. This could have had an effect on the message expressed by the work, or on the work's overall impact.

The argument that certain types of works should not have to explicitly cite a source that is "implicitly known to [an] onlooker" was raised and rejected in *Michelin* (para. 112). However, it could have been argued that as a result of the SCC's decision in *CCH*, a Canadian court could have held that the recognition implicit in a parody is sufficient to satisfy the source requirement. As is the case with the first step in the fair dealing analysis, given the incorporation of a separate parody category within fair dealing in the amended Copyright Act, it is unlikely that future defendants will need to rely on this argument.

The third step in the pre-amendment fair dealing analysis required the court to determine whether the original source work upon which the parody was built was dealt with fairly. As noted above, the first factor to be considered in assessing whether the original copyright-protected work was dealt with fairly was the purpose of the dealing. The purpose of the dealing was fair if it was for one of the purposes set out in the Copyright Act (viz., research, private study, criticism, review, or news reporting; *CCH* para. 54). The SCC in *CCH* stated that these purposes should not be given a restrictive interpretation (para. 54). Those parodies that could not be considered to fall under any of the listed purposes would not have been protected by fair dealing. For acts with respect to parodies that were done for one of the listed purposes, this factor would have tended towards a finding of fairness.

The second factor to consider, the "character of the dealing," examined how the source work was dealt with. In *CCH*, the SCC noted that the wide distribution of multiple copies of works will tend to be unfair (para. 55). Parodists generally add additional content to the work being parodied in the form of verbal commentary, written commentary, additional images, text, video, or music. As a result, even though some parodies are distributed widely, it cannot be said that multiple copies of the original work are distributed widely. Whether this factor tends to fairness or unfairness, however, depends on a variety of factors, including how broadly the original work was distributed and how broadly the parody was distributed.

The amount of the dealing, the third factor to have been considered, varied depending on the parody in question. Some parodies use only small portions of copyright-protected works. Other parodies use larger portions of works. This distinction could imply that parodies that use small snippets of copyright-protected works might be considered "more fair" than parodies that use large portions of copyright-protected works. The fact that parodies may use large portions of copyright-protected works, however, does not necessarily preclude the application of the fair dealing defence. In *Allen* v. *Toronto Star Newspapers Ltd.* (1997), for instance, it was determined that the reproduction of a photograph in its entirety was a fair dealing.

Another factor to have been considered in determining whether the dealing is fair asks whether there are "alternatives to the dealing." In *CCH*, the SCC stated that it is "useful for courts to attempt to determine whether the dealing was reasonably necessary to achieve the ultimate purpose" (para. 57). If the ultimate purpose of a parody is to critique a specific artist by imitating or inverting his or her work, a strong argument may be made that it was "reasonably necessary" to use the artist's work in the process of developing that critique. If the purpose of the parody is to critique society, on the other hand, then the argument that it was "reasonably necessary" to use an individual author's work in the process of doing so may be weaker.

The nature of the work is another factor that should have been considered by the courts in determining whether a dealing is fair. Although the fact that the work used was confidential may "tip the scales towards finding that the dealing was unfair," the use of unpublished but non-confidential works may tend towards a finding of fairness (*CCH* para. 58). As many parodies are created using published works that have been disseminated broadly, this factor – at least in the context of published versus unpublished works – would not have played much of a role in the fairness analysis.

The last factor to have been addressed in determining whether the dealing was fair is the effect of the dealing on the original source work. In discussing this factor, the SCC noted that "if the reproduced work is likely to compete with the market of the original work, this may suggest that the dealing is not fair" (*CCH* para. 59). Very few parodies, if any, compete with the market for the original work. For instance, individuals who wish to purchase Roy Orbison's song "Oh, Pretty Woman" will not be satisfied, instead, with 2 Live Crew's bawdy "Pretty Woman" parody (*Campbell* 1994). In this type of situation – where there is no market substitution – this factor should tend to fairness.

Based on these factors, particularly the last factor addressing the effect of the dealing on the work, many parodies created and distributed in Canada would probably have been considered fair. However, as discussed above, many non-critical parodies, and some types of critical parodies, would not have satisfied the first step of the fair dealing defence under the pre-amendment Copyright Act and, as a result, would not have been protected from a claim of copyright infringement.

Following the SCC's decision in *CCH*, in which defences and exceptions to copyright infringement were recast as user's rights, it could be argued that under the pre-amendment Copyright Act, fair dealing (and, particularly, the fair dealing category of criticism) could have provided some protection for critical parodies. It was an open question, however, whether courts would interpret "weapon parodies" (or satire) as falling within the category of "criticism" for fair dealing purposes. Furthermore, those parodies that could not be seen as critical would have fallen outside of the scope of this fair dealing category. Thus, under the pre-amendment Copyright Act, parodists' rights were limited, in large part because of the structure of fair dealing itself. In order to achieve more robust protection for acts related to the creation and dissemination of parodies, legislative reform was necessary. This reform was recently achieved through amendments to the Copyright Act.

Parodists' Rights under the Amended Copyright Act

In the amended Copyright Act, fair dealing has been expanded by the incorporation of three additional fair dealing categories, two of which are parody and satire. These categories have been added to the same section of the Copyright Act as the fair dealing categories of research and private study (s. 29). Consequently, as is the case with research and private study, under the amended Copyright Act, persons engaging in acts done for the purpose of parody and satire will not be required to cite the source of the work and the author of the work in order to satisfy the fair dealing analysis. As described above, given the nature of parodies, this attribution requirement can serve as an artificial barrier that may prevent persons engaging in acts related to the creation and dissemination of parodies from benefiting from fair dealing or that may alter the impact of the parody itself.

Particularly when viewed in light of the SCC's statement that fair dealing categories should be given a "large and liberal" interpretation (*CCH* para. 51), the incorporation of parody and satire categories into fair dealing, in the same section as research and private study, will accommodate expansive conceptions of these types of expression. Amending the Copyright Act in such a manner can be seen as an affirmation, on the part of the Parliament of Canada, that parody is important, that acts related to the creation and dissemination of parodies benefit Canadian society, and that these acts ought to be protected against claims of copyright infringement. The amended Copyright Act thus protects a robust vision of parodists' rights. This amendment also maintains a balance between parodists' rights and those of copyright owners, as the requirement that any dealing with the copyright-protected work must be fair helps ensure that this additional protection for parody and satire does not unreasonably encroach upon the rights of the latter.

The manner in which the amended Copyright Act provides protection for technological protection mechanisms (TPMs), however, risks undermining the protections that it grants to parodies and satire. TPMs – sometimes referred to as "digital locks" – are technological measures used by copyright owners and distributors to prevent unauthorized access to or use of a work. The amended Copyright Act makes it an offence to circumvent an access control TPM for any purpose save those that are expressly excepted. Although several exceptions are listed, none of these exceptions encompass fair dealing usages. As a result, although the amended Copyright Act gives individuals the right to use a substantial portion of copyright-protected expression for the purpose of parody or satire, provided the dealing is fair, this right can be trumped through the application of a TPM by a copyright owner or distributor.

To ensure that the societal benefits that result from the creation and dissemination of parodies are not diminished because of restrictive copyright laws and laws protecting TPMs, the amended Copyright Act should be further amended to indicate either that it is not an offence to circumvent a TPM in order to exercise one's right to fair dealing, or, more broadly, that it is not an offence to circumvent a TPM for an otherwise lawful purpose (see Reynolds 2010b). Such revisions would ensure that individuals cannot be enjoined from creating or disseminating parodies simply because of the application of a TPM by a copyright owner or distributor.

Conclusion

Despite concern over the manner in which legislative protection for technological protection mechanisms might have an impact on parodists and parodies, the amended Copyright Act can be seen to have significantly expanded parodists' rights in Canada. The addition of parody and satire categories to fair dealing will provide protection to a much broader range of expression than was protected under the pre-amendment Copyright Act. The addition of these two categories also provides parodists and satirists with a level of assurance that what they are doing does not infringe copyright. In so doing, these reforms may further encourage the creation and dissemination of parodies in Canada, acts that will ultimately lead to the development of a stronger Canadian democratic culture.

19 Robin Hood of the Avant-Garde

KENNETH GOLDSMITH

UbuWeb can be construed as the Robin Hood of the avant-garde, but instead of taking from one and giving to the other, we feel that in the end, we're giving to all. UbuWeb is as much about the legal and social ramifications of its self-created distribution and archiving system as it is about the content hosted on the site. In a sense, the content takes care of itself; but keeping it up there has proved to be a trickier proposition. The sociopolitical maintenance of keeping free server space with unlimited bandwidth is a complicated dance, often interfered with by darts thrown at us by individuals calling foul play on copyright infringement. Undeterred, we keep on – after seventeen years, we're still going strong. We're lab rats under a microscope: in exchange for the big-ticket bandwidth, we've consented to be objects of university research in the ideology and practice of radical distribution.

But by the time you read this, UbuWeb may be gone. Cobbled together, operating on no money and an all-volunteer staff, UbuWeb has become the unlikely definitive source for all things avant-garde on the Internet. Never meant to be a permanent archive, Ubu could vanish for any number of reasons: our ISP pulls the plug, our university support dries up, or we simply grow tired of it. Acquisition by a larger entity is impossible: nothing is for sale. You might remember the climax of the film *24 Hour Party People* (2002), where a large record conglomerate swoops in to buy the stubbornly independent Factory Records for millions of pounds. Factory head Tony Wilson muses in the coda that, although it was financially worthless, Factory Records was a great success, a fantastic conceptual art project that never had to make a single compromise. UbuWeb is similar, except unlike pop music, what we host has never made money. Instead, the site is filled with the detritus and ephemera of great artists – the music of Jean Dubuffet, the poetry of Dan Graham, Julian Schnabel's country music, the punk rock of Martin Kippenberger, the films of John Lennon, the rants of Karen Finley, and pop songs by Joseph Beuys – all of which was originally put out in tiny editions and vanished quickly.

However, the Web provides the perfect place to restage these works. With video, sound, and text remaining more faithful to the original experience than, say, painting or sculpture, Ubu proposes a different sort of revisionist art history, one based on the peripheries of artistic production rather than on the perceived, or market-based, centre. How does it all work? Most importantly, UbuWeb functions on no money: all work is done by volunteers. Our server space and bandwidth is donated by several universities, who use UbuWeb as an object of study for ideas related to radical distribution and gift economies on the Web. In terms of content, each section has an editor who brings to the site his or her area of expertise. Ubu is constantly being updated, but the mission is different from the flotsam and jetsam of a blog; rather, we liken it to a library that is ever-expanding in uncanny – and often uncategorizable – directions. Seventeen years into it, UbuWeb hosts over five thousand artists and several thousand works of art. You'll never find an advertisement, a logo, or a donation box. UbuWeb has always been and will always be free and open to all.

The future is eminently scalable: as long as we have the bandwidth and server space, there is no limit as to how big the site can grow. For the moment, we have no competition, a fact we're not happy about. We're distressed that there is only one UbuWeb: why aren't there dozens like it? Looking at the art world, the problem appears to be a combination of an adherence to an old economy (one that is working very well with a booming market) and a sense of trepidation, particularly in academic circles, where work on the Internet is often not considered valid for academic credit. As long as the art world continues to prize economies of scarcity over those based on plentitude, the change will be a long time coming. But UbuWeb seeks to offer an alternative by invoking a gift economy of plentitude with a strong emphasis on global education. And it seems to be working: UbuWeb is visited by more than 20,000 individual computers from every continent daily. We're on numerous syllabi, ranging from kindergarteners studying pattern poetry to postgraduates listening to hours of Jacques Lacan's *Séminaires*.

And yet – it could vanish any day. Beggars can't be choosers, and we gladly take whatever is offered to us. We don't run on the most stable of servers, or on the swiftest of machines; crashes eat into the archive on a periodic basis; sometimes the site as a whole goes down for days; occasionally, the army of volunteers dwindles to a team of one. But that's the beauty of it: UbuWeb is vociferously anti-institutional, eminently fluid, refusing to bow to demands other than what we happen to be moved by at a specific moment, allowing us flexibility and the ability to continually surprise our audience – and even ourselves. There is a two-pronged thrust to keeping UbuWeb alive. One is the reaping and posting of content and the other is the work that it takes to keep that content there. When a cease-and-desist notice comes in, we immediately send a personalized form letter to the concerned party (Figure 19.1).

Nine times out of ten, this approach succeeds and we get permission to host works. Occasionally, if someone still insists on the works being removed from the site, we remove them immediately. After all, the content belongs to the artists and if they, for whatever reason, don't wish their works to be on Ubu, then that's their right. We never force the issue.

I have been told by the station manager of WFMU, Ken Freedman – an expert in these areas – that a cease-and-desist order will most often happen in three stages:

1 A letter is sent saying to please remove the content. If there is no response,
2 A second letter is sent saying that you have been asked to remove their content from your site once. Now they are asking you again to remove it before they take legal action.
3 A third letter is sent saying that they have been asked two times to remove the content from your site and you have not responded. Now they say they have no choice but to take legal action.

We've never let it get past the first step (the same policy as WFMU, which hosts untold numbers of unpermissioned files on their site), engaging in dialogue minutes after the first notice is received. A quick response is often appreciated and encourages dialogue, which is more likely to allow files to remain on Ubu's servers.

It seems to be working: As of this writing, July 2013, a total of thirty-two artists have been removed from the film and video section, which is currently made up of 652 artists, and under a dozen from the sound section, which comprises nearly one thousand artists. That makes a total of about forty-five of nearly fourteen hunded whose works of media

---

Dear ___________,

Thank you for getting in touch.

We assumed that since these wonderful videos for most people are very hard – if not impossible – to see, making them available wouldn't be hurting anyone. Please correct us if we've made a wrong assumption and if so, we apologize in advance for this and will take whatever steps necessary to remedy this.

UbuWeb is an educational, not-for-profit site: we take no money, we make no money. Our hearts are pure. We work in the spirit of making difficult to find, though very worthwhile work available to an interested audience. UbuWeb is primarily used in curriculums from K-12 on up through the post-graduate level. It has become the major resource for study of the historical avant-garde ...Would you consider giving permission to host ________'s videos? We're happy to provide support materials for you and your organization, as well as links where necessary.

Since no one's making money here and the intent is to get the work out, we hope it's a win-win situation for everyone. And I can imagine that ________'s videos being loved on other people's sites can only help ________'s exposure and reputation. How could it be otherwise?

UbuWeb has been extensively written about in Parkett, Artforum, Bookforum and Art in America. In addition, I think if you ask some of your artists about Ubu, you'll find you have an ally here.

Thank you for your understanding.

Sincerely yours,
Kenneth Goldsmith
UbuWeb
http://ubu.com

Figure 19.1. UbuWeb personalized form letter in response to a cease-and-desist notice.

(sound and film/video) have been removed since the site's beginnings in 1996 (and this doesn't include hundreds of other artists in our contemporary, historical, outsiders, and papers sections, for which we've never received any takedowns). It's an attitude that independence affords us. It's hard to imagine a university, for example, taking such an attitude. In fact, at PennSound, where I am a senior editor, only works that have been cleared for permissions reside; anything that is grey in any way is not allowed on the servers.

When UbuWeb began in 1996, we were simply scanning dusty old concrete poems and posting them. We never received a cease and desist for concrete poems (or any textual matter, for that fact), and to this day haven't. A couple of years later, when RealAudio made its appearance, we began streaming sound poetry collections, in small file formats that were cheap to host; to this day, we've rarely received a cease and desist for sound poetry, either in streaming or downloadable form.

By the summer of 2001, with the advent of MP3 and broadband, everything had changed. We could no longer afford either the server space or the bandwidth to host what, at the time, appeared to be huge files. Fortunately, Loss Pequeño Glazier and Charles Bernstein generously offered a solution and allowed UbuWeb's media files to live on the Electronic Poetry Center's servers, thus giving us the green light to post as much material as we could possible rip. And rip we did: by the summer of 2005, we had accumulated the largest collection of avant-garde MP3s on the Web, available to anyone at no cost.

In 2004, emboldened by our success with MP3s and with more access to higher-speed broadband, we decided to host moving images. Plucked mostly from file sharing – and free from the financial concerns of bandwidth and server space thanks to the EPC – by the summer of 2005, we were able to offer a substantial number of avant-garde films in various formats. Then, in May 2005, Charles Bernstein called me with some bad news. It seemed that agents for the artist Bruce Connor had written a letter to the president of the University of Buffalo, claiming that illegal materials were being hosted on their servers. According to Bernstein, they made all sorts of threats including reimbursement for each video downloaded, legal suits, and so forth. Had the letter gone to myself, Bernsteing, or Glazier, we would have done what we normally do in such situations: issue an apology, explain how the site's mission is education and non-commercial, and immediately remove the offending materials from the server. However, the letter went to the head of a university, who, in turn, put everything in the offending directory under lock and key, which, in the case, meant all of UbuWeb's media files. Suddenly, after nearly a decade of quiet accumulation, nothing was available. Furthermore, the university had become conscious of the fact that we were using an insane amount of bandwidth and a significant amount of hard disk space, further threatening to clip our wings. It was clear to me that, in spite of the incredible generosity of Glazier and Bernstein, it was time to move on.

But where to? Who would take on this massive risk and technical burden? Other institutions were able to offer us bits and pieces – Sandy Baldwin at the Center for Literary Computing gave us redundancy, backup, and audio streaming, and Bernstein generously offered to host all of our permissioned materials on PennSound, but that left us with finding a home for all the other stuff, which comprised a substantial portion of the site. In the summer of 2005, when I couldn't find any takers, we hung a sign on the front page of UbuWeb stating that after nearly a decade, our experiment in radical forms of distribution was shutting down. I went as far as to put the domain name up for sale when I received an email from Ken Freedman, who offered to take the entire site, risks and all. Over the course of the summer, UbuWeb was rebuilt on the WFMU servers, and relaunched in that fall with over one hundred films (Bruce Connor was not among them).

Almost immediately, we received a slew of cease-and-desist letters from people claiming to be representatives of several filmmakers. Under siege, we shuttered the newly relaunched film section, sending out a letter that, again, explained our good intentions, the reasoning behind our project, and our eagerness to support – not offend – artists. Ken Freedman strongly objected to our shuttering of the whole film site. Why not just take down the films that were specifically complained about and leave everything else up? "If it comes to it, you can always remove them," he said. And that's what we did. Since the relaunch, we've been slowly building up the film collection; we now host over three hundred films and very rarely do we receive a complaint.

Once more, though, we are playing musical chairs with hosting. That summer we were told by WFMU that we had to vacate our media files from their servers by the end of the month. Fortunately, York University offered to give us a "permanent" home, and that's where we were for several years, linked to the Artmob project. When that situation lapsed, we found ourselves at home on the servers of CENTRO, an art school in Mexico City, where we have unlimited bandwidth and server space free of charge.

I feel that there's a sort of non-economy around the types of things we host on UbuWeb. Take, for example, concrete and sound poetry: I can't imagine anyone's ever made much money from these things. The same goes for avant-garde film and books of innovative poetry. This was confirmed a few years ago when I signed a contract to edit a posthumous collection of interviews with Andy Warhol with a large commercial publisher. Just to make sure I wasn't stepping on their toes, I contacted the Warhol Foundation to get their blessing that it was OK for me to republish these interviews. They laughed and said, in effect, "Take them, please; we're busy chasing around forgeries worth millions of dollars and negotiating worldwide t-shirt deals. You want Andy's words? You can have them."

The Warhol experience also confirmed that our attitude of posting first, asking later was the right one to take. I spent more than my advance on permissions for my book; the process of getting permissions took over a year, and even then, I wasn't able to track down all the information I needed. In fact, if we had to ask permission to host materials, UbuWeb most certainly wouldn't exist. I often think that we are doing the work that museums should be doing; our online holdings far outpace what the Museum of Modern Art offers on their site, even though their physical holdings dwarf ours. The reason is obvious: the Museum of Modern Art or any other proper institution has to get permissions and draw up contracts in order to host what they own in digital form; hence, their hands are tied.

As long as we stay within the margins of culture, we're pretty much safe. When we occasionally dip our toe into the more profitable or mainstream side of the avant-garde, we do get slapped around. For example, we got a letter from the BBC's legal department demanding that we take down some old BBC Beckett and Pinter audio files. We obeyed; Beckett and Pinter are big business. Sometimes, however, a bit of conversation goes a long way. A few years back, I got a phone call from Maureen O'Hara, sister and executor of Frank O'Hara's estate, concerned about MP3s of Frank's that appeared on some old Giorno Poetry System LPs. I told Ms. O'Hara that we neither take nor make money on UbuWeb, that our materials are for educational use only, and that we are accessed daily by dozens of students ranging from K-12 to the postgraduate level. Once she heard this, she acquiesced and cheerfully permitted the work to stay on UbuWeb.

Speaking of John Giorno, years ago we ripped every single Poetry System LP of his without asking permission. When we were finally introduced, he gave me a big hug and thanked me for putting these gems back into a circulatory system – the Internet – that, to his mind, was the obvious technological successor to his telephone-driven Dial-A-Poem methodology. In UbuWeb's rhetoric, Giorno recognized the kernel of his own thinking, hammered out in the 1960s, that innovative poetry, art, and music is a utopian gift economy, freed from the tyranny of copyright, moving freely from one node to another; put another way, radical works deserve radical distribution.

Ubu can be a game of cat-and-mouse. In 2008, we removed ourselves from the Google search engine. If you search for UbuWeb, you'll only find links to the site, but not the site itself. Likewise, you won't find any of Ubu's content directly indexed on Google either. (But we're still on all the "bad" search engines: DuckDuckGo, Ask.com, Bing) Reflecting the nature of our content, UbuWeb is now an underground resource and functions in the way that underground culture always has: by word of mouth, except here it's link to link. You have to be hipped to the site by someone hip in order to know about it. What does it matter? We don't care about numbers. We don't make more money if we have more page views. There's no revenue. It doesn't matter if there's three people or three thousand daily that view the site.

Yet, it's resulted in a crazy skewing of the playing field. Over the years, Ubu has accrued enormous cultural capital by simply operating illegally. Everyone from the Serpentine Gallery in London to the Canadian Centre for Architecture in Montreal wants to partner with UbuWeb. In fact, the CCA presented a show featuring works from several prominent collections: NASA, the National Film Board of Canada, the Smithsonian, and UbuWeb. When the curators asked for works from Ubu, they had to have known that they were being hosted there without permission, yet made a decision to get proper display copies and gather permission from the artists and their representatives at great cost and legal entanglement. When I suggested that the exhibition mirror the outlaw policies of Ubu, they were not able as a proper institution to take that route.

Other large institutions are equally in awe of Ubu: The Academy of American Poets calls UbuWeb "arguably the most comprehensive online repository of experimental and avant-garde documents," and the London *Sunday Times* exclaims that "like all the best galleries, UbuWeb somehow creates its own distinctive space, and one perfectly suited to its brilliant collection." Clearly, UbuWeb's vision is perceived as an authoritative carrier of history. While this is flattering, it is problematic on many levels and, to make a larger point, it is symptomatic of shifting notions and standards of the ownership of historical narratives in these early chaotic years of the Web. Some of the problems are the following:

- UbuWeb is basically an overgrown fanzine or private archive: randomly curated according to whim, not to any rigorous standards.
- UbuWeb has never intended to provide a comprehensive art historical perspective. Although we do have expert editors, the site has a wild bias based on a certain flavour of history – in this case the history of the avant-garde (a slippery slope if there ever was one) – drenched in subjectivity.
- The site is riddled with holes and gaps. Since most of our materials come from donations or file sharing, we post what we can get our hands on willy-nilly. In any given artist's catalogue, there are huge pieces missing without explanation, making a poor argument for context and historicity. If we have a hunch that it's "important" we post it – admittedly a very sloppy and subjective method of curation.
- The taxonomy of the site is misleading. We have broad categories that things get shovelled into: historical, contemporary, sound, film and video, etc.

So, it appears that UbuWeb's grip on a certain historical narrative – which grows more "authoritative" by the year – is, in fact, a faulty one. But, and this is important, it's the only one that exists on the Web. The larger institutions that could do this the "right" way are showing no signs of doing it at all.

If this all sounds very Web 2.0, it is – and it isn't. UbuWeb is not a democracy. And that's why it's so good. Not everything goes; not everyone can participate; there is a rigorous vetting process by a group of experts, which happens before anything can go on the site. Most submission requests are ignored; not everybody gets a fair shake. In the fall of 2009, for example, after a rapid slew of cease and desists from Video Data Bank (many of whose films and videos are featured on Ubu), I entered into a dialogue with them asking, "Why so many so soon?" Their representative declared that artists were not so upset with their films being on Ubu as they were with the fact that they were downloadable. This statement made me reconsider why we offer downloadable film – huge files sucking up massive amounts of server space and bandwidth – and when I thought about it, I realized that such artefacts are a holdover from a time when streaming media (RealVideo) was proprietary and sluggish. Recently, we upgraded our streaming player to be able to go full screen and to embed. When I examined my own viewing habits, I realized that I rarely downloaded, choosing instead to stream. As a result, we have removed the downloadable media from film and video. We must keep adapting in order to meet the demands of changing times, attitudes, and technologies.

Yet, we've always kept a disclaimer on our film page, drawing attention to the fact that the quality of our hosted material is poor, and no match for the real thing – and thereby hoping to instil in our viewers appreciation for the sources themselves. But, for many people, UbuWeb is the real thing inasmuch as, say, the Van Gogh poster in my teenage bedroom for all intents and purposes became the real thing as I wasn't able to go to Europe to experience that "real thing" until I was in my twenties. Hence, our histories, based on our experiences, become extremely localized and subjective based on our access.

Are we crazy? Yes. Are we exposing ourselves to great risk? Yes. Could we get screwed? Yes. What we're doing is clearly wrong, and we wouldn't have a foot to stand on in a court of law, even though we don't sell anything. But we – and the art/cyber/academic/communities – seem to think the good greatly outweighs any damage. And the amount of emails and feedback generated by the site confirms our hunch. Every day, dozens of appreciations are sent worldwide; once every other month, or so, we get a complaint. Oddly enough, in spite of all, it seems to be working.

20 Remixing bpNichol: Direct Dealing and Recombinatory Art Practices

JUSTIN STEPHENSON

Language today no longer poses problems of meaning but practical issues of use; the relevant question being not "what does this piece of writing mean?" (as if meaning was somehow a represented essence in a sign the activity of reading substantially extracts) but "how does this writing work?"

Steve McCaffery (2000 [1986]: 148)

For artists to produce the kind of culturally complex recombinatory art or remixing (Amani, this volume) that is fundamental to contemporary digital art practices, they need to either engage in acts of plunder or go through an onerous bureaucratic process to obtain the rights through middle men such as clearance agencies. Alternatively, they can do the work of dealing with the rights holders directly. I argue that this third way of dealing, through negotiations with authors or original rights holders – what could be called "direct dealing" – is the most practical and arguably the most advantageous way for digital artists to legally remix creative materials that fall under copyright. Sometimes such negotiations are very difficult, but sometimes they are surprisingly pleasant.

This observation was born of my efforts working on a digital video project based on the ouevre of Canadian poet bpNichol, tentatively called *The Complete Works*, conceived of as a translation of Nichol's writing into video form. The idea of translation has developed to encompass the idea of "remixing" his work in digital moving image. As a remix, the video relies heavily on Nichol's published work, all of which is protected by copyright, and all of which would be next to impossible to clear using standard legal practices given the working methodology of the video. Through this initiative, I became involved in designing the cover for Nichol's recent collected works, *The Alphabet Game* (2007), and the major art for the accompanying website, the *Online Archive for bpNichol* (bpNichol.ca).

For a creator proceeding according to the letter of Canadian copyright law, the normal process of working with materials by authors living or dead but still under copyright would be to secure an assignment of numerous rights to specific published and unpublished materials (Murray and Trosow 2007). Moreover, it would seem that artists wanting to remix copyrighted materials would also need to establish how and if the integrity of the work would be maintained in their remix, a rather difficult question to answer because it is one that has an irredeemably subjective element. Further, the ways in which work would be used in conjunction with other cultural material, and the potential danger thereby posed to the reputation of the author, would have to be assessed to ascertain how or if an author or his estate might lay claim to moral rights infringement. All such determinations rely on digital artists having a specific preconceptualization of what they are doing creatively, and to what end, before they engage in the process of doing it, which is rarely the case for many artists working in this genre.

Instead of going through this "normal process" for my project, I went to bpNichol's estate directly to ask for permission to use his work in my film – I gave Ellie Nichol, bpNichol's widow and executor, an idea of what I was doing, and the nature of my creative process, and she agreed to allow me to work with the materials I found most useful and promising. This approach is only possible when an author has not assigned his copyright, and thus where rights remain with a creator or her descendants. The possible benefits of such direct negotiations, I believe, provide some potential reasons why authors and artists might want to refrain from assigning their copyright to collective bodies or from waiving their moral rights. Authors and their families can negotiate in ways far more sensitive to the nuance and context of subsequent digital works and their relationships to the original author's values than corporate copyright collectives are likely to have any interest in doing. What is a purely bureaucratic and economic transaction for a collective is a matter of professional reputation and artistic community for the original creator; direct dealing provides an opportunity to publicly commemorate a loved one for the artist's descendants.

Directly negotiating permission for my project from the estate had a number of unanticipated benefits. When I began the video, in 1999, there were no substantial online archives of bpNichol's work. An important part of his creative process was publishing poems in small runs as chapbooks or as various forms of "ephemera" associated with the events at which he composed and performed. These ephemeral works are very hard to find outside of private collections and the holders of such collections were largely unknown to me. Not only was Ellie Nichol able and happy to provide me with access to bp's personal library of published works, she introduced me to filmmaker Brian Nash, who generously gave me access to the considerable digital audio tape archive of Nichol recordings that he had compiled, organized, and logged for his 1997 film, *bp: Pushing the Boundaries*. One introduction led to another, unlocking a cascade of new and formerly unknown materials from people and institutions in Nichol's personal and artistic networks of friends and colleagues. Working through a collective would never have yielded such a rich treasure trove of work to add to the record of Canadian cultural heritage.

With introductions from Ellie Nichol and Brian Nash, I made contact with Roy Miki, Stephen Ross Smith, Stephen Scobie, Daphne Marlatt, Douglas Barbour, Lia Paz, Gil McElroy, Darren Wershler, Nicki Drumbolis, and Paul Dutton, to name a few, all of whom contributed bibliographic leads, actual chapbooks and ephemera, analysis, and even unknown recorded performances of Nichol's work. Coach House Books has been, and continues to be, an important source of support and information regarding Nichol's work. The Simon Fraser University Library Special Collections provided a wealth of materials. Only with Ellie Nichol's permission and her introduction would the late Gene Bridwell have given me the hours of assistance he did, navigating the countless manuscripts and notebooks held in the SFU collection. In addition to helping me build a rich body of material from which to draw for the video, dealing directly with all of these people and institutions helped me develop a much richer historical and socially contextualized understanding of bpNichol and his oeuvre. The subsequent development of digital archives will enable these conversations to continue with a wider group of fans, friends, and admirers online, while continually adding to the cultural knowledge we have of the man, his work, and his community. With such new forms of electronic distribution, access to the Nichol materials is much more easily facilitated than when my project began. One can find an array of his work at the Online Archive for bpNichol (bpnichol.ca), at PennSound (www.writing.upenn.edu/pennsound/x/Nichol.php), on the Coach House Books website (www.chbooks.com/online), at Karl Young's Homepage Away from Home for bpNichol (www.thing.net/~grist/l&d/bpnichol/bp.htm), Jim Andrews' digital restoration of First Screening (www.vispo.com/bp/introduction.htm) and on UbuWeb (www.ubuweb.com).

A defining aspect of contemporary digital video making is the ability to easily combine a range of materials from a variety of sources to create something new. As other scholars in this volume elaborate, the remix reiterates something that has been a part of textuality and creativity since the beginning of language in the form of the quotation (Lessig 2008). The quotation is ubiquitous in written texts, speeches, and everyday discourse. With contemporary digital technology, quoting, an integral part of creative practice, as contributors Amani, Boon, and Reynolds (this volume) suggest, becomes both more compelling and more complex. Images, audio, text, and video are all usually held in complicated entanglements of copyright and artists and curators have little sense of how the criteria for "fair dealing" pertaining to whether they have taken a substantial part, or engaged in "review" or "criticism" are likely to be determined with respect to their own work of quoting multimedia works in online remixes.

Recombinatory practices are a defining aspect of contemporary digital art. Paul D. Miller (2004), aka DJ Spooky, takes the idea of quotation further to see remixing in the form of sampling as a method of composition in and of itself: "This is a world in which all meaning has been untethered from the ground of its origins and all signposts point to the road that you make up as you travel through the text" (5). The road is the work the artist is creating – selection and combination of materials are compositionally or methodologically determined rather than being determined by semantics or the original context of the source material. The complex network of contexts built up from the combinations of samples become intertextual properties rather than clearly defining or supporting the direction of the work. This poses an even greater challenge to the notion of the integrity of the original materials.

As a hip hop artist operating in the United States, Miller is working in a different medium, country, economy, and cultural context than bpNichol, and a different context from what I operate in as an independent digital media artist in Canada. The available sounds he uses for his remixes come from libraries that have been produced purposely for his work, copyrighted materials that he has privileged access to, or work that is now in the public domain. Sampling does not obviously fall under the fair use exception in the United States or the fair dealing clauses in Canada (see Boutros, this volume). If a remixed work is to be legally legitimate in either country, copyright permission is usually considered necessary for recognizable source materials.

The remix is a culturally complex object that is built up from layers of quotations that originally "belonged" elsewhere. As my work with Nichol's record illustrates, and the work of users of the digital archives of his work will continue to illustrate, such remix is not only a unique combination of creative materials, but also a social network that layers the cultural, political, and economic contexts in which the materials were created and collected. For digital artists working in this recombinatory mode, access to such materials is significant not only in the practical aspects of production (what can and cannot be used), but also in the creative development of the new work: the degree of access changes the kind of creative processes in which an artist can engage, and ultimately, the kind of work that can be produced.

Improvisation, deconstruction, fragmentation, and free play are important aspects of bpNichol's poetics that inform the working methodology of the video I created. His work contains a veritable catalogue of textual strategies, techniques, and processes. "If I can keep moving the structure of the poem around, hopefully I can encompass different realities and different ways of looking at things" (Nichol 2002: 276). The spirit of Nichol's own poetics of reconfiguration is thus the basis of the working methodology for my Nichol video and, in this sense, extends and projects his moral rights by embodying his personal mode of creativity. In *Rational Geomancy* (1992), for example, Steve McCaffery and Nichol discuss translation as a creative act in which one aligns the signs in the destination text to create a new version of the source text. Their idea of translation resonates strongly with the contemporary notion of the remix. It necessarily involves rereading and reinscribing a work. To translate Nichol's work in this spirit means to cut it up, rearrange it, put it though translational systems, to see it in and from a different range of contexts. For digital artists working in recombinatory modes, to really *work* with a work is to deploy it in a manner that may challenge the idea of its integrity. For some authors, this is precisely in line with their own values, but others and their estates and publishers who hold moral rights posthumously may well voice strong opposition to such practices.

It should be clear that rights holders have the potential to act as gatekeepers not only to cultural materials, but also to their meanings through their rights to prohibit transformative reproductions (Bowrey

2005, Coombe 1998). Moreover, section 14.1 of the Canadian Copyright Act (2010) states that the copyright holder has a moral right to maintain the integrity of the work. This could be interpreted in many different ways, however, depending on the intentions and philosophy of the author. McCaffery (2000) describes a poetic in which a literary work becomes a "methodological field" rather than a "fixed object of analysis" (148). The integrity of a poem as method, such as Nichol's *Translating Translating Apollinaire* (1979) is in its continual manipulation, reformulation, and mutation into alternative and sometimes-unrecognizable forms. A more conventional sense of what the integrity of a work means might completely misread the authorial intent of this work. Rights holders, who may be far removed from the original author in commercial contexts where rights are repeatedly assigned, thus have the potential to regulate how a work is read and what it ultimately means.

In my remixes of Nichol's work, I am often putting the poems through processes that radically change their content and appearance. An example would be the sound and visual text for *Interrupted Nap* (1990), which I am using to create new animated visuals to attach to a sound recording made by Nichol (1982). From a conventional perspective, it might be argued that the integrity of the text has been completely mutilated or distorted because I have chosen to entirely reformulate it based on the possibilities available in my digital video practice and those posed by the recording. I am using and inverting a "see-and-say" method that Nichol himself used to create the original performance of the poem so as to produce a new animated visual text that no longer uses the original visual text at all. If a holder of moral rights were to consider the integrity of the piece to lie in its content or in the visual configuration of the original text rather than its method, moral rights could be invoked to prevent this segment of the video from being made, despite the fact that my work carries out the intentions of the author and his personal vision for the original.

Although Nichol's poetic methodologies resonate with contemporary digital practice, the publishing environment is now radically different than the one in which he composed his work. As a poet active from the 1960s into the 1980s, Nichol's work was rarely distributed electronically, nor did it for the most part exist in a networked environment where it would be publicly searchable (although Nichol cofounded the BBS-based e-magazine *Swiftcurrent* in 1984, so some such pieces do exist). The materials Nichol drew upon in the production of his work – "found texts" and otherwise – were not widely known and not easily located and identified. Nichol did not have access to the kind of casual searching that Internet search engines now allow, but neither were the kinds of cultural appropriation in which he engaged so susceptible to the claims of copyright holders who can now, through the same means, easily learn about remixes of their work. Networked cultural environments simultaneously pose new opportunities and new dangers for works of quotation and translation.

In such environments, the social and professional context in which cultural practitioners work and the symbolic capital they are able to claim become especially important. As an independent digital media artist, my credibility was buttressed by my history of relationships with the Nichol family; I first read *Gorg, a Detective Story* some twenty years ago and began a correspondence with Ellie Nichol at that time. As a graduate student who was able to turn this video project into a Master's research project, I was able to build on this social capital as well as the fact that the video received both Canada Council and Ontario Arts Council funding. Such a history of validation provided a context that furnished me with ongoing privileges in terms of my access to copyright materials that might otherwise have been foreclosed. Nichol's estate has granted me open-book access to his material, musicians have granted me formal and informal permissions to use their work, and authors and performers have generously agreed to appear and/or have their work included in the video without charge. I allocated a small fee for the estate, which I paid using grant money received from both the Canada Council and the Ontario Arts Council. Such open access allows an artist considerable leeway in drawing upon the material for improvisation – it allows for an open dialogue with the work in which the process of creation is not driven by a defined outcome, as is usually the case in commercial contexts.

In my role as an independent media artist, I am in a very different position with respect to rights issues than when I am acting as a professional/creative director. These differences involve both practical and conceptual considerations, based on different approaches to securing access to source materials, which in both instances serves as a primary driver in creative development. Professionally, I work primarily in the United States on commercial, broadcast design, and interactive media projects for broadcasters and advertising agencies. Copyright issues are dealt with by multiple legal teams representing the client, the agency, the broadcaster, and my company. In this environment, I have seen projects live and die around mere seconds of music and video belonging to rights holders.

In some cases, it is clear what can be used and what cannot; in others, rights agreements are so subtle and complex that any use becomes the subject of speculative interpretation. In one instance, a large-scale interactive project that took us six months and countless resources to produce was "shelved" after completion because of ongoing uncertainty around the usage of music that had been previously cleared for use in radio promotional contexts. Despite the fact that the project had proceeded on the basis of consulting lawyers' approval of the use of the music in our own radio promotion effort, we found that no one would host the site for fear of litigation. Huge amounts of energy, creativity, resources, and time are often wasted because of such legal uncertainties. In a professional commercial context, all uses of protected materials need to be defined, interpreted, and cleared ahead of time.

The more general the specification of the use, the more expensive the licence to take advantage of the material becomes. Licences to use protected cultural content will often be accompanied with new and further detailed restrictions on how it can be used and specifications for the contexts of its association with other cultural materials, all of which creates further interpretive dilemmas as well as new costs. It also compels different ways of working. When navigating rights agreements in a commercial context, a clear statement of the nature of the use needs to be made – where it will be used, for how long, on what platforms, in what territory, and, depending on the material, in what creative framework. Placing an end result on the use of the material, even if one is working with a friendly rights holder, puts pressure on creative work in a way that limits potential avenues of exploration, combination, and interpretation. As a consequence, improvisational remix methods are not commonly used in commercial contexts because they are too expensive and approvals too onerous.

It might be argued that my experience with bpNichol's work is unique because his estate continues to allow his work to circulate within what Pauline Butling and Susan Rudy (2005) describe as a small-press "gift economy" typified by a surplus of goods that were often given away for the good of the community. Nichol certainly produced an excess of material; he donated thousands of hours of writing, publishing, and editing work. He gave away armloads of copies of his magazine *grOnk*, which published the work of Canadian and international avant-garde poets. Such reciprocal gifting produced a closely linked network of artists who collectively developed much of the contemporary poetry of that historical period. The Nichol estate's generosity in providing access to his art, poetry, and ephemera supports continued interest, distribution, and artistic engagement with his work, which arguably ensures its ongoing social and symbolic value. It allows his work to be explored in new ways, and to continue to develop. The continued circulation of his work ensures that it remains vital and relevant. My own creative work contributes to establishing his significance in Canadian cultural history while keeping the legacy of his way of doing cultural work alive.

All of this is not to suggest that bpNichol had no institutional or commercial presence, and where he did, my own creative efforts are transformed in instructive ways. Where his work is part of media program, such as Phyllis Webb's interview with him on CBC TV's *Extensions* (1967), I would have to pay for materials. In correspondence with staff at the CBC Archives (https://archivesales.cbc.ca/), I was quoted the sum of $85 per second with a thirty-second minimum for worldwide rights in all media in perpetuity – the rights required for use in a video that may be broadcast, shown at festivals, and made available online. In addition to the fee, I need to provide proof that I have permission to use the material from any underlying copyright holders. This is onerous because it requires me to ensure that all rights were cleared to make the original television program from which I am quoting (an impossible task when the program is over 40 years old). Radio clips will cost me $42.50 per second. These are prohibitive costs for a creative project of this nature and will almost certainly ensure that I will not use materials in the public record, which for many viewers provide an important aura of authenticity. As Asquith (this volume) suggests, it seems especially unfair when publicly funded institutions, who should hold these historical records for the public, price this material so as to make it impossible for artists to comment and reflect upon our country's cultural history.

The law and jurisprudence of fair dealing make no allowances for the creative work I do and the kind of cultural history to which I contribute. The bpNichol video project exemplifies a creative practice of remixing that by necessity uses materials protected by copyright. The copyright law under which I have had to work has provided no practical way for digital artists like myself to engage in recombinatory creative practices. It is impossible to submit for the consideration of all rights holders a specific description of all the possible permutations that the source material might take in a recombinant work. The legislative amendments that are now promised to enable non-commercial transformative work as fair dealing give me little comfort, given the ambiguous condition that one's work has no effect upon the market for the original, which is a highly speculative exercise. The overwhelming public perception is that one is still effectively forced to either "steal" the work or go through the requisite clearing agencies. Instead, I'd advocate doing the hard work of directly dealing with the copyright holders, publishers, archivists, peer communities, and institutions to arrange the kinds of access and permission required to legally engage in a remixing practice. Such direct dealing is only possible where the original authors and artists have not assigned their copyright-protected materials to corporations and licensing collectives. Where such windows of opportunity exist, creators need to do a tremendous amount of work, but it is, ironically, the only practical way for independent artists to access the richness of cultural expression that the law of copyright ideally promises yet materially withholds.

PART C

Making Our Digital Heritage a Dynamic One

21 Copyright Dramas: Theatre Archives and Collections Online

DAVID M. MEURER

The mandate of libraries, archives, and museums (LAMs) is to preserve and provide access to cultural resources to research communities and the public. In digital communications environments, copyright law is among the greatest challenges facing LAMs in the fulfilment of this mandate. At stake in whether or not a cultural institution can make cultural resources accessible in online, non-commercial, educational contexts is its relevance for a public increasingly accustomed to seeking and finding information online. As communication and research practices evolve, LAMs must adapt in order to meet changing expectations. Licensing initiatives have become the most common and most frequently recommended path to respond to these changes and communicate and promote culture. However, uncertainties for cultural institutions abound. Clearing copyrighted works requires substantial resources and reliance on precarious funding sources. Making works available under fair dealing provisions, conversely, is subject to a determination of the nature and purpose of the dealing. But in the absence of case law pertaining to digital archives and collections and the applicability of fair dealing exceptions to them, the copyright status of publicly accessible digital reproductions remains uncertain to cultural institutions.

In this chapter, digital collections and archives of theatre materials provide the context for a case study that illustrates how the negotiation of intellectual property (IP) laws, cultural policies, and information and computing technologies shapes the availability of cultural resources online. Legal scholars have drawn attention to the implications of copyright law for the digitization initiatives of cultural institutions both generally (Pessach 2007) and focusing on specific nations (Hudson and Kenyon 2007). The specific copyright challenges of digitizing archival materials as well as the particular characteristics of archival materials in the performing arts have also been explored (see Dryden 2006 and Marini 2007, respectively). In what follows, I will focus on the collaborative, dynamic, and varied labour conditions under which performing arts are produced and supported, and argue that these conditions pose special challenges for initiatives to license cultural resources for online publication.

My research is supported by interviews conducted with representatives of four digital theatre archives and collections based in Ontario, and it reflects actual processes, procedures, decisions, and ramifications rather than theoretical concerns. I thus focus less on policies and law, and more on how they are perceived and negotiated by decision makers. Of the projects considered, two are university based, and were undertaken by senior scholars with academic research grants. A third project is the initiative of a large cultural institution with a multitude of archival holdings and special collections. The fourth is a smaller theatre organization with significant physical holdings but few digitization projects. Interviews were open-ended, and the participants discussed the holdings, digitization projects, and online initiatives of their institutions, as well as challenges relating to copyright. Although each project varied significantly with respect to ownership of source materials, funding sources, level of expertise, and institutional context, all interview subjects articulated a sense that copyright law is ill-suited to accommodate the particularities of digitally archiving performing arts materials.

There is an acute need for a clearer path forward. As commentators have rightly pointed out, copyright law is fundamentally oriented towards the production, reproduction, and distribution of cultural goods in market contexts, and insufficiently addresses the role of non-profit cultural institutions that enable access to knowledge (Pessach 2007: 282). In the present media climate, discussions of copyright and digital communications often position copyright as an adversarial conflict that pits creators and owners against users. Under these discursive conditions, cultural institutions are exiled from the public imagination.

LAMs provide bricks-and-mortar access to cultural resources for education, research and scholarship, cultural documentation and promotion, and preservation of the historical record, among other purposes. Yet, their ability to extend functions across digital communications networks is fundamentally limited by copyright law. Unless exemptions can be applied, "digital cultural preservation always involves reproduction of cultural works … that is exclusively reserved to copyright owners of the reproduced works" (Pessach 2007: 255). Copyright law does not adequately address the particular constraints of reproducing the full range of cultural materials preserved and managed by cultural institutions. Archival funds and special collections often include materials created to support performing arts productions, such as posters, theatre programs, and playbills. As archivist Jean Dryden (2006) explains, "although not created for commercial exploitation, archival material is subject to the same copyright rules as Margaret Atwood's novels, Yousef Karsh's photographs, or Denys Arcand's films. This causes considerable difficulty for archival institutions and those who use archival records as the raw material for their own creations" (167).

Such difficulties substantively undermine the Canadian government's Canadian Culture Online Strategy "to ensure a dynamic and diverse Canadian cultural presence in both English and French on the Internet" (Canadian Culture Online Strategic Statement). They also exacerbate what has been described as a "Canadian Internet deficit" (Dayton-Johnson 2002) – a lack of high-quality Canadian content online. Interest in theatre materials is broad, and theatre-focused digitization projects have the potential to bring cultural resources closer to students at the secondary, postsecondary, and graduate level. Digital archives present an opportunity to enrich and invigorate the cultural industries by making the living history of the performing arts in Canada accessible to researchers, scholars and critics, members of the public, and – perhaps most importantly – the performing arts professionals capable of building on the ideas and innovations of earlier practitioners.

Clearing and Licensing Challenges of Theatre Materials

LAMs dealing with theatre materials encounter a range of sociological, economic, and organizational factors that complicate efforts to license cultural resources for non-commercial, online uses. Materials collected by archives can include set and costume designs, promptbooks, stage plans and models, promotional and documentary photographs, programs, posters, playbills, and other materials (see Marini 2007). These resources are typically secondary marketing materials designed to promote and support a theatre and its productions. If an archive wishes to digitize, reproduce, and publish a theatre's programs and materials online, it is reasonable to assume that securing permission from the theatre company is sufficient. Indeed, under section 13(3) of the Canadian

Copyright Act, an employee or person under contract is not, "in the absence of any agreement to the contrary," the first owner of copyrighted works produced for an employer. However, as Murray and Trosow (2007) note, this is not an easy statement to interpret – a court of law might consider whether contrary arrangements or contracts had been agreed upon, whether standard industry practices are relevant, and in the case of freelancers, whether other areas of the law, including taxation, might complicate or clarify ownership matters (75–6).

The production of a collective work, such as a theatre program, may bring many of these considerations into play, as a theatre may hire or interact with a diverse range of creators and authors from a variety of cultural fields. Any number of photographers, designers, illustrators, and writers might contribute copyrightable works to a program or poster. Advertisements may introduce additional layers of permissions to clear. Industry practices vary in each of these fields, so blanket determinations are unlikely to cover a theatre group's ownership of subsidiary works contained in a performing arts program. And for all but the largest theatre companies, graphic design and photography are unlikely to have been created by full-time employees. Theatre programs are sometimes produced by the performance venue rather than by the theatre company itself, which further complicates the copyright status of the materials. Work in the performing arts is also frequently itinerant: roles and contributors may change from one season, production, or performance to the next. As a consequence, locating all applicable rights holders may not guarantee an opportunity to simultaneously secure permissions for numerous works spanning a lengthy period of time. If digitization project leaders are determined or bound to adhere to a full clearance process and to retrace the often incompletely documented agreements and contracts under which volunteer, contract, and freelance work was performed, they commit to an extremely time-consuming process with few guarantees of a return on the time and resources invested.

Among the most interesting documents for theatre researchers are the programs, promotional photographs, and posters illuminating the social contexts of theatrical performance. Actors and theatre professionals wishing to clarify or confirm their own involvement in productions also heavily use these records. Programs provide a trove of information about the artistic, social, and economic relations that develop around the staging of a theatrical production. The conditions under which such resources are created, however, involve a complex intermingling of interests that is not always fully documented by theatre administrators. In such documents, rights in different kinds of works are layered with different copyright implications, and may contain complex combinations of different materials, each of which may have its own subset of rights holders. Unified strategies for producing such collective works also do not exist.

A good example is an issue of *Playbill News Magazine*, the house program of the St. Lawrence Centre for the Arts, which contains a theatre program for the Toronto Arts Productions Theatre Company's 1975 production of Robertson Davies' *Question Time*. The Toronto Arts Productions Theatre Company was later renamed CentreStage, and then merged with Toronto Free Theatre to become the Canadian Stage Company in 1988. The program in question contains reproductions of several creative works, some of which are credited, while others are not. A photograph of two actors meeting Prime Minister Trudeau in Ottawa is not credited, and neither is a portrait of Robertson Davies accompanying his bio, nor a production photo of an upcoming performance of *Trelawny of the "Wells."* A studio photograph of the Beaux Arts Trio is signed only "Boris," and the program further contains costume sketches by Marie Day, an illustration by "Swain Sr.," and photographs by Eberhard Otto reproduced from *artscanada* magazine. The program text includes an introduction by Robertson Davies as well as an uncredited adaptation of an article on Shamanism by Peter T. Furst, published originally in *artscanada* magazine.

Many of these works were not created by employees of either the St. Lawrence Centre or the Toronto Arts Productions Theatre Company, and the agreements permitting their reproduction may differ considerably. Some works may have been created by volunteers, or contract workers. Even if the theatre company, in its reorganized state, is comfortable asserting ownership over the program based on agreements governing its original creation, the company may be unwilling or unable to give a third-party permission to reproduce the document online as part of a larger digital archive of theatre materials. Teasing apart the details for all of these individual works might require archival research into the administrative files of both the venue and the theatre company, materials that are archived separately in the example provided above. In the absence of a full declaration of ownership, permission would need to be secured from each designer, photographer, illustrator, and writer whose work appears in the program – or from their estates. In an ideal situation, theatre archive projects wishing to license and digitize collective works for online collections could turn to a reasonable and manageable set of guidelines. However, no such guidelines exist in either Canada or the United States (see Besek 2003 for commentary on the US situation).

If theatre groups and other corporate rights holders were prepared to assert ownership over these cultural resources and license them for non-profit, educational use in online archives, the processes would be simplified, and the possibilities for promoting Canadian culture greatly enhanced. However, fear of legal consequences prevails among stakeholders, as is manifest not only in the protocols followed by institutional initiatives in their digitization and online presentation efforts, but also in the unwillingness of theatre groups to assert ownership over promotional materials produced in the past. Moreover, large cultural institutions – with their seemingly vast budgets and substantial liability insurance coverage – may be attractive targets for legal claims and, therefore, feel compelled to avoid exposure where possible. Theatre groups are fundamentally hesitant to wade into legal matters or to tangle with actors' unions, and neither have the resources to pay for counsel nor a desire to alienate past, present, or future members of the theatre community who might object, whether rightfully or not, to the reproduction and publication of materials.

When licensing efforts move ahead, the challenges are great. Photographs inserted into programs may feature actors, directors, artistic directors, and other personnel employed by the theatre, and even when these individuals hold no copyrights they may possess other legal rights (Murray and Trosow 2007: 185). As a result, the licensing protocols followed by digital archives and collections often seek permission from all recognizable subjects, a strategy that introduces additional problems. One interviewee, for instance, tells of an actor appearing in a cast photograph who refused permission to use the photo for a book on the grounds that it was unflattering. Another interviewee reported a case in which an actor was reluctant to permit the use of a photo from an old theatre production because it was considered politically incorrect by contemporary standards (even though it was of scholarly interest for precisely that reason, and to no discredit of the actor).

Expectations of remuneration following permission requests are a further difficulty. Our media climate polarizes discussions of copyright by positioning creators against consumers, so that a request for permission may be considered tantamount to a declaration of economic value, in response to which the assertion of economic interests is only reasonable. One project reported that while production staff continuously emphasized to rights holders the costs of digitizing and making cultural resources available online for educational uses, and stressed the benefits that a digital archive would provide, rights holders nonetheless often expected licensing fees to be paid.

The older the resources for which licences are sought, the greater the challenges: theatre community members move domestically or overseas, their whereabouts may be unknown, or they may have passed away, in which case next of kin or the creator's estate must be identified. Efforts to identify, locate, and contact all rights holders and to secure permissions from each in order to reproduce a single program created many years prior can drain resources dramatically, and rarely yield certainty about the results achieved. But without permission from all rights holders, the work is not considered cleared, and legal counsel, institutional administrators, project partners, and grant-lending agencies may not endorse use of those materials.

Once established, contact with rights holders may initiate negotiations with parties who are unfamiliar with the circumstances in which the works were created, or who may have been unaware of their existence. Strict observance of licensing protocols also impacts communication between rights holders and the producers of digital archives, because the effort to secure permissions through the use of legal forms and contracts invariably formalizes dialogue: several interview subjects reported that rights holders were often happy to provide informal permission for the use of their works, but were less forthcoming if that process required formal written contracts. Rights holders may find contracts laden with unfamiliar terminology, or filled with references to communications technologies they do not use and whose implications they do not fully comprehend. Asking rights holders to sign contracts can further erode trust between the parties. In some instances, agents or legal representatives intervened, and unrealistic requests for remuneration resulted: on occasion, not-for-profit cultural institutions were asked for hundreds or even thousands of dollars for single non-exclusive licences granting permission to use materials in non-commercial contexts. If such requests are multiplied by the number of works in an archive, it becomes clear that few, if any, Canadian cultural digital archive projects can afford to bear these licensing costs over and above the already substantial costs of organizing, clearing, digitizing, and disseminating a database of theatre materials. As one interviewee admitted, "the clearance process brought us to our knees."

Orphan Works and the Consequences of Clearance Culture

The likelihood of successfully clearing collective works such as programs diminishes greatly if all materials must be licensed before use. Organizations may expend vast amounts of resources only to be stalled when efforts to trace the chain of title in works lead to dead ends caused by destruction or loss of records; undocumented verbal, informal, or implicit agreements, or failure to locate a known rights holder. Such cases yield "orphan works," and copyright law ostensibly accounts for such situations by enabling application for permissions to the Copyright Board, which is authorized to stand in for unlocatable copyright owners. However, the procedure is "onerous, unpredictable, and particularly unsuited to Internet materials" (Murray and Trosow 2007: 226–7; Bucholz, this volume). Clearing such works through the Copyright Board can only be done on an individual basis, which further encumbers projects with the responsibility of administering numerous individual requests and payments. Having expended many hours in failed attempts to track down rights holders for a single theatre program in a comprehensive collection, institutions may have neither the appetite nor the resources for additional administrative processes. The resource-intensive licensing procedures of the Copyright Board may be manageable for projects requiring a limited number of licences, but hardly for expansive cultural database projects valued precisely for their breadth and comprehensiveness.

Lack of clarity over clearance requirements has numerous implications for digital arts archives and collections. Institutions operating archival or special collections may "cherry pick" easy-to-clear materials. An Australian study finds that for LAMs, copyright is "significantly influencing the selection of materials to digitize and their availability to the public" (Hudson and Kenyon 2007: 204). Frequently, studies recommend that libraries and cultural institutions should consider copyright before all other factors, as "the place to begin" (Lopatin 2006: 276, 279). According to such recommendations, institutions should produce digital reproductions only after all permissions have been secured, and consider redefining projects if permissions cannot be easily obtained (see Hazen, Horrell, and Merrill-Oldham 1998). Such a conservative approach may help institutions to steer clear of legal thickets, but in the performing arts, where chain of title is difficult and at times impossible to unravel, it can mean the wholesale attenuation of a project's scope.

It means shaping a project not to the needs and wants of performers, researchers, or the public, but to the risk management decisions of administrators and legal counsel.

Although all projects discussed by my interviewees followed slightly different approaches, all considered copyright to be a vast "grey area" incapable of providing legal assurances for anything but a full permissions-based clearance process. In the pursuit of certainty at the outset of a project, one interviewee reported consulting a number of lawyers and receiving different advice from each, including, in one case, a suggestion that the project was to have clearance efforts vetted on an item-by-item basis by legal counsel. Needless to say, the digital archiving project could not afford this proposition. In some cases, certainty was a hard requirement enforced by institutional bodies or funding agencies, which ultimately reduced the scope of the digitization initiative. Although works created by an individual can be easy to clear, collective works such as theatre programs were described as the informational "lynch pins" connecting performers, performances, cultural contexts, communities, and organizations. At the same time, these documents were also described as simply "not worth the effort." There is thus a very real danger that archives abandon contemporary subject matter altogether, in favour of public domain projects with no complex licensing implications (Hudson and Kenyon 2007: 204). Worse, institutions may not bother with digitization projects at all.

For one group, a large and experienced institution with a portfolio of numerous prior digitization projects, developing a digital collection of theatre materials covered by copyright protection proved to be a much greater challenge than they were able to anticipate, budget, or fund. The results were substantial in view of the challenges, but they were viewed both internally and externally as only moderately successful in relation to the original project scope. Consequently, in the absence of legislative change or other solutions, the institution's appetite for pursuing anything other than small or entirely public domain projects was virtually non-existent. In fact, while admitting that a "big pot of money" would have made things easier, the interviewee made it clear that no sum of money alone could solve all of the problems encountered. In another case, a group successfully completed a smaller digitization project involving a single collection of primary works donated by the creator and rights holder, but it also had no plans to develop further comprehensive online representations of its holdings. The interviewee felt that Canadian copyright law was still in its formative stages with respect to online digital archives, with no practicable regulations and guidelines yet worked out.

Two projects, however, enjoyed a measure of success – partly because of the funding agency's lack of insistence on copyright clearance in digital communications contexts. The imperative to deliver the funded project (in order not to have funding withheld in the future) and the influence of scholarly citation practices here seem to have outweighed the largely unknown risks of incorporating low-resolution reproductions into Web-based educational resources. Team members of one project felt that following the legal advice they received would mean to have everything "vetted through a lawyer," allowing them to get only "a tiny portion" of the project online. These projects by no means neglected to request permission where possible. Rather, the project leaders developed their own best practices around permission and principles of respect for creators – a "politesse" or "decorum" – and did not consider the failure to reach a rights holder after a well-documented "reasonable effort" to be grounds for exclusion. The communication practices they followed focused on in-person conversations or personal phone calls, and agreements were supported by email confirmation rather than through the use of permission forms and opaque contractual language. The same project incorporated scholarly citation practices and a disclaimer indicating that every effort had been made to contact rights holders. Another project similarly limited its use of images to small, low-resolution reproductions accompanied by attributions of the source. Between them, the two projects reported only one request to take material down from the website, and this was because permission had been granted for a limited time period, the expiration of which had gone unnoticed.

New Policies for Digital Archives?

The expectations of archive users have changed dramatically over time. Undergraduate students increasingly rely on online resources to conduct research (Van Scoyoc and Cason 2006), and the absence of Web-accessible resources in a particular cultural field can impede scholarship at all levels of study. Unsurprisingly, the general mandate of providing the public with access to knowledge resources has not changed for cultural institutions with the rise of digital communications. However, the lack of nuanced legal policy specific to LAMs severely restricts their ability to deliver on this mandate. Extensions and reformulations are needed to grant LAMs in Canada the ability to make materials available to the public in digital communications contexts, and not just bricks-and-mortar facilities. Through legal or cultural policy changes, restrictions on non-commercial and educational use of materials by not-for-profit cultural institutions must be loosened. So far, Canadian cultural policy has been insensitive to the copyright hurdles encountered in creating digital archives and collections, and copyright was deemed "irrelevant" by more than one interviewee. The importance of LAMs and online access to resources received no mention, for example, in a government-commissioned "comprehensive" report on emerging technology and Canadian cultural policy (Bélanger 2007), or in the final report funded by the Department of Canadian Heritage Culture and Technology Round Table (Watson 2007).

In the absence of policy revisions, legislative change, or clear guidelines for the applicability of copyright exemptions for non-commercial, educational digital archiving projects, access to treasure troves of cultural resources will remain limited to those in close geographical proximity to special collections and archives, and to an academic elite with access to travel funds. At present, a fundamental incompatibility exists between copyright laws and non-profit cultural digitization initiatives. Rich collections of cultural resources that define Canada's heritage and may be capable of invigorating it are kept offline by outdated policies. Such resources are undoubtedly of great interest to students, researchers, performers, and the public, but potential users are currently unable to access them using the digital communications methods they are most accustomed to.

22 Streaming a Digital Scream: Archiving Toronto's Barbaric Yawp

SUZANNE ZELAZO

Lovers and madmen have such seething brains,
Such shaping fantasies, that apprehend
More than cool reason ever comprehends.
The lunatic, the lover and the poet
Are of imagination all compact …
And as imagination bodies forth
The forms of things unknown, the poet's pen
Turns them to shapes and gives to airy nothing
A local habitation and a name.

A Midsummer Night's Dream

For Shakespeare's characters, this "habitation" is a woodland setting outside of Athens, and "the airy nothing," all the potency of a dream. This same conflation of imaginative virtuality and the physicality of the forest was central, in 1993, to the creation of what was, until its conclusion in 2011, Canada's largest single-day poetry festival: Scream in High Park (later, the Scream Literary Festival). Conceived by the enterprising twenty-one-year-old poet Matthew Remski, the Scream took place on the site of the Canadian Stage Company's annual production *Dream in High Park*. The lush hillside amphitheatre was essential to figuring the artistic democratization, reciprocity, and access that inhered in the spirit of the Scream. For nearly two decades, on the second Monday in July, before an audience regularly exceeding a thousand, the pay-what-you-can event celebrated narrative, performative, and poetic exchange. Run by a host of dedicated volunteers, the Scream, and the attempts currently underway to archive its history, offered a poignant paradigm for understanding cultural and legal attempts to challenge prohibitive restrictions of access and copyright within digital media in Canada.

Poet, Web-designer, and third Scream festival chair (after Remski and Peter McPhee) Bill Kennedy is currently spearheading the archival preservation and presentation of seventeen years' worth of festival material. Kennedy's purpose is straightforward and simple: to put into circulation an enormous body of largely ephemeral Canadian cultural expressions in order to promote, as the Creative Commons (CC) mandate indicates, "scholarly and cultural progress by making it easy for people to share their creations and to collaborate by building on each other's work" (Abelson et al. 2008: 3), all the while adhering to the premise of "fair dealing." Admittedly, the very concept of fair dealing is difficult to discuss in the context of a digital archive in which everything – by its very nature – is already a copy. For the sake of argument, however, the author asks the reader to suspend his or her disbelief (to think of electronic "copies" as original work) in reflecting upon what the Scream archive might engender as outlined below.

Certainly, the archive makes manifest the festival's spirit of generosity, organicism, and altruistic perpetuity. Indeed, as Darren Wershler-Henry (2002) reminds us, "the Net exists in the first place because of the generosity of others" (5). Currently in its trial phase, the Scream site is running on a non-release pilot version of the Artmob content management system (CMS) software. This current consideration of the archive is, more precisely, *A Midsummer Night's Dream* of what it might be when publicly launched. However, Kennedy's company Stop14Media, together with ProComp Consulting, has developed an open source (OS) framework for the archives, built on the Drupal CMS (https://drupal.org/) and licensed under version 2 of the GNU General Public License (GPL).

Despite the free distribution of the software that supports the archives, Kennedy and Artmob must nonetheless contend with prohibitive copyright laws that, geared as they are to a corporate economy, are resolutely at odds with the fluid, accessibility-driven digital age. Copyright laws also often seem at odds with the streaming spirit of the Scream itself, which is akin to the gift economy of small-press poetry culture in Toronto, where manuscripts, chapbooks, and even finished books are as likely to be given away or traded as purchased. In its very conception, copyright is destined to expire, eventually releasing all work to the public domain. In Canada, this usually happens fifty years after the artist's death. The illusion on which digital rights management (DRM) and other sorts of restrictions on the circulation and use of digital media are founded is based on fears that free access can result in financial harm for the works' creators. However, considered in a broader sense, the by-products of accessibility, including the possible increase of popularity and reputation may, in fact, lead to even greater compensation for artists. After all, as Wershler-Henry (2002) insists, the paranoia inherent in popular sociocultural perceptions of the Internet as operating according to a gift economy is strongly exaggerated, and it is doubtful that the Internet does, in fact, pose a severe threat to intellectual property (IP) and to the systems that manage its distribution and trade. Wershler-Henry reasons, "The gift economy and the regular economy are opposite sides of the same coin, one can't ever entirely replace the other" (xi). As the current case study makes clear, access is crucial not simply for cultural growth, but potentially, and even paradoxically, for the artist's own gains. Marjorie Perloff (2005) articulates this principle with the example of critics who claim that increasing digitization is resulting in diminished sociocultural value of the literary work: "The Modernist 'masterpiece' – that term of opprobrium – seems to be reasserting its auratic claims upon us, even as Internet discourse, held, in some quarters, to be responsible for the loss of literary 'quality,' is ironically reinforcing its presence" (12).

And yet, preserved material cannot currently be uploaded wholesale onto archival websites. First, copyright must be cleared for each and every embedded contribution, a task that constitutes an administrative nightmare (see Meurer, this volume). Consider, for example, the archivist's efforts to post a recording of an entire night at the Scream – all five hours, from the MC's introductions to the musical interlude of intermissions and to the closing remarks. Easy enough, one might think: post a link to an MP3 file and away you go. What would happen, however, when the archivist encounters an objection from the first performer in the third set, who fears the prospect of her work being made available for easy and free download? Should you block her out, render her performance in a blackout mode? What would such a lacuna do to the integrity and continuity of the remaining four hours and fourty minutes minutes of the performance? What does such an objection convey about an artist's relationship, indeed responsibility, to his or her audience, and to the work itself?

At times, the resistance comes not from the producers of the primary content being displayed (i.e., the poets and other performers), but from those who have contributed copyrightable support material of marginal importance. Kennedy explains these complications through an example involving the National Ballet Company. Imagine an attempt to archive season programs from the National Ballet: every quote, logo, and dancer head shot has its own copyright that must be cleared before people will be able to look up who the character Clara's understudy was in the 1991 performance of *The Nutcracker* (cf. Meurer, this volume). In the concrete efforts to archive Scream, the task just outlined is complicated by the enormous amount of ephemera often passed around to the festival's audiences, material that constitutes an essential part of the event itself. Such ephemera, including the free poems, handbills for upcoming readings, announcements for book sales and art shows, are all part of the musculature of the evening's performance. Quite often, such work is purposefully anonymous, but copyright for all of it must be cleared so that it can be uploaded. Where, however, does one even begin to search for rights holders in such a context?

Kennedy conceptualizes user involvement in the construction of the site itself through the Creative Commons. As in the model of social networking sites, users would be invited to help identify orphan works, locate rights holders, and contribute essential metadata, as well as link material to other sources that would enrich the site's content, "make[ing] visible," as Adalaide Morris (2006) comments, "the historical contexts occluded by variorum print editions" (15). The Creative Commons enables "'some rights reserved,'" rather than "'all rights reserved' … [or] 'no rights reserved'" (Lessig 2004: 11). By using the CC licences, Kennedy's design for the archive will allow "creators [and] content owners … [to] take voluntary action by marking their content with a tag that expresses a kind of freedom" (ibid.).

Established to mollify outdated and often misunderstood copyright laws, the Creative Commons reasserts the fair use and fair dealing standards of being able to utilize copyrighted material without procuring often highly restrictive permissions and exorbitant fees in instances when the social benefit of doing so outweighs the private loss to the copyright holder. In this way, Kennedy envisions the Scream archive as an ongoing work in progress capable of creating its own version of Peter Jaszi's "Best Practices Model," thereby establishing precedents for a repertoire of fair use dealings. As Patricia Aufderheide (2009) insists, "since judges take into consideration the practice of any creator or user community in fair use litigation, identifying a community's norms and values has great utility" (14). Together with Peter Jaszi, Aufderheide has created a number of such codes of best practices in the United States (see, e.g., Aufderheide and Jaszi, 2004, 2008a, 2008b, 2011), and the Scream site aims to extend this approach in Canada.

To be sure, the establishment of this kind of benchmark necessitates quality control, and the Scream archive site will have a board made up of scholars in the fields of law, communication studies, cultural studies, and English, as well as Web developers and consultants who will vet and verify all contributed data. Nonetheless, by making material digitally available for study and appreciation, the public begins to have a say in constructing cultural value. Excessive copyright provisions can adversely affect the potential for open adjudication of artistic credibility and value. Current copyright laws in Canada decidedly work against the possibility of extending the arbitration of cultural value to the public, and often even to the artists themselves. A collective and democratic archive such as the Scream site will expand what Walter Benjamin intuited in 1936, when he noted that "the distinction between author and public is about to lose its basic character" and that "at any moment the reader is ready to turn into a writer" (Benjamin 1968: 232). Visitors to the Scream site will be able to respond instantly to the archival material in public forums such as Artmob's own blog, foregoing the restrictions that characterize the archives of special collections and rare book libraries, far exceeding anything Benjamin might have presaged.

Perloff (2005) champions Benjamin's reader-turned-writer in the broadening of critical discussions about literature through customer reviews at amazon.com – what she calls the "naïve enthusiasm and assessment" of material by non-academic readers (6). She posits a refreshing confirmation of human ability to appreciate art, even if on the simple grounds that it "*give[s] pleasure*" (6, original emphasis). By calling our attention back to the perhaps more obvious, but often critically neglected, aspects of a work of literature, such as the "the charm of its distinctive rhythm and its deployment of a language that is somehow extraordinary," entry into the work shifts and amplifies, and artists earn new audiences as a result (ibid.). For Perloff, Ezra Pound's assertion in *The ABC of Reading* that "poetry is news that STAYS news," is paradoxically paramount to a preservation of the text as object in the digital world (Pound 1934: 29). In fact, thanks to Kenneth Goldsmith's archiving at UbuWeb (a site that was hosted on the Artmob servers for many years; see Goldsmith, this volume), we can now listen to Pound reading any number of his *Cantos*, or from "Hugh Selwyn Mauberly," or one of his many "Impressions" – his is certainly poetry that has stayed new, permitting expanded ways of re-entering or entering for the first time his works in print. The process of "staying news" by earning new audiences is achieved in part by what Goldsmith refers to as "nude media" in his theorization of the workings and success of UbuWeb. Goldsmith (2006) explains:

> What I mean by [nude media] is that once, say, an MP3 file is downloaded from the context of a site such as UbuWeb, it's free or naked, stripped bare of the normative external signifiers that tend to give as much meaning to an artwork as the contents of the artwork itself. Unadorned with branding or scholarly liner notes, emanating from no authoritative source, these objects are nude, not clothed. Thrown into open peer-to-peer distribution systems, nude media files often lose even their historical significance and blur into free-floating sound works, traveling in circles that they would not normally reach if clad in their conventional clothing. (52)

As it is for Pound, Perloff, and Goldsmith, the insistence on "staying news" is at the heart of Kennedy's archival pursuits – indeed of all the archives under construction through Artmob, dedicated as it is to cultural preservation in Canada.

Significantly, the Scream archive digitally replicates the community-based, separate-but-connected audience of the Scream festival – wherein the audience actually becomes part of the piece, as in John Cage's groundbreaking composition *4'33,"* his four minutes and thirty-three seconds of "silence," during which the coughs, shuffling, and audience anxiety constitute the artwork. Similarly, digital archiving of Scream recordings and videos captures the squeals of impatience from children on the hill, registers the merging of performances with the sound of rain, the immediately recognizable laugh of poet Christian Bök, or the mix-ups and mispronunciations of names and titles by those introducing the artists – in short, the organic flaws that underscore the eventuation of the event.

Such seemingly extraneous material creates what Jerome McGann, in his work on textual materiality, describes as a text's linguistic and bibliographical codes. Appropriated to the stage, these codes can be understood as performative codes. In *The Textual Condition*, McGann (1991) explains:

> Every literary work that descends to us operates through the deployment of a double helix of perceptual codes: the linguistic codes, on the one hand,

> and the bibliographical codes on the other. We recognize the latter simply by *looking* at a medieval literary manuscript – or at any of William Blake's equivalent illuminated texts … In each of these cases the physique of the "document" has been forced to play an aesthetic function, has been made part of the "literary work." (77, original emphasis)

In investigating the contexts (social, institutional, or otherwise) in which a text is produced, McGann's plurality of perspective insists on the text (or in our case performances of texts) as a continuous assemblage and reassemblage between various editions, but also in terms of the text's constitution and ongoing reception. Although McGann appears here at odds with Goldsmith's concept of "nude media," both Goldsmith and McGann underscore the social reception of a text as a redeployment. For Goldsmith, this is achieved via the freedom of unrestricted accessibilty, whereas for McGann this liberation is achieved because "texts are produced and reproduced under specific social and institutional conditions, and hence … every text, including those that may appear to be purely private, is a social text" (ibid.). In performance, of course, the social context has an even greater significance. According to Charles Bernstein (1998):

> The [poetry] reading is the site in which the audience of poetry constitutes and reconstitutes itself. It makes itself visible to itself … For poetry is constituted dialogically through recognition and exchange with an audience of peers where the poet is not performing to invisible readers or listeners, but actively exchanging work with other performers and participants. (22–3)

Through reading and listening, writing is written. The spatio-temporal complexity (and freedoms) of digital media engages the social context in even more extensive ways, in a profound democratization of access. The Center for Social Media's 2008 study of trends in online video making highlights the potentiality of this very access. In "Recut, Reframe, Recycle: Quoting Copyrighted Material in User-Generated Video," Aufderheide and Jaszi (2008a) document the marked sense of ease with which former audiences who themselves turned creative practitioners use pre-existing material and even assert new meaning for pop cultural productions, heavily quoting copyrighted material and redeploying it, and their own work, to an ever-widening online viewership. Aufderheide and Jaszi reason:

> This is of course a result of the way culture becomes "popular." It comes to have meanings beyond its immediate utility and is used by the people once known as consumers to express their own identities through association and transformation. Thus, it is no surprise that, in order to use and express the meanings and associations popular culture has come to have in their lives, online video creators turn to its performances and products. These copyrighted works have effectively become a part of these makers' vocabularies. (6)

Similarly, by listening to and viewing the Scream performances in the digital format of the archive, audiences necessarily engage in the content anew: digital code and the computer screen bisect, and the audiences' engagement constitutes a "recutting, reframing," and thereby "recycling" of the archived material.

Starting to Scream

Like Remski, I was twenty-one when I went to my first Scream. I volunteered at a book table selling the wares of Coach House Books, Insomniac Books, and ECW Press. My eyes were full of wonder at the poets whose voices bellowed over the buzz of mosquitoes, echoed against the muffled sigh of the Gardiner Expressway and the QEW as they stretched their motorized limbs against Lake Ontario, and lingered over couples giggling amid pine cones – bursts of love sounding between sets on stage.

What I have of that night is a memory, some recorded thoughts in a rapidly yellowing notebook, and the community of artists that has been my own ever since. But, to be able to see, hear, and relive the performances that night with twelve years of reading and writing and living behind me – as I now can, thanks to Kennedy's initiative and my preview of what the site will be when launched publicly, making available audio and video recordings as well as amazing amounts of ephemera – enables me to explore how I myself have redeployed what I watched and listened to that summer night back in 1997. The streamed video and sound performance on the Scream website and similar archives allows the work to be "augmented, amplified, and filtered by the user's body" (Morris 2006: 17), through multisensual engagement, but also through the ability of users to pause, stop, and skip around the site and linked resources. The result is an ever-increasing reduction in the distance between producer and produced, creator and created.

In his introduction to *Carnival: A Scream in High Park Reader*, Peter McPhee (1996), the second artistic director of the Scream, explains:

> We wanted a celebration of poetry and storytelling. We wanted to be lost for an evening on a midway of voice. Voice like caramel, sticking to our fingers. Voice of adrenaline, of inspiration. Exhilarating, head spinning. We wanted carnival … Scream in High Park became an eclectic meeting of background, viewpoint, and writing style. A momentary blend of voices forming a single, unrepeatable expression of the possible. The carny wasn't asking to buy, just to come in and discover. (xi)

Like a great, amorphous anthology, the Scream archive is a spatially constrained editor's dream. Allowing readers the chance to bridge the present and the past, and gesture to the future, in digital archiving bolsters artists' work and its critical reception by keeping it "new/s." In a prescient foretelling of the digitization of Scream material, McPhee (1996) explains the publication of the *Carnival* anthology as:

> an attempt to capture some of the magic that is Scream in High Park, cast it in a slightly different direction, and create a new spell. It listens to voices that have gathered in the summer air and asks how they will interact when you, the reader, can choose how to free them from the page. (xii–xiii)

McPhee's comments illuminate how the link between performance and the spatio-temporal liberties of digital media enables alternative contexts for theorizing and understanding both. The documenting of emergent poetries and ephemera of the visual and sonic Scream performances, and the presentation of them through a digital interface, enables sites such as the Scream archive to showcase a lineage of contemporary electronic literature. Doing so, Morris (2006) urges, enables us "to understand the computer as an expressive medium" (5). She reasons that "to its advocates, [hypertext] … appeared to materialize the still vibrant post-structuralist dream of processual, dynamic, multiple signifying structures activated by readers who were not consumers of fixed meanings but producers of their own compositions" (12). The recorded and digitally streamed performances of artists at the Scream become material through which viewers/readers can navigate/construct their own compositions, thereby penetrating, integrating, and appreciating the work in new and meaningful ways.

"I will never forget reading at the first Scream," writes McPhee (1996). "The sun had just set and the silhouettes of the people at the top of the hill were blending into the sky, mixing with my voice, and approaching infinity. I think one's sense of place becomes distorted" (xiii). As in its digital environment, the Scream archive mimics this distortion in a re-writing and recreation of form and content, a polyvocal cross-pollination and perpetual deterritorialization. Thanks to Kennedy's efforts, (and my sneak preview of what will soon by publicly available), this generative process was recently underscored for me while listening to an audio file of Nicole Brossard's reading at the 2002 Scream. Tuning into the site, I am, in effect, permitted to hear myself hearing the poems for the first time as I sat on the hillside in High Park. Listening to myself listening to Brossard's beautiful voice – her charmingly tentative English in stark contrast to the slippages into her mother tongue, where her speech is assured, yet fluid – is an amazing experience. In the recording, Brossard dances between linguistic registers, between genres, and between the interfaces of my memory and the screen. "We swim upstream against certainties," she intones:

> between my lips the night poured out its sensations … At night we think loosely about things, our hands on well-chosen verbs, we venture out into the improbable. With the surest instinct we linger in the most daring places of delirium and words. At night existence absorbs us like an obsession … the ineluctable form of desire. At night I always write. My hand on the verb to be. (Transcribed from the Scream Artmob Website; the audio file is currently available directly on the Scream Literary Festival website.)

Brossard's poetics effect what she calls in the poem a "mobile landscape" – one on the verge not only of language and genre, but space and time, the very liminality that the digital interface both cultivates and effects. From the page, the stage, to the infinite dream of cyberspace, attempts to preserve and promote our cultural heritage should not only be embraced and facilitated by less prohibitive policy, but also sounded loudly and fearlessly against the rooftops of the world in a streamed and barbaric yawp.

23 The NFB, Canada's Experimental Documentary Tradition, and Found Futures

MARTIN ZEILINGER AND ELI HORWATT

To anyone who has perused the online listing of freely available films produced by Canada's National Film Board, the institution's recently adopted (but always practised) motto – "The World Changes. Our Stories Live On" – surely appears as a true blessing. For seventy years now, the NFB has embraced a mission of facilitating the production of Canadian film and video works, mediating between the filmmaking community and the movie-going public, and archiving the results of its activities for broad access and both educational and recreational purposes. However, as a result of current copyright licensing practices, not all NFB-produced stories can be guaranteed to "live on." With the market orientation of contemporary intellectual property (IP) policy, a copyright clearance culture has emerged in which some publicly funded films may have to be removed from circulation because of prohibitively high relicensing fees.

Although the NFB does not track and release statistics of the difficulties it encounters with rights management, in a recent conversation with one of the authors of this chapter, Dominique Aubry, the director of the NFB's legal services, expressed dissatisfaction with Canada's current legal climate. Current copyright laws, she noted, produce manifold problems pertaining to rights and permissions, which are only amplified by the NFB's efforts to secure rights in perpetuity and across a wide spectrum of media (from DVD copies to downloadable online copies and, soon, cloud-based services) for all its productions. Given the complexities that often arise during licensing negotiations, it is sometimes necessary for the NFB to recommend changes to works in progress or, indeed, even to remove films from circulation. The public, which contributes to the funding of Canadian filmmakers, may then find itself cut off from access to works whose creation it has supported – a result that goes against the NFB's own goal of making as much as possible of its catalogue available to Canadians.

Taking note of this issue, a copyright survey conducted by Kirwan Cox, David Fewer, and Howard Knopf in 2005 cites the representative example of Paul Cowan's 1982 NFB-produced documentary *The Kid Who Couldn't Miss* (Cox 2006: 33). The film, which conveys contentious details about the First World War Canadian flying ace Billy Bishop, was kept in circulation for sixteen years, despite the political controversy it incurred, and perhaps thanks to the popularity it enjoyed for this very reason. In 1998, however, the NFB decided the documentary was not generating enough revenue to justify the expensive relicensing of some of the archival footage it featured. "In the end," the survey states, "the public lost access to this film not because of political censorship, but because of copyright censorship" (ibid.).

South of the Canadian border, similar examples can be found, as in the 1987 Public Broadcast Service documentary series *Eyes on the Prize*, hailed as one of the most important audiovisual accounts of the US civil rights struggle. Not long after its initial release, this work, too, was taken out of circulation because of licensing issues. In both cases, it is not the funding bodies or the distributors who are at fault for the public's loss of access to these works; rather, what stands in the way of fair access to the films in question is a combination of prohibitive licensing schemes and the narrow fair dealing and fair use provisions by which cultural institutions seek to abide.

Today's prohibitive licensing practices are widely understood to negatively affect the creation and production of future works. In a white paper based on the above-cited survey and prepared for the Documentary Organization of Canada, Howard Knopf (2006a) points out that thanks to the current clearance culture we find ourselves in a situation in which many films "that should be made are not being made" (7). As many of the contributors to this collection argue, there are a number of reasons for this: fair dealing provisions are not phrased in ways that encourage their use; licensing for copyrighted materials to be included in new works can be unaffordable; and, finally, we have entered an era of widespread fear of possible litigation should licences not be obtained. In the present chapter, we extrapolate from these issues the concern that because of potential relicensing issues, the current clearance culture could begin to have equally negative effects for back catalogues of works already in existence. What might be the consequences of applying the insistence on strict licensing schemes that we see applied to contemporary creative expressions to past creations? Given the trajectory of IP regulations throughout the twentieth century, we fear that without significant changes in the legislative attitude towards fair dealing and fair access, the public may find itself in danger not only of losing future works of art – as is already the case – but also of losing access to important works from the canon of existing, publicly funded works.

Fortunately, *The Kid Who Couldn't Miss* is today, once again, available to the public and can be viewed free of charge on the NFB's website (visit www.NFB.ca). *Eyes on the Prize*, too, is back in circulation (although not freely available), after roughly US$ 850,000 in grants and donations was raised to pay for relicensing costs (Anonymous 2005). We take the resistance often triggered by the fencing in of such works to be representative of the public's vexation with policies that cut off its access to works dealing with important aspects of our shared cultural heritage. Yet, even in the face of such resistance, issues of "copyright censorship" pose a potential threat to many entries in the large NFB catalogue. Considering the NFB's pledge to Canadians to keep their stories alive, what changes to the current system are necessary so that publicly funded Canadian films are ours not only culturally, but also legally?

As other contributions in this volume argue, there is a strong need for fair dealing provisions that provide creators with the access to pre-existing cultural matter needed to complete their works. By extension, such provisions should also safeguard the public's continued access to the works it has made possible in the past. As Knopf has shown for the general context of documentary filmmaking, this is currently not the case. Instead, what we see emerging is a body of what Pat Aufderheide and Peter Jaszi (2004) have called "untold stories" – works that are not created because they depend on the use of pre-existing materials that cannot be accessed. To curb this development, it is necessary to broaden current perspectives on fair dealing in filmmaking, and to extend them to the question of fair access to already-existing publicly funded works.

What might happen if highly restrictive copyright policies and licensing concerns were to be applied, retroactively, to single films or even to whole catalogues of works that have so far gone unharmed? Problems may arise when copyrighted materials featured in the works in question need to be relicensed; but could danger also lurk for works featuring copyrighted materials for which licences were never obtained because their production preceded the current rampant clearance culture? In what follows, we apply this logic to one example of the NFB's catalogue of films, and consider how the strict application of existing copyright and licensing regulations might impact viewers' access to this work. In conducting this thought experiment, we focus on Québécois filmmaker Arthur Lipsett's highly successful experimental short film *Very Nice, Very Nice* (1961), which is freely accessible on the NFB's website. Its creation predates the obsession with IP rights we are currently witnessing in the global cultural landscape, and hails from a time when filmmakers, producers, and rights holders had much less awareness of the legal implications of using existing materials without permission. Lipsett was notoriously opaque about his creative process and about the sources of most of the materials used in his films, many of which were produced at night, with materials scavenged from the trim bins of the NFB's editing studios. Because of this practice, the NFB has little information regarding whether permissions were sought or secured for much of the visual and sound footage used in *Very Nice, Very Nice*, and legal complaints by rights holders could, in theory, still arise.

Very Nice, Very Nice is a concise and witty non-narrative critique of the complications and discontents of contemporary urban life in a world of capitalist commerce, commodified culture, and rampant consumerism. Despite its age, the film continues to garner high critical acclaim decade by decade. For a period of time, *Very Nice, Very Nice* even enjoyed relatively great popularity – a unique achievement for a non-narrative, experimental work. The film was Lipsett's first work for the NFB. It could be described as a short, experimental documentary or, more fittingly, as a found footage film consisting almost entirely of appropriated, pre-existing images and sound recordings. In more concrete terms, the film consists of snippets of discarded film strips salvaged by the director in the NFB's editing studios, and of fragments from audio recordings stemming from a broad variety of sources, including radio commercials and news reports. In existing literature, nothing suggests that licences were obtained for these materials. *Very Nice, Very Nice* is thus an ideal subject for our purpose in this chapter: first, because it challenges traditional IP practices by making copying its primary mode of production without seeking permission to do so; and second, because in the authors' view, the film's underlying theme – a critique of consumer culture and of the hollow desire for private property it spawns – renders the artist's reuse of potentially copyrighted materials a relatively clear-cut case of fair dealing for critical purposes.

Lipsett's oeuvre is now considered an important piece of Canadian cultural heritage, and it is celebrated as part of the international canon of experimental cinema. In 1962, the year after its release, the *Very Nice, Very Nice* was nominated for an Academy Award in the category of Best Live Action Short Subject. Such mainstream success remains extremely rare for experimental films, and it is no surprise that this enthusiastic reception catapulted Lipsett into the centre of the Canadian experimental film scene. Today, such a high measure of success would likely also draw the close scrutiny of those who hold copyrights in the materials used, but to the authors' knowledge, this never occurred. Within a few years of the film's release, two hundred copies were in circulation, and Lipsett's oeuvre became widely available to viewers in Canada and around the world. In *Very Nice, Very Nice*, we have thus a film that by today's standards might easily be accused of violating copyrights, and which broadcasters and festival programmers would likely be reluctant to screen. At the same time, *Very Nice, Very Nice* continues to be appreciated by large audiences because it is thematically and formally representative of how we can creatively and critically engage with our sociocultural environment.

In film scholarship, found footage filmmaking refers to the practice of reusing pre-existing film footage and recasting it to reflect new ideas and meanings. Thanks to the malleability of film (both analogue film stock and digital video images can be easily edited, recopied, or otherwise manipulated), found footage filmmaking has been practised since the advent of cinema. Historically, the process has been employed in documentary films, in the creation of newsreels and political propaganda, and in avant-garde films. Today, it must also be understood as closely related to music video culture, to "mash-up" techniques that remix TV and video footage for online viewing, to "machinima" (the re-editing and narrativizing of footage taken from video games and other digital sources; see Horwatt 2010), and to audio sampling. Art works that use found footage are thus particularly relevant to the discussion of issues surrounding IP rights and licensing issues. Accordingly, just like documentary filmmaking, found footage films frequently trigger debates about the permissibility and legitimacy of the modes and techniques underlying their creation.

Despite being a marginal practice prior to the 1960s, found footage techniques were instrumental in defining the editing processes foundational to feature filmmaking and the construction of cinematic narrative continuity. Important forerunners were the early Soviet filmmakers

Sergei Eisenstein, Lev Kuleshov, and Dziga Vertov (all of whom acted as both theorists and experimental practitioners of montage techniques), and Esther Shub, an influential Ukrainian editor who pioneered the so-called compilation film, in which pre-existing, often disparate footage was reassembled to spread the propaganda of the nascent Bolshevik revolution. These figures were also noted for a technique in which Western films were re-edited to reflect pro-labour/anti-capitalist ideology – a technique whose blatantly propagandistic features Eisenstein described as a game both "wise and wicked" (Tsivian 1996: 336). The discoveries made by these directors – that the meaning of a film sequence is based on numerous elements external to the footage itself, and can be easily manipulated through the addition or recontextualization of sound, music, and text – was the springboard for the future of appropriation-based filmmaking. The film communities perfecting early editing techniques placed a high value on the innate reproducibility of film and on the possibility to creatively remix and recirculate ideas communicated cinematically. They were much less interested in approaching film images as originals that could be exclusively and privately owned. This attitude continues to be expressed in the works of found footage filmmakers and video artists (as well as by appropriation artists in general) to this day.

After a brief rebirth at the hands of the American surrealist artist Joseph Cornell in the mid-1930s, found footage was not used significantly by filmmakers until the late 1950s, when the neo-Dadaist filmmaker Bruce Conner created *A Movie* (1958), a whimsically catastrophic commentary on humanity's progress wrapped up in sexuality and death that remains the highest-acclaimed and most-viewed found footage film in the Western canon of experimental cinema. Upon its release, *Very Nice, Very Nice* quickly became part of this canon. The film is now seen as the Canadian counterpart to Conner's *A Movie*, thanks to Lipsett's masterful creation of a complex interplay between already-authored sound and images that enables him to convey, in a very accessible manner, the humour and irony characteristic of his exploration of mass culture and the alienation it produces.

Very Nice, Very Nice focuses on issues of consumerism and the global economic systems of capitalism and technological progress to which it is linked. As such, the film has a timeless quality that makes its social criticism as relevant today as it was when the film was originally released. Accordingly, *Very Nice, Very Nice* continues to be shown in retrospectives and classrooms around the world. The year 2010 marked the release of an NFB-produced animated documentary on Arthur Lipsett's life (entitled *Lipsett Diaries*), as well as a retrospective screening of his work organized by the Toronto-based experimental film screening series Pleasure Dome. A similar retrospective toured Montreal and Strasbourg, France, in 2007. One reason for the film's continued critical and popular appeal may be the immediacy with which it engages its subject matter. Besides some still images shot by Lipsett on the streets of Montreal, the film contains glamour shots of actors and politicians, movie stills, reproductions of artworks, advertisements, and newsreel footage, all of which are edited into a fast-paced visual montage, and paired with a soundtrack consisting of fragments taken from interviews, political speeches, film voice-overs, and commercials.

Arguably, *Very Nice, Very Nice* works so well as a critical commentary on consumer culture because large amounts of its visual and sonic components are taken directly from "real life." Indeed, Lipsett could hardly have produced such an effective critique of modern consumerism and the psychological conditions it creates without reusing the media that blanket and refract our culture. In other words, to adequately engage with the cultural and social conditions of our time, Lipsett, like many other found footage filmmakers and appropriation artists, fully embraced his dependence on a variety of copyrighted materials taken from billboards and magazine advertisements, logos and brands, music, commercials, radio shows, television, cinema, etc.

Addressing this effort to heighten the effectiveness of critical artworks through collage and montage practices that reuse ephemera from the everyday world, the eminent cultural theorist Peter Bürger (1984) has written that the purpose of such techniques is, essentially, to integrate "art into the praxis of life" (22), an integration that facilitates critical reflection on the circumstances and conditions under which cultural artefacts are created, consumed, and circulated. This motive fits well with certain aspects of the function of fair dealing, and it is reminiscent, in particular, of the Canadian Copyright Act's provision that copying for the purpose of review and criticism may not be considered copyright infringement. With its insistence on the importance of accessing and using pre-existing, already-authored materials, Lipsett's work also shares important formal similarities with documentaries that use archival footage, as well as with contemporary art forms and Web-based activities that make use of mash-up techniques. As such, *Very Nice, Very Nice* would without doubt be considered legally problematic if it were to be created today – particularly if we consider the success

Lipsett's film garnered in the 1960s. Very likely, producers, distributors, and festival programmers would feel unable to support the film, and they would either discourage the filmmaker from creating and commercially circulating such a work or impose conditions on its production (e.g., requests for permissions and licences) that might be so prohibitive as to dissuade the artist from his plans.

And even though *Very Nice, Very Nice* is now over fifty years old, the film still has the potential for representing a liability. The film was created in a far less litigious era, but, as far as it is possible to discern today, the various still images, sounds, and film footage it reused were never cleared by the NFB. Indeed, at the time of the film's release, the NFB executive Gérard Bertrand expressed concern over Lipsett's use of copyrighted materials (particularly elements produced outside of the NFB studios). In an internal memo on this subject, Bertrand wrote:

> in building his sound-track, [Lipsett] made use of pieces of sound material, which he had recorded on tape or collected over a period of years from a wide variety of sources. Most of these sound elements are used in so fragmentary a form as to be unidentifiable: however a few may be sufficiently identifiable to constitute a possible infringement of copyright, but their source cannot be located… . [T]he Board is willing to pay the usual fee for the rights to use this material if and when the owners of the copyright approach the Board. (Cited in Dancsok 1998: 29)

Written several decades ago, this statement encapsulates worries about and approaches to current practices for dealing fairly with copyrighted materials and, in particular, orphan works (see Bucholz and Meurer, both this volume). What the NFB memo fails to address is the question of whether Lipsett's copying might not be considered a fair dealing per se. After all, reviewers of *Very Nice, Very Nice* by and large agree that the film, with its humorously condemnatory take on consumer culture, serves edifying, educational, as well as parodic purposes, and offers a strong critique of the cultural environments from which its source materials are appropriated. But instead of assuming that Lipsett's creative practice was legitimate, Bertrand subscribed to the concern that the filmmaker's use of pre-recorded sounds may amount to an infringement of IP rights, and could result in legal complaints at a later point in time. Currently, Canadian copyright legislation generally entitles rights holders to protect their ownership interests for fifty years beyond the death of the original's author. If we estimate, very conservatively, that no authors of the materials reused by Lipsett lived for more than forty years past the 1961 release date of *Very Nice, Very Nice*, claims for material used in the film could potentially still be filed until 2051. (For those copyright-protected materials whose authors are unknown, the copyright term prescribed in the Canadian Copyright Act ended in 2011.)

Arthur Lipsett's work continues to enjoy both critical and popular acclaim. These days, litigation for copyright infringement rarely results from the obscurity of a derivative work; rather, it is generally the popularity of such a work, and its perceived aesthetic qua monetary value, that attracts attention. *Very Nice, Very Nice*, because its message is of a timeless quality that should confirm its status as a fair dealing consistent with the Copyright Act's "review and criticism" language, continues to be subject to the broad exposure that today raises the threat of copyright litigation. If legal complaints concerning the film were filed, or if rights holders were to demand licensing fees, the NFB would be compelled to enter into negotiations that could result in high expenses, and it is not inconceivable that the NFB might have to withdraw *Very Nice, Very Nice* from circulation, pending agreements with the rights holders.

We must, therefore, consider the extent to which the rich legacy of Canadian film and the Canadian public's access to works such as Lipsett's film are contingent on the scope of existing fair dealing provisions. Have we reached a point where, because of legal restrictions, public institutions such as the NFB or the CBC (see Asquith, this volume) can no longer guarantee their stakeholders' access to publicly funded works? What happens to publicly funded films and other creative expressions that we assume to be contained in a broadly conceived public domain when we no longer have access to them? Although the cultural consequences of IP enforcement are commonly discussed in the context of present media use and future media creations, these consequences may be equally devastating when they are extended to existing works. Stronger fair dealing provisions are needed to ensure that a clearance culture does not wholly bury Canada's archives of cultural heritage properties.

By definition, found footage films tend to retain a close thematic and material proximity to the pre-existing, already-authored cultural matter on which they comment. Like most documentary-style works, they also contain information, images, and/or sounds that predate the director's creative act. By bypassing the traditional *instrumentarium* of the filmmaker (cinematography, direction, lighting, set design, etc.), and by incorporating the act of copying and reusing as part of their thematic concern, found footage films can force copyright issues to the foreground much more strongly than other audiovisual works – see, e.g., Craig Baldwin's *Sonic Outlaws* (1995), and Zeilinger and Coombe's (2013) discussion of John Greyson's film *Un©ut*. The very originality and efficacy of found footage film often depends on its derivative use of pre-authored materials. Indeed, Lipsett's combination of documentary and experimental montage traditions in *Very Nice, Very Nice* poses new challenges and opportunities for understanding fair dealing guidelines. On the one hand, the aesthetic purpose of artists such as Lipsett demands that they incorporate real-life footage, much like a documentary filmmaker would. On the other hand, the fair dealing provisions currently included in the Canadian Copyright Act do not offer strong protection of this practice.

And yet, not only was it once possible to create, publicly fund, produce, and distribute a film like *Very Nice, Very Nice* – as noted, the work even received an Oscar nomination. It appears to us that this very clearly speaks to the value, validity, and legitimacy of the creative practices employed by Lipsett and appropriation artists like him. *Very Nice, Very Nice* has become a beloved part of Canadian cultural heritage, and offers a perspective on contemporary culture and society that continues to be highly relevant. During the 1960s and 1970s, Lipsett was one of Canada's best-known filmmakers, which was and is an unprecedented achievement for an experimental filmmaker (Kashmere 2004). But today, expansive IP rights and tendencies to overcommodify creativity pose a real danger to creative expression, with the result that works such as Lipsett's collage film might be found unlawful by proxy.

As the NFB's legal services director Dominique Aubry noted, the National Film Board is in the lucky position of being able to take some risks in interpreting fair dealing provisions, since the organization self-insures its productions (i.e., it does not have to rely on third-party errors and omissions insurers who will generally not allow fair dealing as a justification for the use of any unlicensed materials). The NFB can provide its own legal advice on matters of fair dealing, and stage its own legal defences should complaints be filed. Nevertheless, Aubry commented, the organization has in the past certainly felt compelled to clear rights where it should not have had to, at considerable cost. The NFB's relative autonomy can also be a mixed blessing in the reality of circulating its own productions, since many international distributors (especially in the US) insist on obtaining clearance for all used materials as a matter of principle, and will not pick up films that include materials "covered" by nothing but fair dealing arguments.

Despite ongoing efforts to reform the Canadian Copyright Act and to encourage broad interpretation of its fair dealing provisions, the fact remains that in the current cultural climate thick with the fear of copyright litigation, few producers and distributors are inclined to support the creation of new cinematic works similar to *Very Nice, Very Nice*. How is it that a practice such as Lipsett's found footage collage, once broadly admired by critics and popular audiences, has fallen into such disrepute? The film's continued popularity suggests that public perception of Lipsett's appropriation-based practice has remained unchanged. The problem is, rather, that public appreciation of and access to this type of creative expression is today hampered by copyright legislation and the fear of litigation it engenders. Only further copyright activism and reform measures can ensure that institutions such as the National Film Board can honour their mandate of providing fair access to the archived troves of Canadian culture.

24 Chipmusic, Out of Tune: Crystal Castles and the Misappropriation of Creative Commons–Licensed Music

MARTIN ZEILINGER

A recent controversy surrounding the internationally successful Toronto-based band Crystal Castles provides unique insight into emerging intellectual property (IP) norms. Throughout 2008, it became evident that the band had repeatedly and unapologetically sampled Creative Commons (CC)–licensed music without seeking permission from the original creators, and without crediting them appropriately. Two points complicate this issue in interesting ways: first, the sampled works were protected by licences designed to enable, rather than prevent, the creation of derivative works; second, the band's illicit sampling involved *chipmusic*, an experimental type of electronic music created by repurposing sound chips from electronic devices and using them as instruments. Although Crystal Castles was accused of misappropriating other artists' work in their music, chipmusic itself is at its core an appropriative practice that reuses existing, proprietary hardware and produces recognizable sounds often associated with copyrighted, trademarked, or patented cultural content such as video game soundtracks.

Chipmusic has strong conceptual links to traditions of software hacking and open source (OS) culture, and based on this background, it is often purposefully created and circulated in contexts in which the creative expressions it yields can remain free to be shared and reworked by others. Crystal Castles, however, remains outside of this cultural community: its actions served to pull creative expressions meant to be freely accessible into the purview of copyright law – the band releases its music on commercial labels, and claims conventional intellectual property (IP) rights in it. This unfair collision of different collective and private stakes begs the question of how alternative creative communities can ensure fair access to works they seek to protect against commercial misappropriation.

The specific CC licences used for the original works in question require attribution, non-commercial use, and release of the derivative work under the same licence. Crystal Castles' use violated all of these requirements. To date, the chipmusic community has exposed six Crystal Castles' songs as partly or almost entirely based on samples from creations of the two chipmusic artists Covox and Lo-Bat (for the full list of sampled songs, see Kumar 2008). In response to these allegations – none of which were brought to court – Crystal Castles, as well as the band's management, have displayed a disgraceful unwillingness to acknowledge, let alone undo their offence. Given the ideological background of the infringers, who are celebrated stars on a "new punk" firmament, as well as that of the victims, who, as noted, are more closely linked to OS culture, the fact that no infringement action was ever brought in this dispute is particularly interesting for my following discussion. As I will show, arguments surrounding misappropriations by Crystal Castles have effectively taken the shape of open, Web-based debates about fair practices of accessing already-authored works, rather than following the litigious path of today's clearance culture. The public, quasi-democratic sphere of blogs and online discussion forums thus emerges as an alternative, extra-juridical legal space that is more appropriate for negotiating Crystal Castles' offence than the established system of enforcing IP rights.

In retracing some of these negotiations, my discussion of the Crystal Castles case will suggest that underground culture no longer provides the kinds of lawless or law-free spaces previously associated both with punk culture's mockingly nihilist approach to property and with the ethos of hacking. Furthermore, these debates represent a partial result of artists' growing acknowledgment that, in the past, murky definitions of an artwork's legal status have facilitated the expansion of capitalist enterprises' foothold in the realm of cultural production, rather than protecting creators from such advances. In this sense, the reactions to Crystal Castles' unauthorized sampling of works released under CC licences indicate that creators are becoming more aware of the shortcomings of copyright and IP provisions (including alternative models), and that they may prefer to take recourse, instead, to non-juridical measures and collectively agreed-upon ethical principles that seem better suited to keeping the collective creative current running.

Accordingly, creative communities such as the independent chipmusic scene more frequently aim to negate the capitalist property relations underlying different national IP legislations by forming alternative moral economies of collaboration, fair exchange, and sharing (see Zeilinger 2012). CC licences provide one such alternative, but have been recognized as unable to protect artists' interests according to the ideals to which they may subscribe. Alternative principles of regulating access to creative expressions are not always framed in legal language, and the issues to which they respond are commonly not negotiated in courtrooms. What follows is a discussion of the "para-legal" creative community of chipmusic artists, and observations of how they deal with issues of the unauthorized reuse of expressions that are designed both for fair access and for a certain measure of creators' control over them. The Crystle Castles case, it will be seen, pinpoints the need for creative communities to consider establishing intricate discourses of fair dealing founded on ethical, rather than legal rhetoric.

Misappropriation and "Applied Fair Dealing"

The discussions that followed Crystal Castles' sampling of CC-licensed chipmusic took the shape of an open debate regarding the lived praxis of fair dealing and the self-governing capacities of contemporary underground culture. However, since the actual enforcement of IP rights in the conventional sense was never at stake in these debates, their most interesting aspects concern not legal theories of fair dealing, but rather what we might call "applied fair dealing," that is, the ways in which artists and audiences themselves go about the constitution and implementation of models of fair exchange, collaboration, and circulation of creative expressions.

Crystal Castles is a two-member electronic music act founded in around 2003 in Toronto. According to the founding myth the band itself likes to maintain, everything began when an unrehearsed microphone test, recorded in a basement in April 2005, was accidentally released onto the Internet and became an instant hit. The band's singer Alice Glass, it is said, didn't know about the recording until a British label asked for permission to release it officially (Gillen 2009). Such stories of accidental genius, which Crystal Castles has promulgated in numerous interviews, were received enthusiastically by the mainstream music press, and have been used to cast the band as a creative phenomenon rather than a commercial construct, as an incident without any precedents very much in line with traditional concepts of Romantic genius. This kind of reception also allowed reviewers to compare Crystal Castles' rise to fame to the historical emergence of punk. The BBC, for example, has noted that listening to Crystal Castles' music "is to be cast adrift in a vortex of deafening pain without a safety net … [feeling that] you could do anything in the world, but that nothing would ultimately mean anything" (Hammer 2008: n.p.). This description is strongly reminiscent of how punk aesthetics were often described, and Crystal Castles has indeed been eager to embrace punkish attitudes, for example by violently casting off any suggestions of conceptual links between their music and other genres. This freed the band to do "anything in the world" as if that really meant "nothing" to its members – including the use of other artists' creations without permission or acknowledgment. With this attitude, a pseudo-anarchic stage presence, and a sound sufficiently dissonant to disguise Crystal Castles' indebtedness to a variety of mainstreamed genres, the band went on a quick rise to international fame, and, before too long, was hailed as "the most … original band in the world right now" (Stubbs 2010).

Chipmusic itself had briefly appeared on the stage of popular media attention even before Crystal Castles' stellar rise to fame, namely, when Malcolm McLaren (the self-declared "creator" of the Sex Pistols, who had played a central role in the commodification of the punk phenomenon) announced his "discovery" of the form in a 2003 article for *Wired Magazine* (McLaren 2003). McLaren described chipmusic as a new kind of electronic punk, music made by "reverse engineering" video game hardware from "the antediluvian 8-bit past," with a sound "as though Twiggy were somehow stuck inside *Space Invaders*" (n.p.), a description that can also be applied to Crystal Castles' eponymous 2008 debut album. McLaren, it seemed, wanted to commandeer chipmusic just as he had commandeered the punk phenomenon several decades earlier, and recounted how he had discovered this new type of punk in Paris, in an "Ali Baba's cave of outdated studio equipment," where he explored music made on old Nintendo Game Boys, by artists he described as "the Velvet Underground of the 21st century" and "the new ABBA" (n.p.). Yet, the world didn't seem ready for McLaren's discovery, and it was not until five years later that Crystal Castles brought the term chipmusic back to broader public attention when the band fulfilled McLaren's vision and emerged as a seemingly radical subcultural phenomenon able to take the music world by storm as punk once had.

What both McLaren and Crystal Castles failed to notice (or chose to ignore) was that a vibrant chipmusic scene had, in fact, existed for quite some time, and that it was by no means a fledging art form in need of a maestro or a headliner. Conceptually, chipmusic is related to the precursors of today's OS movement, and its practitioners tend to have a sophisticated understanding of what it means to appropriate, reuse, and share in a fair manner. Unsurprisingly, the community took offence both at McLaren's attempt to seize the chipmusic phenomenon and then, several years later, at Crystal Castles' denials of any connections to existing musical scenes, denials that laughed in the face of the band's proven misappropriations. McLaren's 2003 "discovery" was quickly denounced in a politely cynical open letter posted online (see gwEm 2004). Crystal Castles' transgression, however, couldn't be tossed out so quickly. The band already had a reputation for disrespectfully ill-treating peers, which had earlier surfaced in its unauthorized use of visual artist Trevor Brown's drawing "Black-Eyed Madonna" as an album cover and on band merchandise. Now, Crystal Castles' unauthorized sampling of openly accessible chipmusic spawned an ongoing debate on artistic integrity in the age of reproductive media, on the ethics of collaboration, and on the considerable difficulties of regulating access in an open artistic community.

Chipmusic Past and Present

Chipmusic has been created for at least two decades. The form is hard, if not impossible to pin down as a genre. Over time, chipmusic artists have ventured into the realms of techno, pop, jazz, and even classical music. Rather than referring to any one musical genre, chipmusic is thus better defined as implying the use of a specific technology, and the term designates the use of a particular medium for musical expression. In chipmusic's most purist definitions, this medium takes the form of sound chips found in early video game consoles such as the Nintendo Entertainment System and the Nintendo Game Boy, or in obsolete home computer systems including the Commodore 64 and the Atari ST. Chipmusic artists use the sound chips contained in these machines as instruments, and "play" them much like one would play any other sound-generating device. In the term's literal sense, chipmusic thus refers to the appropriative use of outdated sound chips for the real-time synthesis and sequencing of chip-generated sounds. A considerable part of the aesthetic appeal of these appropriated instruments lies in the skill and knowledgeability required for their use. Equally important are chipmusic's referential qualities; many of the sounds produced are strongly reminiscent of the early days of personal computing, of specific video game consoles, etc. This positions the art form in a contentious relationship with patented sound synthesis technology, with proprietary cultural artefacts such as video game soundtracks, as well as with the production contexts and cultural environments evoked by such artefacts.

Perhaps the most important characteristic of chipmusic, however, are the principles of openness and collaboration underlying many chipmusic creations. Representing an art form in which lines between listeners, creators, and critics are extremely blurry, chipmusic is often circulated under no copyrighted licences or very open licences, parly because the form lists early manifestations of radical OS culture among its conceptual and ideological precursors. The biggest influence among these is the *demoscene* of the the 1970s and 1980s, which grew out of the practice of removing copy protection from computer games so that they may be freely circulated. When such hacked games were booted, a signature identifying the hacker would briefly be displayed. Soon, instead of using simple signatures, hackers began to show off their skills by programming more elaborate audiovisual sequences – the "demos" from which the scene derived its name. In order to work with the limited capacities of early personal computers and to keep files small, demos were written and circulated as executable code, rather than as large audiovisual files. This meant that every time they were triggered, demos were thus executed (or performed) in real time by the host machine's hardware. At the same time, most demos were also created in the spirit of collaboration and collective ownership: whoever opened them was free not only to use the cracked software they accompanied, but also to access the files containing the demo code and to manipulate it.

Today, some chipmusic is sample based and recorded conventionally. However, many of the most acclaimed chipmusic artists follow in the traditions of the demoscene and cast chipmusic as a primarily collaborative art form produced (and sometimes circulated) as editable, executable code, rather than as conventional sound recordings (e.g., audio CDs or MP3 files). The code represents a kind of instructional sheet music (similar to piano rolls), used to generate a composition anew each time it is executed. Code-based chipmusic, in other words, is a form of creative expression whose important ideals of openness, copyability, and shared access are built in on a technological level. In technical terms, chipmusic's existence as editable code that is used to generate sounds in real time has important implications for what copyright discourse might call the "fixity" of chipmusic works, as it suggests that chipmusic has traditionally not favoured fixed, copyrightable expressions. More importantly, it can be derived from this tradition that code-based chipmusic has little to do with the simple sampling and replaying of pre-recorded sounds – instead of referring to unalterable, DRM-protected sound files such as those found on audio CDs, the concept of chipmusic originally foregrounded reusable, editable read/write code similar to the demos described above.

With the emergence of high speed Internet and the availability of convenient audio formats such as MP3, the modalities of circulating chipmusic have drastically changed. Today, many artists make their work available in the form of conventional recordings, often bound in downloadable but otherwise unalterable formats. This may appear puzzling, as it seems to render chipmusic a less open and collaborative form. However, this shift to new modalities of distribution serves, in fact, to explain the chipmusic community's predilection for alternative IP licensing schemes. In scaling down their reliance on the technologically built-in openness of early chipmusic technologies, many musicians quickly embraced a different type of collectivity, namely, one regulated by agreed-upon fair dealing practices and the use of alternative licences such as those offered by the Creative Commons. Because such licences are commonly designed to enable rather than prevent access and redistribution, this transition allows chipmusic to retain its ties to technological and ideological precursors on a conceptual level. This insistence on fair dealing practices also shaped the community's response to Crystal Castles' unauthorized sampling.

While protecting chipmusic's non-commercial ideals, the CC licences simultaneously ensure artists' continued ability to creatively rework each other's compositions. What the chipmusic scene may seem to have lost in adopting more rigid formats of distributed music, it thus made up for by embracing a licensing system that accommodates and safeguards the community's legacy of collaborative artistic creation, and embodies chipmusic's adopted ethics of fair dealing. Furthermore, even in the face of the easy availability of digital sampling tools and high speed Internet connections, the form's focus on technological minimalism and its aesthetics of openness means that outdated sound chip hardware, such as the Nintendo Game Boy, continue to be the most-used tools of chipmusic artists. Overall, the shift from open, inherently modifiable technologies to the use of the CC licences thus denotes the continued implementation of open access practices by other means.

How Can Alternatives to Conventional IP Models Be Enforced?

Clearly, Crystal Castles' sampling practices have really very little to do with the aesthetics of chipmusic. The commercial nature of the band's unauthorized uses constitutes a strong breach of the ethical principles governing chipmusic. The most important question emerging from the Crystal Castles' offence, consequently, is how chipmusicians and other creative communities embracing openness and sharing as part of their creative approach can "handle 'unlawful' use ... by mainstream artists and companies" (Carlsson 2008: 162).

The chipmusic community's reactions ranged from flattered to furious. Some of the implicated artists felt that Crystal Castles has actually improved their creations. One of them, a musician known as Lo-Bat, does not perceive Crystal Castles as having stolen from him, and rather than asking them for compensation argues that the band has essentially enriched the community as a whole – "the twist they've put on it makes it sound better than anything the community could ever create, myself included ... thanks to them, people know more about chiptune, and ... want to hear this music" (Kirn 2008a: n.p.). Most chipmusic artists, however, felt outraged that Crystal Castles had not honoured any of the requirements stipulated in the specific licences used for the works in question. To make matters worse, in a display of punkish mockery, Crystal Castles and its management denied their actions, as well as any general knowledge of or interest in the ethics of chipmusic. This denial violated not only the relevant licensing conditions, but also the community's principles of ethical and fair conduct, which encourage sharing and collaboration. Accordingly, one representative comment posted on a popular electronic music weblog notes that "the notion that hipsters can co-opt the chip music scene's cultural currency without dues paid ... really bother[s] folks," and goes on to complain that Crystal Castles were "disingenuous about their process, fabricating some sort of creation myth ... rather than owning up to technical aspects of their craft" (Kirn 2008a: n.p.). Crystal Castles' retorts to such criticisms certainly did not help – in one interview, the duo stated, "We both hate video games. We were just breaking apart electronics and toys to get annoying sounds" (Boles 2008: n.p.). On numerous occasions, Crystal Castles have also insisted that their sound is absolutely original, a result from simply "wiring an old keyboard to an Atari computer soundboard" (n.a. 2010: n.p.); and, in still more interviews, the band asserted that they learned about the "8-bit [chipmusic] scene" only peripherally: "[We] really don't have anything to do with [it]. It's a completely different world" (Lindsay 2008: n.p.). The chipmusic community, angered by what it considered a mix between PR ploy and arrogant ignorance, was quick to refute each of these statements in turn. It pointed out that the name Crystal Castles is, in fact, the name of a highly influential 1980s arcade video game; it showed how impracticable the band's simplistic idea of "circuit-bending" (the rewiring of electronic hardware) is; and, most importantly, it proved, with the help of sophisticated homebrew spectral graph audio analyses, that rather than not having "anything to do with" chipmusic, Crystal Castles had illicitly used it in at least six of their songs (see nitro2k01 2008).

The debates surrounding Crystal Castles' illegitimate sampling peaked in late 2008, but arguments concerning the legitimacy and "fairness" of the band's sampling practice continue to dominate the comment sections of articles and Web postings speaking to the band's "originality" and genius. Likewise, heated conflicts concerning the ethical implications of the activities of Crystal Castles continue to play out in discussion forums across the Internet. It is interesting to note that even though the misappropriated works are covered by alternative copyright licences, wherever litigation of Crystal Castles' activities is brought up as a possible response it is commonly dissuaded as inappropriate. Instead, discussion continues to focus on the band's attitude, and on exposing their actions to unknowing fans. There appears to be a consensus, among the chipmusic community, that the real problem is not the missing compensation for infringed IP rights. Indeed, such compensation would only serve to reinforce the notion that chipmusic can be treated as just another type of property. Instead, online discussions commonly identify the main problem as the purposeful misinterpretation of licences "designed to encourage sharing" (Kirn 2008a: n.p.). The artists in question have recognized, it seems, that the most obvious reaction to the actions of Crystal Castles, namely, to file a legal complaint for copyright infringement, would mean to betray efforts to keep chipmusic outside the realm of traditional cultural ownership and property exchanges.

As the chipmusic artist M-.-n comments, the lack of understanding of copyright-related concepts such as fair use and fair dealing is "quite a big deal since a LOT of artists are trusting creative commons and this story puts the license to doubt, since it seems people can break it" (Kirn 2008a: n.p.). It is "laughable," another comment reads, that "these kids are playing in Lo-Bat's home country in the largest club now and the promo text states they invented the genre" (ibid.). Again, such comments show that the payment of licensing fees or royalties is clearly not the real issue – what angers and concerns the community, instead, is that "the mainstream music community can just pillage ideas from a less commercial almost hobby community [sic] and get away without paying a bit of respect" (nitro2k01 2008: n.p.).

Perhaps Lo-Bat, the chipmusic artist whose work was misappropriated in as many as five Crystal Castles' songs, should have the last word in this survey of opinions. His perspective on the controversy is exemplified well by the fact that most of his public postings on the matter are published anonymously (although they have been attributed to him by insider observers within the community). Lo-Bat is vehement in his insistence that his complaints are not voiced in order to draw attention to his own work (see, e.g., comments in Kirn 2008a). By explicitly stating that the chipmusic community should focus on collectivity instead of foregrounding individual artists, Lo-Bat condemns the egomania of Crystal Castles. In his critique, the conviction that the practices of Crystal Castles are unethical remains intact, but, the artist states, the band's misappropriation simply makes it more important for the community to now take advantage of the attention it is receiving as a collective. Stating that true talent will prevail where illegitimate copying will fail, he provokes his peers by asking, "Imitators, impostors and 'thieves' will fizzle, and now that the spotlight is on you, what will you do to prove your longevity?" (Kirn 2008a: n.p.).

From the survey of perspectives surveyed above, three interrelated reasons for the chipmusic community's reaction to Crystal Castles' unfair sampling can be distilled: first, chipmusic itself is based on the repurposing of existing technologies, and its practitioners therefore tend to be sympathetic – at least in principle – towards the general concept of cultural appropriation; second, the legal status of chipmusic itself is not entirely clear, since the form is essentially based on the repurposing of patented (if obsolete) technology, and yields works that imitate copyright-protected works; lastly, and most importantly, the chipmusic scene established itself in conscious opposition to conventional discourse on the commercial production and circulation of cultural commodities and is, therefore, highly reluctant to use mainstream copyright licences.

Online, the fans and supporters of Crystal Castles often appear wilfully oblivious to the sampling controversy, and condemn posters that challenge the band's integrity as "flamers" (i.e., incandescent Internet posters) who envy the duo's genius. And still, the affected chipmusic artists will not go down the vengeful path of litigation. As one commenter very accurately noted on a blog entry devoted to the issue, "this isn't about the law – it's about a very nebulous code that [Crystal Castles] broke" (Kirn 2008b). It appears to be difficult for the chipmusic community to formalize this code. Regardless of this fact, it is clear that Crystal Castles' unauthorized sampling was perceived as offensive in several ways: the band ignored licensing schemes designed to ensure the possibility of collaboration while safeguarding fair dealing conventions; the band members wrongfully denied any practical or conceptual connections to the chipmusic community (which violates both relevant licences and the community's ethical ideals); and lastly, Crystal Castles committed the aesthetic fallacy of sampling prerecorded sounds rather than write or manipulate executable code to generate their own music, again contradicting certain established traditions of chipmusic creation.

"What's the point of starting a band if you're not going to do something new?," Crystal Castles' singer asked in an interview (2010: n.p.). As nitro2k01's spectral graph analyses have conclusively shown, however, Crystal Castles' approach to creating music is hardly original in any sense of the term, and certainly does not always produce "new" material. At least the band's unauthorized sampling and the reactions it triggered has raised some new, rarely discussed questions that go beyond obvious issues related to unlicensed uses of intellectual property. How can a creative community effectively protect its works when it does not subscribe to conventional copyright models and when it refuses to invoke such models as a response to infringement? Are there practicable alternative ways of enforcing such protection, beyond denouncing misappropriation after the fact? And finally, are punkish views on ownership boasted by bands such as Crystal Castles viable in a cultural landscape in which underground cultures are well networked and organized, and better informed than ever before about law and discourses on practices of fair access to creative expressions?

Amateur spectral graph analyst nitro2k01 comments on these issues in an appropriately tongue-in-cheek fashion by identifying a commercial trend behind the band's violation of an open community's fair dealing practices and calling it "[t]he new kind of punk, copyright infringement for money" (nitro2k01 2008: n.p.). Meanwhile, Crystal Castles is, supposedly, putting together a "compilation of [their] favourite 8bit songs for release on Lies Records" (Kumar 2008: n.p.) – a gesture meant to restore the band's standing with the chipmusic community, but in fact symptomatic of a further attempt to pull alternative artists into a world of commercial music with which they do not wish to be associated.

Conclusion

Music critics still tend to shy away from discussing the legal implications of Crystal Castles' chipmusic sampling controversy, and, all too often, continue to take the band's energetic live shows and commercial success as a guarantee for its originality. In the long run, however, commenters both from inside and outside the chipmusic scene agree that Crystal Castles "were doing themselves no favour with the 'so what, who cares' attitude … [I]t loses them the respect of more mature music fans and critics" (Thiessen 2008: n.p.). At least in the alternative music press, Crystal Castles has been dethroned as the "next big thing" precisely because of the attitude the band brings to serious infringement allegations involving their peers (Topping 2008).

But how much can be expected, in the long run, from an industry whose economic success depends on a mix between the assimilation of underground artists into the higher echelons of commercial success and the subsequent exploitations of these artists? Awareness of the problems that commercially informed copyright regimes raise for independent artists who believe in collective creativity will not likely be highlighted by the music industry, nor by policy makers. It may be a more viable trajectory for underground cultural movements such as the chipmusic scene to establish their own ethical codices of fair dealing and to fortify their collaborative approaches to creativity in this way. As evidenced by commentary such as the following by John Darnielle of the highly successful indie band The Mountain Goats, creative communities' rallying cries for fair alternatives to conventional copyright models are not falling on deaf ears: "Sure, they made one of my favourite albums of the year so far, but … Crystal Castles can go to Hell and stay there" (Darnielle 2009).

25 "My Real'll Make Yours a Rental": Hip Hop and Canadian Copyright

ALEXANDRA BOUTROS

At the heart of current debates about "copyrights" and "copywrongs" is the hope that copyright will protect and promote the best interests of both artists and the public, but also fears that it will simply promote corporate interests, undermining artistic practices and stifling audience participation and access to culture in the public sphere. Such discussions about who owns culture and who has access to it are particularly loaded in the context of hip hop music. Hip hop's history as a black cultural form, its early social location as a cultural movement for disenfranchised black youth in the United States, and the current debates around its commercialization have meant that hip hop inevitably raises questions about what it means to produce, distribute, and own black culture. If balancing artists' rights to reimbursement with audiences' rights to easy access to artistic and cultural work is at the heart of copyright discourse, then unpacking the nuances of this hoped-for balance in the context of hip hop is an important part of ensuring that copyright reform takes into account diverse forms of cultural production.

What do debates about the intersection of digital sound technology and copyright violation signify in the context of hip hop? Given the centrality of the United States both to the origins of hip hop and to what some see as an increasingly homogenized global response to copyright infringement and digital sharing, how do current developments in the United States impact Canada? This chapter focuses on how debates around intellectual property (IP) encode certain assumptions about cultural production, and explores Canadian hip hop culture's relationships to copyright and (illegal) digital file sharing, or piracy. Some of the most vocal advocates of copyright reform have noted that the easy accessibility of digital, inherently reproductive media has animated a new public interest in copyright issues. Michael Geist (2005), for example, has argued that "the public's interest in copyright ... is the result of the remarkable confluence of computing power, the Internet, and a plethora of new software programs, all of which has not only enabled millions to create their own songs, movies, photos, art, and software but has also allowed them to efficiently distribute their creations electronically without the need for traditional distribution systems" (2). Although current copyright reformers hope for a copyright revolution spearheaded by a digital generation that is newly energized by its participation in the digital public sphere, the history of hip hop tells the story of another (earlier) populace energized by the accessibility and affordability of (analogue) technologies. The history of hip hop, from the uptake of fading sound production technologies to the first suits for copyright infringement brought against artists, suggests that it takes more than technologically facilitated access to the public sphere to bring about the reform Geist and contributors in this volume may hope for.

Owing much of its development to the transplanting of Jamaican dub music to New York's Bronx neighbourhoods, early hip hop artists reclaimed the near-obsolete sound technologies of vinyl and turntables, creating new music sampled from older albums. Hip hop culture didn't just give voice to socially disenfranchised poor, black youth, it also turned those youth into participants in the production of popular music. As such, it generated an understanding of culture as shared, collaborative, intertextual, and built on the past. Hip hop's social successes (in its capacity to make visible black experience) and commercial successes are tied to the repurposing of sound production and distribution technologies that predate the digital remixing some see as only now blurring the distinction between copyright users and copyright creators (Geist 2005: 3). Forecasting concepts like the "prosumer," hip hop tells a history of what could have been. The digitization of music could have destabilized notions of individual ownership over music production. After all, digitized music (or digital data) makes us remember that music is not only a thing (a record, a CD) waiting quietly on a shelf, but a dynamic entity (a packet of information) always in motion, always accessible for the repack(ag)ing of improvisation.

Early hip hop sampling initially occurred in a copyright grey zone. Throughout the 1980s, samples were used without permission. It was not until 1991, with the now famous lawsuit launched against rap artist Biz Markie, who sampled the Gilbert O'Sullivan piece "Alone Again

(Naturally)" on his album *I Need a Haircut*, that sampling became an issue within US copyright law. To shorthand this much-discussed case, presiding judge, Kevin Thomas Duffy, ignored the nuances of fair use and likened sampling to stealing. As Siva Vaidhyanathan (2001) has argued, Duffy's heavy-handed application of US copyright law ended the productive era of 1980s hip hop sampling, forcing artists to obtain permission for samples, at often exorbitant cost (141–4). What had once been a mode of cultural production allowing disenfranchised youth to be heard in the public sphere became legally accessible only to already wealthy recording artists who could afford to clear every sample they used.

Despite the cost, the practice of reaching back into popular music's past through sampling has remained characteristic of hip hop. Tricia Rose (1994) has argued that sampling insists upon cultural literacy and intertextuality in ways that affirm "black musical history" (89). When copyright legislation contributes to a discourse that insists on individual (rather than collaborative) notions of cultural ownership and prohibits sampling and remixing for free or minimal cost, it risks negating the intertextuality inherent in black cultural history. It is worth considering which (or whose) past is being remixed in hip hop culture, and what the implications of this remixing are, both for how hip hop carves a space out for itself in a commercial popular music culture guided by copyright discourses and in terms of how cultural ownership (and authenticity) is understood.

The history of hip hop culture is undeniably an American one. The inner city experiences of African American youth were the defining social conditions that gave rise to this genre. Canada's proximity to the United States has meant that Canadian hip hop artists have found themselves branded outsiders and imitators of American hip hop culture. This identity of the uneasy outsider shapes the reception of Canadian hip hop not only in the United States, but also in Canada. In *Black Like Who*, Rinaldo Walcott discusses the telling title of Maestro Fresh-Wes' 1994 release, *Naaah, Dis Kid Can't Be From Canada?!!* Walcott (2003) suggests that Maestro's title "targets the narrative of Hip Hop as an African-American invention" and disturbs "what appears to be a mimetic identification" (42). This uneasy mimesis seems to render Canadian hip hop like and yet unlike its American counterpart. It haunts endeavours for commercial success, and gives rise to, at times, acute frustration. In a recent interview, Toronto-based Kardinal Offishall lamented that "in Canada, we look at American Hip Hop as this big shiny thing, and we put it on a pedestal, no matter what the quality is, just because it comes from south of the border ... we're still looking outside of the country for good music before we look inside" (Mallory 2008: 34–9). This tension between inside and outside is very much part of the discourse around what counts as "good" or "authentic" Canadian hip hop.

Cultural production in Canada inevitably raises "difficult questions concerning the slippery language of popular culture and national belonging when questions of blackness enter into the conversation" (Walcott 2001: 124). In Canada, blackness is always imagined as coming from elsewhere (the Caribbean, Africa, or even the US). Historic black presence in Canada is often overwritten (129), and black Canadian cultural production thus falls under the complex rubric of multiculturalism, where blackness is equated to "heritage," a reified origin that always belongs to places outside the boundaries of the nation state. This relationship between the inside and outside of the nation, between belonging and what Walcott (2003) calls "elsewhereness" (134) plays out in Canadian hip hop culture where complex issues of authenticity circulate.

An example of tensions around authenticity can be found in the now infamous 2006 dust-up between hip hop artists K'naan and k-os. K-os is a first-generation Canadian artist who has had significant success in Canada with the release of platinum albums *Joyful Rebellion* (2004) and *Atlantis: Hymns for Disco* (2006). K'naan is a Somalia-born artist who has also been successful in Canada, having received a Juno for *Dusty Foot Philosopher* (2005). K'naan is also well known for his single "Wavin' Flag," used as the Coca Cola anthem for the 2010 FIFA World Cup. Although both of these artists are celebrated as successful musicians, the Canadian press often evokes their backgrounds (or heritages) as emblems of their "elsewhereness." K-os, in turn, has an important connection to Trinidad, where he spent his childhood. Canadian media often represents this as "a key period in [k-os'] musical journey" (Cowie 2002: n.p.). Similarly, the press never fails to remind audiences of K'naan's Somali heritage, reiterating time and again that he was "born into a violent country with little opportunity" (CBC Radio Two 2010). In both cases, the roots of these artists signify a type of authenticity that lends credence to their hip hop productions. In Canada, where hip hop is often derided as a pale imitation of its more authentic American counterpart, connections outside the nation are ways of establishing authority and authenticity.

When K'naan shot a video for his single "Soobax" in Somalia in 2005, K'os, it is told, thought that K'naan's video shoot was exploitative, representing Africans simply for the purpose of commercial gain. It is widely believed that K'naan is the subject of pointed lyrics in k-os' hit "*B-Boy Stance,*" which seems to accuse K'naan and his crew of being "great pretenders": "They took cameras to Africa for pictures to rhyme/ Over; Oh, yes, the great pretenders." Speaking about the disagreement to the CBC, K'naan theorizes about what could have troubled k-os: "He made me out to be some kind of colonialist, but he didn't take into account that [Africa] is where I'm from. That's my people; I'm representing their struggle. So I thought he was out of line" (McKinnon 2005: n.p.). The controversy between these two artists shows how Trinidad and Somalia, Africa and the Caribbean function as signifiers of Walcott's "elsewhereness" where connection to geographies (outside of Canada) lend a kind of uneasy authenticity to hip hop productions.

K'naan's work often references Africa in ways that remind audiences of his heritage, reinforcing this mode of authenticity even while offering up critiques of the politics of authenticity in hip hop culture. Issues of authenticity run throughout much of his work. If the opposite of being a pretender is "keepin' it real," then K'naan responds to K'Os' criticism with his 2009 single "ABC," where he raps: "You real, but my real is tenfold / My real'll make yours a rental." In "ABC," the evocation of K'naan's African heritage supersedes, or at least circumvents, the authenticity that US. hip hop derives from voicing the experiences of black ghettos. As McKinnon observes, "where Eminem would rhyme about handguns, K'naan talks about rocket-propelled grenades. His horror stories are real; the violence in his past is *bigger* than that of his American peers" (McKinnon 2005: n.p., emphasis added).

K'naan's also connects Africa and the United States through his use of samples. In "ABC," he opens with a sample from Ethiopian musician Mulatu Astake, followed by samples from one of hip hop's pioneers Chubb Rock ("Treat 'Em Right"). Here, K'naan demonstrates his familiarity with hip hop history even while insisting on his African heritage, or, more specifically, on that which makes him different from (and more "real" than) his Canadian peers. K'naan's work is conditioned both by the cultural borrowing and mixing that is characteristic of hip hop and by what Walcott (2001) describes as the Canadian "demand … for black people to belong elsewhere" (127). K'naan's mixing of "African" and American music functions as a commentary on cultural ownership where authentic hip hop is very much bound up in issues of race and ethnicity. The ways in which authenticity is constructed and performed and how these intersect with issues of ownership within Canadian hip hop culture are important to explore when thinking about how assumptions about ownership intersect with copyright practice and discourse.

Copyright itself forces a refiguring of the hip hop artists' relationship to practices like sampling. One possible yet rarely successful defence against using uncleared samples can be found in the fair use doctrine in the United States and fair dealing practices in Canada. Behind Canada's fair dealing exception is an effort to balance the rights of the user (the reviewer, the critic, the researcher, etc.) with the rights of the copyright holder, and the belief that such exceptions are necessary to allow cultural works to circulate and be accessible in the public sphere. Fair dealing arguments are generally made under the assumption of post-Enlightenment (and Western) notions of individual authorship or creativity. Because of this, hip hop suffers from the assumption that use of any sample should be "original," bearing little resemblance to the initial piece of music from which it is lifted. Insistence on the use of samples that are "original" and do not repeat elements of the sampled music, however, is for all intents and purposes a bastardization of the ethos of sampling. Although samples are brief passages that may be difficult to recognize, the whole point of sampling in hip hop is to draw musical connection between one work and another. This may be done in order to pay tribute to older musicians or to transnational music traditions, or as a way of foregrounding the legacy of black music production. The sample, the original, and the cultural history it references are all *meant* to be recognizable. They are echoes of older works and, as such, are very much about repetition. Having to prove a lack of direct imitative relationship between sample and original subverts the cultural precepts underlying hip hop production. Although this seems to impact Canadian and American hip hop artists alike, sampling, as K'naan's work demonstrates, is a way for Canadian hip hoppers to negotiate both the history of hip hop as a US genre and their own diasporic connections, while producing within the borders of the nation.

The insistence that blackness originates outside the boundaries of the Canadian nation state – an insistence that at least partially shapes Canadian hip hop culture – implicitly extends into the realm of institutional regulation. Copyright laws in Canada are linked to international copyright agreements that seek to ensure that those holding copyright in one country will have that copyright recognized in another. It has been argued that such international agreements generate hegemonic perspectives on intellectual property and copyright that favour so-called developed nations (e.g., Menescal 2005). In *Stealing Empire: P2P, Intellectual Property and Hip-hop Subversion*, Adam Haupt (2008) goes a step further and argues that "multilateral agreements ensure that corporate America's interpretation of intellectual property effectively gets globalized" (xvii). A common critique of the Agreement on the Trade-Related Aspects of Intellectual Property (TRIPs) and the World Intellectual Property Organization (WIPO) administration of it has been that any globalized perspective on copyright cannot account for local specificity (see Toner 2008). In Canada, for example, markets (particularly for hip hop) are smaller than in the United States, and so the funds required to clear samples can become disproportionately exorbitant for Canadian artists and their labels. By making it difficult to compete in the local commercial sphere, the Americanized discourse around copyright furthers the tension between belonging and elsewhereness that conditions Canadian hip hop production when commercial success means attaining recognition outside of Canada.

As Walcott (2001) observes, black popular culture in Canada is simultaneously situated between the difficult dynamics of nation-state regulation, discipline, and governmentality and a diasporic deterritorialized desire (127). Artists such as k'os and K'naan, who generate a discourse of authenticity, are defined by their transnational connections even as they are constituted by the institutions of the nation state. The discourses around cultural ownership that have come to surround copyright and IP discussions only intensify this tension between inside and outside, something that is problematic for Canadian hip hop production on multiple levels. The difficulty of creating music that is both "authentic" *and* commercial has occasioned much debate in the United States. Where socially conscious rhymes meant for a disenfranchised black population once flourished, it is assumed that white middle-class suburban youth – the primary audience that can afford to legally buy hip hop – increasingly shape hip hop production (Kitwana 2005). The same story has not caught on in Canada.

Although artists like Kardinal Offishall steadfastly point to a lack of support for Canadian urban music (where hip hop is categorized) via radio airplay and other institutional structures (Young 2006), piracy is the story frequently told to explain the lack of commercial success for Canadian hip hoppers and the primary reason why these artists fail to garner large sales numbers, even when their music is critically successful. Urban recording artist Jully Black was held up by the Canadian Recording Industry Association (CRIA) as an artist harmed by digital file-sharing practices; in a 2005 speech titled "A National Dialogue on the Need To Safeguard and Promote Products of the Mind," then-CRIA president Graham Henderson used Black to argue that P2P networking ultimately hurts individual artists (rather than big name recording labels); "If you are Jully Black … you watch Canadians make 2.8 million attempts to [illegally] download your new album; and you end up selling 30,000 copies. You may become a household name this way, but you will never own a house" ("CRIA"). Henderson's evocation of ownership is interesting: despite his concern for the economic welfare of urban artists such as Black, the question remains, who gets to own black culture? What does it mean when the CRIA lobbies both for copyright reform and for tighter controls around P2P networking? Exactly "whose products of the mind" are at stake here? Henderson's speech is particularly illuminating in light of accusations by Toronto-based DJ group Lunatics of Sound, that Black's label, Universal, was using one of their commissioned remixes of Black's song "Seven Day Fool" without remuneration. Mark Quail, lawyer for Lunatics, pointed out the irony of the situation: "The thing is, Universal Music sues people all the time for file sharing and downloading, and here it is they've taken all rights and sold it without permission" ([sic], Soul Matters n.d.).

Piracy is tricky for Canadian hip hop artists to negotiate, because the social consciousness that is part of the history of Canadian hip hop dictates that the music should be accessible (cheaply) to the communities it speaks to. And yet, the desire to produce a commercially viable product is always there. K'naan released his 2009 album *Troubadour* on MySpace, where, although it was freely accessible for online listening, K'naan – in a personal message to his fans – entreats his fans to "actually buy" the album. K'naan dances around the issue of piracy, although he does speak to the commercial and economic consequences of low sales: "I know intimately many would-be great artists who are being shackled by the business of music today. Sales are low across the board, because most people are not really interested in buying music. I had a theory for a long time that this is because a lot of the music being made today isn't worth people's money anyway." K'naan, of course, distinguishes his work from "worthless" music, in part, by evoking the ever present trump card of "realness"; "If you love it, I ask that you actually buy it. This is when supporting *real music* becomes critical … Tell everyone you know also, because it's one thing to commend me for my efforts and integrity, but it's another thing to help me continue to do it" (Van Evra 2009). Here, K'naan has connected authenticity and integrity to commercial success (or the selling of an album). Implicitly, then, commercial success depends, at least in part, on K'naan's ability to convince his fans not to download his album for free. Once again, K'naan locates his authenticity in geographical and cultural connections outside of Canada: "I could never lower myself to make music that I don't believe in. This is why I made Troubadour, and there is a reason why I recorded it in Bob Marley's home studio in Jamaica" (Van Evra 2009). Here, the elsewhereness of the Caribbean, and the authority of Bob Marley, is evoked in a bid for an authenticity that feeds into commercial viability.

Yet, K'naan's message remains ambiguous, never directly speaking against the practices of digital file sharing that are so often cited as a reason for hip hop's struggles for commercial success in Canada. The ambiguity of this message is, perhaps, thrown into relief by K'naan's outspoken stance on the actuality of Somalian piracy. In one interview, K'naan recognizes the controversial nature of his stance: "A lot of people don't like me for saying this but I'm in support of the [Somalian] pirates. Massive western companies would come to Somalia and dump nuclear toxic waste containers on the shore because there was no government controlling the shorelines. So these pirates initially went into the ocean to make them pay for that sort of thing. So they just take everything for ransom. That actually helped us clear our environment" (Dow 2009). In the same way that some copyright reformers challenge the assumption that copyright is in the public or artists' best interest, arguing instead that it serves the interests of large, Western, multinational corporations, K'naan challenges the assumption that Somalian piracy is illegitimate, arguing that it is instead a response to the corrupt practices of Western corporations.

While K'naan (whose song "Waving Flag" was picked up by Coca-Cola as the anthem for its $300 million 2010 FIFA World Cup campaign) clearly makes money from means other than selling records, his ambivalence towards digital piracy illustrates a desire for commercial success that may fly in the face of the history of hip hop culture. Initially, hip hop and rap were ways of reclaiming public space, voicing the underrepresented experiences of socially disenfranchised racial and ethnic minorities. When copyright and anti-piracy legislation insist on limiting access to hip hop based on its commercial valuation, the idea is reinforced that access to this culturally specific public forum must be paid for. Embedded in the historicity of hip hop culture is a legacy of subversion. Early black and Latino adaptors of hip hop turned away from up-scale clubs and discos in New York, created their own parties in the parks of the South Bronx, tapping into streetlights and "stealing" electricity. It is hard not to hear the echoes of this subversive thievery when we consider the implications of locking up access to hip hop. Whether in the context of pirated electricity, bootleg copies, or digital down loading, hip hop has always enjoyed a circulation that circumvents more traditional means of distribution. This makes Canadian hip hoppers wary of chastising their fans for piracy, even as their desire for commercial success comes up against the limitations of production conditions in Canada. If there is an ambivalent relationship between black citizenship and constructs of the multicultural nation state in Canada, it follows that there is an equally ambivalent relationship between this citizenship and state laws around cultural production. If the multicultural state positions blackness, as Walcott suggests, outside the boundaries of the nation, then those citizens, artists, and cultural producers also inevitably imagine themselves as belonging to an "elsewhere," where different relations to cultural production exist.

In K'naan's production and marketing of his music, we witness this ambivalence towards both the constructs of the Canadian multicultural nation state and state laws that limit access to cultural products. Despite the continued success of artists such as K'naan, the future of Canadian hip hop remains unstable, in part, because it is located on shifting terrain. Despite the conditions of "elsewhereness" so prevalent in Canadian hip hop, the genre is subject to the laws of a nation state that fails to understand the collaborative and intertextual nature of the genre, insisting instead on universalizing a highly individualized understanding of cultural production. When we look at the history of hip hop culture, we see that the participatory nature of the culture that is evolving around digital technologies and the related public interest in greater access to cultural products is not perhaps all that new. If calls for copyright reform advocating the free flow of cultural goods are made in the best interests of artists and audiences, future legislation might also take into account what it means to be a cultural producer in a genre like hip hop.

26 Friction over Fan Fiction

GRACE WESTCOTT

In October 2007, J.K. Rowling startled the world with the revelation that Albus Dumbledore was gay. Although this announcement was widely reported, the remark she made following that revelation is less well known: "Oh my God, the fan fiction now, eh?" Fan fiction? Unknown to many people, there is a burgeoning online community of Harry Potter fans who amuse themselves by writing their own stories set in Rowling's fictional world. And this phenomenon is not confined to Hogwarts. Fascination with the imaginary worlds of television shows, films, and books has prompted many fans to respond with their own amateur creations. *The Man from U.N.C.L.E.*, *Buffy the Vampire Slayer*, *Star Wars*, *X-Files*, *Xena: Warrior Princess*, and, of course, *Lord of the Rings* are among the many works that have inspired fans to write their own stories using the characters and settings they love.

This is fan fiction, and it is all over the Internet. Although its roots are in the world of print-based science fiction, the phenomenon really took off with the TV series *Star Trek*. By the time the series' second season aired in 1967, fans were busy writing their own episodes and sharing them with like-minded friends. Drawing on familiar *Star Trek* characters and settings – referred to as *the canon* – they placed the characters in narratives not contemplated by the show's writers, often with subversive results. Most famously, these early fan writers perceived a repressed sexual passion between Mr. Spock and Captain Kirk. As a result, a roaring subculture of fan writing began, largely by women and for women, about homoerotic relations between ostensibly heterosexual male characters. Stories of such relationships, known as *slash* (from the "/" used to connote a pairing of characters, such as Harry Potter/Severus Snape), continue to comprise much of fan fiction.

Social scientist Camille Bacon-Smith, in her book *Enterprising Women* (1992), identifies a number of subgenres beyond slash, including mpreg (a man gets pregnant), deathfic (a major character dies), curtainfic (the characters, typically a gay male pairing, go domestic and engage in such comfortably bourgeois exercises as shopping for curtains together), and AU ("alternative universe"; the characters are displaced into an entirely new fantasy setting, such as Harry Potter in Mordor). Sexually explicit subgenres – often tagged as "kink" or "with plumbing" – include PWP (porn without plot or "Plot? What plot?") and BDSM (bondage, discipline, and sadomasochism). Universally deplored as the worst cliché in the genre is the *Mary Sue* story, in which the fan writer writes her thinly veiled self into the plot. "Infinite diversity in infinite combinations" is fandom's motto.

Originally published in hand-stapled mimeographed pages called fanzines, collections of fan fiction stories were distributed in the early days as a kind of pop-cultural samizdat – undercover publications handed out from boxes under tables at fan conventions or covertly mailed to fan community members from volunteers' basements. Within these intimate communities, fans met to share their enthusiasm, to collaborate, to compare interpretations, to edit, criticize, and encourage each other. In the mid-1990s, fan fiction migrated to the Internet, where it has since exploded in size and scope, creating a vibrant virtual fan community and generating vast ad-supported fan archives, blogs, and countless individual fan websites. The fandom of Harry Potter alone has generated hundreds of thousands of fan fiction works, ranging in size from exactly 100 words in length (tiny vignettes called *drabbles*) to full-length novels. Today, a Google search of "fan fiction" brings up about eighty-six million hits, a number that has doubled over the past two years. As a consequence, fan fiction has become increasingly visible. A poster child for the new ethos of participatory culture, fan fiction is at the heart of a free culture movement celebrating the making of user-generated works and "appropriation art," seeking to liberalize laws to let individuals remix others' copyrighted works to create their own. Today, most of us have the sophisticated digital tools to mash up and post our own amateur works using others' content. Not coincidentally, all this is happening at a time when debate over what is fair in the fair use of copyrighted works is receiving more attention than ever before.

Today what's fair is everybody's business. As Henry Jenkins (1992), argues, the impulse to write fan fiction is no different from the creative impulse driving any other narrative genre. It is part of a fundamental human need to tell stories, part of a "shared cultural tradition" dating from Homer onward. According to Jenkins, the works on which fan fiction is based serve for fan communities the same purpose as myths and folklore served in earlier times. They are a source of shared, instantly recognizable references, and therefore ideal raw material for fans' own creative works. Contemporary Web culture, Jenkins argues, is the traditional folk process working at lightning speed on a global scale.

On this reasoning, Mr. Spock has every bit as much validity as a cultural reference within the fan context as has Ulysses within the poetry of Tennyson. Reworking stories of Homer and of Homer Simpson, the argument goes, is much the same thing. Technically speaking, this may be true, but this rather elevated argument is asking fan fiction to carry a lot of freight. Advocates for fan fiction are trying to counter a general perception of fan fiction as a marginal endeavour, a bizarre pastime for emotionally immature people obsessed with reworking ephemeral works of popular entertainment to produce amateurish, second-rate writing. With even fan-generated websites subscribing to such perceptions, advocates are facing a considerable challenge. The idea that cultural works build on their predecessors is incontrovertible, and to say all art is influenced by what has gone before is to admit the obvious. Moreover, a flourishing public domain that allows creators to build on ideas contained in others' works is desirable. It is not unwise, however, to elide the difference between cultural influence, intrinsic in the creative process, and the deliberate appropriation of existing works' key elements, as is done in the writing of fan fiction. Such a conflation empties the term "fan fiction" of much of its distinctive meaning and ignores its essential appeal. Further, an obvious contrast to mythology and folklore is the fact that most iconic works in popular culture are commercial in nature, authored by identifiable writers and still under copyright, which gives rise to potential conflicts and complicates the process of retelling as defined by Jenkins. In the midst of the rapidly evolving cultural norms and expectations of the Internet, fan fiction must carefully negotiate this conflict of creative interests.

To start with: is fan fiction legal? Fans are nervous. To date, there have been no court decisions on the point in either Canada or the United States, so the legal status of fan fiction remains uncertain. Fan fiction typically appropriates fictional characters and settings from copyrighted media works. In the United States, where most of this discussion takes place, copyright law offers significant copyright protection to distinctive fictional characters as such. And a copyright owner's exclusive rights in a work extend explicitly to derivative works based on the original work. Derivative works are fairly broadly conceived in US law:

> A "derivative work" is a work based upon one or more pre-existing works, such as a translation, musical arrangement, dramatization, fictionalization, motion picture version, sound recording, art reproduction, abridgement, condensation or any other form in which a work may be recast, transformed or adapted. (17 U.S.C. ss. 101, 106(2))

Most fan fiction would fall within this definition, and so presents a prima facie case of copyright infringement under American copyright law. Unsure of whether courts will find fan fiction to be fair use, many commentators and fans operate on the rueful assumption that fan fiction is technically infringing.

Undaunted by this, Rebecca Tushnet, a professor of law at Georgetown University and a keen fan fiction writer herself, wants to take fan fiction out of the legal shadows where it has operated, more or less at sufferance, for decades. She has recently helped found the Organization for Transformative Works, with the mandate to establish fan fiction within the parameters of the US doctrine of fair use. As Tushnet (2007c) argues, the writing of non-commercial fan fiction is fair, first, because it takes the source material as raw material and creatively transforms it in ways that copyright law is meant to encourage (it expands covert meanings perceived to be implicit in the original text, presents new viewpoints, or reflects critically on the original content), and second, because the form is extremely unlikely to damage the market of the original work or substitute for it economically: "Like a book review that quotes a work in order to criticize it, a retelling of a story that offers the villain's point of view or adds explicit sexual content can be a transformative fair use" (83).

An opposing view holds fan fiction to be an insufficiently transformative expression. Sonia Katyal (2006), otherwise a polemicist for slash fiction as feminist empowerment, writes:

> the law tends to protect only appropriative works that either assimilate or oppose their originally intended meaning. Works that negotiate meanings fall within a separate category of speech and tend to be afforded almost no protection within the spheres of both copyright and trademark because they produce works that are not fully transformative of the original. Instead, they represent examples of "appropriation art," art that utilizes a

> pre-existing text to create a new work of art that builds upon, but does not completely transform the original. (2006: 498)

Although the characters used in fan fiction may be harnessed to a different story vision, or set in an alternative universe, fan fiction is essentially a narrative reworking of key elements of the original; a derivative work, not a critical work, unlike a book review. According to this view, copyright owners are entitled to protect their characters and stories against fans' distortions.

Under both Canadian and American law, characters from fiction or television, such as *Anne of Green Gables*, can be protected by copyright, as long as the characters are sufficiently creative, distinctive, thorough, and complete, or constitute a substantial part of the work itself. Although the Canadian Copyright Act has no explicit concept of derivative works, it does confer on artists and authors the exclusive right to control the production of their works in other media and adaptations. The basic question is whether a substantial amount of the source has been produced or reproduced, in any material form whatever.

In Canada, construing fan fiction as fair within the Canadian concept of fair dealing remains iffy, despite the 2012 passage of the Copyright Modernization Act and useful language provided that same year by the Supreme Court in five major copyright cases (discussed in the introduction to this book). Unlike the open-ended American fair use concept, fair dealing is defined by a specific list of purposes: criticism and review, research and private study, news reporting, and, since 2012, education, as well as parody or satire. Of these, criticism and parody/satire are possible fits for fan fiction made public on the Internet. It's in the nature of a fan to be an enthusiast, mind you, and much fan fiction may lack the needed critical elements to qualify as criticism, parody, or satire, despite the Supreme Court's insistence on the importance of a liberal interpretation of the concept of criticism.

This question may never need to be decided, however, given the recent introduction in the Copyright Modernization Act of a new exception for non-commercial user-generated content, of which fan fiction is a prime example. This new exception will largely obviate the need to rationalize fan fiction as fair dealing, given the new exception's breadth and permissiveness and given that fan fiction as a phenomenon is almost entirely non-commercial in nature.

There remain, however, the author's moral rights to consider. The US analysis of fan fiction makes barely a passing nod at moral rights. No wonder: in the United States, the notion of moral rights is fairly slight. (And a media corporation cannot have moral rights; it is strictly a personal right.) But, in Canada and much of the rest of the world, an individual author has the moral right both to be credited as the author and to have the integrity of the work protected. That integrity is infringed if the work is, to the prejudice of the honour or reputation of the author, distorted, mutilated, or otherwise modified, or associated with any product, service, cause or institution. Obviously, a moral right protecting a work from being "distorted, mutilated, or otherwise modified" poses a serious legal impediment to the fan fiction writer. It is a significant fetter on the fan's freedom to rework the canon without having this act viewed as an attack on the artistic integrity of the source work and, ultimately, on its author's reputation. After all, an author may well feel that something she has spent years researching and creating is a finished work, not a literary buffet or a cultural spare parts counter for others to rummage in. An author, therefore, may reasonably object to distortions of her characters when they are appropriated to the divergent narrative sensibilities of fan imaginations.

That said, fan fiction generally does not try to pass itself off as the work of the original author. The use of disclaimers – a widespread practice, if not a reliable constant in fandom – goes some distance to meeting author concerns; disclaimers typically cite the source work, disclaim ownership of the borrowed characters, pay homage to the author, and frequently beg not to be sued. But, although this undoubtedly shows good intentions, it does not completely address the problem. The legal position of fan fiction, therefore, remains precarious, and fan writers, knowing this, have tended to keep their heads down from the beginning. To a large extent, this strategy has worked. Fan fiction has generally been either tolerated or ignored by copyright owners. Gene Roddenberry, creator of *Star Trek*, turned a blind eye to fan fiction and Trekkers thrived. Lucas Films, owner of *Star Wars*, officially permitted fan fiction after an initial cease-and-desist skirmish, so long as it was not sexually explicit. Media companies recognize fans as the most devoted viewers of their television programs, and have understood that permitting or even fostering fan sites keeps fans engaged.

Broader benefits may flow from fan fiction as well. Fan fiction allows fan writers – especially children, in educational settings – to develop their writing skills using their favourite characters as a starting point. The fan community provides an important social network for this. On occasion, fanwriters go on to professional writing careers. Canadian science fiction author Cory Doctorow, for example, started out writing *Star Wars* stories at age six, and *Conan the Barbarian* stories at age twelve.

Media companies may judge that the promotional value of creatively engaged fans outweighs the risks of fan fiction. For individual book authors, however, the risk calculation is somewhat different. Although some authors flinch, many find it flattering to have readers identify so deeply with their work. All authors appreciate their fans. But, they have a legitimate concern that fan fiction – operating in the medium of the written word, as the authors themselves do – may put their reputations at risk. A fan, aware of the nature of the genre, might not consider a piece of fanwork to reflect one way or the other on the author of the source work. But, a non-fan, innocently coming upon the same thing out of context, very well might. Now that fan fiction is readily searchable on the Web, a young Harry Potter reader who stumbles inadvertently upon a fan depiction of a sado-masochistic Hagrid could have the image of him – and of J.K. Rowling – indelibly tarnished. Alternatively, a reader might assume that the source author was somehow associated with the fanwork, or approved of it. Fan fiction may potentially compromise the writer's work in the non-fan world by connecting it with substandard writing, or with causes the author deplores.

An author may also perceive his or her economic rights to be under threat. Fans sometimes approach authors for permission. But authors have to safeguard rights in their work for business reasons. To license valuable film and television subsidiary rights, for example, the rights must be free, clear, and exclusive. Authorizing amateur fanworks could complicate rights sales. For writers who write a series of novels – such as Edgar Rice Burroughs, who wrote twenty-five Tarzan novels – the risks are particularly acute. The caution authors have to exercise around managing their rights can be both frustrating to fans and difficult for authors who do not want to discourage their fans, but must.

There is nothing to say that fan fiction cannot be good or even become a phenomenon of sorts. In December 2007, for example, an unofficial fan prequel to the Harry Potter series was written and posted to the Internet. The author was George Norman Lippert, an American Web designer by trade and a keen Potter fan. His novel-length fan fiction, entitled *James Potter and the Hall of Elder's Crossing*, about the lives of Harry's parents, was posted on a professional-looking personal website, where it was noticed and commented on by the Australian press, who speculated it was a secret release by Rowling herself. When the story broke, the site received an avalanche of visits. Rowling, who, fortunately for Lippert, has a liberal attitude towards fan fiction, had to officially deny she had anything to do with the piece.

Another concern is that an author working on a series might encounter in fan fiction an idea similar to the author's own. Ironically, an author who goes ahead and makes use of his or her own idea after having seen the fan fiction in question may risk infringing upon the fan's own copyright. Such a case may not be successful – a court in the United States has held copyright could not be used to "arm an infringer" (*Anderson* v. *Stallone* 1998) – but it could nevertheless be costly to defend or settle. Again, the problem is particularly acute in serial writing, where authors tend to foreshadow in one book or episode a development intended for a future book or episode. Attentive fans might spot the authors' intention and pre-empt the story. Even without a lawsuit, a fan writer's online speculation that the series writer plagiarized his or her idea may be enough to seriously damage the author's reputation.

Some authors use release forms to protect themselves against such eventualities, but this would avail only in cases where the fan writer has directly contacted the author. Many authors, however, opt to shun contact with fan fiction altogether. Some would like to disallow it entirely. Others have permitted fans to create fan stories, subject to restrictions. J.K. Rowling officially encourages fan writing, provided it remains online and not in print, is non-commercial, does not purport to be written by her, and if it contains graphically violent or sexually explicit material, is placed behind an age-verification wall. But, the fact remains: fans post their work to the Internet to facilitate participation in the fan community, not to turn a profit. Confined to fandom, this fannish purpose is essentially personal and non-commercial, in contrast to that of the author's activities.

Where does this leave fan fiction? Perhaps, its shadowy status – largely tolerated, but legally vulnerable – leaves it just where it ought to be, in a healthy state of tension between fans and authors. So far, fan fiction has been able to operate as a tolerated use, if not a fair dealing. Both parties have good reason to accommodate the concerns of the other. No author wants to crush a fan, and fans don't want to damage their favourite author's livelihood or reputation. Fan fiction, particularly under Canadian law, and in view of authors' moral rights, requires the author's forbearance, and probably deserves it.

There is a danger, in this balancing game, in taking a militant stance. We should recognize how the legal landscape is shaping – or misshaping – the arguments here. It is not necessary to contort the discussion with heroic arguments for the lofty transformative nature of slash as feminist emancipation text, or with definitions of *fanfic* as equivalent to Tennyson. To do so, it seems to me, fundamentally miscasts the thing. Fans, for the most part, are writing for fun.

"It's our hobby. We love it," Tushnet (2008) told me. There you have it. What is needed is a kind of digital civility, an online code of respect in engaging with cultural works that recognizes and addresses authors' rights and legitimate concerns. This, together with recognizing fan fiction as coming from "a good place," should encourage authors, rights holders and fans to develop a code of fair practices defining what is fair in fandom, enabling fans to engage creatively with the works they love.

27 Child-Generated Content: Children's Authorship and Interpretive Practices in Digital Gaming Cultures

SARA M. GRIMES

The Internet offers users of all ages opportunities to collaborate in the creation of shared cultural artefacts and experiences. But, while children's use of information communication technologies (ICTs) has been the subject of numerous policy and legal debates in recent years, the emerging role of children as creators of digital content continues to slip under the regulatory radar. In contrast to high-profile issues such as videogame violence and copyright infringement, very little attention is paid to the contributions children make to online cultural production. Yet, ICTs provide children with increasingly important opportunities to create and distribute content across a variety of cultural forums, from emerging spaces such as virtual worlds and social networks to traditional media formats such as television. This is particularly the case now that increasing numbers of children have gained access to "Web 2.0" – second-generation Web applications greatly enhancing the ease with which non-expert users are able to produce and distribute content (often called user-generated content or UGC) online.

Children's role in the Web 2.0 phenomenon is rarely discussed in terms of authorship, ownership, or immaterial labour. However, as with any other user group producing content online, children have become embroiled in complex economic relationships that raise ethical and legal issues demanding of further analysis and consideration. Of primary concern is the way in which children's contributions to UGC culture are frequently exploited for commercial gain. From market research preying upon children's trust (Pybus 2007, Steeves and Kerr 2005) to viral marketing tactics exploiting children's peer relationships, to corporate claims of intellectual property (IP) ownership over children's online submissions, industry standards of practice threaten to undermine the democratic potential of children's digital cultural participation and engagement. Using examples drawn from a number of popular children's online (and Internet-enabled) games and other applications, this chapter provides an overview of the unfolding relationship between child-generated content and the ongoing commercialization of children's digital culture, as well as the implications for children's emerging privacy, authorship, and cultural rights within the digital public domain.

Children as Cultural Producers

Emerging studies of social-networking sites and UGC tools reveal growing participation rates among increasingly younger users. Although a study conducted in 2005 by the Pew Internet and American Life Project described more than half of American teens as "media creators" – producing blogs and websites, posting original artwork and videos, and "remixing" pre-existing content into new compositions (Jenkins 2008) – more recent research conducted by the National School Boards Association (2007) found more than a third (37%) of "students with online access" aged nine to seventeen years to have created websites and online profiles, and nearly a third (30%) to be maintaining their own blogs. Although comparable data on Canadian children is not currently available, previous research suggests that children across North America follow similar patterns when it comes to ICT usage, visiting many of the same websites and exhibiting many of the same (or similar) preferences and behaviours (Steeves 2005, NPD Group 2009).

One of the most significant ways children engage in the production of UGC is within the context of digital games (including game-themed virtual worlds, computer games, and console/handheld games). Digital games represent an immensely important part of children's online experience. A survey commissioned by the Entertainment Software Association of Canada (2011) found that, in 2009, 91 per cent of Canadian children aged six to twelve years had played a video game at least once in the previous four weeks, and 26 per cent reported gaming on a daily basis. As in other areas of digital gaming culture, a growing number of children's games now feature tools for producing and distributing UGC among social networks (Shuler 2007). Coinciding with the Web 2.0 phenomenon, the emphasis within the children's game industry has shifted towards providing players with greater opportunities to collaborate and contribute directly to the games' contents.

An example of this shift is the recent rise in popularity of virtual worlds designed specifically for children (Rusak 2008). Beginning with the massive success of two Canadian virtual worlds in 2006, *Club Penguin* and *Webkinz*, the children's market for virtual worlds has mushroomed over the past few years. In 2008, industry analyst Virtual Worlds Management claimed there were over two hundred virtual worlds for children and youth either live or in development. The vast majority of these were either game-themed (also known as "massively multiplayer online games," or MMOGs) or otherwise centred on play (featuring virtual paper dolls, virtual pets, mini-games, or tools for make-believe play). The top-ranking virtual worlds for children currently claim "populations" of over ten million players, and industry analysts estimated that over 24 per cent of children visited a virtual world at least once a month in 2007 (Oser 2007).

Research into children's engagement with virtual worlds is still in the early stages; nevertheless, preliminary findings suggest child players adopt many of the same behaviours found among teens and adults, including community building, collaborative play, and UGC production (Fields and Kafai 2010; Jackson, Gauntlett, and Steemers 2008; Marsh 2008; Crowe and Bradford 2006). These findings are supported by preliminary user trend surveys, such as the National School Boards Association (2007) report, which found that even before the children's virtual worlds boom had taken place, approximately one in six students with online access had used online tools to create and share virtual objects commonly found in virtual worlds and MMOGs, such as "houses" and "clothing" and virtual characters. Although children's virtual worlds generally contain fewer affordances and design features than those created for teens and adults (Grimes 2010), child players, it appears, are nonetheless able to use these worlds for a variety of creative practices.

In addition to virtual worlds, children have access to UGC tools in a variety of further gaming formats. Console and computer games both have a long history when it comes to enabling high levels of user customization and creativity, as seen in early titles such as Mattel's *Barbie Fashion Designer* (1996) and EA's *The Sims* (2000). With the introduction of Internet-enabled console systems, opportunities not only for generating but also for sharing and distributing game content have expanded significantly. Like MMOGs, a growing number of "UGC games" now allow players to create and exchange virtual items. Some even include tools for constructing entire levels and missions, which allow non-expert players to contribute directly to the game design.

Examples can be found in two highly acclaimed titles released in 2008, which centre almost entirely around the creation and manipulation of UGC: Media Molecule's *LittleBigPlanet* (rated "E" for "Everyone") and EA's *Spore* (rated "E10+" for "Everyone aged 10 years and over," with a number of sequels rated "E"). Because the games are Internet enabled, players can share their finished products (game levels, species of creatures, costumes, etc.) with other players, contributing to vibrant networks of user-creators. Although *LittleBigPlanet* and *Spore* are not specifically "children's games," but rather games targeting a broad demographic, they nonetheless represent important new opportunities for children to engage in increasingly sophisticated forms of UGC. In addition to their E ratings, the games' child-friendly designs and numerous child-targeted marketing initiatives (including cross-promotions for tie-in toys and children's merchandise) indicate that the games' developers perceive children as a key market segment for these particular titles, as well as for UGC more generally.

The introduction of UGC tools into children's gaming cultures is significant for a number of reasons. For one, younger children rarely have the technical knowledge and skills required to engage with complex technological systems at the level of design, such as hacking or programming code (Brin 2006, Donovan and Katz 2009). UGC solves this problem by providing accessible, and increasingly child-friendly, tools for both creating and disseminating content. In this respect, the term "user-generated content" can be confusing, because it does not tend to include more specialized forms of content creation, such as coding, or technological interventions requiring technical expertise, such as hacking. The current discussion is in keeping with common applications of the term as encompassing only those forms of content production and generation made accessible to "everyday" (layperson) users through some type of WYSIWYG ("what you see is what you get") interface. These tools thereby have the potential to greatly facilitate children's entry into media and cultural production.

Second, despite widespread enthusiasm about the democratic potential of Web 2.0, the majority of social-networking sites, MMOGs, and other UGC forums formally prohibit users under the age of thirteen years. Although children are frequently celebrated within popular discourses for their seemingly innate ability to navigate ICTs (Banet-Weiser 2004, Narine and Grimes 2009), they also remain the subjects of numerous moral panics about the potential dangers of life online. This social ambivalence has produced a complex regulatory climate both in the United States and Canada, wherein children's participation in online culture is at once encouraged and restricted by public funding initiatives, child-specific legislation, and self-regulatory expectations (around privacy, e.g.), as well as mutable public concern. As a result, many developers have hitherto appeared unwilling to take on the added legal and ethical responsibilities associated with child users, which are thereby minimized through the inclusion of formal age restrictions (Montgomery 2007, Livingstone 2008). While many children may access the sites anyway, their participation is inevitably limited by the terms of service (TOS) contracts and other mechanisms working to exclude them. The introduction of child-friendly forums for UGC thus provides a surprisingly rare outlet for children to participate in peer interaction and creative self-expression within a digital community of interest.

Another important aspect of this development is that it affords new opportunities for children to engage directly and collaboratively with elements of their shared culture. To date, many of the most popular children's UGC games have centred on themes and characters drawn from pre-existing media texts and toy lines (Grimes 2010). Even within titles that contain original themes, tools, and characters, such as *LittleBigPlanet*, copyrighted content occupies a prominent role. For instance, players of *LittleBigPlanet* can purchase branded downloadable content, such as official Marvel and Disney costumes. Concurrently, the creation of content that pays "unofficial" homage to popular media texts and characters has emerged as a notably common trend among (at least some) of the players of these games (Pigna 2008).

The incorporation of corporately produced content within forums seemingly designed to encourage user appropriations and interpretation should not be underestimated. Children's culture is heavily dominated by wide-reaching media brands using transmedia intertextuality to extend characters and storylines across an expansive array of formats and consumer products. Popular media brands come to function as key features of children's "symbolic culture" (Griffiths and Machin 2003), providing a shared frame of reference through which children organize their play and various social interactions. While the impact this has on the diversity and richness of children's cultural experience is beyond the scope of this chapter, studies do reveal that through creative engagement and collaborative play, children can exert high levels of agency, creativity, and even resistance in their engagements with these texts (Willis 1991, Götz et al. 2005, Formanek-Brunell 1998). Work by Schwartzman (1978) and Sutton-Smith (1986) suggests that the flexible, parodic, and subversive nature of children's play makes it a particularly conducive context for transformative forms of interpretation. Others maintain that children's playful interactions with corporately produced texts can actually function as important forums for assessing, negotiating and challenging dominant ideologies (Gussin Paley 2004).

The introduction of spaces where children are able not only to engage, modify, and reinterpret corporately produced texts, but furthermore to publish their appropriations in a public domain could represent an important reconfiguration of existing power relations within children's culture. Traditionally, children's uses and reinterpretations of corporately produced texts have taken place almost solely within the private sphere – in the bedrooms, playgrounds, and classrooms of contemporary childhood – and they have, thereby, been largely limited to individual (or immediate community) experience. In this respect, UGC games could fill a key function, by providing not only spaces where children can explore content creation in a playful setting, but also opportunities for children to collaboratively interact with elements of their shared cultural landscape.

The idea that engaging in creative appropriation of copyrighted works has broader cultural value has found additional support in current regulatory initiatives, including the recent amendments to the Copyright Act (see Reynolds, this volume). In addition to broadening the general definition of fair dealing to include exceptions for education, parody, and satire, the amended Act provides a section delineating a set of easily attainable conditions under which non-commercial user-generated content that uses some form of copyrighted work does not constitute an infringement. Although several questions remain as to the strength and viability of these particular clauses in relation to the amended Act's broader privileging of copyright owners' ability to extend their control over how their works are used (through technological protection measures and rights management information), the amended Act's articulations of fair dealing and user-generated content nonetheless represent a significant step towards a formal acknowledgment of the cultural rights of the everyday user, which necessarily (albeit not explicitly) extends to child users as well.

Authorship, Distributed Agency, and Fair Dealing

UGC games may, indeed, hold a significant amount of potential; however, they also draw attention to a number of important, and as yet unresolved, questions about the role and status of children as content producers. This includes a number of difficult questions pertaining to authorship, intellectual property (IP) ownership, and fair dealing, each of which are further complicated because the users in question consist of minors with limited – and oftentimes ill-defined – legal rights and responsibilities when it comes to issues of cultural participation. Western culture has traditionally contained very few opportunities for children to participate directly in the large-scale production and dissemination of content, and as such, it is still largely perceived as created for children by adults. Thus, while child-generated content clearly presents a unique new problematic to existing relationships of (cultural) production, it remains unclear how children's special needs and vulnerabilities will be accounted for as they move into various realms of cultural production.

Within adult and teen-oriented gaming cultures, a similar set of issues has already emerged as a key source of debate and legal conflict. For example, Coombe, Herman, and Kaye (2006: 194) describe many MMOGs and virtual worlds as relying quite heavily on "distributed agency," which refers to the "network sociality of cultural production" generated by a game's players. This production process includes both everyday player practices, such as community building, role playing, and creating UGC, as well as more sophisticated (and technically specialized) appropriations of the games' code and contents, such as machinima, "modding," and distributing game patches. As Coombe, Herman, and Kaye (2006) argue, distributed agency is a form of collaborative co-creation that replaces and challenges traditional notions of authorship.

Although collaborative, as well as highly dependent on players' creativity and immaterial labour, the products emerging from distributed agency are nonetheless almost always framed in proprietary terms within the games' end-user licence agreements (EULAs) and TOS contracts. In most cases, the contracts also assign ownership and copyright of that property to the games' corporate owners. These claims raise serious questions about where the players' authorship and ownership rights fit in, questions that in some cases have surfaced as full-fledged legal disputes over whether or not players have the right to sell their in-game creations, or whether game owners have the right to revoke a player's access to their in-game creations (Lastowka and Hunter 2004).

A complicating factor here is the embeddedness of these virtual products within corporately owned game code, as well as their derivation from copyrighted themes, imagery, and narratives. Within this context, "distributed agency" manifests as a "hybrid joinder of the positions of producer and consumer," a position evoked within the Lister et al. (2003) notion of the "prosumer" (34). Thus, while many of the arguments against EULA claims are highly compelling, and although the language of EULAs is clearly "subject to legal scrutiny" (Lastowka 2010), the contracts have yet to be successfully challenged within a judicial system. As such, deeply ambiguous questions about authorship, control, and the potential rights of "prosumers" are mired in a de facto resolution supplied by corporately delineated and enforced EULAs.

By focusing almost solely on adult players, those engaged in this debate have avoided addressing how the situation is further problematized by the involvement of minors. For instance, minors' contracts are voidable in Canada and the United States, which presents a weighty challenge to claims dependent on the validity of TOS contracts and EULAs. With increasing numbers of children creating and sharing content across a growing array of media, it is becoming more crucial than ever to include in this discussion a broader consideration of these types of exceptions, along with an examination of how relationships between players and corporate game owners might be transformed to better accommodate children's special rights and legal status. In the meantime, the corporate owners of children's UGC forums will continue to attempt to address these issues on their own terms and prerogative. In some cases, this might result in important advances for children's cultural rights. For instance, players of *LittleBigPlanet* retain ownership of their UGC under the terms and conditions delineated in the TOS. In other games, however, more dubious solutions will be implemented, as in the case of a fairly common TOS stipulation seeking to enrol parents as agreeing parties in the contractual relationships "entered into" (albeit often unknowingly) by their children.

Another key issue is what space (if any) will be allotted to fair dealing within children's cultural production. The marked emphasis placed on branding and cross-promotion throughout children's culture means that questions of distributed agency become even more complex when applied to child-generated content. Within commercial games and virtual environments, children's production of UGC is not only embedded in corporately owned game code, but is in many cases even more heavily derived from existing (corporately owned) content than the products at the centre of the IP debates described above. For example, the UGC tools provided within children's virtual worlds are often significantly more limited than those available in teen and adult-oriented titles, and frequently they conform to parameters set by established media and toy brands (Grimes 2010). By confining children's creative "prosumption" to a limited range of pre-approved, brand-friendly options, the technological design of virtual worlds such as *Club Penguin, Barbie Girls,* and *Nicktropolis* affords a type of UGC more closely resembling customization than creative appropriation.

In some children's virtual worlds, UGC conforming to the "official" texts is highly encouraged, as long as it abides by the terms of service and appears within the context of a corporately controlled channel. For instance, children are invited to submit artwork and fan fiction based on the *Club Penguin* universe for publication in an in-game, weekly newspaper edited by the game's moderators. Conversely, children's creative reinterpretations of existing media content are frequently under threat of removal or ban, particularly if these don't accord with the desired brand image. In other cases, both forces work in concert. In the example of *LittleBigPlanet*, purchasing the "official" Disney-branded content gives players a limited licence to use the items in their user-generated level designs. At the same time, levels containing player-made, do-it-yourself versions of Disney characters are formally restricted by the game's EULA, and can be removed from the PlayStation Network at any time.

The increasingly symbiotic relationship between child-generated content and copyrighted materials within UGC games makes explorations of player authorship and distributed agency within these contexts all the more challenging. Yet, this relationship must also be examined in terms of its congruency with the wider cultural practices of North American children. As described above, children's symbolic culture is filled with traditions of appropriation, subversion, and other forms of engagement with the media characters and brands permeating their everyday lives. That children might, in fact, have an impetus to extend these interpretive practices into the digital realm is not at all surprising. As it currently stands, however, transporting these types of practices online implies subjecting them to corporate copyright claims and brand management tactics. These tactics, in turn, work to undermine children's sense of ownership over the products of their digital participation, as well as to limit children's freedom to manipulate the contents of their shared culture. Through such processes, child-generated content becomes reconfigured as little more than a new, "interactive" form of consumer practice. This makes it easier to suppress traditions of media appropriation, interpretation, and bricolage that have long occupied a legitimate and valued place within children's cultural practice. Instead, children's UGC is configured to both support corporate ownership claims over its productive dimensions and pre-empt children's authorship rights before they have even been properly introduced.

Notions of fair dealing offer a promising entry point for formulating child-centred alternatives to these corporately biased frameworks. Rather than simply approaching these issues via the proprietary terms introduced in EULAs, we might instead begin to consider how children's cultural rights can also be advanced through a better delineation and protection of their right to access and manipulate elements of their shared culture. One of the major questions to be answered is whether children's creative engagements with popular texts will ultimately continue to be understood as intrinsic, beneficial, or otherwise valuable facets of children's cultural participation. If so, what provisions will be set in place to ensure children's ability to engage with these materials in their play, socialization, and informal learning processes without undue levels of corporate interference and control, both on- and offline?

Conclusion

Despite the discourses of empowerment often associated with Web 2.0 and user-generated content, nothing indicates that increased user participation alone will lead to a more democratic culture. The North American cultural climate remains characterized by strong tendencies towards corporate monopolization, privatization, and expanding copyright regimes (Coombe 2003). In the absence of adequate government intervention, corporate interests have taken the lead role in redefining the foundational tenets of our culture, including authorship, ownership, fair dealing, and the public domain. As users continue to engage in practices of distributed agency and share content online, the need for a formal acknowledgment and delineation of their rights (and responsibilities) as cultural producers, authors, and consumers has become critical. This is particularly true of children, whose participation in the process of cultural production introduces an entirely new set of issues, questions, and responsibilities, with very little historical precedence to fall back on. As children's involvement in cultural production and media has been identified as a key entry point for the advancement of all children's rights (Hamelink 2008), it is crucial that their emerging status as cultural producers be properly addressed, protected, and fostered, within both regulatory frameworks and industry standards of practice.

AFTERWORD

Reflections

Deal with It

LAURA J. MURRAY

"Fair dealing" is an odd phrase, when you think about it. The word "fair" drops us into childhood, to sudden betrayals at dusk just before the streetlights come on, or to the sound of a parent's footsteps coming down the basement stairs to break up a fracas. We can all remember times when we said, "It's not fair!" and the big kids laughed in our face. And we can remember times when somebody else said, "It's not fair," and the adult took the football or candy away from us, *our* football or candy, that *we deserved*. If we're lucky, we recall the vindication of unfairness righted, the doll back in our arms again, if only for "a turn." Self-interest and community interest jostle for power within the word "fair." Fairness is a widespread cultural aspiration: although we all know that "life's not fair," we still keep after it. Fairness is the first ground on which we learn to argue, to mobilize evidence, and it's also the first ground on which we learn to accept compromise or stalemate. Children know that if they can't agree on what's fair, they risk imposed accommodation or deprivation. But unless you're just talking of cutting a piece of cake exactly in half (you cut; I choose), there is hardly ever a formula for fair. Decision depends on a range of contextual facts and implicit or explicit norms. We have to know who had it yesterday, who is bigger or littler, who behaved better, and what the alternatives to "it" are, and we also have to know which of these matters and in what way. In some families, for example, the younger child will be given advantage when all else is equal; in others, the older. Fairness is local. You can't work fairness out once and for all: you have to practise, improvise, defend yourself, every time.

Then there's "dealing." Wheeling and dealing. Plain dealing. Drug dealing. Dealing with it. The *Oxford English Dictionary*'s first meaning is "division; distribution (of gifts, blows, cards, etc.); sharing," from which they move on to "intercourse, friendly or business communication, connection," and "trading, trafficking; buying and selling." At its essence, dealing seems to be orderly interaction, with a notable amplitude of reference from play to combat to commerce. There is an emphasis on human *activity*: selling is an ongoing practice, not a mechanical exchange of objects for cash. Thus, even *Black's Law Dictionary*, which sees the term "dealing" more narrowly as "transactions in the course of trade or business," evokes a continuity of practice that dealing serves and subtends. Dealing is about keeping things moving, keeping them calibrated, keeping relationships alive even when they are adversarial.

Which leads us to "fair dealing." What is fair dealing, anyway?

The usual answer is that it is an exception within the Copyright Act that allows works to be used without permission under certain specified conditions. Much more than that the Act famously does not say, however, and despite fair dealing's history in the courts, including some major Supreme Court cases, it remains somewhat elusive. So, it's a major achievement that several of the essays in this book seek to clarify the scope of fair dealing as a statutory instrument. How can we place fair dealing with regard to other legal concepts such as the public domain or Charter rights (Craig, Amani, this volume)? What filmmaking or archiving or artistic or scholarly practices does it enable (Zeilinger and Horwatt, Meurer, Reynolds, Westcott, this volume)? These are crucial areas for illumination, partly because a lot of creators do their work in institutional or commercial contexts where people other than themselves decide the risk tolerance. A scholar or an archivist may be willing to take chances where his or her funders or producers or Web hosts are not (Goldsmith, this volume). Thus, any argument that can reassure an institution or its representatives that permission and payment are not always required is a Very Good Thing. And any tool that can render fair dealing as routine as the ubiquitous click-through licence is also of great value: the "fair dealing button" for access to copyrighted digital materials is a lovely little bit of pragmatism (Sale et al., this volume).

But, the main thing that will strike any reader of this volume is that many essays depart entirely from fair dealing as Parliament, courts, and lawyers might recognize it. There's a chapter on net neutrality; another on geo-blocking. There's a chapter on "open teaching." We hear about why the CBC shouldn't be locking down its content, and how one might go about devising a digital arts archive. There are discussions of Indigenous cultural rights and children's online user generated content, which speak to the idea of group rights and cultural policy. Zeilinger calls for acknowledgment of "what we might call 'applied fair dealing,' that is, the ways in which artists and audiences themselves go about the constitution and implementation of models of fair exchange, collaboration, and circulation." Wagman and Urquhart "move some distance from the conventional, strict, meaning of fair dealing and … invoke what we call the various 'deals' media consumers are offered, the relative 'fairness' of these deals, and demonstrate how media consumers through their concrete actions 'deal' with the conditions they are presented with."

In such breadth, the collection mobilizes a plural and informal definition of fair dealing that transcends the strict legal definition. When Che, for example, writes that "the transparency of code in open source software enables and promotes expanded prospects for peer review and, consequently, an ethic of fair dealing," he is using the term "fair dealing" to mean something much broader than the statute indicates. Is he wrong? In the technical sense, without doubt – but perhaps he's onto something. In its (welcome) championing of fair dealing in *CCH* v. *Law Society of Upper Canada* (2004), the Supreme Court elevated fair dealing to the status of a "user's right"' And, yet, is not "user's right" a less capacious and more constraining category than "fair dealing"? "User" puts the action in a combative light (user vs. creator/owner), and "right" contains us within an individual rights discourse. Dealing, as we have seen, is relational and process based; use seems terminal and finite and individual. Fairness is a discourse of practice; right is a discourse of law. The two terms seem to come from entirely different political cultures or cultural politics. This book suggests that fair dealing has a meaning, or is participating in a contest of meanings, prior to and parallel with statute, and that as a term it is more alive in our culture than user's rights are.

Various contributors make this point, in very different ways. Seeking to foster more active engagement with fair dealing, Boon asserts that practice "is a matter of value and competence, rather than right. One does not need to own in order to practice. If anything, a practice owns us, reshapes and reconfigures us, and inserts us in a dynamic collectivity." Amani points out that "the inability to know at any given time with certainty what cultural content is fenced in as a protected *work*, and what is available for *play* in the protean space beyond." Craig seeks to place fair dealing within "a cultural commons that is distributed and disaggregated," urging us to focus "on uses as opposed to works (or parts of works) as [the] relevant unit of analysis." Lorimer claims that "the point of open access is to make what would come under fair dealing the rule, rather than a legal exception. Indeed, open access wants a wide swatch of uses to be recognized as entirely legitimate." Maxwell invokes Barrie and Moss's critique of the Creative Commons as reinforcing the misconception that copyright is "all rights reserved" when, in fact, copyright is a finite bundle of rights within a broader and established practice of circulation of scientific knowledge.

In the *CCH* case, there's one little sentence that has always resonated louder with me than all the others: "it may be relevant to consider the custom or practice in a particular trade or industry to determine whether or not the character of the dealing is fair." Relevant, indeed. This sentence imposes a serious responsibility on all of us working and playing with cultural and intellectual expression. It means that *our practice* is *legally weighty*. We can't cower waiting for the law to tell us what to do; *we* make it; the law waits for *us*. This is absolutely essential to understand, because the "grey areas" of fair dealing, even with the *CCH* tests, are frustrating. We just want to *know*. Is it fair dealing, or not? Well, it seems true to the etymology and affective aura of both "fair" and "dealing," as sketched above, that a simple answer is just not available. But, it might also follow from the resonances I've sketched above that we shouldn't be frightened of that. I didn't evoke the world of childhood to belittle discussions about fairness. On the contrary, my point is that adjudicating and working out fairness is something that we really know how to do. We have been practising it since before we learned to talk. It isn't always pleasant or easy, but we can deal with it.

There is something specifically Canadian about this, too, despite fair dealing's counterparts in the legal traditions of other nations. Its recently expanded permitted purposes (review, criticism, news reporting, research, private study, education, parody, and satire) indicate that it's a way to calibrate advantage between creators, publishers, and producers, on one the hand, and education, research, cultural commentary, and journalism, on the other. All good things; all, in Canada, vying for government support. If the resources mostly come from the same source, and the component actors aspire to the same broad goals of supporting democracy, literacy, and creativity, cooperation rather than competition is the most appropriate behaviour. Monetizing every exchange would be as pointless as monetizing every exchange between siblings. The relationship between the arts and postsecondary education in Canada, for example, is not only a commercial one, although students and universities buy many cultural products: affordable postsecondary education is a support for emerging artists, and much art is produced and exhibited within postsecondary institutions. Journalism sometimes borrows through fair dealing and sometimes lends. Free excerpts from books or movies draw readers or viewers to newspapers or TV, and also (if the review is not a pan) draw viewers to the source. Many individuals work in more than one of these sectors and find themselves on both the donor and recipient end of fair dealing.

With the occasional contest and adjustment to accommodate technological change (let's face it: actual copyright lawsuits are all but unknown in Canada), this has all been fairly routine and uncontroversial for a long time. But, it has become controversial as we enter into a neoliberal economic vision of entrepreneurialism and competition. Artists, art galleries, educational institutions, and public broadcasters alike, feeling funding squeezes and much competition for audience attention, are urged to look for "new revenue streams." As they try to garner more corporate support and provide more "market value" to "growing their customer base," they also eye each other to help meet that relentless "bottom line." Why should they forego any potential revenue capture, even from each other? Large media corporations, after all, don't give free rides to artists who want to remix their "properties" and try to leverage new technologies to buy once (from a freelancer, say) and sell many times (in different media); these are the role models we're supposed to be following; and so the Canadian way of sharing public resources starts to seem rather soft and old-fashioned. Along with musical instruments in schools, public broadcasting, and museums, it might seem that fair dealing is a luxury we can't afford any more.

But, this book shows that fair dealing is not a luxury and we can afford it. In fact, it's lawsuits that are the luxury we can't afford, even if we wanted to or thought we could win, and whatever reforms to the statute we might propose or achieve. Lawsuits are only within reach for large moneyed interests. So, the law can be there as a threat, or a touchstone, but it can and should never replace improvisation, discussion, and attempted fair dealing between ordinary people.

Pull Up the Stakes and Fill in the Ditches

The Materiality of Intellectual Property

DARIN BARNEY

Mine! Mine! Mine! Mine! Mine! Mine! Mine! Mine!

A flock of seagulls, expressing proprietary interest in Nemo the clownfish and Dory the blue tang in Andrew Stanton's *Finding Nemo*

Pierre-Joseph Proudhon's 1840 anarchist masterpiece, *What Is Property? Or, an Inquiry into the Principle of Right and of Government*, is most famous for the answer its author gives to the volume's titular question. "*La propriété*," Proudhon declares, "*c'est le vol!*" Property is theft. Aside from (or, perhaps, because of) its manifest clarity, the claim famously became a target in Marx's ongoing battle with anarchist thinkers for proprietary control over the revolutionary program in nineteenth-century Europe. In a letter to J.B. Schweizer, published in 1865 in *Der Social-Demokrat*, Marx praises Proudhon for his "muscular style" and "revolutionary earnestness," while chiding him for "only reproducing old stuff," pointing out that "the same words: "*La propriété c'est le vol!*" had previously appeared in 1789, in a text by the Girondist pamphleteer Jacques-Pierre Brissot. Beyond the charge of not having cleared his samples, Marx criticizes Proudhon for assuming the possibility of a generic form of property abstracted from the particular historical conditions – specifically the mode and relations of production – that alone give property its definitive character in any given milieu. It is not only that, as Marx points out, "theft, as a forcible violation of property, *presupposes the existence of property*" (original emphasis) but, moreover, that this "property" whose existence is presupposed is really just the historically specific form of bourgeois property raised to the level of an abstract, universal generality. Thus, the question *What is property?* "is so badly formulated it cannot be answered correctly." According to Marx, "instead of regarding *economic categories as the theoretical expression of historical relations of production, corresponding to a particular stage of development in material production,* he garbles them into pre-existing *eternal ideas,* and in this roundabout way he arrives once more at the standpoint of bourgeois economy" (original emphasis). For Marx, there is no such thing as property outside property *relations,* historical relations that are specific to particular modes of production (ancient, feudal, bourgeois, etc.). Property is a material fact or, perhaps more accurately, a set of material relations, a "real form," not an abstract concept that exists independently of those relations. To treat property as a concept already concedes too much to the beneficiaries of its historically contingent bourgeois form.

The implication of Proudhon's declaration is that if we could just manage to start thinking of property as theft rather than, say, as the "natural" right to unlimited appropriation and accumulation of value promoted by bourgeois apologists such as John Locke (1980: 23–4), private property and the inegalitarian social relations it supports might vanish altogether. And so Proudhon proceeds to enumerate a list of ten "propositions" aimed at "demonstrating" the "impossibility" of property at the level of its very concept. These include the propositions that "Property is Impossible, because it demands Something for Nothing"; that "Property is Impossible, because, wherever it exists, Production costs more than it is worth"; that "Property is Impossible, because, if it exists, Society devours itself"; that "Property is Impossible, because it is the Mother of Tyranny"; that "Property is Impossible, because it is the Negation of Equality," and so on. As the essays in this volume attest, in the age of non-rivalrous "intellectual" property that is digitally produced, reproduced, circulated, and recycled, each of these reasons for the conceptual impossibility of property is amply demonstrated. And yet, despite its demonstrable impossibility – i.e., despite that, as Carys Craig writes, "almost everything ... in intellectual property law is a metaphor" or that, as Suzanne Zelazo argues, legal mechanisms of digital copyright are founded on an "illusion" – intellectual property and its attendant social relations remain a stubbornly material fact. This is not merely because intellectual property is being studiously cultivated as individual property, or because the legality and morality of fair dealing are being wilfully misrepresented. It is because for at least 250 years the economy of the capitalist world has been organized around the right of a minority to hoard wealth and exclude the majority of others from its enjoyment, and a number of powerful people and institutions would like to keep it that way. For these people, the bonanza represented by the monetization of digital commodities is simply too great to pass up, and certainly not worth foregoing simply because the technological possibility of multiple, non-degraded copies at little or no cost also opens the radical prospect that all of us might finally learn to share.

Incidentally, among this volume's considerable virtues is the clarity with which it insists that, even under a system of widespread fair dealing, the material interests of those whose livelihoods depend on a degree of control over the distribution and use of the products of their culture and intellect would have to be protected somehow. Where you stand depends on where you sit. And as the contributions from Nicholas, Coombe, and Aylwin should remind us, unreconstructed calls for "free culture" sound a lot like colonialist plunder to those whose historical experience of others "taking what they need" has not been a happy one. Put bluntly: a tenured, salaried professor, fat on the public teat, hungry for nothing but affirmation and the veneer of coolness is in no position to tell a freelance poet or Indigenous Elder that information wants to be free.

Something of the current predicament is illuminated by this iconic passage from Rousseau's *Discourse on the Origins of Inequality*:

> The first person who, having enclosed a plot of land, took it into his head to say *this is mine* and found people simple enough to believe him, was the true founder of civil society. What crimes, wars, murders, what miseries and horrors would the human race have been spared had someone pulled up the stakes or filled in the ditch and cried out to his fellow men: "Do not listen to this impostor. You are lost if you forget that the fruits of the earth belong to all, and the earth to no one!" (1987: 60)

It is tempting to believe that we find ourselves in something like this original moment as far as *intellectual* property is concerned – that the Internet is the state of nature and all we need to do in the face of powerful corporations who, like hungry seagulls, have seized upon it barking "Mine! Mine! Mine!" is to disbelieve them and demonstrate the impossibility of their concept. It would be nice if we could do away with what John Maxwell calls "copyright maximalism" simply by doing away with the thought of it. However, given that we have reached the point where intellectual property has become a material reality despite its conceptual impossibility, and fair use of cultural material is presumptively regulated to secure the empires of Disney and U2, maybe covering our ears and shouting, "I can't hear you!" won't quite cut it. As Maxwell explains, "we are headed towards a 'total information awareness' model of IP rights, a world in which every piece of intellectual and cultural material is explicitly owned and licensed and/or marketed, with increasingly hefty and complex requirements for rights discovery, clearance, and marketing, even in the case of so-called free culture and open access movements." It is hard to believe that such a complex might succumb to the force of mere argument. Instead, the situation would seem to call for forms of action that more directly contest the ways in which the idea of intellectual property is being materialized on the capitalist model in concrete relationships. Perhaps confronting the crime of capitalist intellectual property is less about exposing the impossibility of its concept and more about pulling up the stakes and filling in the ditches.

This raises the question of the role of critique and its relationship to other forms of political action. Marx's (1865) attack on Proudhon was predicated on the view that while exposing the impossibility of the concept of property might serve the effort to "abolish" it in "a utopian manner," when it comes down to transforming the specific relations in which property is actually materialized, the job belongs to "history itself" (which is to say, it belongs to the political action of human beings in the world). Property is not a philosophical problem but rather a political one. Thus, as Marcus Boon puts it, the task is not so much "to think beyond or through the frameworks of appropriation that support concepts of property, intellectual or otherwise, towards a depropriated subject and object" but rather, as he writes later, "to render visible once more the instability of all the terms and structures that hold together existing IP regimes, and to point to the madness of modern, capitalist framings of property." In this way, that which appears to be abstract, necessary, and generic is shown to be material, contingent, and historically specific – and, therefore, open to change. Demonstrating that intellectual property makes no sense is nothing compared with demonstrating that it is a system for making sure the rich get richer while the poor get user fees and restricted access, that this has nothing to do with the intrinsic character of property per se but rather is a function of who gets to make and enforce the rules (and design the tools), and that therefore there could be other ways of distributing access to cultural goods and compensating those who create them. Critique will always have a role to play in denaturalizing reified structures and relationships of exploitation and domination, but adventurous endeavours such as UbuWeb suggest that, in relation to intellectual property, this work will probably be accomplished most effectively by simply pulling up the stakes and starting to do things differently.

What "history itself" will hold for the sustainability, extension, or transformation of social relations built on capitalist IP frameworks is impossible to predict. If property only becomes what it is in the context of a specific mode of production, then perhaps the question is whether the emergence of digital networks is facilitating a historical shift towards relations of production, circulation, and consumption that are significantly different from those that prevailed under the auspices of industrial capitalism. In many ways, the present volume is a series of meditations on this possibility, but the balance of evidence suggests it is probably premature to declare that the network society is something other than a capitalist society. As Marx (1854) writes in *The Eighteenth Brumaire of Louis Bonaparte*:

> Men make their own history, but they do not make it just as they please; they do not make it under circumstances of their own choosing, but under circumstances existing already, given and transmitted from the past. The tradition of all dead generations weighs like a nightmare on the brains of the living. And just as they seem to be occupied with revolutionizing themselves and things, creating something that did not exist before, precisely in such epochs of revolutionary crisis they anxiously conjure up the spirits of the past to their service, borrowing from them names, battle slogans, and costumes in order to present this new scene in world history in time-honored disguise and borrowed language. (n.p.)

It is well known that the so-called digital revolution has borrowed not only the disguise and language, but also the basic substance and priorities of the capitalist mode of production. The circumstance we have inherited is a contradictory one, in which emergent technologies have intensified the extension of bourgeois property relations to the domains of art, culture, and intellect, even as these same technologies hold out the promise of a radical alternative (a promise upon which the technology itself cannot automatically deliver). The nightmare that presently weighs on the brains (and bodies) of those who would seize the digital moment to make the world more interesting and egalitarian is the tradition of industrial capitalism that institutionalizes the right of powerful commercial interests to suck value out of the labour of producers and consumers by cultivating artificial scarcity. The digitization of intellectual and cultural material, and the networking of its producers and consumers, could trouble this arrangement, or they could confirm it. It is this contingency, and the stakes and risks it implies, that makes gambits such as UbuWeb and the fair dealing button not only material, but also political. Kenneth Goldsmith's candour – "Are we crazy? Yes. Are we exposing ourselves to great risk? Yes. Could we get screwed? Yes." – is no idle boast. In the digital gold rush, those who pull up the stakes and fill in the ditches are putting things on the line in more ways than one.

References

Statutes Cited

Canadian Charter of Rights and Freedoms. 1982. Part I of the Constitution Act, 1982 being Schedule B to the Canada Act 1982, esp. s. 2.
Consolidated Appropriations Act, 2008. PL 110–161 (US).
Constitution Act 1867 (Canada). Justice Laws Website. http://laws-lois.justice.gc.ca/eng/Const/page-1.html
Constitution Act 1982 (Canada). Justice Laws Website. http://laws-lois.justice.gc.ca/eng/Const/page-15.html#h-38
Copyright Act 1911 (United Kingdom). National Archives. http://www.legislation.gov.uk/ukpga/Geo5/1-2/46/contents
Copyright Act 1968. (Australia). Australasian Legal Information Institute (AustLII). http://www.austlii.edu.au/au/legis/cth/consol_act/ca1968133/
Copyright Act of 1976, esp. s. 107, 17 USC.
Copyright Modernization Act 2012 (Canada). Parliament of Canada. http://www.parl.gc.ca/HousePublications/Publication.aspx?Language=E&Mode=1&DocId=5697419
Department of Justice, Canada. 1985. Copyright Act, RSC, C-42. http://laws-lois.justice.gc.ca/eng/acts/C-42/FullText.html (accessed 23 Oct. 2011).
Digital Millennium Copyright Act 1998 (United States). Copyright.gov. http://www.copyright.gov/legislation/pl105-304.pdf
Millennium Copyright Act, US, 1998.
Parliament of Canada. 2010. Act to Amend the Copyright Act, C-32. Ottawa: Department of Justice. http://www.parl.gc.ca/HousePublications/Publication.aspx?Docid=4580265.
Parliament of Canada. 1991. Broadcasting Act of Canada. Ottawa: Communication Canada.

Statute of Anne 1710 (United Kingdom). Primary Sources on Copyright. http://copy.law.cam.ac.uk/cam/tools/request/showRecord.php?id=record_uk_1710

Telecommunications Act 1993 (Canada). Justice Laws Website. http://laws-lois.justice.gc.ca/eng/acts/t-3.4/page-8.html

Telecommunications Act of 1996, esp. s. 104, 18 USC.

Cases Cited

Alberta (Education) v. Access Copyright, 2010 FCA 198.

Alberta (Education) v. Access Copyright, [2012] SCC 37.

Allen v. Toronto Star Newspapers Ltd., [1997] 36 OR 3D 201.

Anderson v. Stallone, [1998] 150 F3d (2nd Cir.).

Armory v. Delamirie, [1722] KB, 1 Strange 505, 93 ER 664.

BMG Canada Inc. v. John Doe, 2004 FC 488, [2004] 3 FCR 241.

Boudreau v. Lin, [1997] 150 DLR (4th) 324.

Bridges v. Hawkesworth, [1851] 21 LJQB 75.

Campbell v. Acuff-Rose, [1994] 510 US 569.

CCH Canadian Ltd. et al. v. Law Society of Upper Canada, (1999) CanLII 7479, [2000] 2 FC 451 FCTD, 1999.

CCH Canadian Ltd. et al. v. Law Society of Upper Canada, (2002) FCA 187 (CanLII), [2002] 4 FC 213.

CCH Canadian Ltd. et al. v. Law Society of Upper Canada, [2004] 1 SCR 339, 2004 SCC 13.

Cie Generale des Établissements Michelin-Michelin & Cie v. C.A.W.-Canada et al., [1996] 71 CPR 3D 348.

Delrina Corp. v. Triolet Systems Inc., (2002) 58 OR [3d] 339, [2002] OJ No. 676 (QL) (Ont CA).

Fraser Health Authority v. Hospital Employees' Union, 2003 BCSC 807.

Hager v. ECW Press Ltd., [1998] FCJ No. 1830.

Hill v. Church of Scientology of Toronto, [1995] 2 SCR 1130.

Hollinrake v. Truswell, [1894] 3 Ch. 420 (CA).

Irwin Toy v. Quebec, [1989] 1 SCR 927.

Nichols v. Universal Pictures Corporation, (1930) 45 F.2d 119 (2d Cir.).

Parker v. British Airways Board, [1982] 1 QB 1004 (Can).

RJR MacDonald Inc. v. Canada (Attorney General), [1995] 3 SCR 199.

Robertson v. Thomson Corp, [2006] 2 SCR 363, 2006 SCC 43.

SOCAN v. Bell Canada, [2012] SCC 36.

Théberge v. Galerie d'Art du Petit Champlain Inc., [2002] 2 SCR 336, 2002 SCC 34.

Zamacois v. Douville, (1943), 2 DLR 257 (Ex Ct).

Bibliography

24 Hour Party People. 2004. Revolution Films.

Abelson, Hal, Mike Linksswayer, Ben Adida, and Nathan Yergler. 2008. *ccREL: The Creative Commons Rights Expression Language*.. http://wiki.creativecommons.org/ccREL (accessed 20 Sept. 2009).

About "A" Channel Foundation. FAQ. http://www.atv.com/ottawa/5798_18238.aspx (accessed 20 sept. 2009).

Abrell, Elan. 2010. *Implementing a Traditional Knowledge Commons: Opportunities and Challenges*. Developments following the Traditional Knowledge Commons Workshop, Cape Town, South Africa, 14–15 Dec. 2009. Capetown: Natural Justice and Access and Benefit Sharing Capacity Development Initiative for Africa. http://naturaljustice.org/wp-content/uploads/pdf/Implementing_a_TKC-2009.pdf

Access Copyright. 2006. *Unlocatable Copyright Owners*. http://www.accesscopyright.ca/creators/unlocatable-copyright-owners/ (accessed 23 Oct. 2011).

Acheson, Keith, and Christopher Maule. 2001. *Much Ado about Culture: North American Trade Disputes*. Ann Arbor: Michigan University Press.

Ahmed, Mohsen, Nicole Aylwin, and Rosemary J. Coombe. 2009. Indigenous cultural heritage rights in international human rights law. In *Protection of First Nations Cultural Heritage: Laws, Policy and Reform*, ed. Catherine Bell and Robert Paterson, 311–42. Vancouver: UBC Press.

Akester, Patricia. 2010. The impact of digital rights management on freedom of expression: The first empirical assessment. *International Review of Intellectual Property and Competition Law* 41 (1): 31–58.

Albro, Robert. 2005. Managing culture at diversity's expense? Thoughts on UNESCOs newest cultural policy instrument. *Journal of Arts Management* 35 (3): 247–53.

Albro, Robert. n.d. *Cultural Rights in the Context of Cultural Policy*. ZUNIA Knowledge Exchange. http://zunia.org/post/cultural-rights-in-the-context-of-cultural-policy-0

Albro, Robert, and Joanne Bauer, eds. 2005. Cultural rights: What they are, why they matter, how they can be realized. *Human Rights Dialogue Series* 2 (12). Special issue.

Amani, Bita. 1999a. Fact, fiction or folklore? It's time the tale were told …: Part I. *Intellectual Property Journal* 13 (2): 237–73.

Amani, Bita. 1999b. Copyright, cultural industries and folklore: A tall tale of legal fiction – Part II. *Intellectual Property Journal* 13 (3): 275–303.

Anaya, James S. 2004. *Indigenous Peoples in International Law*. Oxford: Oxford University Press.

Anderson, Chris. 2006. *The Long Tail: Why the Future of Business Is Selling Less of More*. New York: Hyperion.

Anderson, Nate. 2009. *FCC Chairman Wants Network Neutrality, Wired and Wireless*. http://arstechnica.com/tech-policy/2009/09/fcc-chairman-wants-network-neutrality-wired-and-wireless/ (accessed 12 Oct. 2009).

Anonymous. 2005. Renowned civil rights documentary *Eyes on the Prize* (1987) is receiving much needed funding for rebroadcast and DVD release. *Afterimage* 33 (2): 9.

Anthony, Denise, Sean W. Smith, and Tim Williamson. 2007. *The Quality of Open Source Production: Zealots and Good Samaritans in the Case of Wikipedia*. Dartmouth College Computer Science Technical Report. . http://www.cs.dartmouth.edu/reports/abstracts/TR2007-606/ (accessed 23 Oct. 2011).

Antons, Chris. 2008. Traditional cultural expressions and their significance for development in a digital environment: Examples from Australia and Southeast Asia. In *Intellectual Property and Traditional Cultural Expressions in a Digital Environment*, ed. Christoph B. Graber and Mira Burri-Nenova, 287–301. Cheltenham: Edward Elgar.

Appadurai, Arjun. 1990. Disjuncture and difference in the global cultural economy. *Public Culture* 2 (2): 1–24. http://dx.doi.org/10.1215/08992363-2-2-1

Arantes, Antonio A. 2007. Diversity, heritage and cultural politics. *Theory, Culture and Society* 24 (7–8): 290–6. http://dx.doi.org/10.1177/02632764070240072506

Artmob. n.d. *About Artmob*. http://artmob.ca/about (accessed 23 Oct. 2011).

Arzipe, Lourdes. 2010. The cultural politics of intangible cultural heritage. In *Safeguarding Intangible Cultural Heritage: Challenges and Approaches*, ed. Janet Blake, 25–42. London: Institute of Art and Law.

Attallah, Paul. 1996. Narrowcasting: Home video and DBS. In *The Cultural Industries in Canada*, ed. Michael Dorland, 257–80. Toronto: James Lorimer.

ATV. n.d. *About "A" Channel Foundation: FAQ*. http://www.ctv.ca/ottawa/5798_18238.aspx (accessed 20 Sept. 2009).

Aufderheide, Patricia. 2009. Expanding the utility of fair use in copyright: The best practices model. *Amsterdam Law Forum* 2 (1): 11–17.

Aufderheide, Patricia, and Peter Jaszi. 2004. *Untold Stories: Creative Consequences of the Rights Clearance Media/Project on Intellectual Property and the Public Interest*. http://www.centerforsocialmedia.org/sites/default/files/documents/UNTOLDSTORIES_Report.pdf (accessed 23 Oct. 2011).

Aufderheide, Patricia, and Peter Jaszi. 2008a. *Recut, Reframe, Recycle: Quoting Copyrighted Material in User-Generated Video*. http://www.centerforsocialmedia.org/sites/default/files/CSM_Recut_Reframe_Recycle_report.pdf (accessed 21 Oct. 2011).

Aufderheide, Patricia, and Peter Jaszi. 2008b. *Code of Best Practices in Fair Use for Online Video*. Center for Social Media. http://www.centerforsocialmedia.org/fair-use/related-materials/codes/code-best-practices-fair-use-online-video

Aufderheide, Patricia, and Peter Jaszi. 2011. *Reclaiming Fair Use: How to Put Balance Back in Copyright*. Chicago: University of Chicago Press. http://dx.doi.org/10.7208/chicago/9780226032443.001.0001

Austin, Graeme W. 2010. Four questions about the Australian approach to fair dealing defenses to copyright infringement. *Journal of the Copyright Society* 57: 611–30.

Australian Research Online. n.d. *A Union Catalogue of Australian IRs*. http://www.oclc.org/oaister.en.html?urlm=168646 (accessed 8 Sept. 2010).

Aylwin, Nicole, and Rosemary J. Coombe. 2008. Taking inventory: (Re)constructing cultural diversity and the possibilities of intellectual property. In *Traditional and Indigenous Knowledge*, ed. V. Veena, 101–11. Bangalore: Icfia University Press.

Babe, Robert E. 1990. *Telecommunications in Canada: Technology, Industry, and Government*. Toronto: University of Toronto Press.

Babe, Robert E. 1995. *Communication and the Transformation of Economics: Essays in Information, Public Policy, and Political Economy*. Boulder: Westview.

Bacon-Smith, Camille. 1992. *Enterprising Women: Television Fandom and the Creation of Popular Myth*. Philadelphia: University of Pennsylvania Press.

Baeker, Greg. 2002. Sharpening the lens: Recent research on cultural policy, cultural diversity and social cohesion. *Canadian Journal of Communication* 27 (1): 179–96.

Bailey, Jane. 2005. Deflating the Michelin Man: Protecting users' rights in the Canadian copyright reform process. In *In the Public Interest: The Future of Canadian Copyright Law*, ed. Michael Geist, 125–66. Toronto: Irwin Law.

Bakan, Joel. 2011. *Childhood under Siege: The Corporate Assault on Children and What We Can Do to Stop It*. New York: Simon and Schuster.

Baker, Paul M.A., and Douglas S. Noonan, with Natahan Moon and Art Seavey, for Red Hat, Inc. 2009. *Open Source Software Index*. http://www.redhat.com/about/where-is-open-source/activity/ (accessed 2 Nov. 2011).

Balkin, Jack M. 2004. Digital speech and democratic culture: A theory of freedom of expression for the information society. *New York University Law Review* 79 (1): 1–54.

Barney, Darin David. 2000. *Prometheus Wired: The Hope for Democracy in the Age of Network Technology*. Vancouver: UBC Press.

Banet-Weiser, Sarah. 2004. Surfin' the net: Children, parental obsolescence, and citizenship. In *Technological Visions: The Hopes and Fears that Shape New*

Technologies, ed. Marita Sturken, Douglas Thomas, and Sandra J. Ball-Rokeach, 270–92. Philadelphia: Temple University Press.

Baron, Paula. 2007. The Moebius strip: Private rights and public use in copyright. *Albany Law Review* 70: 1227–54.

Barratt, Neil, and Leslie R. Shade. 2007. Net neutrality: Telecom policy in the public interest. *Canadian Journal of Communication* 32 (2): 295–305.

Barrett, Tom. 2005. *To Censor Pro-Union Web Site, Telus Blocked 766 Others*. http://thetyee.ca/News/2005/08/04/TelusCensor/ (accessed 15 Dec. 2007).

Bataille, Georges, and Robert Hurley. 1988. *The Accursed Share: An Essay on General Economy*. New York: Zone Books.

Baudrillard, Jean. 1994. *Simulacra and Simulation*. Ann Arbor: University of Michigan Press.

Beale, Alison. 2002. Identifying a policy hierarchy: Communication policy, media industries and globalization. In *Global Culture: Media, Arts, Policy, and Globalization*, ed. Diana Crane, Nobuko Kawashima, and Kawasaki Ken'ichi, 80–9. New York: Routledge.

Beck, Kent. 2000. *Extreme Programming Explained: Embrace Change*. Reading, MA: Addison-Wesley.

Bélanger, Pierre C. 2007. *New Technologies and Cultural Policies: Comprehensive Report*. http://www.culturescope.ca (accessed 6 Mar. 2008).

Belder, Lucky. 2007. Cultural expressions: From common source to public domain. In *New Directions in Copyright Law*, vol. 4, ed. Fiona Macmillan, 35–55. Cheltenham: Edward Elgar.

Bell, Catherine E., and Val Napoleon, eds. 2008. *First Nations Cultural Heritage and Law: Case Studies, Voices, and Perspectives*. Vancouver: UBC Press.

Bell, Catherine E., and Robert K. Patterson, eds. 2009. *Protection of First Nations Cultural Heritage: Laws, Policy, and Reform*. Vancouver: UBC Press.

Benjamin, Walter. 1968 [1936]. The work of art in the age of mechanical reproduction. In *Illuminations: Essays and Reflections*, ed. Hannah Arendt, 217–52. New York: Schocken.

Benkler, Yochai. 1999. Free as the air to common use: First amendment constraints on enclosure of the public domain. *New York University Law Review* 74 (2): 354–446.

Bently, Lionel, Jennifer Davis, and Jane C. Ginsburg, eds. 2010. *Copyright and Piracy: An Interdisciplinary Critique*. Cambridge: Cambridge University Press. http://dx.doi.org/10.1017/CBO9780511761577

Berger, John. 1972. *Ways of Seeing*. London: Penguin.

Berners-Lee, Tim, James Hendler, and Ora Lassila. 2001, 17 May. The semantic web. *Scientific American Magazine*.

Bernstein, Charles. 1998. *Close Listening: Poetry and the Performed Word*. New York: Oxford University Press. http://dx.doi.org/10.1093/acprof:oso/9780195109924.001.0001

Berry, David. 2008. *Copy, Rip, Burn: The Politics of Copyleft and Open Source*. London: Pluto Press.

Berry, David, and Gilles Moss. 2005. On the "Creative Commons": A critique of the Commons without commonallty. *Free Software Magazine*. http://www.freesoftwaremagazine.com/articles/commons_without_commonality (accessed 23 Oct. 2011).

Besek, June M. 2003, Jan. *Copyright Issues Relevant to the Creation of a Digital Archive: A Preliminary Assessment*. Council of Library and Information Resources. http://www.clir.org/pubs/reports/pub112/contents.html (accessed 23 Oct. 2011).

Bey, Hakim [Peter Lamborn Wilson]. 1991. *T.A.Z.*. Brooklyn: Autonomedia Press.

Biagioli, Mario, Peter Jaszi, and Martha Woodmansee, eds. 2011. *Making and Unmaking Intellectual Property: Creative Production in Legal and Cultural Perspective*. Chicago: University of Chicago Press.

BioMed Central. n.d. *What Is BioMed Central?* http://www.biomedcentral.com/about/whatis (accessed 23 Oct. 2011).

Birnhack, Michael D. 2006. More or better? Shaping the public domain. In *The Future of the Public Domain: Identifying the Commons in Information Law*, ed. Lucie Guibault and Paul B. Hugenholtz, 59–86. Alphen aan den Rijn: Kluwer Law International.

Blake, Janet. 2007. *Safeguarding Intangible Cultural Heritage: Challenges and Approaches*. London: Institute of Art and Law.

Blake, Janet. 2009. UNESCO's 2003 Convention on Intangible Cultural Heritage: The implications of community involvement in "safeguarding." In *Intangible Heritage*, ed. Laurajane Smith and Natsuko Akagawa, 45–73. London: Routledge.

Blunden, Andy. 2005. *Transcription of Walter Benjamin's "The Work of Art in the Age of Mechanical Reproduction.* http://www.marxists.org/reference/subject/philosophy/works/ge/benjamin.htm (accessed 24 Oct. 2009).

Bodmer, Karl. 2004. *Karl Bodmer's North American Prints*. Ed. Brandon K. Ruud. Omaha, NB: Joslyn Art Museum.

Boles, Benjamin. 2008. Crystal Castles: "We predict a riot." *Now* Magazine. http://www.nowtoronto.com/music/story.cfm?content=161851 (accessed 28 Sept. 2011).

Bollier, David. 2002. *Why the Public Domain Matters: The Endangered Wellspring of Creativity, Commerce and Democracy*. Washington, DC: New America Foundation.

Bonadio, Enrico. 2011. File sharing, copyright and freedom of speech. *European Intellectual Property Review* 10: 16–28.

Boon, Marcus. 2010. *In Praise of Copying*. Cambridge, MA: Harvard University Press.

Bower, Tom. 1988. *Maxwell: The Outsider*. London: Aurum.

Bowrey, Kathy. 2005. *Law and Internet Cultures*. Cambridge: Cambridge University Press.

Bowrey, Kathy. 2011. Indigenous culture, knowledge, and intellectual property. In *Emerging Issues in Intellectual Property*, ed. Kathy Bowrey, Michael Handler, and Dianne Nicol, 46–67. Melbourne: Oxford University Press.

Bowrey, Kathy, and Jane Anderson. 2009. The politics of global information sharing: Whose cultural agendas are being advanced? *Social and Legal Studies* 18 (4): 479–504. http://dx.doi.org/10.1177/0964663909345095

Boyle, James. 1996. *Shamans, Software, and Spleens: Law and the Construction of the Information Society*. Cambridge, MA: Harvard University Press.

Boyle, James. 1997. A politics of intellectual property: Environmentalism for the Net? *Duke Law Journal* 47 (1): 87–116. http://dx.doi.org/10.2307/1372861

Boyle, James. 2003. The second enclosure movement and the construction of the public domain. *Law and Contemporary Problems* 66 (2): 33–74.

Boyle, James. 2008. *The Public Domain: Enclosing the Commons of the Mind*. New Haven: Yale University Press.

Boyle, James. 2009, 6 Sept. A copyright black hole swallows our culture. *Financial Times*. http://www.ft.com/intl/cms/s/0/6811a9d4-9b0f-11de-a3a1-00144feabdc0.html#axzz2ZFPV7uEh (accessed 23 Oct. 2011).

Bradbury, Danny. 2007, 11 Oct. The cost of copyright. *The Age*. http://www.theage.com.au/news/web/thecostofcopyright/2007/10/10/1191695921443.html (accessed 23 Oct. 2011).

Branje, Carmen. 2006. *LiveDescribe – Can Amateurs Create Quality Video Description?* Master's thesis, Ryerson University. http://www.carmenbranje.com/Thesis-LiveDescribe-CanAmateursCreateQualityVideoDescription_final.pdf (accessed 23 Oct. 2011).

Bratt, E.C. 1937. A suggested reprint service. *American Economic Review* 27 (4): 768–9.

Breakthrough Films. 2004. *Re Licence Application by Breakthrough Films & Television Inc. (Unlocatable Copyright Owners)*. 53 C.P.R. (4th) 240.

Brin, David. 2006, 14 Sept. Why Johnny can't code. *Salon*. http://www.salon.com/2006/09/14/basic_2/ (accessed 23 Oct. 2011).

Brown, Deidre, and George Nicholas. 2010. Protecting Canadian First Nations and Maori heritage through conventional legal means. Paper presented at New Zealand and Canada: Connections, Comparisons and Challenges

Conference, Wellington, New Zealand, 9–10 Feb. http://www.sfu.ca/ipinch/outputs/presentations/protecting-canadian-first-nations-and-maori-heritage-through-conventional-lega (accessed 31 Oct. 2011).

Brown, Laura, Rebecca Griffiths, and Matthew Rascoff. 2007. University publishing in a digital age. *Journal of Electronic Publishing* 10 (3). http://quod.lib.umich.edu/cgi/t/text/text-idx?c=jep;view=text;rgn=main;idno=3336451.0010.301 (accessed 23 Oct. 2011).

Brown, Michael F. 2003. *Who Owns Native Culture?* Cambridge, MA: Harvard University Press.

Brown, Michael F. 2005. Heritage trouble: Recent work on the protection of intangible cultural property. *International Journal of Cultural Property* 12 (1): 40–61. http://dx.doi.org/10.1017/S0940739105050010

Brown, Steven D., and Robert W. Lent. 1984. *Handbook of Counseling Psychology*. New York: Wiley.

Buccafusco, Christopher J. 2007. On the legal consequences of sauces: Should Thomas Keller's recipes be per se copyrightable? *Cardozo Arts and Entertainment Law Journal* 24: 1121–56.

Buchloh, Benjamin. 1982, Sept. Allegorical procedures: Appropriation and montage in contemporary art. *Artforum*, 43–56.

Bürger, Peter. 1984. *Theory of the Avant-Garde*. Trans. Michael Shaw. Minneapolis: University of Minnesota Press.

Burrell, Robert, and Allison Coleman. 2005. *Copyright Exceptions: The Digital Impact*. New York: Cambridge University Press. http://dx.doi.org/10.1017/CBO9780511666964

Burri-Nenova, Mira. 2008. The long tail of the rainbow serpent: New technologies and the protection and promotion of traditional cultural expressions. In *Intellectual Property and Traditional Cultural Expressions: Legal Protection in a Digital Environment*, ed. Chrisoph B. Graber and Mira Burri-Nenova, 205–36. Cheltenham: Edward Elgar.

Burri-Nenova, Mira. 2009. Digital technologies and traditional cultural expressions: A positive look at a difficult relationship. *International Journal of Cultural Property* 17 (1): 1–31.

Burrows, Peter, and Olga Kharif. 2008. The FCC, Comcast, and Net neutrality. *Bloomberg Business Week*. http://www.businessweek.com/stories/2008-02-26/the-fcc-comcast-and-net-neutralitybusinessweek-business-news-stock-market-and-financial-advice (accessed 27 Feb. 2008).

Butling, Pauline, and Susan Rudy. 2005. *Writing in Our Time: Canada's Radical Poetries in English (1957–2003)*. Waterloo: Wilfrid Laurier University Press.

Buyatert, Dries. 2008, 3 Mar. *Report from Formal Drupal Usability Testing at the University of Minnesota Libraries*. http://buytaert.net/files/usability-testing-minnesota.pdf (accessed 31 Oct. 2011).

Byrne, David, and Brian Eno. 1981. *My Life in the Bush of Ghosts.* (Audio CD.) Sire Records.CAB. 2008.

CAB. 2008. *Closed Captioning Manual.* http://www.cab-acr.ca/english/social/captioning/

Cahir, John. 2007. The structure of control – communication systems and copyright law. In *Emerging Issues in Intellectual Property: Trade, Technology and Market Freedom – Essays in Honour of Herchel Smith,* ed. Guido Westkamp, 73–87. Cheltenham: Edward Elgar.

Callon, Michel. 1986. Some elements of a sociology of translation: Domestication of the scallops and the fishermen of St. Brieuc Bay. In *Power, Action and Belief: A New Sociology of Knowlege?* ed. John Law, 196–233. London: Routledge and Kegan Paul.

Cameron, Fiona, and Sarah Kenderdine. 2007. *Theorizing Digital Cultural Heritage: A Critical Discourse.* Cambridge, MA: MIT Press.

Canadian Association of University Teachers (CAUT). 2008, Dec. *Intellectual Property Advisory.* http://www.caut.ca/pages.asp?page=785 (accessed 23 Oct. 2011).

Canadian Culture Online Strategic Statement. 2008. Summative Evaluation of the Canadian Culture Online Strategy. http://www.pch.gc.ca/pgm/em-cr/evaltn/2008/2008-09-2/index-eng.cfm

Canadian Institutes of Health Research (CIHR). 2007, Sept. *Policy on Access to Research Outputs.* http://www.cihr-irsc.gc.ca/e/34846.html (accessed 7 Nov. 2011).

Canadian Intellectual Property Office (CIPO). 2005, Jan. *A Guide to Copyrights.* http://emd.athabascau.ca/resources/cpguide_e.pdf (accessed 23 Oct. 2011).

Canadian Radio-television and Telecommunications Commission (CRTC). 1995. *Public Notice CRTC 1995-48.* http://www.crtc.gc.ca/eng/archive/1995/PB95-48.htm (accessed 23 Oct. 2011).

Canadian Radio-television and Telecommunications Commission (CRTC). 2007. *Broadcasting Decision CRTC 2007-246.* http://www.crtc.gc.ca/eng/archive/2007/db2007-246.htm (accessed 23 Oct. 2011).

Carlsson, Anders. 2008. Chip music: Low-tech data music sharing. In *From Pac-Man to Pop Music: Interactive Audio in Games and New Media,* ed. Karen Collins, 153–62. Farnham: Ashgate.

Carpenter, Kristen A., Sonia K. Katyal, and Angela R. Riley. 2009. In defense of property. *Yale Law Journal* 118: 1022–5.

Carr, Nicholas. 2003, May. IT doesn't matter. *Harvard Business Review* 81 (5): 41–9, 128. Medline:12747161

CBC News. 2007. *Rogers Accused of Hijacking Other Web Pages.* CBC. http://www.cbc.ca/news/technology/story/2007/12/11/tech-rogers.html (accessed 15 Dec. 2007).

CBC Radio Two. 2010. Blog. http://www.cbc.ca/radio2/blog/2009/05/07/knaan.html (accessed June 2010).

CBC TIMES. 1949. 4–10 Dec.

Chander, Anupam, and Madhavi Sunder. 2004. The romance of the public domain. *California Law Review* 92 (5): 1331–71. http://dx.doi.org/10.2307/3481419

Chanthaphonh, Chip, and Thomas J. Ferguson, eds. 2008. *Collaboration in Archaeological Practice: Engaging Descendant Communities*. Lanham: AltaMira Press.

Chartrand, Harry Hillman. 2006. *The Complete Canadian Copyright Act: Present, Past and Proposed Provisions, 1921–2006*. Saskatoon: Compiler Press.

Chase, Mary. 2002. Igniting change in scholarly communication: SPARC, its past, present, and future. *Advances in Librarianship* 26. http://www.sparc.arl.org/bm~doc/SPARC_advances-4.pdf (accessed 23 Oct. 2011).

Chester, Jeff. 2007. *Digital Destiny: New Media and the Future of Democracy*. New York: New Press.

Christen, Kimberly. 2005. Gone digital: Aboriginal remix and the cultural commons. *International Journal of Cultural Property* 12 (3): 315–45. http://dx.doi.org/10.1017/S0940739105050186

Christen, Kimberly. 2012. Does information really want to be free? Indigenous knowledge systems and questions of openness. *International Journal of Communication* 6: 2870–93.

Christen, Kim. n.d. *Long Road*. http://www.kimberlychristen.com (accessed 30 Aug. 2010).

Christen, Kim. n.d. *About: Kim*. http://www.kimchristen.com/about.html (accessed 30 Aug. 2010).

Chua, Hannah Faye, Janxin Leu, and Richard E. Nisbett. 2005, July. Culture and diverging views of social events. *Personality and Social Psychology Bulletin* 31 (7): 925–34. http://dx.doi.org/10.1177/0146167204272166. Medline:15951364

Clarke, Roger. 2000. *Information Wants to be Free ...* http://www.rogerclarke.com/II/IWtbF.html (accessed 23 Oct. 2011).

Clemmensen, Torkil. 2009. *Towards a Theory of Cultural Usability: A Comparison of ADA and CM-U Theory*. Paper presented at HCI International, San Diego. http://dx.doi.org/10.1007/978-3-642-02806-9_48

Coen, Joel. 2000. *O Brother, Where Art Thou?* Burbank: Touchstone Pictures.

Cohen, Don, and Laurence Prusak. 2001. *In Good Company: How Social Capital Makes Organizations Work*. Boston: Harvard Business School Press. http://dx.doi.org/10.1145/358974.358979

Cohen, Julie E. 2006. Copyright, commodification, and culture: Locating the public domain. In *The Future of the Public Domain: Identifying the Commons in Information Law*, ed. Lucie Guibault and Paul B. Hugenholtz, 121–66. Alphen aan den Rijn: Kluwer Law International.

Coleman, Elizabeth, and Rosemary Coombe. 2009. A broken record: Subjecting "music" to cultural rights. In *The Ethics of Cultural Appropriation*, ed. Conrad Brunck and James O. Young, 173–210. Malden: Wiley-Blackwell. http://dx.doi.org/10.1002/9781444311099.ch8

Collins, Steve. 2010. Digital fair: Prosumption and the fair use defence. *Journal of Consumer Culture* 10 (1): 37–55. http://dx.doi.org/10.1177/1469540509354014.

Comaroff, John L., and Jean Comaroff. 2009. *Ethnicity, Inc.* Chicago: University of Chicago Press. http://dx.doi.org/10.7208/chicago/9780226114736.001.0001

Conner, Bruce. 1958. *A Movie.* (Film.)

Coombe, Rosemary J. 1991. Objects of property and subjects of politics: Intellectual property laws and democratic dialogue. *Texas Law Review* 69: 1853–80.

Coombe, Rosemary J. 1998. *The Cultural Life of Intellectual Properties: Authorship, Appropriation, and the Law*. Durham, NC: Duke University Press.

Coombe, Rosemary J. 2003. Fear, hope, and longing for the future of authorship and a revitalized public domain in global regimes of intellectual property. *De Paul Law Review* 52 (1): 1171–91.

Coombe, Rosemary J. 2004. Commodity culture, private censorship, branded environments, and global trade politics: Intellectual property as a topic of law and society research. In *The Blackwell Companion to Law and Society*, ed. A. Sarat, 369–91. Malden: Blackwell. http://dx.doi.org/10.1002/9780470693650.ch20.

Coombe, Rosemary J. 2005. Legal claims to culture in and against the market: Neoliberalism and the global proliferation of meaningful difference. *Law, Culture and the Humanities* 1 (1): 35–55. http://dx.doi.org/10.1191/17438721 05lw010oa

Coombe, Rosemary J. 2006. Cultural rights and intellectual property debates. *Human Rights Dialogue* 2 (1): 34–6.

Coombe, Rosemary J. 2009. The expanding purview of cultural properties and their politics. *Annual Review of Law and Social Science* 5 (1): 393–412. http://dx.doi.org/10.1146/annurev.lawsocsci.093008.131448

Coombe, Rosemary J. 2011a. "Possessing culture": Political economies of community subjects and their properties. In *Ownership and Appropriation*, ed. Mark Busse and Veronica Strang, 105–27. London: Berg.

Coombe, Rosemary J. 2011b. Cultural agencies: "Constructing" community subjects and their rights. In *Making and Unmaking Intellectual Property: Creative Production in Legal and Cultural Perspective*, ed. Mario Biagioli, Peter Jaszi, and Martha Woodmansee, 79–86. Chicago: University of Chicago Press.

Coombe, Rosemary J., and Nicole Aylwin. 2011. Bordering diversity and desire: Using intellectual property to mark place-based products. *Environment and Planning A, New Borders of Consumption* 43 (9): 2027–42.

Coombe, Rosemary J., and Andrew Herman. 2001. Culture wars on the Net: Intellectual property and corporate propriety in digital environments. *South Atlantic Quarterly* 100 (4): 919–47.

Coombe, Rosemary, Andrew Herman, and Lewis Kaye. 2006. Your second Life? Goodwill and the performativity of intellectual property in online digital gaming. *Cultural Studies* 20 (3): 184–210.

Coombe, Rosemary J., and Joseph F. Turcotte. 2012. Indigenous cultural heritage in development and trade: Perspectives from the dynamics of intangible cultural heritage law and policy. In *International Trade in Indigenous Cultural Heritage*, ed. Christoph Graber, Karolina Kuprecht, and Jessica C. Lai, 272–305. Cheltenham: Edward Elgar.

Copeland, Tom. 2008. *Application by the Canadian Association of Internet Providers Requesting Certain Orders Directing Bell Canada to Cease and Desist from "Throttling" Its Wholesale ADSL Access Services*. www.cata.ca/files/PDF/caip/CAIP-PartVII__Traffic- Shaping _ Final_v2.pdf (accessed 25 Aug. 2008).

Corneliussen, Hilde G., and Walker Rettberg, eds. 2008. *Digital Culture, Play, and Identity: A World of Warcraft Reader*. Cambridge, MA: MIT Press.

Coté, Mark, and Jennifer Pybus. 2007. Learning to Immaterial Labour 2.0: MySpace and social networks. *ephemera: theory and politics in organization* 7 (1): 88–106.

Couros, Alec V. 2008. *Examining the Open Movement Possibilities and Implications for Education*. Ottawa: Library and Archives Canada.

Cowie, Del F. 2002, Feb. *Organized K-OS*. Exclaim! http://exclaim.ca/Interviews/FromTheMagazine/organised_k-os (accessed 31 Oct. 2011).

Cox, Kirwan. 2006. Censorship by copyright: Report of the DOC Copyright Survey 2005. In *The Copyright Clearance Culture and Canadian Documentaries*, 33–4. New York: Knopf. http://www.macerajarzyna.com/pages/publications/HPK_white_paper.pdf (accessed 31 Oct. 2011).

Craig, Carys. 2005. The changing face of fair dealing in Canadian copyright law: A proposal for legislative reform. In *The Public Interest: The Future of Canadian Copyright Law*, ed. Michael Geist, 437–61. Toronto: Irwin Law.

Craig, Carys. 2006. Putting the community in communication: Dissolving the conflict between freedom of expression and copyright. *University of Toronto Law Journal* 56 (1): 75–114. http://dx.doi.org/10.1353/tlj.2006.0002

Craig, Carys. 2010. The Canadian public domain: What, where, and to what end? *Canadian Journal of Law and Technology* 7: 221–41.

Craig, Carys, and Joseph F. Turcotte, with Rosemary Coombe. 2011. What's feminist about open access? A relational approach to copyright in the academy. *feminists@law: An Open Access Journal of Feminist Legal Scholarship* 1 (1). http://journals.kent.ac.uk/index.php/feministsatlaw/article/view/7/54

Crane, Diana, Nobuko Kawashima, Kenichi Kawasaki, and Alison Beale, eds. 2002. *Global Culture: Media, Arts, Policy, and Globalization*. New York: Routledge.

Creative Commons. n.d. *About the Licenses*. http://www.kimchristen.com/about.html (accessed 23 Oct. 2011).

Crowe, Nic, and Simon Bradford. 2006. "Hanging out in Runescape": Identity, work and leisure in the virtual playground. *Children's Geographies* 4 (3): 331–46. http://dx.doi.org/10.1080/14733280601005740

Crowne, Emir. 2012a, July. Supreme Court of Canada rules that "private study" need not be done in "splendid isolation" to satisfy fair dealing provisions. *Journal of Intellectual Property Law and Practice* 7 (2): 852–4. http://jiplp.oxfordjournals.org/content/7/12/852.short (accessed 23 Oct. 2012).

Crowne, Emir. 2012b, July. Supreme Court of Canada rules that music previews are a form of "research" covered under the fair dealing provisions of the Copyright Act. *Journal of Intellectual Property Law and Practice* 7 (2): 850–1. http://jiplp.oxfordjournals.org/content/7/12/850.short (accessed 23 Oct. 2012).

Crowne-Mohammed, Emir. 2009. Parody as fair dealing in Canada: A guide for lawyers and judges. *Journal of Intellectual Property Law and Practice* 4 (7): 468–72. http://dx.doi.org/10.1093/jiplp/jpp070

Cunningham, Ward, and Bill Venners. 2003. Exploring with Wiki: A conversation with Ward Cunningham. *Artima Developer*. http://www.artima.com/intv/wiki.html (accessed 31 Oct. 2011).

Daggett, Becca V. 2007. *Localizing the Internet: Five Ways Public Ownership Solves the US Broadband Problem*. Minneapolis: Institute for Local Self-Reliance. http://dx.doi.org/10.1017/CBO9780511611421.041

D'Agostino, Pina. 2008. Healing fair dealing: A comparative copyright analysis of Canada's fair dealing to U.K. fair dealing and U.S. fair use. *McGill Law Journal* 53: 309–63.

Dancsok, Michael. 1998. *Transcending the Documentary: The Films of Arthur Lipsett*. Master's thesis, Concordia University. Spectrum Research Repository. http://spectrum.library.concordia.ca/552/ (accessed 31 Oct. 2011).

Darnielle, John. 2009, 5 Dec. *Why Are People Grudgeful?* http://www.lastplanetojakarta.com/2008/04/why_are_people_grudgeful.html (accessed 31 Oct. 2011).

David, Matthew. 2010. *Peer to Peer and the Music Industry: The Criminalization of Sharing*. Thousand Oaks, CA: Sage.

Davies, Gillian. 1994. *Copyright and the Public Interest*. Weinheim: VCH Verlagsgesellschaft.

Dayton-Johnson, Jeff. 2002. The economics of cultural policy in the Internet age. *Canadian Journal of Communication* 27 (4): 447–52.

de Waard, Anita, and Joost Kircz. 2008. *Modeling Scientific Research Articles – Shifting Perspectives and Persistent Issues*. http://elpub.scix.net/data/works/att/234_elpub2008.content.pdf (accessed 31 Oct. 2011).

Deazley, Ronan. 2006. *Rethinking Copyright: History, Theory, Language*. Cheltenham: Edward Elgar.

Deloria, Vine, Jr. 1971. *Custer Died for Your Sins: An Indian Manifesto*. Norman: University of Oklahoma Press.

Demers, Joanna. 2006. *Steal This Music: How Intellectual Property Law Affects Music Creativity*. Athens: University of Georgia Press.

Dentith, Simon. 2000. *Parody*. London: Routledge. http://dx.doi.org/10.4324/9780203451335

Denzin, Norman K., Yvonna S. Lincoln, and Linda Tuhiwai Smith, eds. 2008. *Handbook of Critical and Indigenous Methodologies*. Los Angeles: Sage.

DiBona, Chris, Sam Ockman, and Mark Stone, eds. 1999. *Open Sources: Voices from the Open Source Revolution*. Sebastopol, CA: O'Reilly.

DiBona, Chris, Mark Stone, and Danese Cooper, eds. 2006. *Open Sources 2.0: The Continuing Evolution*. Sebastopol, CA: O'Reilly.

Diffie, Whitfield. 2003, 16 Jan. *Risky Business: Keeping Security a Secret*. http://www.zdnet.com/news/risky-business-keeping-security-a-secret/127072 (accessed 1 Feb. 2010).

DiNucci, Darcy. 1999. Fragmented future. *Print* 53 (4): 32.

Ditchburn, Jennifer. 2011, 8 Sept. Long-awaited copyright bill returns, but top court to wade in too. *Winnipeg Free Press*. http://www.huffingtonpost.ca/2011/09/08/long-awaited-copyright-bi_n_954517.html (accessed 31 Oct. 2011).

Doctorow, Cory. 2008. *Content: Selected Essays on Technology, Creativity, Copyright, and the Future of the Future*. San Francisco: Tachyon. http://www.jus.uio.no/sisu/content.cory_doctorow/sisu_manifest.html (accessed 31 Oct. 2011).

Doctorow, Cory. 2010, 29 June. Canada's copyright laws show Britain's digital legislation is no exception. *Guardian*. http://www.guardian.co.uk/technology/2010/jun/29/canada-copyright-digital-economy (accessed 31 Oct. 2011).

Donders, Yvonne. 2008. The history of the UNESCO Convention on the Protection and Promotion of the Diversity of Cultural Expressions. In

Protection of Cultural Diversity from a European and International Perspective, ed. Hildegard Schneider and Peter Van de Bossche, 1–29. Antwerp: Intersentia.

Donders, Yvonne. 2010. Do cultural diversity and human rights make a good match? *International Social Science Journal* 61 (199): 15–35. http://dx.doi.org/10.1111/j.1468-2451.2010.01746.x. Medline:21132940

Donovan, Gregory T., and Cindi Katz. 2009. Cookie monsters: Seeing young people's hacking as creative practice. *Children, Youth and Environments* 19 (1): 197–222.

Dow, Danica. 2009, 10 Apr. *Somalian Rapper K'naan Defends the Pirates*. http://www.sohh.com/2009/04/somalian_rapper_knaan_def.html (accessed 31 Oct. 2011).

Drahos, Peter. 2002. Negotiating intellectual property rights: Between coercion and dialogue. In *Global Intellectual Property Rights: Knowledge, Access and Development*, ed. Peter Drahos and Ruth Mayne, 161–82. New York: Palgrave Macmillan. http://dx.doi.org/10.1057/9780230522923

Drahos, Peter. 2005. The regulation of public goods. In *International Public Goods and Transfer of Technology under a Globalized Intellectual Property Regime*, ed. Keith E. Maskus and J.H. Reichman, 46–64. New York: Cambridge University Press. http://dx.doi.org/10.1017/CBO9780511494529.003

Drahos, Peter, and John Braithwaite. 2002. *Information Feudalism: Who Owns the Knowledge Economy?* New York: New Press.

Drahos, Peter, and Ruth Mayne, eds. 2002. *Global Intellectual Property Rights: Knowledge, Access, and Development*. New York: Palgrave Macmillan. http://dx.doi.org/10.1057/9780230522923

Drassinower, Abraham. 2005. Taking user rights seriously. In *The Public Interest: The Future of Canadian Copyright Law*, ed. Michael Geist, 462–79. Toronto: Irwin Law.

Drassinower, Abraham. 2008. Authorship as public address: On the specificity of copyright vis-a-vis patent and trade-mark. *Michigan State Law Review* 31 (1): 199–232.

Dreier, Thomas. 2001. Balancing proprietary and public domain interests: Inside or outside of proprietary rights? In *Expanding the Boundaries of Intellectual Property: Innovation Policy for the Knowledge Society*, ed. Rochelle C. Dreyfuss, Diane L. Zimmerman, and Harry First, 295–316. Oxford: Oxford University Press.

Dreyfuss, Rochelle. 2010. Does IP need IP? Accommodating intellectual production outside the intellectual property paradigm. *Cardozo Law Review* 31 (5): 1437–73.

Dreyfuss, Rochelle C., Diane L. Zimmerman, and Harry First, eds. 2001. *Expanding the Boundaries of Intellectual Property: Innovation Policy for the Knowledge Society*. Oxford: Oxford University Press.

Driver, Mark. 2008, 8 Dec. *Gartner Predicts 2009: The Evolving Open-Source Software Model*. http://www.gartner.com/DisplayDocument?doc_cd=164057 (accessed 31 Oct. 2011).

Drotner, Kirsten, and Sonia Livingstone, eds. 2008. *The International Handbook of Children, Media and Culture*. Los Angeles: Sage.

Dryden, Jean. 2006. Is that copyright too strong? Copyright in archival material. *Journal of Canadian Studies/Revue d'études canadiennes* 40 (2): 163–82.

Dutfield, Graham. 2000. The public and private domains: Intellectual property rights in traditional knowledge. *Science Communication* 21 (3): 274–95. http://dx.doi.org/10.1177/1075547000021003004

Dyer-Witheford, Nick, Jonathan Burston, and Alison Hearn. 2010. Digital labour: Workers, authors, citizens. Editors' introduction. *Ephemera: Theory and Politics in Organization*. Special Issue on Digital Labour 10 (3/4): 214–21.

Dyer-Witheford, Nick, and Greig de Peuter. 2009. *Games of Empire: Global Capitalism and Video Games*. Minneapolis: University of Minnesota Press.

Dyson, Laurel E., Max Henriks, and Stephen Grant. 2007. *Information Technologies and Indigenous Peoples*. Hershey, PA: Information Science Publishing.

Easterbrook, Frank H. 1990. Intellectual property is still property. *Harvard Journal of Law and Public Policy* 13 (1): 108–13.

Eichhorn, Kate. 2006. Breach of copy/rights: The university copy district as abject zone. *Public Culture* 18 (3): 551–71. http://dx.doi.org/10.1215/08992363-2006-019

Elkin-Koren, Niva. 2001. A public-regarding approach to contracting over copyrights. In *Expanding the Boundaries of Intellectual Property: Innovation Policy for the Knowledge Society*, ed. Rochelle C. Dreyfuss, Diane L. Zimmerman, and Harry First, 191–221. Oxford: Oxford University Press.

Elkin-Koren, Niva. 2006. Exploring Creative Commons: A skeptical view of a worthy pursuit. In *The Future of the Public Domain: Identifying the Commons in Information Law*, ed. Lucie Guibault and Paul B. Hugenholtz, 325–45. Alphen aan den Rijn: Kluwer Law International.

Entertainment Software Association of Canada. 2011. *2011 Essential Facts about the Canadian Computer and Video Game Industry*. http://www.theesa.ca/wp-content/uploads/2011/10/Essential-Facts-2011.pdf (accessed 31 Oct. 2011).

Erlandson, Robert F. 2007. *Universal and Accessible Design for Products, Services and Processes*. New York: CRC Press. http://dx.doi.org/10.1201/9781420007664

ESearch-Africa. n.d. Google Custom Search. http://www.google.com/coop/cse?cx=012189697858739272261:nppegeei_q4 (accessed 31 Oct. 2011).

European Organization for Nuclear Research (CERN). 2007. *How the Web Began*. http://home.web.cern.ch/about/birth-web (accessed 23 Oct. 2011).

Fagundes, David. 2011. Talk derby to me: Emergent intellectual property norms governing roller derby pseudonyms. *Texas Law Rev*iew 90: 1093–1152.

Farber, Michael. 1990, Mar. Whoa Canada. *Sports Illustrated* 5: 38–43.

Fauchart, Emmanuelle, and Eric von Hippel. 2008. Norms-based intellectual property systems: The case of French chefs. *Organization Science* 19 (2): 187–201. http://dx.doi.org/10.1287/orsc.1070.0314

Feld, Steven. 2004. A sweet lullaby for "world music." In *Popular Music: Critical Concepts in Media and Cultural Studies*, ed. Simon Frith, 62–86. London: Routledge.

Fels, D.I., J.P. Udo, and J.E. Diamond. 2006a. A comparison of alternative narrative approaches to audio description for animated comedy. *Journal of Visual Impairment and Blindness* 100 (5): 295–305.

Fels, D.I., J.P. Udo, P. Ting, J.E. Diamond, and J.I. Diamond. 2006b. Odd Job Jack described – a universal design approach to described video. *Journal of Universal Access in the Information Society* 5 (1): 73–81. http://dx.doi.org/10.1007/s10209-006-0025-0

Fennell, Chad. 2008, 6 Feb. *Drupal Partners with U of M Libraries – Formal Lab Usability Testing of D6*. http://drupal.org/node/204667 (accessed 2 Nov. 2011).

Fewer, David. 1997. Constitutionalizing copyright: Freedom of expression and the limits of copyright in Canada. *University of Toronto Faculty of Law Review* 55: 175–240.

FFAQ. n.d. http://wiki.creativecommons.org/FFAQ (accessed 7 Nov. 2011).

Fields, Deborah A., and Yasmin B. Kafai. 2010. "Stealing from Grandma" or generating cultural knowledge? Contestations and effects of cheating in a tween virtual world. *Games and Culture* 5 (1): 64–87. http://dx.doi.org/10.1177/1555412009351262

Finckenstein, Konrad von. 2008. Speech by Konrad von Finckenstein, QC. news.gc.ca/web/view/en/index.jsp?articleid=405529 (accessed 18 Aug. 2008).

Fish, Stanley. 2011. *How to Write a Sentence and How to Read One*. New York: HarperCollins.

Fisher, William F., III. 2004. *Promises to Keep: Technology, Law, and the Future of Entertainment*. Stanford: Stanford University Press.

Flint, Eric. 2002. *Prime Palaver*, no. 6. Baen Free Library. http://www.baen.com/library/palaver6.htm (accessed 15 Apr. 2002).

Formanek-Brunell, Miriam. 1998. The politics of dollhood in nineteenth-century America. In *The Children's Culture Reader*, ed. Henry Jenkins, 363–81. New York: NYU Press.

Forum Administrator. 2007, 31 Oct. Bell Discussion forum [Msg 4]. Message posted to http://www.supportcommunity.sympatico.ca/pe/action/forums/ displaysinglethread?rootPostID=10138051&returnExpertiseCode

Franz, Vera. 2010. Back to balance: Limitations and exceptions to copyright. In *Access to Knowledge in the Age of Intellectual Property*, ed. Amy Kapczynski and Gaëlle Krikorian, 517–30. London: Zone Books.

Fraser, Nancy. 2000. Rethinking recognition. *New Left Review* 3: 107–20.

Fraser, Nancy. 2005. Reframing justice in a globalizing world. *New Left Review* 36: 69–88.

FreePress. 2008. Comcast Decision "Major Victory" for Open Internet. http://www.freepress.net/node/42937 (accessed 29 Aug. 2008).

Friends of Canadian Broadcasting. 2009. *Ads on CBC Radio: Who Do You Believe?* http://www.friends.ca/fact-sheet/7973 (accessed 23 Oct. 2011).

Frith, Simon, ed. 2004. *Popular Music: Critical Concepts in Media and Cultural Studies*. London: Routledge.

Frow, John. 1996. Information as gift and commodity. *New Left Review* 219: 89–108.

Frow, John. 2000. Public domain and the new world order in knowledge. *Social Semiotics* 10 (2): 173–85. http://dx.doi.org/10.1080/10350330050009416

Gaffield, Chad. 2008, 7 Apr. Research excellence is key to Canadian innovation and prosperity. *Hill Times*, 37.

Gaines, Jane. 1991. *Contested Culture: The Image, the Voice, and the Law*. Chapel Hill: University of North Carolina Press.

Gantz, John, and Jack B. Rochester. 2005. *Pirates of the Digital Millennium: How the Intellectual Property Wars Damage Our Personal Freedoms, Our Jobs, and the World Economy*. Upper Saddle River, NJ: Prentice-Hall/Financial Times.

Gardner, Janet C., Greg Garvin, Andrew J. Nelson, Gian Vascotto, and G. Conlogue. 2004, Oct. Paleoradiology in mummy studies: The Sulman mummy project. *Canadian Association of Radiologists Journal* 55 (4): 228–34. Medline:15362345

Garfield, Eugene. 1972. Reprint exchange. I. The multi-million dollar problem "ordinaire." *Current Contents* 1 (36): 5–6.

Gaylor, Brett, director. 2008. *Rip: A Remix Manifesto*. (DVD.) Washington, DC: Disinformation Co.

Geigner, Tim. 2011. *Academic Publishers Attempting to Eliminate Fair Use at Universities*. http://www.techdirt.com/articles/20110523/00552614397/

academic-publishers-attempting-to-eliminate-fair-use-universities.shtml (accessed 27 May 2011).

Geismar, Haidy. 2012. *Treasured Possessions, Cultured Resources: Intellectual and Cultural Property and Indigenous Rights in the Pacific*. Durham, NC: Duke University Press.

Geist, Michael. 2002. iCraveTV and the new rules of Internet broadcasting. *University of Arkansas at Little Rock Law Review* 23: 223–42.

Geist, Michael, ed. 2005. *In the Public Interest: The Future of Canadian Copyright Law*. Toronto: Irwin Law.

Geist, Michael. 2006. *Our Own Creative Land: Cultural Monopoly and the Trouble with Copyright*. Toronto: University of Toronto Hart House Lecture Commitee.

Geist, Michael. 2007. They're shrinking the Internet. *The Tyee*. http://thetyee.ca/Views/2007/11/06/ShrinkingInternet/ (accessed 5 Dec. 2007).

Geist, Michael. 2010a, 2 June. Geist: Long-awaited copyright reform plan flawed but flexible. *Toronto Star*. http://www.thestar.com/entertainment/2010/06/02/geist_longawaited_copyright_reform_plan_flawed_but_flexible.html (accessed 7 Aug. 2010).

Geist, Michael, ed. 2010b. *From "Radical Extremism" to "Balanced Copyright": Canadian Copyright and the Digital Agenda*. Toronto: Irwin Law.

Geist, Michael. 2011, 3 Sept. Leaks show US swayed Canada on copyright bill. *Toronto Star*. http://www.thestar.com/news/canada/2011/09/03/leaks_show_us_swayed_canada_on_copyright_bill.html (accessed 3 Sept. 2011).

Geist, Michael. 2012, 17 July. Why the Supreme Court's Copyright Decisions Eviscerate Access Copyright's Business Model. http://www.michaelgeist.ca/content/view/6593/125/ (accessed 16 July 2013).

Geist, Michael, ed. 2013. *The Copyright Pentalogy: How the Supreme Court of Canada Shook the Foundation of Canadian Copyright Law*. Ottawa: Ottawa University Press.

Geist, Michael. n.d. *Michael Geist – Blog*. http://www.michaelgeist.ca/.

Geist, Michael. n.d. *Supreme Court of Canada Stands Up for Fair Dealing in Stunning Sweep of Cases*. http://www.michaelgeist.ca/content/view/6588/125/ (accessed 30 July 2012).

Gendreau, Ysolde, ed. 2008. *An Emerging Intellectual Property Paradigm*. Cheltenham: Edward Elgar.

George, Nelson. 1998. *Hip Hop America*. New York: Viking Penguin.

Gibson, Johanna. 2007. Audiences in tradition: Traditional knowledge and the public domain. In *Intellectual Property: The Many Faces of the Public Domain*, ed. Charlotte Waelde and Hector McQueen, 174–88. Cheltenham: Edward Elgar.

Gillen, Kieron. 2009, 29 Sept. Crystal Castles interview. *Plan B Magazine*. http://web.archive.org/web/20080103053445/http://www.planbmag.com/content/view/492/42/

Gillespie, Tarleton. 2007. *Wired Shut: Copyright and the Shape of Digital Culture*. Cambridge, MA: MIT Press.

Ginsburg, Jane C. 1994. A tale of two copyrights: Literary property in revolutionary France and America. In *Of Authors and Origins: Essays on Copyright Law*, ed. Brad Sherman and Alain Strowel, 131–58. Oxford: Clarendon.

Ginsburg, Jane C. 2006. "Une chose publique"? The author's domain and the public domain in early British, French and US copyright law. *Cambridge Law Journal* 65 (3): 636–70. http://dx.doi.org/10.1017/S0008197306007252.

Ginsburg, Jane C. 2011, Jan. *European Copyright Code – Back to First Principles (with Some Additional Detail)*. Columbia Public Law Research Paper No 11-261. http://papers.ssrn.com/sol3/papers.cfm?abstract_id=1747148

Girard, René. 1987. *Things Hidden since the Foundation of the World*. Stanford: Stanford University Press.

Gitelman, Lisa. 2006. *Always Already New: Media, History and the Data of Culture*. Cambridge, MA: MIT Press.

Goffman, Erving. 1979. *Gender Advertisements*. Cambridge, MA: Harvard University Press.

Goldberg, Brianna. 2009. *Radio 2 Blog: K'naan on the Move ... Artistically Speaking*. http://www.cbc.ca/radio2/blog/2009/05/07/knaan.html (accessed 1 June 2010).

Goldschmidt-Clermont, Luisella. 2002. Communication patterns in high-energy physics. 1965. *High Energy Physics Libraries Webzine* 6 (1). http://library.web.cern.ch/library/Webzine/6/papers/1/ (accessed 2 Nov. 2011).

Goldsmith, Kenneth. 2006. The bride stripped bare: Nude media and the dematerialization of Tony Curtis. In *New Media Poetics: Contexts, Technotexts, and Theories*, ed. Adalaide Morris and Thomas Swiss, 49–64. Cambridge, MA: MIT Press.

Google Custom Search – AuseSearch. n.d. *Google*. http://www.google.com/coop/cse?cx=012189697858739272261:yyyqychcumo

Gordon, Wendy. 1989. An inquiry into the merits of copyright: The challenges of consistency, consent and encouragement theory. *Stanford Law Review* 41 (1): 1354–1405.

Gosseries, Axel, Alain Marciano, and Alain Strowel, eds. 2008. *Intellectual Property and Theories of Justice*. Basingstoke: Palgrave Macmillan. http://dx.doi.org/10.1057/9780230582392

Gotz, Maya, Dafna Lemish, Hyesung Moon, and Amy Aidman. 2005. *Media and the Make-Believe Worlds of Children: When Harry Potter Meets Pokemon in Disneyland*. Mahwah, NJ: Lawrence Erlbaum.

Government of Canada. 2003. *Charter of Rights for Creators. Supporting Culture and Innovation: Report on the Provisions and Operation of the Copyright Act*. http://strategis.ic.gc.ca/epic/site/crp-prda.nsf/en/rp00870e.html (accessed Aug. 2008).

Graber, Christoph Beat. 2008. Substantive rights and obligations under the UNESCO Convention on Cultural Diversity. In *Protection of Cultural Diversity from a European and International Perspective*, ed. Hildegard Schneider and Peter Van den Bossche, 141–61. Antwerp: Intersentia.

Graber, Christoph Beat, and Mira Burri-Nenova, eds. 2008. *Intellectual Property and Traditional Cultural Expressions: Legal Protection in a Digital Environment*. Cheltenham: Edward Elgar.

Graham, Lorie, and Stephen McJohn. 2005. Indigenous peoples and intellectual property. *Washington University Journal of Law and Policy* 19 (2): 313–25.

Gredley, Ellen, and Spyros Maniatis. 1997. Parody: A fatal attraction? Part 1: The nature of parody and its treatment in copyright. *European Intellectual Property Review* 19: 339–44.

Griffiths, Jonathan. 2011. Infopaq, BSA and the "Europeanisation" of United Kingdom copyright law. *Media and Arts Law Review* 16. http://papers.ssrn.com/sol3/papers.cfm?abstract_id=1777027

Griffiths, Merris, and David Machin. 2003. Television and playground games as part of children's symbolic culture. *Social Semiotics* 13 (2): 147–60. http://dx.doi.org/10.1080/1035033032000152589

Grimes, Sara M. 2010. *The Digital Child at Play: How Technological, Political and Commercial Rule Systems Shape Children's Play in Virtual Worlds*. Dissertation, Simon Fraser University, Vancouver. https://theses.lib.sfu.ca/thesis/etd6018 (accessed 9 Sept. 2012).

Gross, Grant. 2003, 13 Mar. Does file trading fund terrorism? *PC World*. http://www.pcworld.com/article/109808/article.html (accessed 13 Mar. 2003).

Gross, Larry P., John S. Katz, and Jay Ruby. 2003. *Image Ethics in the Digital Age*. Minneapolis: University of Minnesota Press.

Gross, Robin D. 2006. "Tragedy of the Commons": Intellectual property rights in the information age. In *Human Rights in the Global Information Society*, ed. Rikke Frank Jorgensen, 108–20. Cambridge, MA: MIT Press.

Grossman, Lev. 1998. *New Free License to Cover Content Online*. Toronto: Netly News.

Guédon, Jean-Claude. 2001. In Oldenburg's long shadow: Librarians, research scientists, publishers, and the control of scientific publishing. *Association of*

Research Libraries, 138th Membership Meeting Proceedings. http://eprints.rclis.org/6375/1/ARL_Proceedings_138_In_Oldenburg%27s_Long_Shadow%2C_by_Guedon.htm (accessed 2 Nov. 2011).

Guibault, Lucie, and Paul B. Hugenholtz. 2006. *The Future of the Public Domain: Identifying the Commons in Information Law*. Alphen aan den Rijn: Kluwer Law International.

Gussin Paley, Vivian. 2004. *A Children's Work: The Importance of Fantasy Play*. Chicago: University of Chicago Press.

Gutstein, Donald. 1999. *E.Con: How the Internet Undermines Democracy*. Toronto: Stoddart.

gwEm. 2004, Apr. Dear Malcom [sic: Open letter to Malcolm McLaren]. *micromusic.net*. http://micromusic.net/public_letter_gwEm.html (accessed 31 Oct. 2011).

Haines, Joe. 1988. *Maxwell*. London: Macdonald.

Halbert, Deborah J. 2005. *Resisting Intellectual Property*. London: Routledge.

Hall, Gary. 2008. *Digitize This Book!: The Politics of New Media, or Why We Need Open Access Now*. Minneapolis: University of Minnesota Press.

Hamelink, Cees. 2008. Children's communication rights: Beyond intentions. In *International Handbook of Children, Media and Culture*, ed. Kirsten Drotner and Sonia Livingstone, 508–19. London: Sage. http://dx.doi.org/10.4135/9781848608436.n31

Hamilakis, Yannis, and Phillip G. Duke, eds. 2007. *Archaeology and Capitalism: From Ethics to Politics*. Walnut Creek: Left Coast Press.

Hammer, Sophie. 2008. Crystal Castles review. *BBC Music*. http://www.bbc.co.uk/music/reviews/48p2 (accessed 23 Oct. 2011).

Hand, David. 1937. *Snow White and the Seven Dwarfs*. (Film.) Burbank: Walt Disney Studios.

Handa, Sunny. 2002. *Copyright Law in Canada*. Markham: Butterworths.

Handler, Michael, and David Rolph. 2003. "A real pea-souper": The *Panel Case* and the development of the fair dealing defences to copyright infringement in Australia. *Melbourne University Law Review* 27: 381–422.

Hardin, Garrett. 1968. The tragedy of the commons. Science 162 (13): 1243–8.

Hardison, Preston. 2006. *Indigenous Peoples and the Commons*. http://onthecommons.org/indigenous-peoples-and-commons (accessed 2 Nov. 2011).

Hardt, Michael, and Antonio Negri. 2000. *Empire*. Cambridge, MA: Harvard University Press.

Hardt, Michael, and Antonio Negri. 2004. *Multitude: War and Democracy in the Age of Empire*. New York: Penguin.

Hardt, Michael, and Antonio Negri. 2009. *Commonwealth*. Cambridge, MA: Harvard University Press.

Hardwicke, Catherine. 2008. *Twilight*. (DVD.) Boston: Summit Entertainment.

Hargreaves, David H. 2003. *Working Laterally: How Innovation Networks Make an Education Epidemic*. Nottingham: Dfes Publications.

Harnad, Stevan. 1995. *Scholarly Journals at the Crossroads: A Subversive Proposal for Electronic Publishing*. Washington, DC: Association of Research Libraries.

Harnad, Stevan. 1998. Learned inquiry and the Net: The role of peer review, peer commentary and copyright. *Learned Publishing* 11 (4): 283–92. http://dx.doi.org/10.1087/09531519850146229

Harnad, Stevan. 2001. The self-archiving initiative. *Nature* 410 (6382): 1024–5. http://www.nature.com/nature/debates/e-access/Articles/harnad.html (accessed 26 Apr. 2011)

Harnad, Stevan. 2006, 13 Mar. The immediate-deposit/optional-access (ID/OA) mandate: Rationale and model. *Open Access Archivangelism*. http://openaccess.eprints.org/index.php?/archives/71-guid.html (accessed 2 Nov. 2011).

Harnad, Stevan. 2008. Waking OA's "slumbering giant": The university's mandate to mandate open access. *New Review of Information Networking* 14 (1): 51–68. http://dx.doi.org/10.1080/13614570903001322

Harnad, Stevan, Leslie Carr, and Yves Gingras. 2008. Maximizing research progress through open access mandates and metrics. *Liinc em Revista* 4 (2): 269–73.

Harnad, Stevan, Leslie Carr, Alma Swan, Arthur Sale, and Hélène Bosc. 2009. Maximizing and measuring research impact through university and research-funder open-access self-archiving mandates. *Wissenschafts-management* 15 (4): 36–41.

Harris, L.E. 2001. *Canadian Copyright Law: The Indispensible Guide for Publishers, Web Professionals, Writers, Artists, Filmmakers, Teachers, Librarians, Archivists, Curators, Lawyers and Business People*. Toronto: McGraw-Hill Ryerson.

Hatcher, J.S. 2005. Of Otakus and Fansubs: A critical look at anime online in light of current issues in copyright law. *SCRIPT-ed* 2 (4): 544–71.

Haupt, Adam. 2008. *Stealing Empire: P2P, Intellectual Property and Hip-Hop Subversion*. Cape Town: Human Sciences Research Council.

Havrilla, Jeffrey S. 2001. *CERT Advisory CA-2001-01: Interbase Server Contains Compiled-in Back Door Account*. Software Engineering Institute. http://www.cert.org/advisories/CA-2001-01.html (accessed 28 Dec. 2008).

Hayes, Christina. 2008. Changing the rules of the game: How video game publishers are embracing user-generated derivative works. *Harvard Journal of Law and Technology* 21 (2): 567–87.

Hazen, Dan, Jeffrey Horrell, and Jan Merrill-Oldham. 1998. Selecting research collections for digitization. *Council on Library and Information Resources, Commission on Preservation and Access* 1 (4): 82–94.

Hebdige, Dick. 1979. *Subculture: The Meaning of Style*. London: Routledge.

Hegel, Georg Wilhelm Friedrich. 1967. *Philosophy of Right*. Oxford: Oxford University Press.

Helfer, Laurence. 2007. Toward a human rights framework for intellectual property. *UC Davis Law Review* 40 (1): 971–1020.

Heller, Michael. 2008. *The gridlock economy: How too much ownership wrecks markets, stops innovation, and costs lives*. New York: Basic Books.

Hemmungs Wirtén, Eva. 2008. *Terms of Use: Negotiating the Jungle of the Intellectual Commons*. Toronto: University of Toronto Press.

Henderson, Graham. 2005, 29 Sept. A national dialogue on the need to safeguard and promote products of the mind. Speech to the National Press Club, Ottawa. *Speeches and Letters*. Canadian Recording Industry Association. http://www.cria.ca/news/290905_n.php (accessed 1 June 2010).

Heritage Community Foundation. 2004. Alberta Government Telephones (AGT). http://wayback.archive-it.org/2217/20101208161839/http://www.abheritage.ca/telephone/era/agt.html (accessed 23 Oct. 2011).

Herland, Karen. 2008. Class action: COMS 274: The medium's rare message. *Concordia Journal*. http://cjournal.concordia.ca/archives/20080508/class_action_coms_274_intermedia_i.php (accessed 15 July 2010).

Herrington, TyAnna. 2001. *Controlling Voices: Intellectual Property, Humanistic Studies, and the Internet*. Carbondale: Southern Illinois University Press.

Hesmondhalgh, David. 2010. User-generated content, free labour and the cultural industries. *ephemera: theory and politics in organization* 10 (3–4): 267–84.

Hesse, Carla. 2002. The rise of intellectual property, 700 BC–AD 2000: An idea in balance. *Daedalus* 131 (2): 26–45.

Hill, Benjamin Mako. 2010. Piracy and free software. Presentation at Inlaws and Outlaws, Split, Croatia, http://mako.cc/copyrighteous/piracy-and-free-software (accessed 1 Aug. 2010).

Hirschbiegel, Oliver. 2004. *Downfall/Der Untergang*. (DVD.) Culver City: Sony Pictures.

Hitchcock, Steve M. 2004, 15 Sept. *The Effect of Open Access and Downloads ("Hits") on Citation Impact: A Bibliography of Studies*. Open Citation Project. http://opcit.eprints.org/oacitation-biblio.html (accessed 2 Nov. 2011).

Hitchcock, Steve M. 2006, 7 Apr. *Boost Repository Content with E-Prints "Request E-Print" Button*. University of Southampton School of Electronics and Computer Science, ECS Notices. https://secure.ecs.soton.ac.uk/notices/publicnotices.php?notice=902 (accessed 2 Nov. 2011).

Hitchcock, Steve M. 2010. The effect of open access and downloads ("hits") on citation impact: A bibliography of studies. http://opcit.eprints.org/oacitation-biblio.html

Hogg, Peter. 2006. *Constitution Law of Canada*. 3rd Student ed. Toronto: Irwin Law.

Holder, Cindy. 2008. Culture as an activity and human right: An important advance for Indigenous peoples and international law. *Alternatives* 33 (1): 7–28. http://dx.doi.org/10.1177/030437540803300102

Hollowell, Julie J., and George P. Nicholas. 2007. Archaeological capital as cultural knowledge. Paper presented at the Society for American Archaeology Conference, 72nd Annual Meeting, Austin, Texas.

Hollowell, Julie J., and George P. Nicholas. 2008. Intellectual property issues in archaeological publication: Some questions to ponder. *Archaeologies* 4 (2): 208–17. http://dx.doi.org/10.1007/s11759-008-9073-9

Hollowell, Julie J., and George Nicholas. 2009a. Decoding implications of the genographic project for archaeology and cultural heritage. *International Journal of Cultural Property* 16 (2): 131–220. http://dx.doi.org/10.1017/S0940739109090079

Hollowell, Julie J., and George Nicholas. 2009b. Using ethnographic methods to articulate community-based conceptions of cultural heritage management. *Public Archaeology* 8 (2): 141–60. http://dx.doi.org/10.1179/175355309X457196

Horwatt, Eli. 2008. New media resistance: Machinima and the avant-garde. *CineAction* 73/74: n.p. http://cineaction.ca/issue73sample.htm (accessed 10 Sept. 2011).

Houtman, Gustaaf. 2009. Negotiating new visions: An interview with Anthony Shelton. *Anthropology Today* 25 (6): 7–13. http://dx.doi.org/10.1111/j.1467-8322.2009.00698.x

Howard, Jen. *Comcast Decision "Major Victory" for Open Internet*. http://www.freepress.net/node/42937 (accessed 7 Nov. 2011).

Hudson, Emily, and Andrew T. Kenyon. 2007. Without walls: Copyright law and digital collections in Australian cultural institutions. *SCRIPT-ed* 4 (2): 197–213. http://dx.doi.org/10.2966/scrip.040207.197

Hugenholtz, P. Bernt. 2001. Copyright and freedom of expression in Europe. In *Expanding the Boundaries of Intellectual Property: Innovation Policy for the Knowledge Society*, ed. Rochelle C. Dreyfuss, Diane L. Zimmerman, and Harry First, 343–64. Oxford: Oxford University Press.

Hughes, Justin. 1999. "Recoding" intellectual property and overlooked audience interests. *Texas Law Review* 77: 923–1010.

Hugo, Victor. 1977. *Berne Convention for the Protection of Literary and Artistic Works: Paris Act of July 24, 1971*. Geneva: World Intellectual Property Organization.

Hutcheon, Linda. 1985. *A Theory of Parody: The Teachings of Twentieth-Century Art Forms*. New York: Methuen.

Hutcheon, Linda. 1989. *The Politics of Postmodernism*. London: Routledge. http://dx.doi.org/10.4324/9780203426050

Hyde, Lewis. 2010. *Common as Air: Revolution, Art, and Ownership*. New York: Farrar, Straus and Giroux.

iCopyright Inc. 2009, 31 Mar. Maximizing revenue and minimizing piracy. http://info.icopyright.com/Article-Tools-White-Paper-4-09.pdf (accessed Feb. 2010).

Intergovernmental Committee on Intellectual Property and Genetic Resources. 2010. *The Protection of Traditional Cultural Expressions/Expressions of Folklore: Revised Objectives and Principles*. Geneva: World Intellectual Property Organization. http://www.wipo.int/meetings/en/doc_details.jsp?doc_id=55137 (accessed 2 Nov. 2011).

Internet Archive. n.d. *Internet Archive: Universal Access to All Knowledge*. http://archive.org/ (accessed 6 Oct. 2009).

Internet Indicators: Subscribers, Users and Broadband Subscribers. n.d. International Telecommunications Union, *ICT Eye*. http://www.itu.int/ITU-D/ICTEYE/Indicators/Indicators.aspx (accessed 19 Jan. 2010).

IP Osgoode. n.d. *IPilogue*. http://www.iposgoode.ca/

Ishida, Toru, Susan R. Fussell, and Piek T.J.M. Vossen, eds. 2007. *Intercultural Collaboration I. Lecture Notes in Computer Science*. Berlin: Springer-Verlag. http://dx.doi.org/10.1007/978-3-540-74000-1

Jackson, Lizzie, David Gauntlett, and Jeanette Steemers. 2008. *Children in Virtual Worlds: Adventure Rock Users and Producers Study*. London: BBC.

Jackson, Peter. 2010. *The Lord of the Rings: The Motion Picture Trilogy*. (Blu-Ray.) Los Angeles: New Line Home Video.

Jacobs, Neil, and Alma Swan. 2006. The culture of open access: Researchers' views and responses. In *Open Access: Key Strategic, Technical and Economic Aspects*, ed. Neil Jacobs, 52–100. Oxford: Chandos.

Jameson, Frederic. 1991. *Postmodernism, or, the Cultural Logic of Late Capitalism*. Durham, NC: Duke University Press.

Janus, Kevin A. 2000. Defending the public domain in copyright law: A tactical approach. *Intellectual Property Journal* 14 (3): 379–401.

Jaszi, Peter. 1991. On the author effect: Contemporary copyright and collective creativity. *Cardozo Arts and Entertainment Law Journal* 10 (2): 293–320.

Jaszi, Peter, and Martha Woodmansee, eds. 1994. *The Construction of Authorship: Textual Appropriation in Law and Literature*. Durham, NC: Duke University Press.

Jaszi, Peter, and Martha Woodmansee. 1996. The ethical reaches of authorship. *South Atlantic Quarterly* 95 (4): 947–77.

Jenkins, Henry. 1992. *Textual Poachers: Television Fans and Participatory Culture.* New York: Routledge.

Jenkins, Henry, ed. 1998. *The Children's Culture Reader*. New York: NYU Press.

Jenkins, Henry. 2006. *Fans, Bloggers and Gamers: Exploring Participatory Culture.* New York: NYU Press.

Jenkins, Henry. 2008. *White Paper on Digital Media and Learning*. Chicago: John D. and Catherine T. MacArthur Foundation.

Jesdanun, Anick. 2007. Publishers seeking Web controls. *Washington Post.* http://www.washingtonpost.com/wp-dyn/content/article/2007/11/29/AR2007112902207.html

Jhally, Sut. 1991. *Dreamworlds.* (VHS.) Northampton, MA: Media Education Foundation.

Jhally, Sut. n.d. *Mission – About MEF*. www.mediaed.org/wp/about-mef (accessed 15 July 2010).

Johnson, Justin. 2006. Collaboration, peer review and open source software. *Information Economics and Policy* 18 (4): 477–97. http://dx.doi.org/10.1016/j.infoecopol.2006.07.001

Joint, Nicholas. 2008. Is digitisation the new circulation? Borrowing trends, digitisation and the nature of reading in US and UK libraries. *Library Review* 57 (2): 87–95. http://dx.doi.org/10.1108/00242530810853973

Joranson, Kate. 2008. Indigenous knowledge and the knowledge commons. *International Information and Library Review* 40 (1): 64–72. http://dx.doi.org/10.1016/j.iilr.2007.09.002

Jung, Courtney. 2003. "Indigenous" is the new "Peasant": The struggle for political identity in the neo-liberal age. *Social Research* 70 (2): 433–62.

Jung, Courtney. 2006. Why liberals should value "identity politics." *Daedalus* 135 (4): 32–9. http://dx.doi.org/10.1162/daed.2006.135.4.32

Jung, Courtney. 2008. *The Moral Force of Indigenous Politics: Critical Liberalism and the Zapatistas*. Cambridge: Cambridge University Press. http://dx.doi.org/10.1017/CBO9780511551222

Jungen, Brian, and Daina Augaitis. 2005. *Brian Jungen*. Vancouver: Vancouver Art Gallery.

Kagedan, Elizabeth, and Tim Legault. 2009, 19 Oct. Busted! *The Varsity*. http://thevarsity.ca/articles/21369 (accessed 21 Feb. 2010).

Kahin, Brian, and Hal Varian, eds. 2000. *Internet Publishing and Beyond: The Economics of Digital Information and Intellectual Property*. Cambridge, MA: MIT Press.

Kansa, Eric C., Jason Schultz, and Ahrash N. Bissell. 2005. Protecting traditional knowledge and expanding access to scientific data: Juxtaposing intellectual property agendas via a "some rights reserved" model. *International Journal of Cultural Property* 12 (3): 285–314. http://dx.doi.org/10.1017/S0940739105050204

Kashmere, Brett. 2004. Arthur Lipsett. *Senses of Cinema* 32. http://sensesofcinema.com/2004/editorial/32index/ (accessed 31 Oct. 2011).

Katyal, Sonia K. 2006. Performance, property, and the slashing of gender in fan fiction. *Journal of Gender, Social Policy and the Law* 14 (3): 461–518.

Kelly, Kevin. 1998. *New Rules for the New Economy: Ten Radical Strategies for a Connected World*. New York: Viking.

Kelty, Christopher M. 2004. Punt to culture. *Anthropological Quarterly* 77 (3): 547–58. http://dx.doi.org/10.1353/anq.2004.0043.

Kelty, Christopher M. 2005. Geeks, social imaginaries, and recursive publics. *Cultural Anthropology* 20 (2): 185–214. http://dx.doi.org/10.1525/can.2005.20.2.185

Kelty, Christopher M. 2008. *Two Bits: The Cultural Significance of Free Software*. Durham, NC: Duke University Press.

Kelty, Christopher M. 2011. Inventing copyleft. In *Making and Unmaking Intellectual Property: Creative Production in Legal and Cultural Perspective*, ed. Mario Biagioli, Peter Jaszi, and Martha Woodmansee, 133–48. Chicago: University of Chicago Press.

Kemp, E., C. Phillips, C. Kinshuk, and J. Haynes. 2001. *Proceedings of the Symposium on Computer Human Interaction*. Wellington: Palmerston North Press.

Keyes, A., and C. Brunet. 1977. *Copyright in Canada: Proposals for a Revision of the Law*. Ottawa: Consumer and Corporate Affairs Canada. http://dx.doi.org/10.1080/00315249.1977.9943424

Khong, Dennis W. 2007. Orphan works, Abandonware and the missing market for copyrighted goods. *International Journal of Law and Information Technology* 15 (1): 54–89. http://dx.doi.org/10.1093/ijlit/eai032

Kim, Eugene E. 2003. *An Introduction to Open Source Communities*. San Mateo: Blue Oxen.

Kirn, Peter. 2008a, 5 May. Chiptune music theft continues; Crystal Castles abuses Creative Commons license. http://sensesofcinema.com/2004/editorial/32index/ (accessed 29 Sept. 2009).

Kirn, Peter 2008b, 29 Sept. CSI: Chiptune – Nitro2K01 gets scientific with alleged violations; Crystal Castles responds. CDM – Create Digital Music. http://createdigitalmusic.com/2008/05/06/csi-chiptune-nitro2k01-gets-scientific-with-alleged-violations-crystal-castles-responds/#more-3418

Kitwana, Bakari. 2005. *Why White Kids Love Hip Hop: Wankstas, Wiggers, Wannabes, and the New Reality of Race in America*. New York: Basic Civitas Books.

Knopf, Howard. 1994. Limits on the nature and scope of copyright. In *Copyright and Confidential Information Law of Canada*, ed. Gordon F. Henderson, 229–58. Scarborough: Carswell.

Knopf, Howard. 2006a. The Copyright Clearance Culture and Canadian Documentaries: A White Paper on Behalf of the Documentary Organization of Canada ("DOC"). www.macerajarzyna.com/pages/publications/HPK_white_paper.pdf (accessed 2 Aug. 2012).

Knopf, Howard. 2006b, 6 Feb. Excess caution. *Excess Copyright*. http://excesscopyright.blogspot.ca/2006/02/excess-caution.html (accessed 2 Nov. 2011).

Knopf, Howard. 2008. Why Canada needs parody parity and comedy comity: Copyright control of Canadian humour. *Les cahiers de propriété intellectuelle* 20 (3): 717–46.

Knopf, Howard. n.d. *Excess Copyright*. http://excesscopyright.blogspot.ca/2006/02/excess-caution.html

Krasilovsky, William M. 1967. Observations on public domain. *Bulletin of the Copyright Society of the USA* 14 (1): 205–29.

Krauss, Rosalind. 1985. *The Originality of the Avant-Garde and Other Modernist Myths*. Cambridge, MA: MIT Press.

Krillidou, Martha. 2004, June. Serials trends reflected in the ARL statistics 2002–2003. *ARL: A Bimonthly Report*, 234. http://old.arl.org/resources/pubs/br/br234/br234serials.shtml (accessed 1 Aug. 2008).

Kumar, Matthew. 2008, 25 June. People who live in crystal castles … http://torontoist.com/2008/06/people_who_live_in_crystal_castles/ (acessed 29 Sept. 2009).

Kundnani, Arum. 1998. Where do you want to go today? The rise of information capital. *Race and Class* 40 (2): 49–71.

Kymlicka, Will. 2007. *Multicultural Odysseys: Navigating the New International Politics of Diversity*. Oxford: Oxford University Press.

Lacoue-Labarthe, Philippe. 1989. *Typography: Mimesis, Philosophy, Politics*. Ed. Christopher Fynsk. Introduction Jacques Derrida. Cambridge, MA: Harvard University Press.

Laddie, Sir Hugh. 1997. Copyright: Over-strength, over-regulated, over-rated? Special Issue: Innovation, Incentive and Reward: Intellectual Property Law and Policy. *Hume Papers on Public Policy* 5 (3): 1–16.

Lametti, David. 2005. Coming to terms with copyright. In *In the Public Interest: The Future of Canadian Copyright Law*, ed. Michael Geist, 480–516. Toronto: Irwin Law.

Landselius, Kyra. 2006. *Natives on the Net: Indigenous and Diasporic Peoples in the Virtual Age*. New York: Routledge.

Lange, David. 1981. Recognizing the public domain. *Law and Contemporary Problems* 44 (1): 147–78. http://dx.doi.org/10.2307/1191227

Lange, David. 2003. Reimagining the public domain. *Law and Contemporary Problems* 66 (2): 463–83.

Lastowka, Greg. 2010. *Virtual Justice: The New Laws of Online Worlds*. New Haven: Yale University Press.

Lastowka, Greg F., and Dan Hunter. 2004. The laws of the virtual worlds. *California Law Review* 92 (1): 1–73. http://dx.doi.org/10.2307/3481444

Laszlo, Krisztina. 2006. Ethnographic archival records and cultural property. *Archivaria* 61 (1): 299–307.

Lave, Jean, and Etienne Wenger. 1991. *Situated Learning: Legitimate Peripheral Participation*. Cambridge: Cambridge University Press. http://dx.doi.org/10.1017/CBO9780511815355

Law, John. 1986. *Power, Action, and Belief: A New Sociology of Knowledge?* London: Routledge and Kegan Paul.

Lawrence, Steve. 2001. Nature debates: Authors willing to pay for instant Web access. http://www.nature.com/nature/debates/e-access/Articles/lawrence.html

Lazzarato, Maurizio. 1996. Immaterial labour. In *Radical Thought in Italy: A Potential Politics*, ed. Paolo Virno and Michael Hardt, 133–47. Minneapolis: University of Minnesota Press.

Leaver, Tama. 2008. Watching Battlestar Galactica in Australia and the tyranny of digital distance. *Media International Australia* 126: 145–54.

Lee, Edward. 2003. The public's domain: The evolution of legal restraints on the government's power to control public access through secrecy or intellectual property. *Hastings Law Journal* 55 (1): 91–110.

Lee, Hye-Kyung. 2009. Between fan culture and copyright infringement: Manga Scanlation. *Media, Culture and Society* 31 (6): 1011–22. http://dx.doi.org/10.1177/0163443709344251

Leetaru, Kalev. 2008. Mass book digitization: The deeper story of Google books and the open content alliance. *First Monday* 13 (10) http://firstmonday.org/ojs/index.php/fm/article/view/2101/2037

Lemley, Mark A. 2005. Property, intellectual property, and free riding. *Texas Law Review* 83 (1): 1031–75.

Lemley, Mark A., Deirdre Mulligan, and Jason Schultz. 2003. *Brief of Amici Curiae the Internet Archive Filed on Behalf of Petitioners*. http://cyber.law.harvard.edu/openlaw/eldredvashcroft/cert/archive-amicus.html (accessed 7 Nov. 2011).

Lessig, Lawrence. 2001. *The Future of Ideas: The Fate of the Commons in a Connected World*. New York: Random House.

Lessig, Lawrence. 2004. *Free Culture: How Big Media Uses Technology and the Law to Lock Down Culture and Control Creativity*. New York: Penguin.

Lessig, Lawrence. 2006. *Code and Other Laws of Cyberspace: Version 2.0*. New York: Basic Books.

Lessig, Lawrence. 2008. *Remix: Making Art and Commerce Thrive in the Hybrid Economy*. New York: Penguin. http://dx.doi.org/10.5040/9781849662505

Lessig, Lawrence. 2010, 26 Jan. For the love of culture. *The New Republic: Google, Copyright, and Our Future*. http://www.newrepublic.com/article/the-love-culture (accessed 2 Nov. 2011).

Levin, Bob. 2003. *The Pirates and the Mouse: Disney's War against the Counterculture*. Seattle: Fantagraphics Books.

Levine, David K., and Michele Boldrin. 2008. *Against Monopoly*. New York: Cambridge University Press.

Levy, Roanie. 2009, 29 July. *Statement at Gatineau Roundtable and Public Hearing on Copyright*. http://www.ic.gc.ca/eic/site/008.nsf/eng/h_04028.html

Liebmann, Matthew, and Uzma Z. Rizvi, eds. 2008. *Archaeology and the Postcolonial Critique*. Lanham: AltaMira Press.

Lindsay, Cam. 2008, Mar. Crystal Castles. http://exclaim.ca/Interviews/WebExclusive/crystal_castles (accessed 2 Nov. 2011).

Linklater, Richard. 2001. *Waking Life*. (DVD.) Burbank: Warner Home Video.

Linklater, Richard. 2006. *A Scanner Darkly*. (DVD.) Burbank: Warner Home Video.

Lipsett, Arthur. 1961. *Very Nice, Very Nice*. (Film.) http://www.nfb.ca/film/Very_Nice_Very_Nice/ (accessed 2 Nov. 2011).

Lister, Martin, Jon Dovey, Seth Giddings, Iain Grant, and Kieran Kelly. 2008. *New Media: A Critical Introduction*. Hoboken: Taylor and Francis.

Litman, Jessica. 1990. The public domain. *Emory Law Journal* 39 (1): 965–1023.

Litman, Jessica. 1994. The exclusive right to read. *Cardozo Arts and Entertainment Law Journal* 13: 29–54.

Litman, Jessica. 2004. Sharing and stealing. *Hastings Communication and Entertainment Law Review* 27: 1–50.

Litman, Jessica. 2006. *Digital Copyright*. Amherst, NY: Prometheus.

Livingstone, Sonia. 2008. Internet literacy: Young people's negotiation of new online opportunities. In *Digital Youth, Innovation, and the Unexpected*, ed. T. McPherson, 101–22. Cambridge, MA: MIT Press.

Livingstone, Sonia, and David R. Brake. 2010. On the rapid rise of social networking sites: New findings and policy implications. *Children and Society* 24 (1): 75–83. http://dx.doi.org/10.1111/j.1099-0860.2009.00243.x

Locke, John. 1980. *Second Treatise of Government*. 1689. Ed. C.B. Macpherson. Indianapolis: Hackett.

Logie, John. 2003. A copyright Cold War: Rhetoric of the peer to peer debates. *First Monday* 8 (7). http://firstmonday.org/ojs/index.php/fm/article/view/1064/984

Lopatin, Laurie. 2006. Library digitization projects, issues and guidelines: A survey of the literature. *Library Hi Tech* 24 (2): 273–89. http://dx.doi.org/10.1108/07378830610669637

Lorimer, Rowland, and Adrienne Lindsay. 2004. Canadian scholarly journals at a technical crossroads. *Canadian Journal of Communication* 29 (3): 253–75.

Lorimer, Rowland, Johanne Provençal, Brian Owen, Rea Devakos, David Phipps, and Richard Smith. 2011. *Digital Technology: Innovation in Scholarly Communication and University Engagement*. http://tkbr.ccsp.sfu.ca/files/2010/04/Lorimer-DigInnovationScholCmn.pdf (accessed Feb. 2011).

Loshin, Jacob. 2008. Secrets revealed: How magicians protect intellectual property without law. In *Law and Magic: A Collection of Essays*, ed. Christine A. Corcos, 123–42. Durham, NC: Carolina Academic Press.

Lowenthal, David. 1985. *The Past Is a Foreign Country*. Cambridge, MA: Cambridge University Press.

Luong, John V., ed. 2010. *New Intellectual Property Issues*. New York: Nova Science.

Lydon, Jane, and Uzma Z. Rizvi, eds. 2010. *Handbook of Postcolonial Archaeology*. Walnut Creek: Left Coast Press.

Mackey, Eva. 1999. *The House of Difference: Cultural Politics and National Identity in Canada*. Toronto: University of Toronto Press.

MacKie-Mason, Jeffrey, and Hal R. Varian. 1992. *Some Economics of the Internet*. Paper presented at the 10th Michigan Public Utility Conference, Western Michigan University, 25–7 Mar. http://deepblue.lib.umich.edu.proxy.lib.sfu.ca/bitstream/2027.42/50461/1/Economics_of_Internet.pdf (accessed 10 Jan. 2008).

MacKinnon, Shauna. 2007. Manitoba Telephones, ten years later. *Public Values*. http://archive.is/Rl8F (accessed 25 Dec. 2007).

Macmillan, Fiona. 2007a. Altering the contours of the public domain. In *Intellectual Property: The Many Faces of the Public Domain*, ed. Charlotte Waelde and Hector McQueen, 98–117. Cheltenham: Edward Elgar.

Macmillan, Fiona, ed. 2007b *New Directions in Copyright Law*, vol. 4. Cheltenham: Edward Elgar.

Macmillan, Fiona. 2008. Human rights, cultural property and intellectual property: Three concepts in search of a relationship. In *Intellectual Property and Traditional Cultural Expressions in a Digital Environment*, ed. Christoph B. Graber and Mira Burri-Nenova, 73–95. Cheltenham: Edward Elgar.

Mallory, Luther. 2008. Kardinal Offishall and Canadian hip hop. *Canadian Musician* 30 (6): 34–9.

Manovich, Lev. 2001. *The Language of New Media*. Cambridge, MA: MIT Press.

Manovich, Lev. 2002. *Avant-Garde as Software*. http://www.uoc.edu/artnodes/espai/eng/art/manovich1002/manovich1002.html (accessed Dec. 2002).

Marini, Francesca. 2007. Archivists, librarians, and theatre research. *Archivaria* 63 (1): 7–33.

Marrie, Henrietta. 2009. The UNESCO Convention for the Safeguarding of the Intangible Cultural Heritage and the Protection and Maintenance of the Intangible Cultural Heritage of Indigenous Peoples. In *Intangible Heritage*, ed. Laurajane Smith and Natsuko Akagawa, 169–92. New York: Routledge.

Marsh, Jackie. 2008. Out-of-School Play in Online Virtual Worlds and the Implications for Literacy Learning. Adelaide: University of South Australia, Centre for Studies in Literacy, Policy and Learning Cultures.

Marshall, Denis S. 2000. First impressions of a troubling case: Some comments on *CCH Canadian Limited* v. *Law Society of Upper Canada*. *Canadian Law Libraries/Bibliothèques de droit canadiennes* 25 (1): 18–23.

Marx, Karl. 1854. *The Eighteenth Brumaire of Louis Bonaparte*. http://www.marxists.org/archive/marx/works/1852/18th-brumaire/ch01.htm (accessed 2 Nov. 2011).

Masango, Charles A. 2009. Understanding copyright in support of scholarship: Some possible challenges to scholars and academic librarians in the digital environment? *International Journal of Information Management* 29 (3): 232–6. http://dx.doi.org/10.1016/j.ijinfomgt.2008.10.003

Maskus, Keith E., and Jerome H. Reichman, eds. 2005. *International Public Goods and Transfer of Technology under a Globalized Intellectual Property Regime*. Cambridge: Cambridge University Press. http://dx.doi.org/10.1017/CBO9780511494529

Mayer, Carol E., and Anthony Shelton. 2010. *The Museum of Anthropology at the University of British Columbia*. Toronto: Douglas and MacIntyre.

McCaffery, Steve. 1986. Language writing: From productive to libidinal economy. In Steve McCaffery, *North of Intention: Critical Writings 1973–1986*, ed. Karen MacCormack, 143–58. New York: Roof Books.

McCaffery, Steve. 2000. *North of Intention: Critical Writings 1973–1986*. 2nd ed. New York: Roof Books.

McCaffery, Steve, and bp Nichol. 1992. [Toronto Research Group]. *Rational Geomancy: The Kids of The Book-Machine: The Collected Research Reports of the Toronto Research Group, 1973–82*. Vancouver: Talonbooks.

McClean, Daniel, and Karsten Schubert, eds. 2002. *Dear Images: Art, Copyright and Culture.* London: Institute of Contemporary Arts.

McCutcheon, Jani. 2007. Property in literary characters: Protection under Australian Copyright Law. *European Intellectual Property Review* 29 (4): 140–51.

McCutcheon, Jani. 2008. The new defense of parody or satire under Australian copyright law. *Intellectual Property Quarterly* 2: 163–92.

McGann, Jerome. 1991. *The Textual Condition*. Princeton: Princeton University Press.

McHenry, Robert. 2004, 15 Nov. *The Faith-Based Encyclopedia.* http://www.ideasinactiontv.com/tcs_daily/2004/11/the-faith-based-encyclopedia.html (accessed 2 Nov. 2011).

McKay, Patrick. 2011. Culture of the future: Adapting copyright law to accommodate fan-made derivative works in the twenty-first century. *Regent University Law Review* 24: 117–46.

McKinnon, Matthew. 2005. *Kicking Up Dust: the Remarkable Hip-Hop Odyssey of Toronto's Ka'naan.* http://www.cbc.ca/arts/music/knaan.html (accessed 1 June 2010).

McLaren, Malcolm. 2003, 7 Oct. 8-Bit Punk. *Wired.com.* http://www.wired.com/wired/archive/11.11/mclaren_pr.html

McLay, Geoff. 1999. Editorial. Being fair to users: The welcome arrival of a new, more liberal approach to fair dealing. *New Zealand Intellectual Property Law Journal* 2: 135.

McLeod, Kembrew. 2001. *Owning Culture: Authorship, Ownership and Intellectual Property Law*. New York: Peter Lang.

McLeod, Kembrew. 2005. Confessions of an intellectual (property): Danger Mouse, Mickey Mouse, Sonny Bono, and my long and winding path as a copyright activist-academic. *Popular Music and Society* 28 (1): 79–93. http://dx.doi.org/10.1080/0300776042000300981

McLeod, Kembrew. 2007. *Freedom of Expression: Resistance and Repression in the Age of Intellectual Property*. Minneapolis: University of Minnesota Press.

McLeod, Kembrew, and Peter DiCola. 2011. *Creative License: The Law and Culture of Digital Sampling*. Durham, NC: Duke University Press.

McLeod, Kembrew, and Rudolf E. Kuenzli, eds. 2011. *Cutting across Media: Appropriation Art, Interventionist Collage, and Copyright Law*. Durham, NC: Duke University Press.

McLuhan, Marshall. 1964. *Understanding Media: The Extensions of Man*. New York: McGraw-Hill.

McNutt, Ryan. 2010, 21 June. Changing Canada's copyright. *Dal News.* http://dalnews.dal.ca/2010/06/20/copyright.html (accessed 22 Feb. 2011).

McPhee, Peter. 1996. *Carnival: A Scream in High Park Reader*. Toronto: Insomniac.

McPherson, Tara, ed. 2008. *Digital Youth, Innovation, and the Unexpected*. Cambridge, MA: MIT Press.

Media Access Group at WGBH. n.d. *DVS FAQ*. http://main.wgbh.org/wgbh/pages/mag/services/description/dvs-faq.html (accessed 23 Oct. 2011).

Mele, Salvatore. 2008. The SCOAP3 project: Converting the literature of an entire discipline to open access. In *Open Scholarship: Authority, Community, and Sustainability in the Age of Web 2.0: Proceedings of the 12th International Conference on Electronic Publishing, Toronto, 25–7 June*, ed. Leslie Chan and Susanna Mornati, 223–33. http://elpub.scix.net/cgi-bin/works/Show?223_elpub2008 (accessed Aug. 2008).

Menescal, Andrea Koury. 2005. Changing WIPO's ways? The 2004 development agenda in historical perspective. *Journal of World Intellectual Property* 8 (6): 761–7. http://dx.doi.org/10.1111/j.1747-1796.2005.tb00277.x

Merges, Robert P. 2004. A new dynamism in the public domain. *University of Chicago Law Review* 71 (1): 1–20.

Meurer, David, and Rosemary J. Coombe. 2009. Digital media and the informational politics of appropriation. In *Lifting: "Theft" in Art*, ed. Atopia Projects, 20–7, Aberdeen, UK: Peacock Visual Arts.

Miller, Paul D. [aka DJ Spooky]. 2004. *Rhythm Science*. Cambridge, MA: Mediawork/MIT Press.

Miller, Toby, Nitin Gofvil, John McMurria, and Richard Maxwell. 2005. *Global Hollywood*. London: BFI.

Miller, Toby, and George Yúdice. 2002. *Cultural Policy*. London: Sage.

Miyamoto, Yuri, R.E. Nisbett, and T. Masuda. 2006, Feb. Culture and the physical environment: Holistic versus analytic perceptual affordances. *Psychological Science* 17 (2): 113–19. http://dx.doi.org/10.1111/j.1467-9280.2006.01673.x. Medline:16466418

Mohammed, Emir A. C. 2009. Parody as a form of fair dealing in Canada: A guide for lawyers (and judges). *Journal of Intellectual Property Law and Practice* 4 (7): 468–72. http://dx.doi.org/10.1093/jiplp/jpp070

Monbiot, George. 2011, 29 Aug. *The Lairds of Learning*. http://www.monbiot.com/2011/08/29/the-lairds-of-learning/ (accessed 23 Sept. 2011).

Montero, Etienne, and Quentin Van Enis. 2011. Enabling freedom of expression in light of filtering measures imposed on Internet intermediaries: Squaring the circle? *Computer Law and Security Review* 27 (1): 21–35.

Montgomery, Kathryn C. 2007. *Generation Digital: Politics, Commerce, and Childhood in the Age of the Internet*. Cambridge, MA: MIT Press.

Moore, Adam D. 2003. Intellectual property: Theory, privilege, and pragmatism. *Canadian Journal of Law and Jurisprudence* 16: 191–216.

Morris, Adalaide. 2006. New media poetics: As we may think/how to write. In *New Media Poetics: Contexts, Technotexts, and Theories*, ed. Adalaide Morris and Thomas Swiss, 1–46, Cambridge, MA: MIT Press.

Morrison, Gavin, and Fraser Stables, eds. 2009. *Lifting: Theft in Art*. Aberdeen: Atopia Projects.

Mossman, Mary Jane, and William Flanagan. 2004. *Property Law: Cases and Commentary*. Toronto: Emond Montgomery.

Mowery, David C., and Timothy Simcoe. 2000. *Is the Internet a US Invention? – an Economic and Technological History of Computer Networking*. Berkeley: Haas School of Business.

Murray, Laura. 2005. Copyright talk: Patterns and pitfalls in Canadian policy discourses. In *In the Public Interest: the Future of Canadian Copyright Law*, ed. Michael Geist, 15–40. Toronto: Irwin Law.

Murray, Laura. 2009. See you in court: Can Canadians practice parody? *FUZE Magazine* 32 (2): 12–17.

Murray, Laura, and Sam Trosow. 2007. *Canadian Copyright: A Citizen's Guide*. Toronto: Between the Lines.

Murray, Laura, and Samuel E. Trosow. 2013. *Canadian Copyright: A Citizen's Guide*. 2nd ed. Toronto: Between the Lines.

Nair, Meera. 2010. Fair dealing at a crossroads. In *From "Radical Extremism" to "Balanced Copyright": Canadian Copyright and the Digital Agenda*, ed. Michael Geist, 90–120. Toronto: Irwin Law.

Narine, Anil, and Sara M. Grimes. 2009. The turbulent rise of the child gamer: Public fears and corporate promises in cinematic and promotional depictions of children's digital play. *Communication, Culture and Critique* 2 (3): 319–38. http://dx.doi.org/10.1111/j.1753-9137.2009.01040.x.

National Research Council of Canada (NRC). n.d. *Publishing Policy*. http://pubs.nrc-cnrc.gc.ca/eng/policy/index.html (accessed Aug. 2008).

National School Boards Association (NSBA). 2007. *Creating and Connecting: Research and Guidelines on Online Social and Educational Networking*. Alexandria: Technology Leadership Network.

Negativland. 2003. Two relationships to a cultural public domain. Special Issue: The Public Domain. *Law and Contemporary Problems* 66 (1–2): 239–62.

Negativland. 2009. *Fair Use: The Story of the Letter U and the Numeral 2*. Olympia: Seeland-Negativland.

Neil, Garry. n.d. *General Agreement on Trade in Services (GATS): A Growing Threat to Cultural Policy*. http://www.incd.net/paper03.html (accessed 21 Aug. 2010).

Netanel, Neil. 2003. Impose a noncommercial use levy to allow free peer-to-peer file sharing. *Harvard Journal of Law and Technology* 17: 1–84.

Netanel, Neil. 2008. *Copyright's Paradox*. Oxford: Oxford University Press. http://dx.doi.org/10.1093/acprof:oso/9780195137620.001.0001

Newman, Michael Z. 2009, Apr. P2P TV: Ethical considerations. *Flow* 9/10. http://flowtv.org/?p=3283 (accessed 29 Sept. 2009).

Nichol, bp. 1979. *Translating Translating Apollinaire: A Preliminary Report*. Milwaukee: Membrane Press. http://www.thing.net/~grist/l&d/bpnichol/lnichol1.htm (accessed 5 July 2010).

Nichol, bp. 1982. 1979. *Ear Rational, B.P. Nichol*. (Audio cassette.) Milwaukee: Membrane Press.

Nichol, bp. 1990. *Art Facts: A Book of Contexts*. Tucson: Chax.

Nichol, bp. 2007. *The Alphabet Game: A bpNichol Reader*. Ed. Darren Wershler-Henry and Lori Emerson. Toronto: Coach House.

Nichol, bp, and Roy Miki. 2002. *Meanwhile: The Critical Writings of bpNichol*. Vancouver: Talonbooks.

Nicholas, George. 2006. Intellectual property issues in archaeology: Addressing the needs of a changing world through negotiated practice. The Burra Conference: Plenary Address to the Cultural Heritage and Indigenous Cultural and Intellectual Property Rights, Flinders University, Adelaide, Australia, 3–5 Dec.

Nicholas, George, and Kelly P. Bannister. 2004. Copyrighting the past? Emerging intellectual property rights issues in archaeology. *Current Anthropology* 45 (3): 327–50. http://dx.doi.org/10.1086/382251

Nicholas, George, and Julie Hollowell. 2007. Ethical challenges to a postcolonial archaeology. In *Archaeology and Capitalism: From Ethics to Politics*, ed. Yannis Hamilakas and Phillip Duke, 59–82. Walnut Creek, CA: Left Coast Press.

Nicholas, George, and Alison Wylie. 2009. Archaeological finds: Legacies of appropriation, modes of response. In *The Ethics of Cultural Appropriation*, ed. Conrad Brunck and James O. Young, 11–54. Malden, MA: Wiley-Blackwell.

Nicholas, George, Catherine Bell, Kelly Bannister, Sven Ouzman, and Jane Anderson. 2009. Intellectual property issues in heritage management – Part 1: Challenges and opportunities relating to appropriation, information access, bioarchaeology and cultural tourism. *Heritage Management* 2 (1): 261–86.

Nichols, David, and Michael Twidale. 2007. The usability of open source software. *First Monday* 8 (1). http://firstmonday.org/article/view/1018/939/ (accessed 22 Dec. 2009).

Nichols, D.M., K. Thomson, and S.A. Yeates 2001. Usability and open-source software development. In *Proceedings of the Symposium on Computer Human Interaction*, ed. E. Kemp, C.P Kinshuk, and J. Yanes, 49–54. Palmerston North: New Zealand.

Nielsen, Jakob. 1993. *Usability Engineering*. Boston: Academic.

nitro2k01. 2008, 5 May. Crystal Castles and chip music copyright infringements. *Gameboy Genius*. http://blog.gg8.se/wordpress/2008/05/06/crystal-castles-and-chip-music-copyright-infringements/ (accessed 12 Apr. 2010).

Nk'Mip Winery. n.d. *Nk'Mip Cellars*. http://www.nkmipcellars.com/winery/default.asp (accessed 2 Nov. 2011).

Norcott, Tanys. 2010. *Oral Tradition into Written Tradition*. (Video, 9:33 min.) SFU School of Communication and SFU Museum of Anthropology and Ethnography, Simon Fraser University, Burnaby, BC. http://www.sfu.museum/wayang/videos/

NPD Group. 2009, 10 Sept. Households with kids up to 12 years of age account for 45 percent of video game industry revenue. *National Purchase Diary*. http://www.npd.com/press/releases/press_090910.html (accessed 27 May 2010).

Nwauche, Enyinna S. 2008. The judicial construction of the public interest in South African copyright law. *International Review of Intellectual Property and Competition Law* 39 (8): 917–42.

O'Donnell, Michael. n.d. *Maximizing Revenue and Minimizing Piracy*. info.icopyright.com/Article-Tools-White-Paper-4–09.pdf (accessed 1 Feb. 2010).

OAIster Database. n.d. *OCLC*. http://www.oclc.org/url/?404 (accessed 2 Nov. 2011).

Ochoa, Tyler T. 2003. Origins and meanings of the public domain. *University of Dayton Law Review* 28 (1): 215–67.

Oliar, Dotan, and Christopher Sprigman. 2011. Intellectual property norms in stand-up comedy. In *Making and Unmaking Intellectual Property: Creative Production in Legal and Cultural Perspective*, ed. Mario Biagioli, Peter Jaszi, and Martha Woodmansee, 385–98. Chicago: University of Chicago Press.

Open Content Alliance – FAQ [Frequently Asked Questions]. n.d. http://www.opencontentalliance.org/faq/ (accessed 2 Nov. 2011).

Open Context: Web-Based Research Data Publication. 2010, 13 Dec. http://opencontext.org (accessed 2 Nov. 2011).

Organisation for Economic Co-Operation and Development (OECD). 2002.*OECD Report: Measuring the Information Economy*. http://www.oecd.org/redirect/dataoecd/16/14/1835738.pdf (accessed Aug. 2008).

Oser, Kris. 2007. *Virtual Worlds Are Trendiest Spot Online for Kids and Teens*. http://www.emarketer.com/Article.aspx?R=1005405 (accessed 27 Sept. 2007).

Partridge, Robert Charles Barrington. 1938. *The History of the Legal Deposit of Books throughout the British Empire*. London: London Library Association.

Patry, William. 1985. *The Fair Use Privilege in Copyright Law*. Arlington, VA: Bna Books.

Patry, William. 2009. *Moral Panics and the Copyright Wars*. New York: Oxford University Press.

Patterson, Lyman R. 1968. *Copyright in Historical Perspective*. Nashville: Vanderbilt University Press.

Patterson, Lyman R., and Stanley W. Lindberg. 1991. *The Nature of Copyright: A Law of Users' Rights*. London: University of Georgia Press.

Peers, Frank W. 1969. *The Politics of Canadian Broadcasting, 1920–1951*. Toronto: University of Toronto Press.

Penalver, Eduardo M., and Sonia K. Katyal. 2009. *Property Outlaws: How Squatters, Pirates, and Protesters Improve the Law of Ownership*. New Haven: Yale University Press.

Perloff, Marjorie. 2005. The aura of modernism. *Modernist Cultures* 1 (1): 1–14. http://dx.doi.org/10.3366/E204110220900001X

Pessach, Guy. 2007. Museums, digitization and copyright law: Taking stock and looking ahead. *Journal of International Media and Entertainment Law* 1 (2): 1–30.

Peukert, Alexander. 2009. A bipolar copyright system for the digital network environment. In *Peer-to-Peer File Sharing and Secondary Liability in Copyright Law*, ed. Alain Strowel, 148–95. Cheltenham: Edward Elgar.

Phillips, Ruth. 2005. Re-placing objects: Historical practices for the second museum age. *Canadian Historical Review* 86 (1): 83–110. http://dx.doi.org/10.3138/CHR/86.1.83

Pigna, Kris. 2008, 9 Nov. *Little Big Planet Levels Being Deleted due to Copyright Issues*. http://www.1up.com/news/big-planet-levels-deleted-due (accessed 9 Nov. 2009).

Poggi, Christine. 1992. *In Defiance of Painting: Cubism, Futurism, and the Invention of Collage*. New Haven: Yale University Press.

Pollack, Malla. 2006. Towards a feminist theory of the public domain, or rejecting the gendered scope of United States copyrightable and patentable subject matter. *William and Mary Journal of Women and the Law* 12 (3): 603–26.

Porsdam, Helle. 2009. *From Civil to Human Rights: Dialogues on Law and Humanities in the United States and Europe*. Cheltenham: Edward Elgar.

Postel, J., and J. Reynolds. 1985. *File Transfer Protocol*. http://tools.ietf.org/html/rfc959

Postigo, Hector. 2008a. Video game appropriation through modifications: Attitudes concerning intellectual property among modders and fans. *Convergence: The International Journal of Research into New Media Technologies* 14 (1): 59–74. http://dx.doi.org/10.1177/1354856507084419

Postigo, Hector. 2008b. Capturing fair use for the YouTube generation: The digital rights movement, the electronic frontier foundation and the user-centered framing of fair use. *Information Communication and Society* 11 (7): 1008–27. http://dx.doi.org/10.1080/13691180802109071

Pound, Ezra. 1934. *ABC of Reading*. New York: New Directions.

Prokesch, Steven. 2008. The media business: Pension changes urged after Maxwell scandal. *New York Times*. http://www.nytimes.com/1992/03/10/business/the-media-business-pension-changes-urged-after-maxwell-scandal.html2008)

PubMed Central. n.d. *PMC Overview*. http://www.ncbi.nlm.nih.gov/pmc/about/intro.html (accessed Aug. 2008).

Pybus, Jennifer. 2007. Affect and subjectivity: A case study of neopets.com. *Politics and Culture* 7 (2). http://www.politicsandculture.org/2009/10/02/jennifer-pybus-affect-and-subjectivity-a-case-study-of-neopets-com/

Quail, Christine. 2009, 24 Oct. The myth of online TV. *Flow* 10/4. http://flowtv.org/?p=4132 (accessed 3 Oct. 2009).

Rajan, Mira T. Sundara. 2011. *Moral Rights: Principles, Practice and New Technology*. Oxford: Oxford University Press.

Ramsey, Nancy. 2005, 16 Oct. The hidden cost of documentaries. *New York Times*. http://www.nytimes.com/glogin?URI=http://www.nytimes.com/2005/10/16/movies/16rams.html&OQ=_rQ3D0&OP=c31900e2Q2FXktCX-Q3DCXzzzXQ5DC7Q2BX9kUQ3EQ7CkkCQ20XQ20PP8XBPXBEX7kf!RQ3EXBEQ7Ce7Q3EQ3CQ5DC7Q2B (accessed 2 Nov. 2011).

Rao, Vijayendra, and Michael Walton, eds. 2004. *Culture and Public Action*. Stanford: Stanford University Press. http://dx.doi.org/10.1596/0-8047-4787-3

Raustiala, Kal, and Chris Sprigman. 2006. The piracy paradox: Innovation and intellectual property in fashion design. *Virginia Law Review* 92: 1687–1777.

Raymond, Eric S. 1997. *The Cathedral and the Bazaar: Musings on Linux and Open Source by an Accidental Revolutionary*. Sebastopol, CA: O'Reilly.

Raymond, Eric S. 1998a. *Homesteading the Noosphere*. Philadelphia: Self-Published.

Raymond, Eric S. 1998b. The cathedral and the bazaar. *First Monday* 3 (3). http://firstmonday.org/ojs/index.php/fm/article/view/578/499 (accessed 13 Dec. 2009).

Raymond, Eric S. 1999c. The revenge of the hackers. In *Open Sources: Voices from the Open Source Revolution*, ed. Chris DiBona, Sam Ockman, and Mark Stone, 207–20. Sebastopol, CA: O'Reilly.

Raymond, Eric S. n.d. *Goodbye, "Free Software"; Hello, "Open Source."* Eric Raymond's Home Page. http://catb.org/~esr/open-source.html (accessed 22 Jan. 2010).

Reardon, Marguerite. 2009. *Net Neutrality Gets a Boost from the Feds*. http://news.cnet.com/8301-1035_3-10278484-94.html (accessed 19 Aug. 2009).

Recommendations of the NISO/ALPSP Working Group on Versions of Journal Articles. n.d. Home – National Information Standards Organization. http://www.niso.org/news/pr/view?item_key=8a7904a59c448610fac0949fcde7d7d1de9923d7

Rees, Manon. 2010. Open access publishing: From principles to practice. In *Access to Knowledge in the Age of Intellectual Property*, ed. Amy Kapczynski and Gaëlle Krikorian, 475–95. New York: Zone Books.

Reyman, Jessica. 2009. *The Rhetoric of Intellectual Property: Copyright Law and the Regulation of Digital Culture*. London: Routledge.

Reynolds, Graham. 2006. A step in the wrong direction: The impact of the legislative protection of technological protection measures on fair dealing and freedom of expression. *Canadian Journal of Law and Technology* 5 (3): 179–94.

Reynolds, Graham. 2009. A stroke of genius or copyright infringement? Mashups and copyright in Canada. *SCRIPT-ed* 6 (3): 639–68.

Reynolds, Graham. 2010a. Necessarily critical? The adoption of a parody defence to copyright infringement in Canada. *Manitoba Law Journal* 33 (1): 241–62.

Reynolds, Graham. 2010b. Towards a right to engage in the fair transformative use of copyright-protected expression. In *From "Radical Extremism" to "Balanced Copyright": Canadian Copyright and the Digital Agenda*, ed. Michael Geist, 395–422. Toronto: Irwin Law.

"RFI – No Charge Licensed Software." n.d. *Welcome to MERX*. http://www.merx.com/English/SUPPLIER_Menu.Asp?WCE=Show&TAB=1&PORTAL=MERX&State=7&id=PW-%24%24EE-015-18733&FED_ONLY=0&hcode=Au64x22Vv9pVNE3IKtFp3Q%3d%3d (accessed 16 Jan. 2010).

Rifkin, Jeremy. 2000. *The Age of Access: The New Culture of Hypercapitalism, Where All of Life Is a Paid-For Experience*. New York: J.P. Tarcher/Putnam.

Riley, Mary, ed. 2004. *Indigenous Intellectual Property Rights*: Legal Obstacles and Innovative Solutions. Walnut Grove, CA: AltaMira Press.

ROARMAP. n.d. *About the Repository*. http://roarmap.eprints.org/ (accessed 23 Oct. 2011).

Robbins, Bruce, and Elsa Stamatopolou. 2004. Reflections on culture and cultural rights. *South Atlantic Quarterly* 103 (2–3): 419–34. http://dx.doi.org/10.1215/00382876-103-2-3-419

Robin, Richard. 2007. Commentary: Learner-based listening and technological authenticity. *Language Learning and Technology* 11 (1): 109–15.

Rodrigues, Eloy. 2006. *DSpace Request Copy Add-on Documentation*. https://wiki.duraspace.org/display/DSPACE/RequestCopy (accessed 2 Nov. 2011).

Rose, Carol. 1985. Possession as the origin of property. *Chicago Law Review* 52 (1): 73–88. http://dx.doi.org/10.2307/1599571

Rose, Margaret A. 1993. *Parody: Ancient, Modern, and Post-Modern*. Cambridge: Cambridge University Press.

Rose, Mark. 2003. Nine-tenths of the law: The English copyright debates and the rhetoric of the public domain. *Law and Contemporary Problems* 66 (1): 75–87.

Rose, Tricia. 1994. *Black Noise: Rap Music and Black Culture in Contemporary America*. Middletown, CT: Wesleyan University Press.

Rothman, Jennifer. 2010. Liberty-based approach to copyright limits. *Cornell Law Review* 95: 463–534.

Rousseau, Jean-Jacques. 1987. Discourse on the Origins of Inequality (1754). In *The Basic Political Writings*, ed. Donald Cress. 25–82. Indianapolis: Hackett.

Rowley, Susan, et al. 2010. Building an on-line research community: The reciprocal research network. http://www.museumsandtheweb.com/mw2010/papers/rowley/rowley.html (accessed 30 Aug. 2010).

Royal Commission on Laws and Regulations Relating to Home, Colonial and Foreign Copyrights: Report, Minutes of Evidence, Appendix. 1878. London: Eyre and Spottiswoode.

Rusak, Gary. 2008. *More than 100 Virtual Worlds Aimed at Kids Market*. http://www.kidscreen.com/2008/04/17/vw-2008/ (accessed 15 July 2008).

Sahlfeld, Miriam. 2008. Commercializing cultural heritage? Criteria for a balanced instrumentalization of traditional cultural expressions for development in a globalized digital environment. In *Intellectual Property and Traditional Cultural Expressions: Legal Protection in a Digital Environment*, ed. Chrisoph B. Graber and Mira Burri-Nenova, 256–86. Cheltenham: Edward Elgar.

Saint-Amour, Paul K. 2003. *The Copywrights: Intellectual Property and the Literary Imagination*. Ithaca: Cornell University Press.

Sale, Arthur. 2006a. The impact of mandatory policies on ETD acquisition. *D-Lib Magazine* 12 (4). http://dx.doi.org/10.1045/Apr.2006-sale

Sale, Arthur. 2006b. Comparison of IR content policies in Australia. *First Monday* 11 (4). http://dx.doi.org/10.5210/fm.v11i4.1324

Sale, Arthur. 2006c. Researchers and institutional depositories. In *Open Access: Strategic, Technical, and Economic Aspects*, ed. Neil Jacobs, 87–100. Oxford: Chandos.

Sale, Arthur. 2006d. The acquisition of open access research articles. *First Monday* 11 (9).

Samuels, Edward. 1993. The public domain in copyright law. *Journal of the Copyright Society* 41 (1): 137–82.

Samuelson, Pamela. 2003. Mapping the digital public domain: Threats and opportunities. *Law and Contemporary Problems* 66 (1): 147–71.

Samuelson, Pamela. 2006. Enriching discourse on public domains. *Duke Law Journal* 55 (1): 101–69.

Save the Internet. 2007. *Frequently Asked Questions*. http://www.savetheinternet.com/sti-home (accessed 13 Mar. 2007).

Scassa, Teresa. 2004, July. Recalibrating copyright law? A comment on the Supreme Court of Canada's decision in *CCH Canadian Limited et al.* v. *Law Society of Upper Canada*. *Canadian Journal of Law and Technology* 3 (2). http://cjlt.dal.ca/vol3_no2/pdfarticles/scassa.pdf

Scassa, Teresa. 2005. Interests in the balance. In *In the Public Interest: The Future of Canadian Copyright Law*, ed. Michael Geist, 41–65. Toronto: Irwin Law.

Scassa, Teresa. 2007a. *Nouvelles approches en propriété intellectuelle dans un monde transsystémique*. Cowansville: Éditions Yvon Blais.

Scassa, Teresa. 2007b. Table scraps or a full course meal? The public domain in Canadian copyright law. In *Intellectual Property at the Edge: New Approaches to IP in a Transsystemic World*, Proceedings of the Meredith Lectures, McGill University, Faculty of Law, 347–76. Cowansville: Éditions Yvon Blais.

Schellekens, Maurice. 2006. Free and open source software: An answer to commodification. In *The Future of the Public Domain: Identifying the Commons in Information Law*, ed. Lucie Guibault and Paul B. Hugenholtz, 303–24. Alphen aan den Rijn: Kluwer Law International.

Schneider, Hildegard, and Peter van den Bossche. 2008. *Protection of Cultural Diversity from a European and International Perspective*. Antwerp: Intersentia Press.

Schur, Richard L. 2009. *Parodies of Ownership: Hip-Hop Aesthetics and Intellectual Property Law*. Ann Arbor: University of Michigan Press. http://dx.doi.org/10.3998/dcbooks.6814160.0001.001

Schwabach, Aaron. 2011. *Fan Fiction and Copyright: Outsider Works and Intellectual Property Protection*. Dartmouth: Ashgate.

Schwartz, Hillel. 1996. *The Culture of the Copy: Striking Likenesses, Unreasonable Facsimiles*. New York: Zone Books.

Schwartzman, Helen B., ed. 1978. *Transformations: The Anthropology of Children's Play*. New York: Plenum.

Science Commons. 2007. *Protocol for Implementing Open Access Data*. http://sciencecommons.org/projects/publishing/open-access-data-protocol/ (accessed 2 Nov. 2011).

Scollan, Becca, Abby Byrnes, Malia Nagle, Maleka Ingram, Paul Coyle, and Cynthia York. n.d. *Drupal Usability Research Report*. http://groups.drupal.org/files/DrupalUsabilityResearchReport.pdf (accessed 19 Jan. 2010).

Scopus. n.d. *About Scopus*. http://www.info.sciverse.com/scopus (accessed 2 Nov. 2011).

Scott, Ben. 2006. *A Victory We Can Hang Our Hats On*. http://www.savetheinternet.com/blog/2006/12/29/a-victory-we-can-hang-our-hats-on/ (accessed 20 Nov. 2007).

Scott, Ben, Mark Cooper, and Jeannine Kenne. n.d. Free press – reform media, transform democracy. *Network Neutrality: Fact vs. Fiction*. http://www.freepress.net/ (accessed 5 Dec. 2007).

Seiler, Joey. 2009. *200+ Youth-Oriented Worlds Live or Developing*. http://www.virtualworldsnews.com/2009/01/virtual-worlds-management-today-released-its-updated-youth-worlds-analysis-based-on-comprehensive-research-available-through.html (accessed 30 Jan. 2009).

Senge, Peter M. 1990. *The Fifth Discipline: The Art and Practice of the Learning Organization*. New York: Random House.

Shakespeare, William. 1997. *A Midsummer Night's Dream* (1594). In *The Riverside Shakespeare*, ed. G. Blakemore Evans and J.J.M. Tobin, et al., 251–83. Boston: Houghton Mifflin.

Shankland, Stephen. n.d. *Borland InterBase Backdoor Detected*. http://www.zdnet.com/news/borland-interbase-backdoor-detected/113384 (accessed 1 Feb. 2010).

Sheffer, Waren. n.d. *Writers' Rights Upheld: The Robertson Decision*. http://www.pwac.ca/files/PDF/Writers.Rights.Upheld.pdf

Sheppard, Tamara. 2009. Putting the public in the public domain: The public library's role in the re-conceptualization of the public domain. *New Library World* 110 (5–6): 207–18. http://dx.doi.org/10.1108/03074800910954244.

SHERPA/RoMEO. n.d. *Publisher Copyright Policies & Self-Archiving*. http://www.sherpa.ac.uk/romeo/

Shuler, Carly. 2007. *"D Is for Digital": An Analysis of the Children's Interactive Media Environment with a Focus on Mass-Marketed Products that Promote Learning*. New York: Joan Ganz Cooney Center.

Silbey, Jessica M. 2010. Comparative tales of origins and access: Intellectual property and the rhetoric of social change. *Case Western Reserve Law Review* 61 (1): 195–267.

Silliman, Stephen W. 2008. *Collaborating at the Trowel's Edge: Teaching and Learning in Indigenous Archaeology*. Tucson: University of Arizona Press.

Silver, Josh. 2008, 1 Aug. *Comcast Decision "Major Victory" for Open Internet*. http://www.freepress.net/node/42937 (accessed 29 Aug. 2008).

Silverman, Helaine, and D. Fairchild Ruggles, eds. 2007. *Cultural Heritage and Human Rights*. New York: Springer. http://dx.doi.org/10.1007/978-0-387-71313-7

Simon Fraser University. n.d. *Intellectual Property Issues in Cultural Heritage (IpinCH): Theory, Practice, Policy, Ethics*. http://www.sfu.ca/ipinch (accessed 2 Nov. 2011).

Singleton, Sharon. 2010. *International Trade Group Calls on G20 to Act on Piracy*. http://www.standard-freeholder.com/2010/06/23/international-trade-group-calls-on-g20-to-act-on-piracy-4 (accessed 15 July 2010).

Smith, Laurajane. 2007. Empty gestures? Heritage and the politics of recognition. In *Cultural Heritage and Human Rights*, ed. Helaine Silverman and D. Fairchild Ruggles, 159–71. New York: Springer. http://dx.doi.org/10.1007/978-0-387-71313-7_9

Smith, Laurajane, and Natsuko Akagawa. 2009. *Intangible Heritage*. London: Routledge Press.

Snyder, Joel. 2007. Audio description: The visual made verbal. *International Journal of the Arts in Society* 2 (2): 99–104.

Soar, Matt. 2000. *Behind the Screens: Hollywood Goes Hypercommercial*. (DVD.) Northampton, MA: Media Education Foundation.

Sookman, Barry. 2009. *Copyright: Cases and Commentary on the Canadian and International Law*. London: Carswell.

Soul Matters. n.d. Is Jully Black Stealing Music? http://www.soulmattersmag.com/index.cfm?pagepath=NEWS_CORNER&id=3577&modeX=BlogID&modeXval=02A5C2F1-2219-19C8-1549A4811CCF2B13&BlogID=02A5C2F1-2219-19C8-1549A4811CCF2B13&action=showcomments (accessed 1 June 2010).

Spence, Michael. 1998. Intellectual property and the problem of parody. *Law Quarterly Review* 114 (2): 594–620.

Sponsler, Ed, and Eric F. Van de Velde. 2001. *Eprints.org Software: A Review*. http://authors.library.caltech.edu/25884/

Stallman, Richard. 1985. *The GNU Manifesto*. http://www.gnu.org/gnu/manifesto.html

Stallman, Richard. 1999. The GNU operating system and the free software movement. In *Open Sources: Voices of the Open Source Revolution*, ed. Chris DiBona, Sam Ockman, and Mark Stone, 53–70. Sebastopol, CA: O'Reilly. http://oreilly.com/openbook/opensources/book/stallman.html

Stallman, Richard M. 2002. *Free Software, Free Society: Selected Essays of Richard M. Stallman*. Boston: Free Software Foundation Press.

Stallman, Richard. 2009. *Ending the War on Sharing*. http://stallman.org/articles/end-war-on-sharing.html (accessed 2009).

Standing Committee on Canadian Heritage. 2003. *Our Cultural Sovereignty: The Second Century of Canadian Broadcasting*. Ottawa: Communication Canada.

Starr, Paul. 2000. The electronic commons: The promise of the new public domain. *American Prospect* 11 (10): 30–44.

Steeves, Valerie. 2005. *Young Canadians in a Wired World – Phase II*. Ottawa: Media Awareness Network.

Steeves, Valerie, and Ian Kerr. 2005. Virtual playgrounds and buddybots: A data-minefield for tweens. *Canadian Journal of Law and Technology* 4 (2): 91–8.

Stefik, Mark. 1997. Shifting the possible: How trusted systems and digital property rights challenge us to rethink digital publishing. *Berkeley Technology Law Journal* 12: 137–60.

Stirling Online Research Repository. n.d. *STORRE*. https://dspace.stir.ac.uk//

Stone, Brad, and Miguel Helft. 2007. New weapon in Web war over piracy. *New York Times*. http://www.nytimes.com/2007/02/19/technology/19video.html?pagewanted=all&_r=0

Striphas, Ted. 2009. *The Late Age of Print: Everyday Book Culture from Consumerism to Control*. New York: Columbia University Press.

Striphas, Ted, and Kembrew McLeod. 2006. Strategic improprieties: Cultural studies, the everyday, and the politics of intellectual property. *Cultural Studies* 20 (2–3): 119–44. http://dx.doi.org/10.1080/09502380500495635

Stubbs, Stuart. 2010, 19 June. Crystal Castles. Album Review. *Loud and Quiet*. http://www.loudandquiet.com/2010/06/crystal-castles-crystal-castles/ (accessed 1 Nov. 2011).

Sturken, Marita, Douglas Thomas, and Sandra Rokeach. 2004. *Technological Visions: The Hopes and Fears that Shape New Technologies*. Philadelphia: Temple University Press.

Suber, Peter. 2004, 21 June. *Open Access Overview: Focusing on Open Access to Peer-Reviewed Research Articles and Their Preprints*. http://legacy.earlham.edu/~peters/fos/overview.htm (accessed Aug. 2008).

Suber, Peter. 2006, 2 Aug. The dual deposit/release strategy. *SPARC Open Access Newsletter* 100. http://www.earlham.edu/~peters/fos/newsletter/08-02-06.htm (accessed 1Nov. 2001).

Sun, Huatong. 2004. *Expanding the Scope of Localization: A Cultural Usability Perspective on Mobile Text Messaging Use in American and Chinese Contexts*. Dissertation submitted to the Rensselaer Polytechnic Institute, New York. 3140970.

Sunder, Madhavi. 1996. Authorship and autonomy as rites of exclusion: The intellectual propertization of free speech in *Hurley* v. *Irish-American Gay, Lesbian, and Bisexual Group of Boston*. *Stanford Law Review* 49 (1): 143–72. http://dx.doi.org/10.2307/1229374.

Surowiecki, James. 2005. *The Wisdom of Crowds*. New York: Random House.

Sutton-Smith, Brian. 1986. *Toys as Culture*. New York: Gardner.

Swan, Alma. 2006. The culture of open access: Researchers' views and responses. In *Open Access: Key Strategic, Technical and Economic Aspects*, ed. Neil Jacobs, 52–9. Oxford: Chandos.

Swan, Alma, and Leslie Carr. 2008. Institutions, their repositories and the Web. *Serials Review* 34 (1): 31–5 . http://eprints.soton.ac.uk/264965/

Swift, Jamie. 2003. *Walking the Union Walk: Stories from CEP's First Ten Years*. Toronto: Between the Lines.

Symonides, Janus. 1998. The implementation of cultural rights by the international community. *Gazette: International Journal for Communications* 60 (1): 7–25. http://dx.doi.org/10.1177/0016549298060001002.

Tananbaum, Greg. 2003. *Of Wolves and Boys: The Scholarly Communication Crisis*. http://www.sparc.arl.org/bm~doc/tananbaum_learnedpublishing.pdf (accessed Aug. 2008).

Tansley, Robert, and Stevan Harnad. 2000. Eprints.org software for creating institutional and individual open archives. *D-Lib Magazine* 6 (10). http://www.dlib.org/dlib/Oct.00/10inbrief.html

Tapscott, Don, and Anthony D. Williams. 2006. *Wikinomics: How Mass Collaboration Changes Everything*. New York: Portfolio.

Tapscott, Don, David Ticoll, and Alex Lowy. 2000. *Digital Capital: Harnessing the Power of Business Webs*. Boston: Harvard Business School Press. http://dx.doi.org/10.1145/341836.336231

Tawfik, Myra. 2005. International copyright law: W[h]ither user rights? In *In the Public Interest: The Future of Canadian Copyright Law*, ed. Michael Geist, 66–85. Toronto: Irwin Law.

Tehranian, John. 2011. *Infringement Nation: Copyright 2.0 and You*. Oxford: Oxford University Press. http://dx.doi.org/10.1093/acprof:oso/9780199733170.001.0001

Thatcher, Sanford. n.d. *Thinking Systematically about the Crisis in Scholarly Communication*. http://old.arl.org/resources/pubs/specscholmono/thatcher.shtml (accessed Aug. 2008).

The Free Software Definition. n.d. *GNU Operating System*. http://www.gnu.org/philosophy/free-sw.html (accessed 1 Nov. 2011).

Theodorou, Roxana. 2010. OA repositories: The researchers' point of view . *Journal of Electronic Publishing* 13 (3). http://old.arl.org/resources/pubs/specscholmono/thatcher.shtml (accessed Dec. 2010).

Therien, John R. 2001. Exorcising the spectre of a pay-per-use society: Toward preserving fair use and the public domain in the digital age. *Berkeley Technology Law Journal* 16: 979–1043.

Thiessen, Brock. 2008, 6 May. *Crystal Castles Accused of Plagiarism*. http://exclaim.ca/News/crystal_castles_accused_of_plagiarism (accessed 28 Sept. 2011).

Thomas, Gordon, and Martin Dillion. 2002. *Robert Maxwell, Israel's Superspy: The Life and Murder of a Media Mogul*. New York: Carrol and Graf.

Toner, Glen, ed. 2008. *Innovation, Science, Environment: Canadian Policies and Performance, 2008–2009*. Montreal: McGill-Queen's University Press.

Tonkin, Emma. n.d. eBooks: Tipping or vanishing point? *Ariadne* 62. http://www.ariadne.ac.uk/issue62/tonkin/ (accessed 30 Jan. 2010).

Topping, David. 2008, 16 Apr. *Untrust Us*. http://torontoist.com/2008/04/crystal_castles_trevor_brown.php (accessed 31 Oct. 2011).

Tor/Forge E-Books Are Now DRM-Free. 2012, 20 July. Tor.com. http://www.tor.com/blogs/2012/07/torforge-e-books-are-now-drm-free (accessed 12 Sept. 2012).

Torvalds, Linus. 1991, 26 Aug. What Would You Like to See Most in Minix? Google Groups, comp.os.minix. http://groups.google.co.uk/group/comp.os.minix/browse_thread/thread/76536d1fb451ac60/b813d52cbc5a044b (accessed 17 Oct. 2011).

Trosow, Samuel. 2009. Copyright submission. *Osgoode Hall Review of Law and Policy* 2 (2): 169–84.

Trosow, Samuel, Scott Armstrong, and Brent Harasym. 2012, 14 Aug. *Objections to the Proposed Access Copyright Post-Secondary Tariff and Its Progeny Licenses: A Working Paper*. http://ir.lib.uwo.ca/fimspub/24/ (accessed 23 Oct. 2012).

Trove. n.d. *National Library of Australia*. http://trove.nla.gov.au/

Tsivian, Yuri. 1996. The wise and wicked game: Re-editing and Soviet film culture of the 1920s. *Film History* 8 (3): 327–43.

Tuomi, Ilkka. 2007. Internet, innovation and open source: Actors in the network. *First Monday* 6 (1). http://dx.doi.org/10.5210/fm.v6i1.824 (accessed 18 Dec. 2009).

Turner, S. Derek. 2007. "Shooting the messenger": Myth vs. reality: US broadband policy and international broadband rankings. www.freepress.net/files/shooting_the_messenger.pdf (accessed 5 Jan. 2008).

Tushnet, Rebecca. 2007a. Copyright law, fan practices, and the rights of the author. In *Fandom: Identities and Communities in a Mediated World*, ed. Jonathan Gray, Cornel Sandvoss, and C. Harrington, 82–98. New York: NYU Press.

Tushnet, Rebecca. 2007b. Domain and forum: Public space, public freedom. *Columbia Journal of Law and the Arts* 30 (1): 101–13.

Tushnet, Rebecca. 2007c. Payment in credit: Copyright law and subcultural creativity. *Law and Contemporary Problems* 70: 135–74.

Tushnet, Rebecca. 2008. Personal interview with author in New York City, Feb.

Tushnet, Rebecca. 2010. I put you there: User-generated content and anticircumvention. *Vanderbuilt Journal of Entertainment and Technology* 12: 889–945.

Udo, J.P., and Deborah I. Fels. 2009a. The beginnings of a new theatrical tradition: Sighted students describe school play for a blind and low-vision audience. *International Journal of Education and the Arts* 10 (20). http://www.ijea.org/v10n20/index.html (accessed 18 Sept. 2009).

Udo, J.P., and Deborah I. Fels. 2009b. Suit the action to the word, the word to the action: An unconventional approach to describing Shakespeare's *Hamlet*. *Journal of Visual Impairment and Blindness* 103 (3): 178–83.

Udo, J.P., and Deborah I. Fels. 2010a. Re-fashioning fashion: A study of a live audio described fashion show. *Universal Access in the Information Society* 9 (1): 63–75. http://digitalcommons.ryerson.ca/trsitm/17/ (accessed 18 Sept. 2009).

Udo, J.P., and Deborah I. Fels. 2010b, Apr. The rogue poster children of universal design: Closed captioning and audio description. *Journal of Engineering Design* 21 (2): 207–21. http://dx.doi.org/10.1080/09544820903310691

Union Catalog of Digital Resources. n.d. *BASE – Bielefeld Academic Search Engine: Basic Search*. http://www.base-search.net/index.php?l=en.

United Nations Educational, Scientific and Cultural Organization (UNESCO). n.d. Convention for the Safeguarding of the Intangible Cultural Heritage. http://www.unesco.org/culture/ich/en/convention (accessed 21 Aug. 2010).

United Nations Educational, Scientific and Cultural Organization (UNESCO). n.d. Convention for the Safeguarding of the Intangible Cultural Heritage. http://www.unesco.org/culture/ich/index.php?pg=00006 (accessed 21 Aug. 2010).

US Copyright Office. 2006. *Report on Orphan Works*. Report of the Register of Copyrights. Washington, DC: Library of Congress.

Usability Testing Report: Summer 2008. 2008. *Wordpress Development*. wpdotorg. wordpress.com/files/2008/10/wp-testreport-205-crazyhorse-1028a08jw.pdf (accessed 8 Jan. 2010).

Vaidhyanathan, Siva. 2001. *Copyrights and Copywrongs: The Rise of Intellectual Property and How It Threatens Creativity*. New York: NYU Press.

Vaidhyanathan, Siva. 2004. *The Anarchist in the Library: How the Clash between Freedom and Control Is Hacking the Real World and Crashing the System*. New York: Basic Books.

Vaidhyanathan, Siva. 2010. *The Googlization of Everything (and Why We Should Worry)*. Berkeley: University of California Press.

Valenti, Jack. 1982, 12 Apr. *Home Recording of Copyrighted Works*. Hearings Before the Subcommittee on Courts, Civil Liberties, and the Administration of Justice of the Committee in the Judiciary House of Representatives Ninety-Seventh Congress, Second Session, On H.R. 4783, H.R. 4794 H.R. 4808, H.R. 5250, H.R. 5488, and H.R. 5705 (Congressional Testimony presented at the Committee on the Judiciary, House of Representatives, Washington, DC). http://cryptome.org/hrcw-hear.htm (accessed 31 Oct. 2011).

Valloppillil, Vinod. n.d. *Open Source Software: A (New?) Development Methodology*. http://iowa.gotthefacts.org/01162007 (accessed 19 Dec. 2009).

Van Evra, Jennifer. 2009, 24 Feb. K'naan asks fans to "actually buy" his new record. *CBC Music Blog*. http://music.cbc.ca/#/blogs/2009/2/Knaan-Asks-Fans-To-Actually-Buy-His-New-Record

Van Scoyoc, Anna M., and Caroline Cason. 2006. The electronic academic library: Undergraduate research behaviour in a library without books. *Portal: Libraries and the Academy* 6 (1): 47–58. http://dx.doi.org/10.1353/pla.2006.0012

Vatrapu, Ravi, and Dan Suthers. 2007. Culture and computers: A review of the concept of culture and implications for intercultural collaborative online learning. In *Intercultural Collaboration I: Lecture Notes in Computer Science*, ed. Toru Ishida, Susan R. Fussell, and Piek T.J.M. Vossen, 260–75. Heidelberg: Springer-Verlag. http://dx.doi.org/10.1007/978-3-540-74000-1_20.

Vaver, David. 1990. Intellectual property today: Of myths and paradoxes. *Canadian Bar Review* 69 (1): 98–128.

Vaver, David. 1997. *Intellectual Property Law: Copyright, Patents, Trade-marks*. Concord: Irwin Law.

Vaver, David. 2000. *Copyright Law*. Toronto: Irwin Law.

Vaver, David. 2006. Intellectual property: The state of the art. In *Intellectual Property Rights: Critical Concepts in Law*, ed. David Vaver. London: Routledge.

Verran, Helen. 2009. On assemblage. *Journal of Cultural Economics* 2 (1): 169–82.

Virtual Worlds Are Trendiest Spot Online for Kids and Teens. 2007, 24 Sept. *EMarketer*. http://www.marketwire.com/press-release/virtual-worlds-are-trendiest-spot-online-for-kids-and-teens-772841.htm (accessed 31 Oct. 2011).

von Lohmann, Fred. 2002. Fair use and digital rights management: Preliminary thoughts on the (irreconcilable?) tension between them. http://w2.eff.org/IP/DRM/cfp_fair_use_and_drm.pdf (accessed 31 Oct. 2011).

Voorhoof, Dirk, and Hannes Cannie. 2010. Freedom of expression and information in a democratic society: The added but fragile value of the European Convention on Human Rights. *International Communication Gazette* 72 (4): 407–23.

Waelde, Charlotte, and Hector L. MacQueen, eds. 2007. *Intellectual Property: The Many Faces of the Public Domain*. Cheltenham: Edward Elgar.

Wahid, Ratnaria. 2011. The fairness of "stealing" knowledge for education. *Journal of International Commercial Law and Technology* 6 (2): 86–95.

Walcott, Rinaldo. 2001. Caribbean pop culture in Canada; or, the impossibility of belonging to the nation. *Small Axe* 9 (1): 123–39.

Walcott, Rinaldo. 2003. *Black Like Who?: Writing Black Canada*. Toronto: Insomniac Press.

Wallace, Kenyon. 2009, 10 Jan. Textbook piracy thriving around city's campuses. *Toronto Star*. http://www.thestar.com/news/gta/2009/01/10/textbook_piracy_thriving_around_citys_campuses.html (accessed 21 Feb. 2010).

Wark, McKenzie. 2004. *A Hacker Manifesto*. Cambridge, MA: Harvard University Press.

Wark, McKenzie. 2006. Information wants to be free (but is everywhere in chains). *Cultural Studies* 20 (2–3): 165–83. http://dx.doi.org/10.1080/09502380500495668.

Watson, Katherine. 2007, 23 Mar. *New Normal: Version 2.07: Final Report*. Report on the Culture and Technology Round Table, Convened by the Culture and Technology Task Force and the Canadian Cultural Observatory, Department of Canadian Heritage. http://www.culturescope.ca/ev_en.php?ID=13716_201&ID2=DO (accessed 6 Mar. 2008).

Watt, Andrew. 2002. Parody and post-modernism: The story of Negativland. *Journal of Law and Arts* 25 (1): 173–94.

Weatherall, Kimberlee. 2007. Of copyright bureaucracies and incoherence: Stepping back from Australia's recent copyright reforms. *Melbourne University Law Review* 31 (3): 967–1016.

Server Survey. n.d. Netcraft. http://news.netcraft.com/archives/web_server_survey.html

Webb, Phyllis. 1967. *Extensions*. Television Program. CBC. http://www.youtube.com/watch?v=eBmxvfktZaM (accessed 31 Oct. 2011).

Webdesign und Webentwicklung aus Berlin. n.d. Ister.ORG. http://www.ister.org/

Weber, Steven. 2004. *The Success of Open Source*. Cambridge, MA: Harvard University Press.

Weber, Steven. 2006. Patterns of governance in open source. In *Open Sources 2.0: The Continuing Evolution*, ed. Chris DiBona, Mark Stone, and Danese Cooper, 361–72. Sebastopol, CA: O'Reilly.

Weinberger, David. 2009. Is Drupal moral? *Drupalcon DC 2009*. http://portland2013.drupal.org/node/4012 (accessed 22 Feb. 2010).

Weitzner, Daniel. 2006. *The Neutral Internet: An Informative Architecture for Open Societies*. http://dig.csail.mit.edu/2006/06/neutralnet.html (accessed 27 Nov. 2007).

Wells, Jane. 2008, 29 Oct. *Usability Testing Report: 2.5 and Crazyhorse*. http://wordpress.org/news/2008/10/usability-testing-report-25-and-crazyhorse/ (accessed 2 Nov. 2011).

Wenger, Etienne. 1998. *Communities of Practice: Learning, Meaning, and Identity*. Cambridge: Cambridge University Press.

Wenger, Etienne, Richard A. McDermott, and William Snyder. 2002. *Cultivating Communities of Practice: A Guide to Managing Knowledge*. Boston: Harvard Business School Press.

Wershler-Henry, Darren. 2002. *FREE as in Speech and Beer: Open Source, Peer-to-Peer and the Economics of the Online Revolution*. Toronto: Financial Times Press.

Westbrook, Steve. 2009. *Composition and Copyright: Perspectives on Teaching, Text-Making, and Fair Use*. Albany: SUNY Press.

WGBH Educational Foundation. n.d. http://www.wgbh.org/

WGBH NCAM. n.d. http://ncam.wgbh.org/

Whedon, Joss. 2010. *Buffy the Vampire Slayer – The Complete Series*. (DVD.) Los Angeles: Twentieth Century Fox Home Entertainment.

Wheeler, David. 2007. *Why Open Source Software/Free Software (OSS/FS, FLOSS, or FOSS)? Look at the Numbers!* http://www.dwheeler.com/oss_fs_why.html (accessed 31 Oct. 2011).

Wikipedia. n.d. *Captain Copyright*. http://en.wikipedia.org/wiki/Captain_Copyright (accessed 22 Feb. 2010).

Wilbanks, John. 2008. Public domain, copyright licenses, and the freedom to integrate science. *Journal of Science Communication* 7 (2): 1–10.

Wilkinson, Margaret A. 2003. National treatment, national interest and the public domain. *University of Ottawa Law and Technology Journal* 1 (1): 23–49.

Williamson, Judith. 1978. *Decoding Advertisements: Ideology and Meaning in Advertising*. London: Boyars.

Willinsky, John. 2004. Scholarly associations and the economic viability of open access publishing. *Journal of Digital Information* 4 (2). http://pkp.sfu.ca/node/440 (accessed 31 Oct. 2011).

Willinsky, John. 2006. *The Access Principle: The Case for Open Access to Research and Scholarship, Digital Libraries and Electronic Publishing*. Cambridge, MA: MIT Press.

Willinsky, John, Sally Murray, Claire Kendall, and Anita Palepu. 2007. Doing medicine differently: Open medicine, open access, and academic freedom. *Canadian Journal of Communication* 32 (3): 595–612.

Willis, Susan. 1991. *A Primer for Daily Life*. London: Routledge.

Winseck, Dwayne. 1998. *Reconvergences: A Political Economy of Telecommunications in Canada*. New York: Hampton Press.

Wong, Mary W.S. 2008. Toward an alternative normative framework for copyright: From private property to human rights. *Cardozo Arts and Entertainment Law Journal* 26: 777–843.

Wong, Tzen, Molly Torsen, and Claudia Fernandini. 2010. Cultural diversity and the arts: Contemporary challenges for copyright law. In *Intellectual Property and Human Development: Current Trends and Future Scenarios*, ed. Tzen Wong and Graham Dutfield, 279–318. Cambridge: Cambridge University Press. http://dx.doi.org/10.1017/CBO9780511761027.011.

Wood, Walter R. 1992. The role of the romantic West in shaping the Third Reich. *Plains Anthropologist* 35 (132): 313–19.

Wordpress. 2008. *Usability Testing Report: Summer 2008*. http://wpdotorg.files.wordpress.com/2008/10/wp-testreport-205-crazyhorse-1028a08jw.pdf (accessed 8 Jan. 2010).

World Intellectual Property Organization (WIPO). 1996a. *World Intellectual Property Organization Copyright Treaty* (adopted 20 Dec. 1996, entered into force 6 Mar. 2002) 36 ILM 65 (WCT). http://www.wipo.int/treaties/en/ip/wct/trtdocs_wo033.html (accessed 31 Oct. 2011).

World Intellectual Property Organization (WIPO). 1996b. *World Intellectual Property Organization Performances and Phonograms Treaty* (adopted 20 Dec. 1996, entered into force 20 May 2002) 36 ILM 76 (WPPT), http://www.wipo.int/treaties/en/ip/wppt/trtdocs_wo034.html (accessed 31 Oct. 2011).

World Intellectual Property Organization (WIPO). 2003, 2 May. Intergovernmental Committee on Intellectual Property and Genetic Resources, Traditional Knowledge and Folklore, *Consolidated Analysis of the Legal Protection of Traditional Cultural Expressions*, WIPO/GRTKF/IC/5/3. http://www.wipo.int/meetings/en/topic.jsp?group_id=110 (accessed 31 Oct. 2011).

World Intellectual Property Organization (WIPO). 2010. *The Protection of Traditional Cultural Expressions/Expressions of Folklore: Revised Objectives and Principles*. Intergovernmental Committee on Intellectual Property and Genetic Resources, Traditional Knowledge and Folklore 17th Session, Geneva, 6–10 Dec. 2010. WIPO/GRTKF/IC/17/4 (7 June 2010) Annex (e).

World Wide Web Consortium (W3C). n.d. *About the World Wide Web Consortium*. http://www.w3.org/Consortium (accessed 28 Sept. 2009).

Wu, Tim. 2010. *The Master Switch: The Rise and Fall of Information Empires*. New York: Knopf.

Yammiyavar, Pradeep, et al. 2008. Influence of cultural background on non-verbal communication in a usability testing situation. *International Journal of Design* 2 (2): 31–40.

Yar, Majid. 2008. The rhetorics and myths of anti-piracy campaigns: Criminalization, moral pedagogy and capitalist property relations in the classroom. *New Media and Society* 10 (4): 605–23. http://dx.doi.org/10.1177/1461444807087911

Young, David. 2006. Ethno-racial minorities and the Juno Awards. *Canadian Journal of Sociology* 31 (2): 183–210.

Young, James O., ed. 2008. *Cultural Appropriation and the Arts*. Malden: Blackwell. http://dx.doi.org/10.1002/9780470694190

Yu, Peter. 2005. P2P and the future of private copying. *University of Colorado Law Review* 76: 653–65.

Yu, Peter. 2007. Reconceptualizing intellectual property interests in a human rights framework. *UC Davis Law Review* 40: 1039–49.

Yúdice, George. 2003. *The Expediency of Culture: Uses of Culture in the Global Era*. Durham, NC: Duke University Press.

Zegers, James. 1994. Parody and fair use in Canada after *Campbell* v. *Acuff-Rose*. *Coalition for Intellectual Property Rights* 11 (1): 205.

Zeilinger, Martin. 2009. *Art and Politics of Appropriation*. Dissertation, University of Toronto.

Zeilinger, Martin. 2011. Remix cultures and the imagining of alternative intellectual property policies. In *Proceedings of the International Society of Electronic Arts Annual Meeting 2011. Leonardo Electronic Almanach*. http://isea2011.sabanciuniv.edu/paper/remix-cultures-and-imagining-alternative-intellectual-property-policies (accessed 8 Sept. 2012).

Zeilinger, Martin. 2012. Chiptuning intellectual property: Digital culture between Creative Commons and moral economy. *IASPM@Journal* 3 (1): 19–34.

Zeilinger, Martin, and Rosemary J. Coombe. 2013. Three Peters and an obsession with Pierre: Intellectual property in John Greyson's *Un©ut*. In *The Perils of Pedagogy: The Works of John Greyson*, ed. Brenda Longfellow, Scott MacKenzie, and Thomas Waugh, 438–49, Montreal: McGill-Queen's University Press.

Zittrain, Jonathan. 2008. *The Future of the Internet – and How to Stop It*. New Haven: Yale University Press.

Acknowledgments

The coeditors would like to thank the contributors for their patience in seeing this project through to its completion. Rosemary J. Coombe and Darren Wershler gratefully acknowledge the support of the Social Science and Humanities Research Council (SSHRC), which supported initial explorations through an Image, Text, Sound and Technology Networking Grant (2006–2008). Prof. Coombe further acknowledges support from Canada Research Chair Program as well as SSHRC assistance through the Major Collaborative Research Initiative (MCRI) grant 'Intellectual Property Issues in Intangible Cultural Heritage' (2008–2015), which supported the work of Aylwin, Coombe, and Nicholas. Prof. Wershler expresses thanks for funding received towards completion of the book from the Concordia University Research Chair program. Martin Zeilinger gratefully acknowledges SSHRC support through a Banting Postdoctoral Fellowship at York University (2011–2013).

Contributors

Bita Amani is an associate professor at Queen's University's Faculty of Law. Among other topics, her research focuses on domestic and international intellectual property law, IP theory and policy, as well as the interactions between IP law and regulating genetics, new technologies, biopiracy, and cultural heritage.

Steve Anderson is the founder and executive director of the civic engagement organization OpenMedia.ca and holds a Masters in Communications from SFU. His work as a digital policy analyst and open Internet advocate focuses on telecom, surveillance, copyright policy, and Internet governance issues. His writing has appeared in numerous print and online publications, and he is a contributing author of the CCPA book *The Internet Tree*.

Kyle Asquith is an assistant professor in the Department of Communication, Media, and Film at the University of Windsor. His research interests include advertising and consumer culture, media history, and the political economy of media industries.

Nicole Aylwin is the assistant director of the Winkler Institute for Dispute Resolution at Osgoode Hall Law School and Executive Officer of the Canadian Forum on Civil Justice. Her research and teaching focus broadly on cultural rights, cultural heritage, access to justice, and transnational cultural policy and cultural diversity.

Darin Barney is Canada Research Chair in Technology and Citizenship in the Department of Art History and Communication Studies at McGill

University. He is the author of several books on digital technology and politics, including *The Network Society*, and *Prometheus Wired: The Hope for Democracy in the Age of Network Technology*.

Marcus Boon is a professor of English at York University in Toronto. He is the author of *The Road of Excess: A History of Writers and Drugs* and *In Praise of Copying* (both from Harvard UP), and co-author of *Nothing: Three Essays on Buddhism and Critical Theory*, with Timothy Morton and Eric Cazdyn (U. of Chicago Press, forthcoming).

Alexandra Boutros is an associate professor of Communication Studies at Wilfrid Laurier University. Her research examines the intersection of media, technology, and identity in the context of religious, social, and cultural movements. Current research, funded by a SSHRC Insight Development Grant, explores transnational networks forged through grass root hip hop communities.

Ren Bucholz is an associate at the litigation firm Lenczner Slaght, where his focus ranges from high tech and intellectual property disputes to insurance and professional liability matters.

Leslie Carr teaches electronics and computer science and is affiliated with the Physical Sciences and Engineering Faculty at the University of Southampton. He is co-director of the Web Science Doctoral Training Centre and the technical director of the EPrints Repository software team. He is also course leader for the MSc in Web Technologies and the MSc in Web Science.

Eliot Che is a researcher who also works in web development, application development and user-experience design. He studies the political implications of technological transformation and the social effects of virtual space.

Rosemary J. Coombe is Senior Canada Research Chair in Law, Communication, and Culture at York University where she teaches in the Communication and Culture and Sociolegal Studies graduate programs. She publishes in the fields of anthropology, cultural studies, geography, law and society, and heritage studies. Her work may be found at www.yorku.ca/rcoombe.

Alec V. Couros is an associate professor of Educational Technology and Media at the Faculty of Education, University of Regina. He is a well-recognized scholar, advocate, and innovator in the area of open and networked education, and a pioneer of Massive Open Online Courses (MOOCs).

Marc Couture, PhD in Physics (Laval), is a professor in the Science & Technology unit of Télé-université (Université du Québec) and head of the general science undergraduate programs. His main research interests are Information Technology for science education, Intellectual Property in the university, and Open Access.

Carys J. Craig is an associate professor at York University's Osgoode Hall Law School. Among her recent publications is *Copyright, Communication & Culture: Towards a Relational Theory of Copyright Law* (Edward Elgar Press, 2011). Carys researches and publishes in the fields of domestic, comparative, and international intellectual property law and policy, with an emphasis on public interest theory and the public domain.

Deborah Fels is an associate professor in the School of Information Technology Management, and director of the Centre for Learning Technologies at Ryerson University. Her research interests include rehabilitation engineering (more specifically access to computing systems for people with disabilities), access to multi-media computer applications, computer-based learning, and video conferencing.

Kenneth Goldsmith is a poet living in New York City.

Sara M. Grimes is an assistant professor in the Faculty of information at the University of Toronto, and visiting professor in Book and Media Studies at the University of St. Michael's College. She researches primarily in the area of children's digital media culture(s), play studies, and critical theories of technology, with a special focus on videogames.

Stevan Harnad is Canada Research Chair in Cognitive Sciences at Université du Québec à Montréal and a professor in Electronics and Computer Science at the University of Southampton, UK. He is founding editor of *Behavioral and Brain Sciences*, past president of the Society for

Philosophy and Psychology, external member of the Hungarian Academy of Science, and author and contributor to over 300 publications. His research is on categorization, communication, and cognition.

Eli Horwatt is a PhD candidate in the Cinema & Media Studies Department of York University, Toronto. His dissertation organizes a topology of the reciprocal relationships between post-minimal art practices, documentary, and experimental film & video art. He is a member of the programming collective Pleasure Dome.

Rowland Lorimer is a professor of publishing, the director of the SFU Publishing program and research institute, and a former board member of Access Copyright. He has undertaken ten-plus client-commissioned studies of books and magazines and is author of *Ultra Libris* (ECW Press), an analysis of Canadian book publishing policy.

John W. Maxwell is an associate professor in the Publishing Program at Simon Fraser University. His research and teaching focus is on the impact of digital technologies in the cultural sector (particularly books and magazines), the history of digital media, and the emergence of digital genres and mythologies.

David M. Meurer is a doctoral candidate in the Joint Graduate Program in Communication and Culture at York and Ryerson Universities in Toronto. His research interests include digital archives, copyright, cultural production, and electronic literature. His work has been published in several peer-reviewed collections and publications including *Dichtung Digital*.

Laura J. Murray is a professor of English and Cultural Studies at Queen's University. She is coauthor with Samuel E. Trosow of *Canadian Copyright: A Citizen's Guide* (Between the Lines 2007, 2013), and with S. Tina Piper and Kirsty Robertson of *Putting Intellectual Property in its Place: Rights Discourses, Creative Labor, and the Everyday* (2014).

George Nicholas is a professor of archaeology, Simon Fraser University, and founding director of SFU's Indigenous Archaeology Program in Kamloops, BC (1991–2005). He is the director of the Intellectual Property Issues in Cultural Heritage (IPinCH) Project. Nicholas's research focuses on Indigenous peoples and archaeology, intellectual property, the archaeology and human ecology of wetlands, and archaeological theory.

Graham Reynolds, BA (Man), LLB (Dal), BCL, MPhil (Oxon.), is an assistant professor at the University of British Columbia Faculty of Law at Allard Hall, where he teaches and researches in the areas of copyright law, intellectual property law, property law, and intellectual property and human rights.

Eloy Rodrigues is the director of the University of Minho Documentation Services. He led the creation of RepositoriUM–UMinho institutional repository (2003), and the definition of UMinho Open Access policy (2004). Eloy actively promotes and advocates Open Access in Portugal, where he is the scientific coordinator of RCAAP (Portugal Open Access Science Repository), and across Europe, through several organizations and EC funded projects.

Arthur Sale is Emeritus Professor of Computer Science at the University of Tasmania. His research focuses on issues of Open Access, bioinformatics, mobile computing, and Internet technologies.

Matt Soar (PhD) is an intermedia artist and filmmaker with a particular interest in the conjuncture of residual and emergent media. He is an associate professor of Communication Studies at Concordia University, and co-director of development for the Korsakow System, an open source software application for creating non-linear database narratives.

Justin Stephenson is an award-winning animator and filmmaker working in Toronto. He has designed and directed feature film title sequences, commercial work, music videos, and short films.

J.P. Udo holds degrees and certificates from McMaster University, Ryerson University, and the Ontario Institute for Studies in Education at the University of Toronto, and works as Strategic Writer for the Heart and Stroke Foundation.

Peter Urquhart is an associate professor of Communication Studies at Wilfrid Laurier University.

Ira Wagman is an associate professor of Communication Studies, with a cross-appointment between the School of Journalism and Communication and the Institute for the Comparative Study of Literature, Art, and Culture at Carleton University. He is also a Research Associate at the Max Zelikovitz Centre for Jewish Studies, the Carleton Centre for Public History, and the Centre for European Studies.

Darren Wershler is the Concordia University Research Chair in Media and Contemporary Literature (Tier 2), Co-Director of the Media History Research Centre and a board member of the Technoculture, Art and Games group. His most recent book is *Guy Maddin's "My Winnipeg"* (2010).

Grace Westcott is a lawyer with Westcott Law, where she carries on a commercial law practice focusing on copyright, media, and the cultural industries, with an emphasis on publishing. She has been heavily involved in matters of copyright reform since the 1990s. Ms Westcott holds an LLB from the University of Toronto, and an LLM from Columbia University School of Law.

Martin Zeilinger currently teaches at the University of Toronto's Institute of Communication, Culture, Information, and Technology, and at the Ontario College for Art and Design's Faculty of Liberal Studies. From 2011–13, he was Banting Postdoctoral Fellow in Law and Culture at York University. Martin is also co-director of the Toronto-based *Vector Game + Art Convergence Festival.*

Suzanne Zelazo teaches at OCAD U and York University and is Managing Editor of Triathlon Magazine Canada.

Index

8–bit, 308, 312

access, 4, 8–9, 14–26, 30, 32–4, 36, 45, 54, 57–8, 73, 74, 76, 78–80, 100, 102–9, 111, 115–6, 120, 124–32, 135–142, 144–5, 147–50, 153, 154, 167, 171, 177, 179–82, 184–86, 188, 189–91, 193–4, 196–200, 201–203, 207, 211, 212, 213, 215, 217, 219, 222, 236, 250, 260, 263–5, 267, 269–70, 273–4, 282–3, 284–6, 290, 294–7, 302, 304, 307, 309–11, 315, 317–9, 325–6, 336–8, 340, 342, 345, 350, 352, 357
Access Copyright (formerly Cancopy), 10–11, 15, 56–9, 61, 105
access to information, 74
Access to Knowledge (A2K) movement ,9, 213, 274
accessibility, 19–21, 24, 73, 91, 116–17, 145, 148, 149, 166, 285–6, 317
Accessible Channel (the), 148
Act to amend the Copyright Act, Bill C–11, 11, 13, 237
activism, 106, 304
activists, 3–8, 12, 14, 18–19, 24–5, 39, 90, 204, 207, 236
adaptations, 174, 331
agency, 10, 15, 48, 105–6, 109, 147, 185, 267, 282, 340–5
Allen v. Toronto Star (1997), 9, 247, 362
alternative copyright models, 35, 306, 315
Amani, Bita, 7–8, 14, 43–55, 98, 204, 261, 264, 350–1
amateur, 16, 19, 144, 150–1, 153, 162, 315, 327, 328–9, 333
amateur audio description, 144, 151, 153
An Act to Amend the Copyright Act, 1988, 58
An Act to Amend the Copyright Act, 1997, 9, 49–52, 54, 247, Anderson, Steve, 7, 20, 133–143, 204
applied fair dealing, 307, 351
appropriation, 25–6, 28–9, 34–5, 37, 52, 60–1, 75–6, 201–2, 204–5, 214, 216–18, 267, 300, 303–4, 328–30, 340–1, 344, 355, 357
appropriation art, 28, 328, 330
archival footage, 295, 300
archival holdings, 274
archival websites, 286
archive, 29, 32, 58, 89, 92, 106, 151, 171, 182–3, 209–10, 223, 251, 253,

259, 262–3, 275, 277, 279, 282, 284–5, 287, 288–9, 291–3, 350
art, 28, 34, 48, 57, 68, 112, 160, 206, 213–14, 216–18, 228, 235, 239, 251, 252, 256, 258–60, 261–2, 264, 269, 287–8, 296, 298, 300, 308, 310, 318, 328–31, 353, 358
artists, 3, 5–6, 28, 33, 35, 48, 63, 90, 127, 141, 157, 211, 252–3, 256, 258–9, 261–2, 264–5, 269–70, 286, 288–9, 291–2, 299–300, 303, 305–326, 331, 351, 353
Artmob, 31–33, 122, 256, 285, 288–9, 293
arts, 5, 7, 29, 33–4, 70, 119, 119, 122, 154, 160, 172, 203, 222, 226, 229, 232, 242, 267, 274, 275–7, 280, 350, 352
Asquith, Kyle, 7, 16, 17, 34, 90–99, 269, 302
assignation of rights, 186
assigning copyright, 262
AT&T, 134–5, 139
attribution, 5, 23, 29, 31–2, 61, 104, 108, 110–11, 249, 306
audience(s), 5–6, 21, 28, 31, 33, 34, 37, 78, 87, 91, 95–6, 125, 144–5, 151, 153, 215, 239, 253–4, 284, 286–291, 298, 304, 307, 317, 320–1, 323, 326, 351, 353
audience participation, 317
audio, 20, 89, 145–6, 148–9, 151–3, 161, 169, 225, 255–7, 264, 291, 293, 295, 297, 298, 303, 310–11, 313
audio description (AD), 21, 144–5, 148–9, 151, 153
authenticity, 233, 269, 320–3, 325
author, 23, 25, 30, 35, 43, 75, 76, 78, 83–7, 107–9, 181, 186, 189, 191– 2, 196–199, 203, 230, 241, 243, 246, 249, 262, 266, 285, 288, 301, 332–4. 345, 354
authorship, 23, 44, 75, 77, 100, 107–11, 322, 336–7, 341–5; ideologies of, 107; trope of, 44
avant garde, 28–9, 35, 48, 62, 63, 251, 254–9, 269, 298
Aylwin, Nicole, 7, 26, 27, 201–12, 215, 223, 225–236, 356

Barney, Darin, 3, 354–9
barriers to access, 79, 144, 166, 181, 185
Bell Canada,12, 135, 140, 141
Benjamin, Walter, 35, 217, 288
Benkler, Yochai, 8, 70, 100
best practices model, 153, 287
Bill C–32, 9, 162
BioMed Central, 182
Black cultural history, 317, 319, 321–2, 326
Black music production, 317–23, 326
blindness/low vision (B/LV), 144–5, 147–8, 150–1, 153
blogosphere, 127
blogs, 155, 160, 166, 171–3, 244, 306, 328, 337
Boon, Marcus, 7, 11, 15, 56–64, 264, 351, 357
bootleg, 326
Boutros, Alexandra, 7, 36, 265, 317–326
Boyle, James, 15, 50, 57, 66, 71–5, 80, 83, 100–1, 107, 204, 213
Broadasting Act (Canada, 1991), 95
broadcast television, 146, 148, 153
broadcasters, 96, 99, 125, 127, 130, 139, 145, 147–9, 157, 267, 298, 353
broadcasting, 90–1, 93–9, 353

Brown, Jesse, 16–17, 23, 26, 91–5, 97–9
Bucholz, Ren, 7, 16, 82–89, 280, 301

Cage, John , 289
Campbell v. Acuff–Rose Music, Inc. (1994), 240, 248
Canada, 3–4, 6–7, 9–14, 16–17, 20, 26–7, 31, 33–4, 45–6, 49, 53–4, 57–8, 67, 70, 78, 83, 85, 90, 95–6, 98, 105, 114, 121, 124–31, 134–6, 138, 140, 141–2, 147, 157–8, 179, 182, 184–7, 194, 204, 208, 210, 214–15, 222, 225–6, 228, 229, 231, 233–6, 237–242, 244, 248–50, 258, 264–5, 267, 275, 277–8, 283, 285, 288, 289, 294–5, 298, 302–3, 317, 319–323, 325–6, 329, 331–2, 337, 339, 343, 352–3; and minority cultural rights, 203, 205, 212, 226, 231, 233–5; and reconfiguration of indigenous heritage, 217, 231
Canadian Association of Broadcasters (CAB), 149
Canadian Association of Internet Providers (CAIP), 140-1
Canadian Broadcasting Corporation (CBC), 16–17, 90–9, 128, 139–40, 269, 302, 320–1, 350
Canadian Charter of Rights and Freedoms, 14, 44, 47, 49–52, 54, 350
Canadian *Copyright Act (1921),* 3–4, 7, 9–10, 12, 14, 29, 43, 45–6, 49, 51, 58, 70, 84–5, 88, 107, 144–7, 151, 153, 162, 194, 237–8, 240–3, 245–7, 249–50, 266, 276, 302–4, 331, 341, 350
Canadian cultural heritage, 6, 225, 263, 298, 303
Canadian cultural policy, 6, 20, 130, 228–9, 233, 283
Canadian cultural policy, problems with, 6, 294
Canadian Culture Online Strategy (CCOS), 275
Canadian Hip Hop, 35–6, 63, 91, 317–26
Canadian Institutes of Health Research (CIHR), 183
Canadian Intellectual Property Office (CIPO), 146
Canadian public domain, 4, 14, 16, 65–81, 90, 98–9, 105, 107, 215
Canadian Radio–Television Telecommunications Act (CRTC), 131, 134, 136, 138, 140–2, 147–8
Canadian Recording Industry Association, 17, 324
Canadian Research Knowledge Network (CRKN), 184
CanCopy, 58
Canon, 28, 102, 105, 196, 296, 298–9, 327, 332
capital, 19, 59, 170, 223, 226, 258, 267
capitalism, 23, 58, 299, 358–9
capitalist property relations, 306
captioning tools, 144, 150
Carr, Emily, 215
Carr, Leslie, 7, 25, 189–200
case law, 16, 39, 273
Compagnie Générale des Établissements Michelin–*Michelin & Cie v. National Automobile, Aerospace, Transportation and General Workers Union of Canada (1997),* 244
CCH Canadian et al. v. Law Society of Upper Canada (CCH), 242
cease and desist orders, 29, 156, 253–6, 259, 332
censorship, 52–3, 295–6

chain of title , 280
Che, Eliot, 7, 18–19, 113–23, 165, 351
child–generated content, 336–345
childhood, 320, 341, 349, 352
children, 37–8, 112, 234, 289, 332, 336–45, 349–50
children's digital games, 37, 337, 340, 344
Chilling Effects Clearinghouse, 156
chipmusic, 305–16
chiptune, 312
Cie Générale des Établissements Michelin– Michelin & Cie v. C.A.W.–Canada et al., *244*
citizens, 4–6, 17–18. 39, 48, 51, 58 64, 81, 90, 92–3, 97, 112, 121, 135, 142, 153, 162, 235, 326
classroom, 21, 58, 154–7, 161, 163
clearance, 18, 53, 102–5, 280–2, 303, 357
clearance agencies, 261
clearance culture, 30, 34, 280, 294–6, 302, 306
clearance processes, 276, 279, 281
Closed Access, 190–1, 193–4, 197–200
closed captioning (CC), 144, 149
Club Penguin, 338, 344
code. *See* source code
collage, 28, 35, 300, 303
collective works, clearance issues with, 276, 280–1
commercial exploitation, 53, 86, 181, 275
commodification, 34, 77, 216–18, 308
commons, 15, 24, 72, 73, 75, 83, 90, 93, 96, 100, 101–2, 106–9, 165, 202, 204, 206, 217, 351
communications, 45–6, 127, 137–9, 180–1, 201, 211, 228, 273, 274, 279, 282–3
community internet networks, 135
community–based participatory research (CBPR), 221–2
conservation, 233
Constitution of Brazil, 235
constitutional rights, 8, 38, 44, 45, 47, 49, 51–2, 54, 73, 77, 101, 204, 239
consumers, 6, 12,29, 31, 35–9, 126, 129, 151, 174, 233, 278, 291–2, 345, 351, 359
consumers as producers, 36–7, 292
content management systems, 19, 113
contracts, 79, 92–3, 111, 197,257, 276, 279, 340, 342–3
Convention Concerning the Protection of the World Cultural and Natural Heritage, *229*
Coombe, Rosemary, 3–40, 51, 53–4, 60, 201–212, 223, 230–4, 236, 266, 303, 342– 3, 345, 356
copies, 11, 16, 22, 23–4, 45, 56–2, 89, 92–4, 156, 185, 189, 194, 247, 258, 268, 285, 294, 298, 324, 326, 356
Copps, Sheila, 228
copy shops, 56, 59
copying, 5, 9–11, 15, 28, 35, 39, 46, 52, 56–7, 59–64, 101, 103, 297, 300, 301, 303, 314
copying and philosophy, 60
copying and the University, 15, 56–7, 59–60
copyleft, 107–9, 165, 172, 174
Copyright Act (of Canada), 3–4, 7, 9, 10, 12, 14, 29, 43, 45–6, 49, 51, 58, 70, 84–5, 88, 107, 144–7, 151, 153, 162, 194, 237–8, 240–3, 245–50, 266, 276, 302–4, 321, 341, 350
copyright anxiety, 154
Copyright Board, 85, 87, 280

copyright censorship, 52–3, 295–6
copyright collectives, 12, 14, 58, 262, 270
copyright holders, 8, 15–16, 20, 29–30, 32–7, 55, 58, 67, 84, 88–9, 103, 144, 153, 179, 261, 265–7, 269–70, 277, 279–80, 282, 287, 297, 301–2
copyright infringement, 9, 14, 29, 36–7, 47, 51–2, 83–4, 104, 163, 195, 237, 240–1, 243–6, 248, 300, 302, 313, 317–8, 330, 336
copyright infringement, definition, .237, 245, 330,
copyright law, 4, 14–15, 20, 26–, 32, 34, 39, 43–5, 50, 54, 57–8, 66–7, 71–2, 74–5, 78–9, 83, 86, 88, 91–2, 97, 101–2, 146, 157–8, 162, 173, 179, 191, 225, 239, 241, 269, 273–5, 282, 305, 319, 329–30
copyright policy, 74, 78 83
copyright protection, 14, 16, 84, 99, 102, 227, 230, 281, 329
copyright, purpose of, 9, 12–4, 39, 43, 48, 78, 241–4, 247
corporations, 59, 133, 136, 206, 270, 325, 353, 356
Couros, Alec V., 7, 21, 164–74
coursepacks, 56–7, 59
courts, 17, 35, 49–50, 66, 193–4, 242, 244–5, 248–9, 330, 350
Couture, Marc, 7, 25, 189–200
Craig, Carys, 7,12, 15–6, 29, 43, 46, 65–81, 90, 101, 350–1, 355
Creative Commons, 8, 71, 98, 102, 105, 106, 108–9, 111, 158, 166, 206–7, 223, 285, 305, 311, 313, 352
Creative Commons , critiques of, 352
creative communities, 306–7, 312
creative finder (of orphan works), 83, 86–9
creative labour, 57, 93
creators, 4–6, 9, 11, 15, 21–2, 25, 28–34, 36, 39, 45, 58, 77, 83, 90–1, 105, 115, 118, 131, 145–6, 151–3, 174, 179, 207, 270, 274, 276, 278, 282, 286–7, 291, 296, 306–7, 310, 318, 329, 336–7, 339, 350, 352
creators' rights, 4, 25, 29, 31, 90, 97, 151, 174, 179, 234, 242, 287
criteria for fair dealing, 193, 264
critical parodies, 245, 248–9
Crystal Castles (band), 35, 305–9, 311–16
cultural capital, 223, 258
cultural commons, 83, 90, 93, 96, 202, 204, 351
cultural content, 4–6, 15, 29, 31, 37, 43–4, 103, 153, 207, 268, 305, 351
cultural copyright, 211
cultural difference, rights to, 208, 233
cultural distinction, 206, 209, 228
cultural diversity, 26–8, 119, 203, 225–6, 228–32, 234–6
cultural exchange, 4, 40, 55, 78, 96, 112
cultural goods, 3–4, 20, 26–7, 46–7, 88, 150, 201–3, 210, 225, 227, 229, 236, 274, 326
cultural heritage, 6, 26–7, 32–3, 74, 85, 89, 201, 203, 205, 208–16, 218–24, 225- 6, 228, 232–6, 263, 293, 298, 303
cultural industries, 4–5, 37, 131–2, 225, 227–9, 234, 275
cultural ownership, 313, 319, 321, 323
cultural participation, 232, 239, 342, 345
cultural policy, 5–9, 27, 30, 38–9, 50,

80, 130–1, 225–6, 228–31, 233–6, 283, 351
cultural production, 6, 28, 31–2, 34, 36, 39, 53, 306, 317, 319, 326, 339, 342–3, 345
cultural resources, 77, 227, 232, 273–5, 278, 279, 283
cultural rights, 21, 26–7, 39, 203–6, 208–12, 231–7, 341, 345, 350
cultural rights claims, 212, 232–3
culture, exchange value of, 226

DAISY Consortium, 149
data, 68, 88, 104, 134–5, 137, 145, 166, 174, 178, 187, 198–9, 223, 259, 288, 318, 337
databases, 23, 32, 83, 89, 150, 182, 208
deaf/hard of hearing (D/HOH), 144, 153
Declaration of the Rights of Indigenous, *Peoples* (2007), *205, 212*
defence of fair dealing, 47, 51, 245
democracy, 18, 74, 227, 259
demoscene, 310
derivative works, 36, 71, 108, 161, 202, 302, 306, 330–1
developed nations, 323
digital age, 80, 90, 101, 127, 132, 285
digital archive projects, 183, 277, 279, 285
digital culture, 3, 6, 44, 48, 337
digital divide, 201
digital environments, 3–4, 6, 7, 11–14, 17, 29, 30, 32, 45, 49, 52, 54, 202–3, 206
Digital games, 37, 337
digital interfaces, 292–3
digital locks (i.e. TPMs), 154, 162, 250
Digital Millennium Copyright Act (U.S.), 162
digital networks, 3, 142, 358
digital reproductions (access to), 80, 273, 280
digital research, 23, 155
digital revolution, 66, 78, 358
digital rights management, 4, 11, 19, 286
digital sharing, 317
digital sound technology, 317
digital technology, 4–5, 13, 31, 36, 88–9, 264
digitization, 4, 122, 201, 273–8, 278, 281, 283, 292, 318, 359
direct dealing, 30, 261–2, 270, 273–4, 278, 283
disabilities, 144–7, 149, 153
disclaimers, use of, 332
distributed agency, 341–5
distribution, 29, 57–8, 96–7, 99, 133, 137, 153–4, 165, 230, 239–41, 247, 251–2, 256, 258, 263, 269, 274, 285, 286, 289, 311, 318, 326, 350, 356
distribution systems, 289
distribution technologies, 318
diversity, 26–8, 119, 121–2, 203, 207–8, 215, 225–6, 228–36, 328, 340
documentaries, 155, 300
Documentary Organization of Canada, 33
dot com bubble, 117
downloading, 17, 179, 194, 324
Dreamworlds (1991), 156
Drupal, 113, 115–16, 121–2, 285
dynamic fair dealing, 5, 13, 32, 80

economy, 39, 62–3, 103, 105, 114, 225–6, 229, 232, 256, 258, 264, 268, 285–6, 355
education, 20, 57–8, 62, 150, 155,

163–7, 170–1, 17, 183, 241, 252, 255, 352–3
educational institutions, 7, 9, 10, 21, 70, 79, 353
educators, 4, 24, 38–9, 58–9, 93, 95, 155, 164–6, 170, 172, 174
email, 94, 189–92, 194–5
enclosure, 80, 100–3, 107
End–User Licensing Agreements (EULAs), 342–5
enlightenment notions of authorship , 322
ephemera, 252, 263, 269, 285, 287, 291–2, 300
EPrints Institutional Repository software, 189, 190–1, 197 errors and omissions (E&O) insurance, 53
estates, 30, 265, 277
ethics, 27, 30, 35, 37, 39, 58, 61, 63, 114, 121–2, 202, 220–3, 311
ethnicity, 156, 322
ethnographic materials, 211
exchange value, 226
executable code, 310
exemptions, 9, 32, 53, 69, 103, 144–5, 147, 153, 206, 274, 283
expanding the reach of copyright, 14, 39
experimental film, 300
extra–juridical spaces, 306

factors tending to fairness/unfairness, 247
fair dealing, 3–7, 9–17, 20–35, 39–40, 46–7, 51–5, 57–8, 69–71, 80, 83–4, 90, 93–4, 97–8, 101–2, 112, 114, 116, 119, 121, 122–3, 126, 147, 153, 155, 157, 163, 173, 181, 190–200, 214, 223, 225, 234, 237–8, 241–50, 264, 269, 273, 285, 287, 295–7, 300–4, 307, 311, 313, 315, 316, 322, 331, 334, 341, 345, 349, 350–3, 359
Fair Dealing Button, 192, 198–200, 350, 359
fair dealing categories, 249
fair dealing defence, 9, 29, 52, 237, 244–7
fair dealing exception, 10, 57, 147, 242, 322
fair dealing exception as user's right, 10, 242, 322
fair dealing guidelines, 303
fair dealing practices, 25, 80, 196, 311, 315, 322
fair exchange, 307, 351
fair use, 8–10, 12–14, 19–20, 29, 53, 57, 62, 69–70, 10, 103, 110, 155–7, 173, 181, 190, 193, 204, 264, 287, 295, 313, 319, 322, 328, 330, 331, 357
fair use (United States), 12, 57, 264, 322
fairness, 20, 29, 47, 111, 126, 132, 193, 241, 247–8, 349,351–2
fairness analysis, 389
fan fiction, 36–7, 44, 48, 327–34, 344
fandom, 324, 332, 334–5
fanzines, 328
Federal Communications Commission (FCC), 134, 139–40
Fels, Deborah, 7, 21, 144–53
feminism, 92
fiction (excluding science– and fan–), 75, 331
file sharing, 19, 82, 112, 179, 255, 259, 317, 324–5
film, 7–8, 22, 34, 53, 95, 125–7, 129, 144–6, 152–3, 157–8, 213, 215–6, 227, 251, 253–4, 256, 258–60, 262–3, 294–5, 297–304, 333

filmmakers, 30, 33, 53, 82, 103, 256, 273, 294, 297–303
filmmaking, 33, 159, 294, 296, 298–9
First Nations, 121, 211, 214–18, 222, 233
Flickr, 18, 109, 112, 173
Folklore, 206, 329
foreign media, 130–1
found footage, 297–304
found footage filmmaking, 297–304
free culture, 57, 91, 96, 104, 328, 356–7
free culture movement, 91, 96, 328
freedom of expression, 8–9, 14, 19, 38, 45, 47–52, 54
funding, 181–5, 197, 267, 273, 281–2, 294–5, 353
funding, public, 340

gaming, 125, 234, 337–9, 342
Geist, Michael, 7, 11, 15, 39, 78, 90, 138, 148, 161–2, 318
geo–blocking, 350
gift economy, 252, 258, 268, 285–6
Girl Talk (artist), 44, 157–8, 160–2
Globe and Mail, 131
GNU General Public License (GPL), 18, 107–9, 165, 285
Goldsmith, Kenneth, 7, 29–30, 48, 251–260, 288–90, 350, 359
Google, 59, 83, 105–6, 112, 126, 173, 258, 328
government, 4, 9–10, 12, 22, 39, 51, 114, 119, 121, 134–5, 138, 179, 236, 283, 345, 352, 354
graduate level, 257, 275
grey area, copyright as, 281, 352
gridlock, 103
Grimes, Sarah, 7, 37–8, 234, 336–45
guidelines, 10, 134, 142, 149, 150, 231, 278, 282, 303

hacking, 306
Harnad, Stevan, 23, 25, 185, 189–200
Harry Potter, 327–8, 333
HBO, 129, 204
Hegel, G. W. F., 60, 63
Heller, Michael, 103
heritage, 6, 22, 26–7, 30–3, 39–40, 74, 85, 89, 95–6, 105, 136, 140, 201, 203–26, 228–36, 263, 283, 293, 296, 298, 302–3, 320–1
heritage management, 22, 26, 209, 229
heritage protection, 220, 229, 230–1
hip hop, 35–6, 39, 52, 63–4, 75, 91, 207, 211, 295, 317–26
Hobbes, Thomas, 62
Honey Bee Network, 208
Horwatt, Eli, 7, 34, 103, 294–304, 350
human rights, 26, 39, 128, 201, 203–7, 226, 233–5

I Need a Haircut (album), 319
iCopyright, 93–9
idea, 43, 50, 52, 57, 68–9, 80, 93, 117, 119, 186, 210, 216, 334
images, 157, 211–12, 214–17, 247, 264, 282, 297–302
immaterial labour, 37, 337, 342
immediate–deposit/optional–access (IDOA),196
In the Land of the Head Hunters (1914, re- titled *In the Land of the War Canoes* in 1974), 215
independent artists, 270, 316
independent ISPs, 136, 140,
Indigenous archeology, 220
Indigenous cultural heritage, 27, 218, 223,
Indigenous peoples, 25–7, 203–6, 212, 214, 216–24, 230–2
Infringement of copyright, 4, 9–11, 14, 29–30, 36–7, 46–7, 51–2, 70,

83–4, 89, 97, 104, 150, 156, 163, 194–6, 213, 217, 237, 241, 243–6, 248–9, 251, 262, 300–2, 306, 313, 315–18, 330, 336, 341
innovation, 31, 67, 70, 78, 80, 90–1, 100, 114, 122, 128, 133, 164, 171, 184
Institutional Repositories (IRs), 183, 189, 197
institutions, 6–7, 9–10, 17, 21–3, 30–1, 33–4, 60, 70, 79, 93, 180, 182–4, 190–1, 196, 198, 209, 221, 256, 258–9, 263, 269–70, 273–5, 278–83, 295, 302, 304, 323, 353, 356
intangible cultural heritage (ICH), 209, 225–6, 228–9, 233–4
intellectual commons, 75, 109
intellectual property (IP), 4–8, 14–15, 20, 25–8, 30–1, 33, 35–9, 43, 56, 58, 60–62, 65, 67, 69, 73, 75–6, 80, 85–9, 90–1, 97, 100, 103, 125–6, 144, 146, 157, 179, 202–5, 213–14, 217, 221–2, 225, 227, 245, 273, 286, 294, 305, 315, 317, 323, 336, 341, 355–8
Intellectual Property Issues in Cultural Heritage (IPinCH) Project, 214, 221
intellectual property rights, 20, 26, 69, 73, 245
intention to possess, 87
International Covenant on Economic, Social and Cultural Right, *231*
International Labour Organization Convention No. 169 (1989), 205
international trade regime, 228
Internet, 19–20, 24, 29, 31–2, 62, 64, 78, 89, 94, 97, 99, 101, 103, 106, 113–17, 119, 124–8, 131–43, 145, 148, 150, 153, 160, 164–5, 170, 178, 180, 189, 198, 215, 218, 251–2, 257, 267, 275, 280, 286, 307, 311, 313–14, 318, 327–9, 331, 333–4, 336–9, 356
Internet infrastructure, 133–4
Internet Service Providers (ISPs), 133
Internet traffic, 133, 139–42, 160
intra–cultural diversity, 235
IP address, 124, 126–7, 129
iTunes, 126

Jenkins, Henry, 36, 125, 328–9, 337
Jhally, Sut, 156

K'naan (artist), 320–1, 324–5
Knopf, Howard, 6, 33, 295
K–os (artist), 320–1

LAMs (libraries, archives and museums), 273–5, 280, 282–3
law, 3–4, 6, 8–10, 14–17, 19–20, 22, 25–7, 29–32, 34, 37, 39–40, ,43–6, 48–52, 54–9, 61–2, 64–7, 71–2, 74–6, 78–9, 83–9, 91–2, 97, 100–2, 107, 111–2, 142, 146–7, 155, 157–9, 162, 173, 178–9, 183, 186–7, 191, 194–6, 207, 212–13, 217, 225, 232, 237, 239, 241–2, 260, 262, 269–70, 273–6, 280, 282, 288, 305–6, 315, 319, 329–31, 334, 350–3, 355
lawful finder, 83, 85–9
learning, 4, 14, 20–1, 36, 38–9, 57, 77, 101, 118, 150, 164–5, 167–74, 222, 345
legal climate, current , 294
legislation, 6, 13, 29–30, 36, 79, 101–2, 112, 134, 137, 145–6, 153, 238, 242, 301, 304, 319, 325–6, 340
legislative reform, 22, 39, 67, 238, 249
legitimacy, 14, 26, 46, 54, 205, 298, 303, 313
Lessig, Lawrence, 18, 90, 102, 157, 161, 234

liability, 4, 14, 21, 84, 278, 301
librarians, 4, 6, 24, 157, 178
libraries, 9, 23, 32–3, 57–8, 70, 79, 125, 177, 182–5, 264, 273, 280, 288
licences, 16, 30, 32, 35, 39, 56, 58, 93–5, 98, 102–5, 108–9, 112, 116, 148, 166, 169, 173, 207, 268, 279–80, 287, 295–7, 301, 305–7, 310–15
licensing, 10, 12, 17–18, 23, 26, 31, 35–6, 45, 51, 54, 58, 71, 93–5, 98–9, 104–5, 107–8, 174, 181, 206, 270, 273, 278–81, 294–8, 302, 311–12, 314–15
licensing collectives, 12, 270
licensing fees, 36, 51, 279, 302, 314
licensing initiatives, 273
Linux, 114, 118, 150, 165
Lipsett, Arthur, 297–304
literature, 7–8, 23, 28, 31, 65, 73, 77, 83, 150, 173, 181–2, 187–8, 213, 217, 240, 244, 266, 286, 288, 289–90, 292, 297
litigation, 43, 45–6, 49–54, 219, 268, 287, 295, 302, 304, 313, 315
LittleBigPlanet (game), 339–40, 343–4
LiveDescribe (software), 151
living culture, 204, 215, 226, 229, 231
living heritage practices, 228, 233
Lorimer, Rowland, 7, 20, 25, 177–88, 352

machinima, 298, 342
mainstream, 63; cinema, 215; music, 307, 314; success, 298
marketplace, 57, 129, 179, 187, 230
Markie, Biz, 318
Marx, Karl, 60, 354–5, 357–8
mash-ups, 160–1
massively multiplayer online game (MMOG), 338
material culture, 126
material heritage, 232
Maxwell, John, 7, 18, 46, 100–12, 352, 356–7
Maxwell, Robert, 177–8
McLaren, Malcolm, 308–9
media, digital, 25, 27–8, 30, 34–5, 37, 45, 50, 90, 98, 101, 103–4, 124, 127–8. 131–2, 144–6, 148–51, 154–9, 163, 164, 167, 171, 173, 201, 216–17, 230, 234, 253, 255–6, 259, 264, 267, 269, 274, 278, 285–6, 289–90, 292, 294, 300, 302, 308–9, 317, 320, 329, 331–4, 336–7, 339–40, 351; news, 8, 17, 57, 91–2, 95–6, 98–9, 128–32, 139, 141–2
media brands, 340
media consumers, 126, 351
media creators, 337
Media Education Foundation, 155, 163
metaphors, 82–3
Meurer, David, 7, 32–4, 201, 273–283, 286–7, 301, 350
mimesis, 60–1, 319
minority cultural groups, 230–1, 233
misappropriation, 35, 305, 314–15
modding, 342
Modernism, 108, 286
montage, 63, 160, 299–300, 303
Moodle, 169
moral rights, 23, 39, 93, 107, 151, 206, 262, 265–6, 331–2, 334
Mozilla Firefox, 115–16
Mukurtu Archive, 209
multiculturalism, 26–7, 91–2, 210, 225, 228, 320
Murray, Laura, 6, 14, 262, 276, 278, 280, 349–53
museum, 30, 63, 209–12, 221, 257

music, 19, 22, 28, 35, 63, 82, 124, 139, 156–7, 159–61, 179, 202, 213–14, 216–17, 247, 251–2, 258, 268, 298–300, 305, 307–12, 314–26
music industry, 22, 316

Nanook of the North (1922), 215
National Film Board of Canada, 34, 95, 258, 294, 303–4
National Research Council (NRC), 182
National Research Council Press, 182
neoliberalism, 227, 353
net neutrality, 20, 124, 132–4, 136–43, 350
networked communications, 46
networked cultural environments, 267
networked teacher, 167
networking, 19, 95, 159, 171, 287,324, 337, 339, 359
networks, 3, 17, 19, 57, 115, 118, 122, 125, 127, 133–7, 142, 154, 164, 167, 170, 172, 174, 263, 274, 336–7, 339, 358
news reporting, 31–2, 94, 102, 193, 195, 241, 243–4, 246–7, 331, 352
Nichol, bp, 261-3, 265–9
Nichol, Ellie, 262–3, 267
Nicholas, George, 7, 27, 204–5, 217–23
non-commercial, 14, 29, 108–9, 194, 207, 243, 255, 270, 273, 275, 279, 283, 306, 311, 330–1, 334, 341
non-critical parodies, 243, 245, 248
non-tangible cultural goods, 227
nude media, 289–90

online access, 189, 283, 337–8
Online Archive for bpNichol, 262–3
online courses, 168–9
Open Access (OA), 21, 213; publishing, 182
open content, 5, 106, 166, 173
Open Content Alliance (OCA), 106
open education, 164, 167, 171
open Internet movement, 140–1
Open Publication License (OPL), 166
open source, 8, 18, 62, 71, 113–17, 119, 122, 158–9, 161, 164, 206, 234, 285, 305, 351; movement, 18, 62; software, 164, 351
Open Source Cinema, 158–9, 161
open teaching, 173–4, 350
OpenCourseWare (MIT), 166
organic society, 48
Organization for Transformative Works, 330
originals, 28, 60
Orphan Works, 16, 83–9, 280, 287, 301
owner rights, 242
owners, 5, 12–13, 19, 24, 32, 43, 45–7, 51–2, 54, 56, 70, 83–5, 88, 137, 139, 240–2, 249–50, 274–5, 280, 287, 301, 331–2, 341–3
ownership, 24, 27, 36, 60, 63–4, 74, 77, 80, 91, 93–4, 98, 104, 108, 116, 137, 142, 146, 154, 174, 202, 207, 213, 217, 225–6, 234, 258, 274, 276–8, 301, 310, 313, 315, 318–19, 321–4, 332, 336, 341–5

P2P (peer–to–peer) sharing, 19, 57, 101, 112, 139, 323–4
parody, 29, 46, 237–41, 243–50, 331, 341, 352; and competition with original work, 29, 238, 240, 241, 245, 247–8. 331
participants, 6, 33, 77, 110–11, 118, 120, 151, 166–71, 233, 274, 290, 318

participation, 26, 49, 74, 77–8, 116–18, 161, 172, 203, 232–3, 239, 317–18, 334, 337, 339–40, 342, 344–5
Participatory Based Research (PAR), 221
participatory culture. 328
pay-per-use licensing agreements, 23, 54
peer review, 23, 114, 116–17, 119, 122, 180–3, 185, 187, 197, 351
peer–to–peer (P2P), 19, 57
perceptual disabilities, 145, 147, 153
performance, 31, 73, 160, 162, 164, 206, 228, 243, 266, 276–7, 286–7, 290– 2
performing arts, 274–6, 280
Perloff, Marjorie, 286, 288–9
permissions, 15, 29–30, 32–33, 36, 39, 58, 98, 103, 108, 157, 255, 257, 267, 276, 279–81, 287, 294, 297, 301
photography, 158, 217, 276
piracy, 30, 36, 46, 57, 94, 317, 323–6
placelessness (of internet), 125–6, 129
play, 37–8, 43–5, 47, 49, 53–4, 76, 313, 337–45, 350; fair, 58, 112
Play Station, 344
Playbill News Magazine , 277
podcasts, 92, 166, 217
poetry, 28–9, 34, 83, 252, 255–8, 269, 284–5, 288, 290, 292, 329,
policy, 91, 110, 131, 133–4; copy right, 80, 83, 85, 182, 192, 194, 196, 234, 294; cultural, 5–9, 13–14, 17, 20, 22–3, 26–8, 30, 36, 38–9, 44, 49–50, 54, 65–66, 74, 77–8, 80, 89, 130–5, 138–9, 141, 174, 182–4, 192, 194, 196, 205, 210, 221–2, 225–31, 233–6, 242, 253, 282–3, 293–4, 336, 351; Internet, 133–5, 141, 162
policy makers, 5, 49, 132, 221, 316
popular culture, 7, 44, 291, 320, 323, 329
possession, 84–5, 87
postcolonial, 27, 214, 219, 220–1, 223
postcolonial ethic of the public domain, 219
post–structuralism, 59, 292
Pound, Ezra, 288–9
power, copyright, 4, 8, 10, 16, 38, 45, 48, 65, 77, 80–1, 105, 107, 132
practice, 4, 6–7, 13, 20, 22–3, 25, 27–8, 30,34–5, 39–40, 50, 54, 61, 63–4, 76–7, 79–80, 87, 98, 108–9, 111–12, 114, 117, 118, 122, 124, 131, 149–51, 153, 155, 166–7, 172, 181–2, 184, 189, 201, 203, 208, 219–20, 223, 228, 231–2, 235, 251, 264, 266, 269–70, 287, 297–8, 301, 303–5, 310, 313, 319, 322, 332, 337, 344–5, 350–2
practice, concept of, 63–4
practices, 3–7, 9–11, 15, 17–18, 20–1, 23, 25, 28–9, 31–2, 34–5, 40, 54, 57, 63–4, 76–7, 79–80, 91, 101, 112, 116, 119, 123, 125, 135, 139–40, 142, 144, 149–53, 155, 158, 196, 204–5, 208, 210, 212, 214, 220, 222–4, 226, 228–9, 231–6, 238, 261, 264–5, 269, 273, 276, 282, 287–8, 294–5, 297, 300–1, 303, 306, 311–12, 314–15, 317, 322, 324, 325, 335, 338, 342, 344–5, 350
pre–authored materials, 303
print, 23–4, 85, 94, 178–81, 185, 287, 289, 327, 334
privacy, 37, 117, 211, 217, 337, 340
privilege, 13, 50, 90, 111, 128
producers, 19, 21, 34, 36–7, 59, 91–2, 97–8, 127, 133, 153, 174, 183, 188, 202, 234, 279, 286, 292, 297, 301, 304, 326, 337, 341, 345, 350, 352, 359

production, 4, 6–7, 18, 21, 28, 31–9, 44, 48, 53, 62, 83, 110, 112, 115–17, 119, 121, 130, 145–6, 152–3, 155, 158–9, 163, 172–3, 178–80, 185–6, 203, 230, 252, 265–6, 274, 276–9, 284, 294–7, 301, 306, 310, 314, 317–20, 322–3, 326, 331, 336–9, 342–3, 345, 354–5, 358
profit, 22–3, 36, 59, 133, 165, 185, 188, 203, 334
program, 18, 89, 91–2, 95, 105, 118, 121, 128–9, 145, 148–9, 159, 184, 269, 276–7, 279–80, 354
programming, 90, 92, 95, 115, 147–8, 310, 339
property, 4–8, 14–15, 18, 20, 22, 25–8, 30–1, 33, 35–9, 43–5, 47, 54, 56–8, 60–2, 64–5, 67, 69, 72–3, 75–77, 80, 82–91, 97, 100–3, 109–11, 125–6, 144, 146, 157, 179, 202–5, 210–11, 213–14, 217–18, 221–2, 225, 227, 230, 232, 245, 273, 286, 294, 297, 305–6, 313, 315, 317, 323, 336, 341–2, 354–8
prosumer, 318, 342–3
protectable elements, 43, 68
protected works, 10, 44, 69–70, 73, 102, 234, 241, 247, 314
protection, 4, 11, 14–16, 24, 44, 49, 54, 57, 68–9, 73–6, 79, 84, 88, 98–9, 101–2, 154, 203–6, 208, 213, 217, 219–20, 223, 225–32, 236–8, 242, 245–6, 249–50, 281, 303, 310, 315, 329–30, 341, 345
provisions, 3, 16, 25, 33, 39, 43, 46, 51, 53, 57, 79, 83–4, 94, 97–8, 105, 139, 151, 153, 155, 162, 165, 190, 193, 196, 205–6, 231, 273, 288, 295–6, 302–4, 306, 345
public broadcasting, 90–1, 93–6, 98–9, 353
public dissemination, 71, 244
Public Domain, 4, 14–16, 19–20, 25–7, 48, 57, 61–2, 65–81, 84–5, 90, 98–9, 101– 2, 104–5, 107–8, 112, 144, 151, 204, 207, 214–15, 217, 219, 221, 223, 230, 234, 264, 281, 285, 302, 329, 337, 341, 345, 350
public domain, definitions of, 72
public funding, 340
Public Library of Science (PloS), 182
public space, 325
public sphere, 16, 34, 36, 54, 234, 317–19, 322
publicly–funded works, 34, 296, 302
publishers, 6, 9–10, 22–4, 53, 58, 61, 105, 111, 127, 151, 177–80, 182–3, 186, 188–91, 193–4, 196–7, 199, 265, 270, 352
publishing, 7–8, 18, 22–5, 57, 137, 157, 177–8, 180–2, 185–8, 197–8, 223, 263, 266, 268
PubMed Central (PMC), 181, 183, 186
Punk, 48, 63, 252, 306–8, 315
purposes of criticism, 70, 241, 243, 246
purposes of review, and fair dealing, 244, 300

Quicklaw service, 186–7
Quoting, 156, 240, 264, 269, 290

radical distribution, 29, 251–2, 258
radio, 16, 90–3, 96–9, 127–8, 131, 134, 141, 147, 238, 268–9, 297, 300, 320, 323
Raymond, Eric, 18, 114–5, 119–20, 165–6, 174
Read/Only culture, 162
Read/Write culture, 162
reading, 23, 36, 147–8, 162, 142, 261, 288, 290–1, 293

Reciprocal Research Network (RRN), 211
recombinatory practices, 264
recontextualization, 299
records, 88, 145, 191, 211, 251, 269, 275–6, 280, 315, 325
Reed Elsevier (publisher), 187
reform, 5–8, 12–13, 15, 22, 29, 31, 36–7, 39, 46, 67, 79, 102, 174, 178, 237, 249, 304, 317–18, 324, 326
region encoding, 129
regulation, 3, 49, 78–9, 101, 103, 107, 137–8, 143, 148, 322–3
release forms, 334
relicensing, 294–6
remix, 44, 157, 159–61, 261–2, 264–5, 268, 298–9, 328, 353
remixing, 14, 44, 261, 264, 269–70, 318–19, 337
repetition, 322
reporting, 5, 31–2, 94, 102, 193, 195, 241, 243–4, 246–7, 331, 352
repositories, 19, 23–4, 29, 183, 186, 189, 197–8
reproduction, 4, 9–10, 31, 35, 46, 48, 53–4, 80, 97, 111, 146, 194, 201, 217, 225, 244, 247, 274, 277–8, 330
research, 5, 9, 11–12, 23, 25, 27, 31, 38, 57, 59, 79, 94, 102, 104, 112, 114, 120–2, 141, 154–5, 166, 177–90, 193-200, 211, 213, 220–3, 241, 243–4, 247, 249, 251, 267, 273, 274, 277, 282, 331, 336–8, 352
researchers, 4, 31, 33, 39, 46, 57, 120–1, 123, 151, 180–1, 183–6, 188–9, 192, 196–7, 199–200, 206–7, 210–11, 221–3, 275–6, 281, 283
resources, 25–6, 44, 51, 69, 73–4, 77–80, 83, 89, 92, 95, 97, 99, 108, 135, 150, 166, 182, 201, 205–7, 209, 212, 221, 227, 232, 236, 268, 273–6, 278–80, 282–3, 291, 352–3
restrictions, 17, 21, 36, 56, 79, 94, 102–3, 106, 108–9, 181, 202, 206, 268, 283, 285–6, 288, 302, 334, 340
reuser, 5, 30, 33–4, 71, 77, 103, 108, 119, 191, 297, 300, 307, 309
review, 5, 9, 15, 31–2, 51, 70, 102, 114, 116–17, 119, 122, 136, 138, 160, 173, 178, 180–2, 185, 194, 221–2, 241, 243–4, 246–7, 264, 300, 302, 330–1, 351–3
Reynolds, Graham, 7, 9, 29, 35, 50, 54, 189, 204, 237–50, 264, 341, 350
rights holders, 29–30, 32–7, 102–3, 179, 261, 265–6, 268–9, 276–80, 282, 287, 297, 301–3, 335
rights management, 4, 11, 19, 46, 154, 286, 294, 341
RiP!: A Remix Manifesto, 157, 159–60
ROARMAP, 190–1, 197
Rodrigues, Eloy, 7, 25, 189–200
rotoscope, 160
Rowling, J. K., 327, 333–4
Royalities, 12, 58, 105, 125, 227, 314

Sale, Arthur, 7, 25, 189–200
sampling, 28, 35–6, 48, 94, 157, 159–60, 202, 264, 298, 305–7, 309, 311– 16, 318–19, 322
satire, 237–8, 241, 243, 245, 249–50, 331, 341, 352
SaveOurNet.ca coalition, 141
SavetheInternet.com Coalition, 139
scholars, 3–8, 14–15, 20, 23–5, 27–8, 30, 36–7, 39, 48, 57, 66, 75, 90, 94, 110, 132, 156, 180, 188, 213, 220–1, 264, 273–5, 288
scholarship, 4, 8, 13, 20, 30, 39, 75, 111, 179–81, 220, 274, 282, 298

science, 7, 24, 104, 111–12, 120, 177–8, 182–3, 187, 189, 227, 327, 333
Science Commons, 104, 111–12
scientific colonialism, 219, 221
Scientific, technical and medical journal publishing (STM), 177–80, 185
SCOAP3 (Sponsoring Consortium for Open Access Publishing in Particle Physics), 182
Scopus, 187–8
Scream in High Park/ The Scream Literary Festival, 284, 292
search engines, 184, 198, 258, 267
Second Life, 170
self–archiving, 185, 190, 193, 196–7
serial writing, 334
shared access, 310
sharing, 5, 7, 15, 17–19, 26–7, 35, 39, 58, 69, 71, 76, 82, 108–9, 112– 13, 115–16, 118, 150, 164, 166, 168, 173, 179, 201, 206–7, 212, 255, 259, 307, 312–13, 317, 324–5, 327, 338, 343, 350, 353
sharing software, 113
Situationism, 28
Soar, Matt, 7, 21, 154–63
social capital, 19, 170, 267
social collectivities , 205
social media, 96, 164, 167, 171
social networking, 19, 95, 159, 171, 287, 337, 339
social regulation, 3, 78
social sciences and humanities (SSH) publishing, 178
Social Sciences and Humanities Research Council (SSHRC),184
social texts , 290
software, 7, 16, 18–19, 25, 31–3, 48, 71, 102, 107, 110, 112–19, 122, 125, 127–8, 145, 151, 159, 164–6, 169, 173–4, 190–2, 206, 210, 234, 285, 305, 310, 318, 337, 351
software hacking, 305
Somalian pirates, 325
Sony, 25
sound chips, 305, 309
soundtracks, 305, 310
source code, 18, 71, 113, 115–17, 165
source materials, 265, 267, 274
sovereignty, 95, 126, 218–19, 227–8, 233
Spore, 339
Standards, 116, 149, 153, 181–2, 196, 223, 258–9, 278, 287, 298, 336, 345
Star Trek, 327, 332
Stephenson, Justin, 7, 30
streaming, 20, 124, 133, 145–6, 171, 255–6, 259, 285
students, 6, 11, 20–1, 23–4, 31, 33, 39, 46, 58–9, 93, 150, 154–5, 158–64, 169–74, 187, 257, 275, 282–3, 337–8, 353
studies, 5, 7–8, 30, 32, 34, 48, 120–1, 132, 141, 154–5, 181, 202, 221– 2, 280, 288, 337, 340
Supreme Court of Canada (SCC), 11, 46, 67, 70, 241–2
System, 12, 19, 29, 31–2, 53, 56–8, 63–4, 68, 71, 75, 78–80, 83, 88, 93–5, 97–9, 115, 118, 124, 127–8, 135, 137–8, 142, 169, 180–1, 183–4, 205, 208, 251, 257, 285, 296, 306, 309, 311, 343, 356, 357

tangible heritage, 229
teaching, 21, 92, 154, 160–1, 164, 166, 173–4, 350
technological protection mechanisms (TPM), 250

technologies, 3, 6–7, 14–15, 17, 19, 21–2, 27, 31, 35, 38–9, 66, 78–80, 104, 113–15, 117–21, 127, 129, 131–2, 149, 157, 166–7, 179, 181, 201, 203, 212–13, 217–18, 226, 228, 238–9, 260, 273, 279, 311, 314, 318, 326, 336, 353, 358
technology, 4–5, 7–8, 13–15, 17, 21, 30–2, 36–7, 57, 70, 88–9, 96, 119, 123, 126, 132, 141, 149, 164, 167, 169, 279–80, 184, 201, 223, 264, 283, 309–10, 314, 317, 358
telecommunications, 46, 127, 131, 133–8, 142–3, 147
telecommunications industry, 136
television, 22, 98, 125, 127–31, 134, 139, 141, 144–53, 157, 227, 238, 269, 300, 327, 331–3, 336
Terms of Service (TOS), 24, 340, 344
texts, 20–1, 25, 28–9, 36, 38, 47, 57, 59–60, 125, 128, 130, 132, 225, 264, 267, 290, 340–1, 344–5
The Agreement on the Trade–Related Aspects *of Intellectual Property* (TRIPs) (1995), 227, 323
The Cathedral and the Bazaar (book), 115, 119, 165
The Contrarians (radio programme), 16–17, 91–3, 95–8
The Convention for the Safeguarding of the Intangible Cultural Heritage (the Intangible Heritage Convention), 226, 229
The Convention on the Protection and Promotion of the Diversity of Cultural Expressions (the Diversity Convention), 226, 228
The Indigenous Knowledge and Resource Management in Northern Australia project, 210
The Past is a Foreign Country (1985), 213
theatre archives, 274
Théberge v. Galérie d'Art du Petit Champlain (2002 decision), 67, 242
tolerated use, 334
tools, 3, 14, 33, 35, 37, 46, 73, 89, 94, 96, 115, 144, 150, 154, 159, 163–4, 166–74, 184, 206, 218, 235, 239, 311, 328, 337–40, 343, 357
trade, 12–13, 23, 58, 119, 131, 138, 213, 226–8, 232–3, 245, 286, 323, 333, 350, 352
trade secrets, 232
trademarks, 213, 232–3
traditional cultural expressions (TCEs), 26, 201, 205
traditional knowledge (TK), 26, 206–8, 214, 217, 223, 233
Traditional Knowledge Commons, 207
traffic, 20, 124, 133–4, 138–42, 154, 160
traffic shaping, 138, 140, 154
transformative reproductions, 265
transparency, 116–17, 119, 166, 169, 174, 351
Trosow, Samuel E., 6, 10, 262, 276, 278, 280
Tushnet, Rebecca, 37, 330, 335
typical techer network, 167

U.K. *Copyright Act* (1911), 12
Ubuntu, 165
UbuWeb, 29, 251–60, 264, 288–9, 358–9
Udo, J. P., 7, 21, 144–53
UN World Decade for Cultural Development (1987–1997), 208
underground culture, 258, 306–7
United Nations Declaration of Human Rights (1948), 203

United Nations Declaration on Human Rights, International Covenant on Civil and Political Rights, *231*
United Nations Educational, Scientific and Cultural Organization (UNESCO), 228
United States, 8, 12, 46, 57, 85, 101, 126–7, 129, 134–6, 157, 162, 182–3, 185, 214, 227, 264, 267, 278, 288, 317, 319, 321–3, 329, 332, 334, 339, 343
universal design theory, 151–2
university, 15, 21, 57, 59–60, 134, 151, 155–6, 163, 192, 199, 221, 251, 254–5, 274
unlocatable copyright owners, 280
unregulated uses, 103, 107
Urquhart, Pete, 20, 124–32, 351
US Copyright Office, 86
usability, 19, 114, 119–23, 159
usage, 23, 106, 111, 198, 268, 337
user–generated content (UGC), 331, 336, 339, 341, 345
user–generated works, 328
users, 4–6, 9–13, 15, 17, 19, 23–4, 31–2, 35–7, 39, 46–8, 54, 58, 79, 83–5, 88–91, 93–6, 98–9, 102, 105, 113, 118, 120–8, 133, 137, 139, 144–8, 150–2, 162, 179, 182, 191, 194–6, 211, 234, 240, 242–3, 265, 274, 282–3, 287, 291, 318, 336–7, 339–42, 345
users' rights, 5–6, 11–13, 19, 39, 47, 79, 194, 234, 243

values, 24–5, 51–4, 72, 83, 86–7, 89–91, 100, 132, 170, 203, 206–8, 210, 213, 216, 220, 239, 262, 265, 287
Vaver, David, 15, 53–4, 242
Very Nice, Very Nice (film), 297–304
VHS, 129, 156–7
video, 20, 30–1, 36, 89, 95–6, 124, 129, 145–6, 149–51, 155–6, 158–61, 169, 171–2, 216, 247, 252–5, 259–69, 290–1, 294, 298–9, 305, 308–10, 312–13, 321, 337
video games, 298, 312
virtual worlds, 37, 336–8, 342–4
von Finckenstein, Konrad, 141

Walt Disney, 64, 340, 344, 357
Waving Flag (song), 325
weapon parodies, 238, 243, 245, 249
Web 2.0, 169, 336–8, 345
Web Content Accessibility Guidelines V2.0, 149
WebCT, 169, 171
Webkinz, 338
website, 6, 18, 58–9, 61, 71, 92–7, 105–6, 128, 139, 155, 157, 159–60, 182–3, 194, 262–3, 282, 291, 293, 296–7, 333
Wershler, Darren, 3–40, 234, 263, 285–6
Westcott, Grace, 7, 36–7, 48, 74, 327–35, 350
Western, 25, 63, 83, 120, 213–16, 219–20, 231, 299, 322, 325, 342
wiki software, 116
Wikipedia, 18, 59, 109–10, 112, 116
wikis, 166
Wiley, David, 23, 166
WIPO (see below), 26, 205–6, 323
WordPress, 113, 115, 120
World Intellectual Property Organization (WIPO), 26, 205–6, 323
World Trade Organization (WTO), 131, 227
World Wide Web Consortium (W3C), 149

writing, 6, 56, 67, 82, 120, 197, 242, 253, 261, 263, 268, 290–2, 327, 329–30, 332–5

Xtranormal, 172

York University, 56, 256
YouTube, 4, 132, 145, 150, 160–1, 172–3, 244

Zamacois v. Douville (1943), *9*
Zeilinger, Martin, 3–40, 60, 103, 234, 294–304, 305–16, 350–1
Zelazo, Suzanne, 7, 33, 284–93, 355